OF MEMORY
AND THE MISPLACED

IRISH CULTURE, MEMORY, PLACE
Oona Frawley, Ray Cashman, Guy Beiner, editors

OF MEMORY
AND THE MISPLACED

Irish Immigrant Life Writing
in the United States

Sarah O'Brien

INDIANA UNIVERSITY PRESS

This book is a publication of

Indiana University Press
Office of Scholarly Publishing
Herman B Wells Library 350
1320 East 10th Street
Bloomington, Indiana 47405 USA

iupress.org

Manufactured in the United States of America

First printing 2023

Cataloging information is available from the Library of Congress.

ISBN 978-0-253-06787-6 (hardback)
ISBN 978-0-253-06788-3 (paperback)
ISBN 978-0-253-06789-0 (ebook)

CONTENTS

ACKNOWLEDGMENTS

This book is predicated on the pioneering work of Kerby Miller, Professor Emeritus of History at the University of Missouri who first brought these life writings to light. I am also indebted to Guy Beiner, Oona Frawley, and Jennika Baines, who offered guidance at critical stages of this book's completion. Liam Mac Mathúna, Professor Emeritus of Irish at University College Dublin, generously read several drafts of the manuscript and offered insightful notes. Mary Immaculate College, Limerick, has been a kind and caring workplace during the writing of the book.

I am deeply grateful to my friend Éilís Murphy, who designed this book's cover. The photograph, which Éilís carefully restored, features Nora O'Connor (center-top), her daughters, and her mother.

My partner, Tadhg O'Sullivan, has been a steadfast companion through long months of writing, inspiring me to think in new ways about the lives at the center of this research.

This book is dedicated to our daughter, Sibéal, who makes every day memorable.

INTRODUCTION

This text responds to a collection of thirty-two memoirs written by Irish immigrants of the post-Famine period in the United States.[1] With few exceptions these life narratives were not published and may have been lost were it not for Professor Kerby Miller. Miller's tireless investigations into the Irish experience in North America led to the discovery and preservation of these precious documents, opening up new corridors of possibility for fledgling researchers like myself.

From the 1980s, firsthand migrant testimony has provided the substance for formative studies of Irish emigration. This has led to the publication of iconic texts that include David Fitzpatrick's *Oceans of Consolation*, Kerby Miller's *Emigrants and Exiles*, Jennifer Redmond's *Moving Histories*, Edmundo Murray's *Devenir Irlandés*, and Enda Delaney's *The Great Irish Famine: A History in Four Lives*.[2] These texts have collectively recovered, altered, and particularized different features of the Irish diaspora, creating, in the words of Richard Kearney, a "hospitality of narratives."[3] Inspired by this scholarship, I have attempted to take the historiography one step further by reconsidering emigrant testimony from a theoretical perspective hitherto lacking in the field. Despite its breadth, this perspective remains encapsulated by the term *memory studies*.[4]

Since 2001, memory studies has irrevocably altered the study of Irish political and cultural history. That year Ian McBride's *History and Memory in Modern Ireland* was published, bringing together a collection of essays that become prototypes for a new body of historical work in Ireland.[5] The movement immediately focused on applying the lens of memory to reevaluate defining national events such as the Great Famine of 1845–50, the War of Independence, the Civil War, and the partition of Ireland.[6] Interest in this line of inquiry has grown to a point where it has now breached the boundaries of the academy and become part of public discourse. This was most recently evidenced through the *Machnamh 100* seminar series, which saw President Michael D. Higgins of Ireland host live televised broadcasts that dealt explicitly with memories relating to the national revolutionary period.[7] As a result, new terms have entered the Irish lexicon, leading to the fluent deployment of phrases such as *collective memory, ethical commemoration,* and *social forgetting.* Initiatives such as the Irish Memory Studies Network of University College Dublin further catalyzed the interest in memory studies, and podcasts of lectures delivered by renowned memory theorists became freely available.[8] The publication of Oona Frawley's four-volume *Memory Ireland* series was another iconic moment in Irish memory studies, illustrating its connections to literature, art, and film as well as historiography.[9] In turn, the 2018 publication of Guy Beiner's *Forgetful Remembrance* added weight to the methodological and theoretical capacities of memory studies and its applicability to events as distant and opaque as the folk memory of the Rebellion of 1798 in Protestant Ulster.[10]

Reports on the experiences of women who survived Irish mother and baby "homes" have intensified public discourse in Ireland around the necessity of memory studies as a window onto the past. This conversation has been heightened by the failure of the Irish state to adequately archive or analyze survivors' orally narrated memories during its investigation of the mother and baby homes.[11] As a result, the antennae of the Irish public are today highly attuned to the importance and vulnerability of memory. Moreover, the Irish public now insists on the application of vigorous methodologies for the interpretation of memory and has experienced firsthand the political and legal tensions that exist between state and public memory. A sense of responsibility for the memories of the repressed and silenced has never been more at the forefront of the Irish collective consciousness.

In spite of these extraordinary developments, the field of Irish emigration studies has remained largely unmarked by the memory turn. To be sure, one volume of Frawley's collection was dedicated to "memory and the diaspora," yet this did not lead to the systematic application of theories of social, collective, or cultural memory to the realm of migration literature.

Two notable exceptions are Marguérite Corporaal's *Relocated Memories* and Emily Mark-FitzGerald's *Commemorating the Irish Famine*, both of which focus on the period of 1845–50 and look, respectively, at literature and art as windows onto Irish and Irish American memory of the Famine.[12] Otherwise, however, the pre- and post-Famine emigrant experience in North America, which encompasses more than 4.5 million people, has been left untouched by memory studies. It seems important to pause at this point and consider what memory studies can offer to explorations of Irish emigration.

Memory studies recognizes interrelationality. It reads personal reminiscence as a socially constructed process, a process that draws from a polyphony of cultural registers.[13] Memory theory draws multiple lines of connection between the remembering mind and its surrounding society, and it perceives that society as existing between a past, present, and future. As such, the study of individual memory is by its nature a recognition of human interdependence. This interplay between personal and social is vital in a field of migration studies preoccupied with individual exceptionalism and singular personalities (take as just three examples the attention paid to Colonel Admiral Browne of the Irish-Argentine diaspora, John F. Kennedy in the American case, and Bernardo O'Higgins in Chile).[14] Recognition of interrelationality is also necessary for a field of study that has frequently characterized Irish emigrants as passive consumers of their environment rather than agents in its co-creation. "Irish emigrants," one historian has commented, "were probably as innumerate and illiterate as the population from which they sprang." He added that they were "virtually unencumbered by training, expertise or accomplishment" and emerged "from a context of enforced idleness and ignorance, full of eagerness to learn how to labour and to serve."[15] Memory studies prohibits such dismissiveness and reductivity. Guided by cognitive psychology, which recognizes that memories operate through reciprocal exchange with the outside world, the field of memory studies acknowledges the social world's influence while tracing through individuals' recollections the ways they integrated or rejected social mores.[16] Memory presents emigrants with a right of reply to the totalizing assumptions of history.

Memory studies accepts that while memory's theoretical address is the past, its matter is the present and future.[17] This encourages Irish emigration scholars to engage with the fluidity and mobility of migrants so that they are not cast as immobilized subjects anchored to one particular epoch but as people constantly being remade in response to their cultural imperatives and environments. As this book will illustrate, the memories of Irish immigrants in the US in 1900 were different from the memories that emerged twenty years later, and twenty years after that they were recast all over again. The immigrants' material pasts had not changed, but their aspirations for the future had, leading them to reframe how they thought about their childhoods, their emigration, their poverty, wealth, gender roles, nationality, and so on. This awareness of memory's relationship to the future has led to exciting new concepts, such as what Guy Beiner calls "prememory," which notices how individuals and groups construct memories of an event even before it takes place.[18] By applying this understanding to Irish migration studies, we resist the old methods of co-relating Irish immigrants to specific moments of their past and instead acknowledge that, like us, they focus their gaze as much if not more on the future. Cormac Ó Gráda, whose studies of the Famine eventually brought him into the realm of memory, concludes that victims of the Famine responded in different ways to its traumas and that most eventually recovered, living better lives than has heretofore been appreciated.[19] Memory studies indexes resilience in a way that history has not.

Memory expands the contours of historical time. Cultural memory studies show that our recollections are drawn not just from direct experience but rather have roots *in illo tempore*. Astrid Erll, for instance, has illustrated how Homer's depiction of the Odyssean voyage created a transnational cultural memory that irrigated the twentieth-century literature of Derek Walcott and James Joyce.[20] In turn, Marianne Hirsch's memory work on the Holocaust suggests that memory is inherited across generations, implanting a sense of a known, shared memory: a past that is unshakably "ours."[21] Astonishingly, such memory emergence is especially evident in families whose older members actively sought to forget and repress their experiences of the Holocaust. This newfound awareness of the expanded temporal coordinates of personal memory allows us to look beyond the immediate environment of the emigrant and to think about these individuals as repositories of imbricated, fossilized memories, drawn from an array of cultural sources and embedded in a richly patterned intergenerational matrix of memory. Through this line of thought, we deepen our appreciation of the complexity of the Irish migrants' mental world. Emigrants can never be simply "innumerate" and "illiterate" through this worldview; rather, they are shining threads in a rich tapestry of Irish cultural memory, individual but connected and worthy of dedicated investigation.

Memory studies insists on considering the significance of a rainbow of social spheres often ignored by historiography.[22] In particular, it encourages investigation of memories relating to childhood, adolescence, domesticity, and the family, since it is within such realms that the first memories are laid down, their eidetic nature enduring across the life span. Awareness of the mnemonic sensitivity of this period (termed the "reminiscence bump") in turn brings into focus the significance of women as vectors of social memory, since it is they who traditionally oversaw these domains and who guided the implantation of memories through tasks such as telling family anecdotes, organizing family events, writing letters, preserving photograph collections, and passing on family traditions.[23] Where Irish migration history has in the past tended to trivialize domains overseen by everyday women, memory studies insists on their centrality for the emergence, preservation, and re-generation of social memories, recognizing the female realm as an essential vector of national and transnational history. Memory studies sees family memory as particularly significant for its filtering, reinforcement, or subver-sion of official memory.[24] Through the intimacy of the family, individuals could gather around the table or fireplace and debate the relevance of stories passed on through the nation-state, the media, cultural outlets, and other of-ficial sources. The methods of family memory are also enviably more effective than these available to agents such as the nation-state. Transmitted through direct communication, reinforced by photographs and objects, enshrined in daily ritual, and subject to frequent repetition, memories passed down through the family burn into the consciousness, enduring far better than those transmitted through the more distant and uneven apparatus of state, religion, and society. In placing such memories alongside official acts of com-memoration, we create a syncopated historical record of Irish emigration that acknowledges the diversity of Irish cultural remembrance across different territories, communities, neighborhoods, and kinship networks.

Finally, memory studies provides an architecture to audit the processes of myth.[25] Irish emigration, as a highly emotive experience that has affected most Irish families across the past three centuries, has required a great deal of mythmaking, both to come to terms with the enormous cultural loss that it has entailed as well as to justify its continuation long after the wane of British colonialism. As discussed in chapter 2, certain myths, or what I have termed "memory narratives," have emerged as a result, ranging from the no-tion of emigration as political exile to the imagining of the Irish diaspora as a unilaterally Catholic and militantly nationalist body.[26] One myth given particular attention in this book (and reflected in its title) is the notion of place and the Irish landscape as an essential vector of memory for Irish people.[27]

To a migration scholar, this overwhelming portrayal of the Irish landscape as a fundamental mnemonic is particularly grating, for it implies that the cultural memories of Irish migrants and their families across the diaspora must somehow be less authentic, given their creation at a physical distance from the fabled Irish landscape. Furthermore, the myth of a monolithic communion between Irish landscapes and people severely underestimates the extent to which class and gender disrupted certain people's access to and relationship with the Irish landscape. By navigating systematically through such people's memories, we can plainly see the irrelevance of such myths to vast numbers of hitherto underrepresented migrants. Memory studies thus hedges and actualizes the all-encompassing nature of cultural myths. This reevaluation of the quasi-mystical belief in place as a detached conduit of memory is visible in contemporary literature across Europe and is especially evident in the writing of women. For example, in her memoir *A Girl's Story* Annie Ernaux writes of her return to the location of an adolescent trauma. Standing on the site, Ernaux expects she might fully come to terms with what had happened to her and thus experience a moment of closure. And yet, she says, "it seemed less familiar than I thought."[28] Ernaux comes to recognize her return to the place as "a kind of propitiatory gesture" that does little to reconstitute her memories of the trauma. It is after this visit that she begins to write—"step by step to move toward an elusive whole."[29] Memory, for Ernaux, would require an inward excavation through writing. Likewise, Maria Stepanova's *In Memory of Memory* describes her journeys across Europe to try to reconstitute a complete memory of her Jewish family.[30] In one episode she travels through the Volga basin to Saratov, in western Russia, in search of the birthplace of her grandfather. With the help of a friend, she is guided to a house that she recognizes with metaphysical intensity as her ancestral home: "It seemed to speak to me, saying: here, you needed to come here. . . . I remembered everything beneath the high windows with such a sense of heightened native precision that I seemed to know it had all been, in this, our place, how we had lived and why we had left."[31] A few days later, still buoyed by her sense of having psychically coincided with her ancestor through the vector of place, she receives a call from her friend. Sheepishly, he admits that his coordinates had been off. The house before which she had stood and through which she had "remembered" her past was in fact the home of a stranger. "And that," Stepanova concludes, "is just about everything I know about memory."[32]

I mention the above not as a complete inventory of the redeeming capacities of memory studies—such a feat is impossible in a field of inquiry of this scale—but rather to signpost the ways that memory studies have particularly informed the production of this book. It is also important to note that concepts of social or collective memory were not sufficient in themselves as frameworks of analysis. Memory has different media, and in the case of this book that media was memoir. To come to terms with the ways that the conventions of memoir mediated memory required an additional framework of interpretation, specific to the technology of writing and particular to the genre of life writing. Far from being considered a reliable preservative of memory, the medium of writing has long been criticized for distorting the organic nature of memory discourse. One of the first and most famous of such criticisms occurs in Plato's *Phaedrus*. Theuth, hoping to win his king's favor by offering him a potion for memory and wisdom, invents the technology of writing. Yet the king is not persuaded. "'In fact,' he says, evaluating the written word, 'it will introduce forgetfulness into the soul of those who learn it; they will not practice using their memory because they will put their trust in writing, which is external and depends on signs belonging to others.'"[33]

As writing became more conventionalized, the influence of "signs belonging to others" extended beyond the learning of elemental skills such as logographs and syllabic systems and into processes of cognition and perception.[34] Writing makes the units of speech explicit, thus altering people's relationship with language. In turn, newspapers, legal texts, academic books, accountancy reports, and novels have developed particular conventions that prime users to arrange their memories in increasingly generic ways.[35] The spatiality of writing, some argue, promotes a linear arrangement of thought and operates along a progressive, pared-back register that enforces the ideological worldviews of Western society.[36] As a result, written memories noticeably contrast with the rhythmic, circular, and repetitive nature of orally narrated memories. Also, where an interlocutor provokes points of connection and prompts further recollection in collecting an oral history, the writing of memories is invariably a solitary task and one as determined by the freighted conventions of writing as by the kaleidoscopic nature of memory.[37] Roland Barthes has also critiqued writing's artificial "reality effect," by which it "continues to signify just that very same thing forever."[38] Where orality permits open-endedness and a lack of resolve, writing demands precision and conclusion. Our memories rarely share these latter features.

In spite of these limitations, the culturally informed nature of writing is extremely efficient at revealing the social ecosystem of the writer. Just as speech betrays features of our identity, such as class and geographical background, an individual's style of writing is akin to a cultural fingerprint that bears the hallmarks of time. Indeed, for Stepanova, "text . . . consists entirely of time." "When you look at the page of an old newspaper," writes Stepanova, "the first thing you feel is a hopeless remoteness": "Writing is a template of time, not 'how it actually was' but written in that concentrated form which gives us a feeling for the age. . . . Even those who behave as if they stood outside the idea of 'typical' suddenly make a linguistic gesture that's common to their contemporaries, without even noticing it, as if they were unaware of the pull of gravity on them."[39]

True to Stepanova's word, the memoirists in this book each reveal through their style of writing their suspension in a particular milieu. The thematic and structural sobriety of Ned Ronayne's life writing (part 2) is reflected in the broader autobiographical literature of 1900s America, while Margaret McGuinness's 1973 memoir bears all the marks of a feminist, consumeristic, and newly liberalized America. By tracing the socially constructed nature of their personal narratives and drawing comparisons between their private manuscripts and the broader culture of autobiographical writing in the United States, we find that the orientation of Irish immigrants to a new cultural world becomes far more obvious than their displacement. Through their life writing, replete with borrowed modes of self-expression and remembrance, Irish immigrants can be seen in the full light of their American surroundings rather than through the distant, half-lit gloom of Ireland.

Notes

1. All of the memoirs addressed in this book are archived in the University of Galway, alongside thousands of Irish emigrant letters.

2. Jennifer Redmond, *Emigration to Britain from Independence to Republic* (Liverpool: Liverpool University Press, 2018); Kerby Miller, *Emigrants and Exiles: Ireland and the Irish Exodus to North America* (New York: Oxford University Press, 1985); David Fitzpatrick, *Oceans of Consolation: Personal*

Accounts of Irish Migration to Australia (Cork: Cork University Press, 1994); Enda Delaney and Donald MacRaild, eds., *Irish Migration, Networks and Ethnic Identities Since 1750* (London: Routledge, 2007); Timothy Guinnane, *The Vanishing Irish: Households, Migration, and the Rural Economy in Ireland, 1850–1914* (Princeton, NJ: Princeton University Press, 1997); Edmundo Murray, *Devenir Irlandés: Narrativas íntimas de la emigración irlandesa a la Argentina (1844–1912)* (Buenos Aires: Eudeba, 2004).

3. Richard Kearney, "Narrative Hospitality: Three Pedagogical Experiments," in *Radical Hospitality,* ed. Richard Kearney and Melissa Fitzpatrick (New York: Fordham University Press, 2021).

4. For three overviews of the memory studies field, see Anna Lisa Tota and Trever Hagen, eds., *Routledge International Handbook of Memory Studies* (NY: Routledge, 2016); Susannah Radstone and Bill Schwarz, eds., *Memory: Histories, Theories, Debates* (New York: Fordham University Press, 2010); Astrid Erll and Ansgar Nünning, eds., *A Companion to Cultural Memory Studies* (Berlin: De Gruyter, 2010).

5. Ian McBride, *History and Memory in Modern Ireland* (Cambridge: Cambridge University Press, 2001).

6. Richard Grayson and Fearghal McGarry, eds, *Remembering 1916: The Easter Rising, the Somme and the Politics of Memory in Ireland* (Cambridge, Cambridge University Press, 2016).

7. Michael D. Higgins, Ciarán Benson, Anne Dolan, Michael Laffan, and Joep Leerssen, "The Challenges of Public Commemoration," *Machnamh 100,* Dublin, December 2020, https://president.ie/en/diary/details/president-hosts -machnamh-100-event/audio; John Horne, Niamh Gallagher, Alvin Jackson, Eunan O' Halpin, Marie Coleman, and Michael D. Higgins, "Empire: Instincts, Interests, Power and Resistance," *Machnamh 100,* Dublin, February 2021; Catriona Crowe, Margaret O'Callaghan, Caitriona Clear, Linda Connolly and John Cunningham, "Recovering Imagined Futures," *Machnamh 100,* Dublin, May 2021.

8. Irish Memory Studies Network, accessed September 13, 2016, http:// irishmemorystudies.com.

9. Oona Frawley, ed., *The Famine and the Troubles,* vol. 3 of *Memory Ireland* (Syracuse, NY: Syracuse University Press, 2014); Oona Frawley, ed., *History and Modernity,* vol. 1 of *Memory Ireland* (Syracuse, NY: Syracuse University Press, 2011); Oona Frawley, ed., *Diaspora and Memory Practice,* vol. 2 of *Memory Ireland* (Syracuse, NY: Syracuse University Press, 2012).

10. Guy Beiner, *Forgetful Remembrance: Social Forgetting and Vernacular Historiography of a Rebellion in Ulster* (New York: Oxford University Press, 2018).

11. Caitriona Crowe, "The Commission and the Survivors," *Dublin Review* 83 (Summer 2021), https://thedublinreview.com/article/the-commission-and

-the-survivors/; Sarah O'Brien, "Art, Oral History and Ireland's Mother and Baby Homes," *Oral History Review* (April 2021), https://oralhistoryreview.org/ethics/art-and-oral-history/

12. Marguérite Corporaal, *Relocated Memories: The Great Famine in Irish and Diaspora Fiction, 1846–1870* (Syracuse, NY: Syracuse University Press, 2017); Emily Mark-FitzGerald, *Commemorating the Irish Famine: Memory and the Monument* (Liverpool: Liverpool University Press, 2013).

13. Maurice Halbwachs, *On Collective Memory*, trans. Lewis A. Coser (Chicago: University of Chicago Press, 1992).

14. Tim Fanning, *Paisanos: The Forgotten Irish Who Changed the Face of Latin America* (Dublin: Gill, 2016).

15. David Fitzpatrick, *Irish Emigration, 1801–1921* (Dublin: Economic and Social History Society of Ireland, 1984).

16. Harald Welzer, "Communicative Memory," in *A Companion to Cultural Memory Studies*, ed. Astrid Erll and Ansgar Nünning (Berlin: De Gruyter, 2010).

17. Keith Ansell-Pearson, "Bergson on Memory," in *Memory: Histories, Theories, Debates*, ed. Susannah Radstone and Bill Schwarz (New York: Fordham University Press, 2010).

18. Beiner, *Forgetful Remembrance*; Guy Beiner, "Probing the Boundaries of Irish Memory: From Postmemory to Prememory and Back," *Irish Historical Studies* 39, no. 154 (2014).

19. Cormac Ó Gráda, "Famine, Trauma and Memory," *Béaloideas* 69 (2001), doi.org/10.2307/20520760.

20. Astrid Erll, "Homer: A Relational Mnemohistory," *Memory Studies* 11, no. 3 (2018).

21. Marianne Hirsch, *The Generation of Post-Memory: Writing and Visual Culture after the Holocaust* (New York: Columbia University Press, 2012).

22. James Fentress, *Social Memory* (Oxford: Blackwell, 1992).

23. Fentress, *Social Memory*.

24. Astrid Erll, "Locating Family in Cultural Memory Studies," *Journal of Comparative Family Studies* 42, no. 3 (2011); Katie Barclay and Nina Javette Koefoed, "Family, Memory, and Identity: An Introduction," *Journal of Family History* 46, no. 1 (2021).

25. E. J. Hobsbawm and T. O. Ranger, *The Invention of Tradition* (Cambridge: Cambridge University Press, 1983); Benedict Anderson, *Imagined Communities: Reflections on the Origin and Spread of Nationalism* (London: Verso, 1983).

26. Sarah O'Brien, "Politics, Community and Nationhood in Irish-Argentine Oral Narrative," in *New Perspectives on the Irish Abroad: The Silent People?*, ed. Míchéal Ó hAodh and Máirtín Ó Cathain (Lanham, MD: Lexington, 2013).

27. Patrick Sheeran, "Genius Fabulae: The Irish Sense of Place," *Irish University Review* 18, no. 2 (1988), http://www.jstor.org/stable/25484245; Angela

K. Martin, "The Practice of Identity and an Irish Sense of Place," *Gender, Place and Culture* 4, no. 1 (1997).

28. Annie Ernaux, *A Girl's Story*, trans. Alison L. Strayer (London: Fitzcarraldo, 2020), 142.

29. Ernaux, *A Girl's Story*. For a review of the book, see Madeleine Schwartz, "A Memoirist Who Mistrusts Her Own Memories," *New Yorker*, April 20, 2020.

30. Maria Stepanova, *In Memory of Memory: A Family Romance*, trans. Sasha Dugdale (London: Fitzcarraldo, 2021).

31. Stepanova, *In Memory of Memory*, 53.

32. Stepanova, In Memory of Memory, 54.

33. Plato, *Phaedrus*, 275a, quoted in Paul Ricoeur, *Memory, History, Forgetting* (Chicago: University of Chicago Press, 2004), 142.

34. David Olson, "Writing and the Mind," in *Sociocultural Studies of Mind*, ed. J. V. Wertsch, P. del Río, and A. Alvarez (Cambridge: Cambridge University Press, 1995); David Olson and Nancy Torrance, "Conceptualizing Literacy as a Personal Skill and as a Social Practice," in *The Making of Literate Societies*, ed. David Olson and Nancy Torrance (Oxford: Blackwell, 2001); Richard Sproat, *Language, Technology, and Society* (Oxford: Oxford University Press, 2010).

35. S. Scribner and M. Cole, *The Psychology of Literacy* (Cambridge: Cambridge University Press, 1981).

36. Walter Ong, *Orality and Literacy: The Technologising of the Word* (London: Routledge, 1982).

37. Ong, *Orality and Literacy*.

38. Roland Barthes, trans. Richard Howard, *The Rustle of Language* (New York: Hill and Wang, 1986), 275.

39. Stepanova, *In Memory of Memory*, 375.

OF MEMORY
AND THE MISPLACED

PART I

Memory and the Irish
in the United States

1

Social Frameworks of Memory

Imagine there are two manuscripts before you. One is the memoir of Henry O'Mahoney, written in 1933. The other is the memoir of his daughter, Mary, written ten years later. Both reflect on moments from their shared past, experienced simultaneously. Yet the way that father and daughter recall these incidents is profoundly different.[1]

Let's take an example. In an early section of Henry's memoir, he describes the day he traveled to Kilmainham jail to present himself as a political prisoner. (Henry was a leading figure in Ballydehob Land League in 1881, a nationalist organization that agitated for tenant rights.) In his memoir this journey to Kilmainham was a public and jubilant affair in which he was hoisted by a crowd of supporters onto a chair and carried through the streets to the train station: "When we were within a mile of Skibbereen, a large crowd from Skibbereen who were attending a fair that day, came out to meet us with a brass band. When the increased crowd reached Skibbereen, they seated me on a chair and hoisted the chair on men's shoulders and took me thus to the barracks which housed a large police force. They dared the police to come out and arrest me. The police did not take the dare."

Mary's memory is barely recognizable as being of the same event. For her, there was no crowd, no brass band, and no policemen. Instead, she recollected her father's journey to Kilmainham as a quiet familial scene, imbued with a rare memory of intimacy between herself and her father. She writes that Henry, accompanied by her and her mother, slipped away quietly to Skibbereen so as not to draw a crowd: "Arriving at the station at night and noticing the lights and noise of the train and having my mother hold me up to the train windows to kiss my father goodbye is one of my earliest remembrances."

The extreme divergence between these two accounts of Henry's departure to Kilmainham is illustrative of the complex task faced by the historian of memory. Clearly, the "truth" of both accounts can be partially corroborated against external sources (there are no contemporaneous reports in the local newspaper of a jubilant crowd, for example), and the fact that Mary was a young child at the time partially explains her memory's focus. However, the question of *why* father and daughter remembered this occasion in such distinct ways remains a conundrum. Memory studies gives us a framework to respond to this problem, if not with clean answers than at least with a clearer sense of what is involved when accounting for this disparity in recollection.

Memory, Individuality, and Society

Henry's and Mary's memoirs are typical examples of what one study defines as the "entangled" nature of memory.[2] In particular, they bear the hallmarks of collective memory, the term coined by Maurice Halbwachs in *Les cadres sociaux de la mémoire (On Collective Memory)*, a text—first published in 1925—that would go on to guide memory scholars over the next century.[3] For Halbwachs, collective memory acknowledges the role of surrounding society in determining personal memories. What and how an individual remembers, Halbwachs believed, was dictated by their social networks and their attendant biases toward selective experiences, personalities, and interpretations of the past. As such, for Halbwachs, any analysis of memory should involve an excavation of the social world, past and present, of the one who remembers. Halbwachs's theory had many effects, not least a shift in the study of memory away from the domain of cognitive psychology and toward the domain of history, wedding the two disciplines in inextricable and sometimes uncomfortable ways.

A cursory scan through Henry's and Mary's social worlds provides some immediate suggestions as to the different collectives that may have shaped their divergent memories of Henry's journey to Kilmainham. Coming of age in the 1860s in Ballydehob, Henry spent the formative years of memory creation within a social group of fervent Irish nationalists. On his way to work as an apprentice cooper, Henry passed the workshop of the famed Fenian

Jeremiah O'Donovan Rossa. Studies of agrarian unrest in West Cork suggest that the O'Mahoney family supported Irish republicanism, allowing Fenians to drill on Henry's father's land in nearby Coomengeh.[4] This local focus on militaristic Irish nationalism was replicated at the national level, as the cultural imperatives of late nineteenth-century Ireland concentrated Irish Catholic society's attention on the cause of Irish freedom from British rule. During Henry's late teenage years, men like Michael Davitt, John Devoy, Charles Stewart Parnell, and O'Donovan Rossa were held up as national heroes, prioritized in the nascent nation's cultural memory through stories, song, plays, and poetry.

On emigrating, O'Mahoney served in the US Civil War, where he came into contact with other Fenians. In the popular transatlantic newspaper the *United Irishman*, he may have read sections of O'Donovan Rossa's memoir and noted the frenetic reception of an Irish American audience to the account of O'Donovan Rossa's nationalist activities. Given this context of glorified Irish nationalist commemoration on both sides of the Atlantic, it is hardly surprising that Henry's own recollections of nationalist involvement would shine so brightly in his memoir. Indeed, O'Donovan Rossa's very production of a memoir may have not only influenced the content of Henry's memoir but may also have provided him with a ready-made narrative schema through which to articulate his own life circumstances. In such intense sociohistorical conditions, the collective nature of Henry's memoir becomes strikingly apparent.

While Henry's social affiliations are made transparent through his formal associational activity in the Land League, Mary's social world, like that of many women of the nineteenth century, is slightly more difficult to determine. She was only eleven years old when the O'Mahoney family emigrated to the US and thus did not experience the overt discourse of Irish nationalism that so shaped her father's social world. As a woman, she was also discouraged by her father from participating in the public arena, and much of her early life was limited to the spheres of home and school. In fact, the most obvious sense of social affiliation that Mary describes relates to her role as a family member. In the opening of her memoir, she expresses a desire to pass on her memories to her grandchildren, and much of what she wrote in her manuscript revolved around documenting the intimacies of a family's life. And yet Mary O'Mahoney was not just a family member: She was also a former schoolteacher and an avid reader, a talented writer and a critical thinker, a woman of limited means who had come of age on the liberalizing American frontier. Likewise, Henry's social affiliations were multidynamic and diasporic, and they fluctuated over time—for many decades he worked as a machinist in Texas and had no contact with any of his old Irish nationalist compatriots. These highly mobile variables problematize the suggestions arrived at earlier and indeed provoke further questions. Why did Henry's short-lived Irish nationalist involvement exert such a strong gravitational pull over his memories? Why was the social framework of the family so much more influential for daughter than father? Why did their shared cultural memory of Irish nationalism not inspire Mary to write about Henry's journey to Kilmainham in a more heroic register? And how does the diasporic nature of both Henry's and Mary's memoirs affect how they remembered these distant events of the Irish past? In short, how can we account for the uneven dispersal and character of memories across different members of the same social group? To address these questions requires greater excavation of memory across individual, gender, family, diaspora, and national lines.

Memory and the Self

According to Jan Assmann, memory is a central constituent of identity. "Memory," says Assmann, "is the faculty that enables us to form an awareness of selfhood, both on the personal and on the collective level."[5] Paul Ricoeur reaffirms the interrelation of personal identity and memory when he writes, "Memory provides a sense of temporal continuity at a deeply personal level, through the 'mine-ness' of memory."[6] Indeed, critics of Halbwachs's *collective memory* argue that the term does not sufficiently account for the individuality of memory, falsely portraying the individual's remembering mind as a blank canvas selectively filled in by a society doggedly pursuing its own concerns. Debate over this tension between individual and collective memory has led some scholars to replace the term *collective memory* with *social memory*. For James Fentress and Chris Wickham, "social memory is better suited for a conception of memory which, while doing full justice to the collective side of one's conscious life, does not render the individual a sort of automaton, passively obeying the interiorized collective will."[7] In turn Astrid Erll's review of family-based memory illuminates the ways that individuals actively resist being subsumed into established narratives of collective memory. Comparing how individuals narrate their family stories in contrast to national histories, Erll argues that "there is obviously a gap between official and private memories, between cultural and communicative memory, between institutionalized commemoration and the dynamics of everyday remembering in social contexts."[8] Though Erll does not deny the social dimensions of remembering, she does emphasize the error of assuming that one form of social memory (e.g., a newspaper article about a national hero) will be as influential for the individual as another (e.g., a story directly communicated from a grandparent to a grandchild). This point is reinforced by Fentress and Wickham, who insist that "however much a novel or schoolteacher's story can affect the content of a memory of an event held by an individual or a social group, it will have much less effect on which sorts of events social groups will characteristically choose to commemorate, which are linked to deeper patterns of identity."[9]

Guy Beiner reasserts this idea, stating that "you can't invent any memory you want; there is a negotiation at play." Beiner adds, "It depends on reaction. To create socially meaningful memory, certain stories require a lot of reception and re-working."[10] Such insight is rendered all the more significant when we are faced with the fact that, as I explore in chapter 2, much of the work in Irish memory studies disproportionately focuses on official memory narratives created by and for Irish American religious, political, and cultural elites. This focus on national and pan-national commemorative practices sidelines exploration of intimately transmitted memories through the less considered spheres of family, friendship, and local communities.

These perspectives lead us toward a different territory of memory studies: that is, how different forms of memory transmission impact the long-term internalization of an individual's memory. For Assmann, the popularized notion of cultural memory, defined by Erll as "the interplay of present and past in sociocultural contexts," unacceptably generalizes the forms and effectiveness of different kinds of memory transmission.[11] Cultural memory, Assmann argues, falsely equates the influence of embodied memory, such as oral storytelling, with disembodied forms of memory, such as national museums.[12] Cultural memory also juxtaposes highly formalized national narratives, such as the Declaration of Independence, with informal narratives told at close proximity, such as the stories a mother tells her daughter. Further, cultural memory expands the temporal parameters of collective memory, encompassing events from mythical time alongside events of the directly remembered past. Additionally, cultural memory involves the study of ever-widening ranges of media: texts, films, icons, dances, and performances, rather than the vernacular oral and literary media indigenous to most memory communities. In an attempt to disentangle and differentiate these forms of memory and their attendant influences, Assmann suggests the use of the term *communicative memory*, which he understands as having special significance for how individuals go on to frame their own life histories. Communicative memories are those accounts of the recent past that individuals share with their contemporaries, the transmission of which generally takes place in intimate family and community settings, akin to the father-daughter dynamic through which Henry conveyed his memories to Mary in 1933.

Assmann's insistence on the exceptionality of communicative memory as a formative mode of transmission is corroborated by cognitive psychology. Harald Welzer, for instance, drawing from cognitive investigation, writes that "the history of our communicative experiences is the element which most strongly individualizes our memory and our self."[13] Reinforcing the role of communicative memory, Welzer's research suggests that humans develop what he calls an "autobiographical memory" by "using the material made available by the previous generation, which they easily modify since they actively exploit their environment instead of simply adapting to it."[14] Welzer's last point enables us to form a more sophisticated hypothesis around the dynamic at play in Mary's recollection of her father. It makes it conceivable, for instance, that Mary was adapting the narrative passed on to her by her father to suit her present-day aspirations: to create a coherent family narrative thematically arranged around the bonds of kinship.

In spite of Assmann's attempts to distinguish communicative memory from cultural or collective memory, further investigation of its boundaries suggests that it cannot exist in isolation. Although the journey to Kilmainham was orally related to Mary by her father during the transcription of his memoir, it was equally a personal memory, one that Mary felt herself to have experienced in a very particular, tactile, and intimate way. At the same time, it was a form of cultural memory, its selection in Mary's memoir influenced by the extent to which it linked with a broader narrative of Irish national history. Thus, while we may now be clearer on the particular power of communicative, family-based memory as a form of transmission, we remain alert to the inevitably entangled nature of memory and of the impossibility of discerning individual from social memories. As J. Olaf Kleist has remarked, whether memories are a result of social circumstances or whether society constructs them is an obsolete question. Simply put, memories are a mediating element of society.[15] This does not preclude us, however, from engaging with the other social elements that may have influenced Mary to "modify and exploit" her memories of her father's journey to Kilmainham. We turn, then, to a leitmotif that resurfaces throughout Mary's memoir: the role of gender in mediating memory.

Memory and Gender

As we progress through Mary's memoir, it becomes clear that Henry O'Mahoney was something of a tyrant in the family. "My father," she writes frankly, "was a rather cold and severe person. His will was law not only with his children but with my mother as well. This attribute was not conducive to those loving confidences that children should have for a father." As the text proceeds, it also becomes evident that the purpose of Mary's memoir is not simply to chronicle the life of the family but also to amend the record established by Henry's memoir a decade earlier: Mary wanted to return to the center of the family narrative someone her father's written account had erased: her mother, Brigie. While we learn nothing of Brigie from Henry's memoir, she is repeatedly brought to life through the writing of her daughter. Mary describes her mother as an accomplished businesswoman who single-handedly ran the Ballydehob family business—a shop, hardware store, and pub—while her husband was in America. In the evenings, after her mother's work was done, Mary remembers the many visitors who would call at the house and her mother's luminous presence in the midst of these social occasions: "Mother always played for these dances on the accordion or the concertina. They would dance in the kitchen while Mother sat by the fire in the big range and played. When she danced, someone would take her place at the instrument. Sometimes Dan Daly would play while Mother danced. Mother was gay and young and enjoyed being with other young people. When Mother played she always had a far-away look in her eyes. She did not look as she usually did."

At another point Mary discusses her mother's role in the local Land League, which Henry excludes from his memoir—a glaring omission, given the attention his narrative lavishes on this organization. As though actively defying her father's memory lapse, Mary describes the precise nature of her mother's political involvement: "Mother also took an active part in the Land League. John Boyle O'Reilly, the Irish patriot who had been transported to a British penal colony in Australia, from which he later escaped and fled to Boston, Massachusetts, at this time published a newspaper supporting the Irish cause. He published a letter written to him about the cause which my mother had written him while Father was in prison."

Later in the memoir, when describing the family's life in Texas, she discloses the pain her mother suffered under the controlling dominion of her father. "He never gave Mother a dollar to spend for anything but necessities," Mary observes: "Around payday, Mother would get up at night after he went to sleep and take out of his pocket as much as she dared without danger of his missing it. She spent this on small things that she had forgotten to buy on the shopping day—threads, buttons, trimmings for dresses or something of that kind." Mary also wrote of the hard physical labor that Henry forced her mother to undertake, describing how her mother had to care for the cattle while heavily pregnant. "He expected Mother and all of us who were old enough to do all that we were capable of," Mary writes. "Mother had to feed the [livestock] every day. She had to climb the latter to the loft. She had to climb the ladder to the loft and throw out hay for them and set out the cottonseed to feed them on. It was hard work, and the winter was bad. Mother did not complain. In the Spring, a baby girl was born." This story is made all the more tragic when Mary reports that the infant "moaned its life away in a week." Mary writes that "Father took the little coffin to the cemetery in the buggy. Mother turned her face to the wall and cried. She always tried to hide her emotion from us children, but I knew how she felt and I went out in the kitchen and washed the dishes and I am afraid dropped my tears into the dishpan." Mary's efforts to represent the heroism and suffering of her mother are so pointed and frequent that they must be understood as a deliberate counternarrative to her father's memoir, challenging in particular his patriarchal authority and jaundiced perspective on the role of women in the O'Mahoney family's past.

In spite of Halbwachs's observation of the influence of social affiliations on memory, surprisingly little research exists on the ways that gender shapes memory.[16] Social groups in memory studies are generally constructed around class, race, or ethnicity, their memories mapped to their respective regional or national territories. The assumption, of course, is that women make up half of each such group and are thus represented within them. However, as feminist history has shown, women's experiences have been historically excluded from the memory traditions of these groups.[17] This is particularly true of the late nineteenth century, as Western European nations' compulsion to "invent traditions" led to the construction of commemorative processes that were overwhelmingly male.[18] Monuments commemorated male patriots; parades emphasized masculine militarism; songs, paintings, and photos depicted male forms of consciousness; and historical narratives focused on male experiences. The conservative Victorian and Catholic values of late nineteenth-century Ireland reinforced the invisibility of women by encouraging their enclosure within the household, limiting their bodily and legal autonomy as citizens, monitoring their access to public spaces, and emphasizing their roles as wives and mothers.[19]

Male dominance over official ideology and forms of narration may have affected women's memory-making in multiple ways. First, because the principal narrative styles for commemorating the past are about male activities and are traditionally performed by men (e.g., military parades on national feast days or tribal drum circles), women have been left without any established narrative format to articulate their own experiences.[20] According to Fentress, this has forced women to use a male perspective in their depictions of the past, thus bolstering male hegemonic memory traditions.

Second, the enclosure of women within the domestic sphere has influenced and notably restricted the content that they relate in their life histories, which overwhelmingly center on home life.[21] Women's life histories give less or different space to "public" history than men's do "for the simple reason that women were less involved in it."[22] However, rather than seeing this entirely as a deficit, the concentration of women's stories around the domestic sphere can also be understood as a reflection of women's ownership and control over this particular domain. As Fentress notes, "it is not only because they often have little experiences outside the family environment that they structure their recollection around such moments but also because such moments are in their hands, rather than men's."[23]

Third, gender roles in Western Europe made women responsible "for sanitizing and moralizing accounts of the experienced past for young children, as part of the process of socialization."[24] As caregivers, European women rather than men were expected to narrate and preserve family history for the younger generations via tasks such as collecting family photographs and sharing family lore. This responsibility has led to the development of a different genre of female, family-centered commemoration (which, frustratingly and ironically, remains nameless). Though similar to the classic male autobiography, it diverges in a number of key ways. For one thing, women autobiographers make more use of the pronouns *we* and *us* where male autobiographers use *I*. This links to another feature of female autobiography, which tends to privilege relationships over specific historical events and which perceives the past from the position of an interrelational group rather than an individual. A different sense of temporality also distinguishes men's and women's autobiographies. Women's autobiographical narratives are more prone to using the imperfect tense, indicating their sense of continuity across time through the perpetuation of the family's life cycle; men prefer the past or future tense, reflecting both a sense of autonomy and psychological distance from the dynamics of the family.

Finally, women's modes of memory, unlike men's, reflect "an absence of emphasis on choice."[25] According to Fentress, women's existence under the control of men has led to the development of a female autobiographical narrative genre "of ironic detachment" textured by an atmosphere of powerlessness. While this is difficult to refute as a general finding, it is undermined by the particularities of Mary O'Mahoney's memoir, which depict a woman's willed efforts to contest the gendered narrative forms that had emerged in her own family. This feature of her memoir suggests the ways that emigration from Europe to North America in the early twentieth century may have provided young women like Mary O'Mahoney with new modes of thinking about gender and the roles traditionally ascribed to men and women in Western Europe.[26] Furthermore, the question of choice, or lack of it, in women's memories may not be so evident in memoirs written by immigrant women. After all, these are women whose lives were effectively defined by their decision to emigrate and who continued to make active choices about their well-being and happiness in the United States.[27] This introduces a new and important element for consideration: memory in the context of diaspora.

Memory and Diaspora

The scholarship on diasporic memory can be categorized into three main themes: reconstruction, continuity, and diversification. The first of these themes, reconstructed memory, is attended to in many different contexts, from Marianne Hirsch's study of postmemory in the Jewish diaspora to

Ghassan Hage's examination of the meaning of food in the Lebanese Australian immigrant enclave.[28] In Oona Frawley's second volume of her *Memory Ireland* collection, memory's reconstruction is given particular weight, with Frawley's overview of the volume serving as a signpost for the essays that follow. "Settlement abroad," Frawley notes in the book's introduction, "necessitates the production of a new kind of memory of 'home,' one that involves the reconstruction of a place through an alchemy of memory and imagination, one that no longer relies on interaction between a landscape and a people. Memory becomes a conduit to a particular past but simultaneously because it distorts and stretches, invents and alters, it constructs a new Ireland."[29]

In assessing the impact of this diasporic reconstruction of memory, we tend to focus on reification and the loss of authenticity. The latter stems, we might argue, from a relic of the twentieth century, when the nation-state was the most authentic and authoritative form of identity. As Simon Schama observes in *Landscape and Memory*, national identity from the nineteenth century was invented by drawing from the "mystique of a particular landscape tradition."[30] By consequence, those migrants outside of the sacralized fulcrum of the native landscape would find their memory acts beleaguered by cries of inauthenticity, both from their homelands as well as from the new host society. Although this is itself interesting, it remains unclear how this shadow of inauthenticity has actually reshaped immigrants' memories.[31] Indeed, the question of inauthenticity may in fact prove to be more of a source of unease for the memory of the nation-state than for its diaspora, since any coagulation of memory acts outside of its borders implicitly challenges its social and cultural dominion.

In terms of reification, Frawley notes how Irish cultural memory in the diaspora "becomes something to be embodied, something to be made plain": "When Ireland is not a geographic possibility or a physical actuality there seems to be a need to convert that absence into a tangible presence."[32] As Frawley's collection of essays makes clear, this tendency to reify memories of Ireland in contexts of diaspora is synonymized in the diaspora's reliance on symbols and material manifestations of ethnicity, such as wearing green on Saint Patrick's Day or sporting tattoos of Celtic symbols. The loss of a "geographic possibility" might also seem to explain the trend among immigrants to write their memoirs, as acts of immobilizing in print specific memories of the homeland that might otherwise disappear. And yet, as we shall see, it is often the case that Irish immigrants' memoirs, especially those written by women, do not actually reflect at great length on memories of Ireland itself. Rather than reviving images of the lost homeland, the memoirs often instead trace out patterns of continuity at a personal level, locating the writers not in pastoral landscapes but in family units. This suggests the bias that continues to exist in the scholarship on Irish diasporic memory, which tends to center on ethnically and nationally overt manifestations of memory, such as Saint Patrick's Day parades, to the detriment of more nuanced explorations of diasporic memory that transcend the boundaries of the nation-state and that reside in the realms of the personal and indeed the universal.

Conversely, it is memory's continuity in contexts of diaspora that is the focus of Andreas Huyssen's work.[33] Going against the grain of diasporic memory scholarship, so much of which highlights the distortion of cultural memory through emigration, Huyssen stresses that "in terms of memory formation, diaspora and nation, rather than being in opposition to each other, may have more troubling affinities than visible at first sight."[34] Huyssen convincingly qualifies this position by pointing out the false sense of homogeneity forced on immigrant groups by the host society and the extent to which this classification of diverse people according to their real or imagined shared qualities mirrors the homogenizing efforts of the nation-state: "Its tenuous and often threatened status within the majority culture, whose stereotyping of otherness combined with its exclusionary mechanisms, may make a given diaspora appear more homogeneous than it is in reality. Precisely because of such pressures the diaspora cannot offer redemption from the national."[35]

Furthermore, Huyssen argues that immigrants' reliance on tangible memories of the homeland, such as food, symbols, or rituals, is simply a more transparent expression of the process of memory making that goes on within the national homeland. "The attempt," says Huyssen, "to create a unified or even mythic memory of the lost homeland and the desire to return may be as much a temptation for the diaspora as the creation of a unitary national memory is for the nation."[36] Yasemin Nuhoglu Soysal supports Huyssen's position, arguing that diaspora is an extension of the nation-state model in that it constitutes foreignness within other nations and ethnicities and implies a congruence between territory, culture, and identity.[37] From this perspective, the only difference between national and diasporic memory is the latter's sense of consciousness over its memory construction. "While national memory usually veils its *Nachträglichkeit*, diasporic memory remains critically aware of it," Huyssen concludes.[38] This in turn suggests the possibility of interpreting diasporic memory as a pure and distilled form of national memory rather than as its deviant, derivative, or impoverished relation.

The third theme of memory's diversification in contexts of diaspora is touched upon in my earlier analysis of Mary O'Mahoney's memoir, where I suggest the influence of the turn-of-the-century American feminist movements in mediating Mary's family memory. To a certain extent this may simply echo Maurice Halbwachs's theory of collective memory, which acknowledges the constellation of cultural influences that inform individual memory. However, the suddenness with which immigrants encounter new cultural norms in the host society, and the expectations traditionally placed on immigrants to interpret and integrate them into their own cultural outputs, must be understood as having specific jolting effects on immigrants' memories. Michael Rothberg's work on multidirectional memory attempts to grapple with this phenomenon, suggesting that memory in such contexts is understood "as subject to ongoing negotiation, cross-referencing and borrowing."[39] In reality, there is nothing very radical about Rothberg's formulation of multidirectional memory, and its usefulness in contexts of diasporic memory may be limited to its reassertion of the ways that individuals borrow and adapt from cultural frameworks that may seem foreign and strange. Even for immigrants who feel themselves to be entrenched in the cultural norms of the homeland, their memories will inevitably be recalibrated by their exposure to cultural trends in the new host society.[40] Rothberg also emphasizes the extent to which the multidirectionality of memory, which gleans from home and host society as it sees fit, becomes a source of "powerful creativity" for the immigrant—a fact confirmed in the immigrant life writing that follows, so much of which shows the imaginative grafting of American cultural norms onto Irish narrative forms.

One theme arguably undervalued in these aforementioned considerations of diasporic memory relates to the elemental connection between memory and belonging.[41] "Remembering," as Assmann writes, "is a realization of belonging."[42] Assmann goes on to remind us that "memory enables us to live in groups and communities, and living in groups and communities enables us to build a memory."[43] It goes without saying that one of emigration's main effects is its disruption of one's sense of belonging, forcing the development of new modes of socialization elsewhere. That memory registers this process with particular accuracy is exciting, for it implies that the seemingly elusive processes that Irish immigrants engaged with to cultivate a sense of belonging in the United States can be traced through the content of their communicated memories. Studying these memories—in this case through immigrants' written memoirs—in turn enables us to harmonize the subjective, ephemeral efforts made by individual Irish immigrants in the US to cultivate a sense of belonging against their more formal manifestations. To date, it is the latter that have received the most attention in Irish migrant scholarship, with associations and institutions like the Ancient Order of Hibernians, the Fenian Brotherhood, Tammany Hall's political machinery, the Knights of Saint Columbus, and Clan na nGael extensively studied as indicators of Irish adaption to American life.[44] It hardly needs to be stated that those who took part in such formal ethnic associations represent a subgroup of atypically zealous individuals for whom ethnicity, religion, or politics was of utmost importance. Moreover, memberships of such associations tend to be predominantly male, thus perpetuating the problems of gendered memory that we encountered earlier in this chapter. Conversely, the intimate writing of vernacular Irish immigrant memoirs opens a window onto the inner world of nonjoiners, providing broader understanding of the complexities of group formation in the US for those who did not feel their nationality, ethnicity, or religion to be at the fore of their social identity. These people's memories can provide insight into the more subtle, everyday journeys toward belonging traversed by Irish immigrant men and women in the US at various points across the twentieth century.

Memory and Place

Emigration engenders, at its most basic level, the loss of a native place. If this sense of loss is shared by emigrant groups globally, it is portrayed as having had a particularly devastating effect on the Irish, a people historically imagined as having an unusually charged sense of native place. This image is stressed in the Irish emigrant literature of the nineteenth and twentieth centuries, which portrays the Irish landscape in anthropomorphic terms, as illustrated in the following extract from Jeremiah O'Donovan Rossa's memoir. Here, O'Donovan Rossa compares Irish immigrants in the US to trees, physically and traumatically uprooted from their native landscape and withering in foreign soil:

> This rooting out of the Irish people; this transplanting of them from their native home into a foreign land, may be all very well, so far as the young

people are concerned; but for the fathers and mothers who have reared families in Ireland, it is immediate decay and death. The young tree may be transplanted from one field to another without injury to its health, but try that transplanting on the tree that has attained its natural growth, and it is its decay and death. The most melancholy looking picture I see in America, is the old father or mother brought over from Ireland by their children. See them coming from mass of a Sunday morning, looking so sad and lonely; no one to speak to; no one around they know; strangers in a strange land.[45]

This idea of Irish emigrants pining for their native landscape from a far-flung immigrant enclave continues to reappear in the Irish cultural consciousness into the present day. John Creedon's popular book *That Place We Call Home*, published in 2020, explores the famed Irish sense of place. In its opening exposition, it evokes the image of the Irish emigrant to confirm the seriousness of the Irish attachment to place: "When you add the story of Irish emigration, you'll better understand why that longing for home has deepened our love of place more than most. Indeed, it's this love of place that sees Irish emigrant gatherings the world over belt out ballads that are often little more than lists of place-names."[46]

Within this place-based discourse, there has been sustained emphasis on the Irish landscape as a cultural mnemonic, for those at home as well as abroad. Kevin O'Neill writes, for example, that the painful dislocation experienced by Irish immigrants in America was due to the strangeness of their new urban environment. For these Irish, "place and landscape formed important structural elements of social memory to communities that were now urban and industrial."[47] Landscape as a canvas for memory is also explored in Elizabeth Grubgeld's analysis of Anglo-Irish autobiographies, where "landscapes take part in human emotion and participate in human consciousness."[48] An iconic article written by Patrick Sheeran in the 1980s further navigates the genesis and evolution of what he calls Ireland's *genius fabulae*.[49] Sheeran's writing assumes the relationship between rural landscapes and memory in Ireland, rhetorically asking, "How many of us remember hearing, as we grew up in the towns and cities, an antiphonal incantation of parish and townland names . . . now grown remote and mysterious, full of the pain of memory?"[50]

A number of respective multidisciplinary studies have focused on the relationship between place and memory in Ireland. Each of these studies was carried out in Northern Ireland, and each observes the peculiar exchange between memory and landscape in the human geography of the border. According to Hastings Donnan, Irish Protestant farmers within these territories "used material elements in the landscape to bring to mind the past."[51] In this context, Donnan argues, "landscapes serve as aide memoirs [sic], recalling the sights, sounds and smells of former times and providing 'frameworks through which people perceive and engage with the present and future.'"[52] Likewise, Ray Cashman's study of Irish Catholics in County Tyrone finds that "in rural Aghyaran, mental connections between places and narrative often focus radically inward, clutching this spot, this land as our birthplace, our birth-right."[53] Henry Glassie's momentous ethnographies, *Passing the Time in Ballymenone* and *The Stars of Ballymenone,* also illuminate memory's reliance on place in the district of Ballymenone, a Fermanagh townland skirting the border between the north and the republic of Ireland.[54] Over the course of the 1970s, when the Northern Ireland conflict was at its height, Glassie recorded what he called the "verbal art" of the men of this district, who gathered nightly by the fireside to tell stories. Glassie was fascinated at how the Ballymenone storytellers carefully referenced the contours of the surrounding landscape to locate, legitimize, and renew their memories of events, stories, and histories that had preceded them. Where academic historians' obsession was with time and chronology, Glassie realized that the chief concern of the vernacular historians of Ballymenone was the location of their histories in a particular place. In Ballymenone, Glassie went on to write, "The landscape we share with the dead swells into an encompassing mnemonic, embodying our history and urging us to judgement."

It is not unexpected that these observations of memory's cleaving to place occurred in Northern Ireland and thus within contested political territory. As Angela Martin notes, "many contemporary social and political movements, especially nationalist movements, rely heavily on associations of place with particular identities."[55] Benedict Anderson's work on imagined communities also asserts the use of landscape in the making of the nation-state as a demonstration of the "antiquity of specific tightly-bound territorial units."[56] Simon Schama adds that "inherited landscape myth and memories share two common characteristics: their surprising endurance through the centuries and their power to shape institutions."[57] These insights force us to question whether place-memory is an actual form of memory or in fact another construction of the nation-state, developed during its search for expression in an appropriate landscape tradition.[58] Indeed, it seems to be precisely this mythic sacralization of place within Irish society in the 1940s (fueled in no small way by the Land League) that led poet Patrick Kavanagh to write his savagely satirical epic, *The Great Hunger*. Through the character of Patrick McGuire, a recognizable Irish bachelor who has forsaken a wife for the family farm, the poem evokes a psychosexual relationship with the Irish landscape, with the love of fields taking precedent over the love of family:

His dream changes like the cloud-swung wind
And he is not so sure now if his mother was right
When she praised the man who made a field his bride

Nonetheless, despite this problematic entanglement of memory with national myths and the blurring of the line between the remembering mind (i.e., people) and the reminding object (i.e., place), there remains evidence to suggest the relevance of place as a social framework of memory. For one thing, the fact that the Irish nation-state drew from images of the Irish landscape to legitimize itself may reflect what Eric Hobsbawm identifies as the nation-state's adoption of traditional symbols and rituals for modern purposes.[59] Beiner continues Hobsbawm's line of thought, pointing out that the agents of nationalism drew "on the deep resources of older memories and ethno-history, so that the traditions of national memory were effectively reinvented rather than invented *ex nihilo*."[60] This implies that the state encouraged the articulation of place-based memories precisely because this was a framework of memory already present in the Irish vernacular tradition and thus likely to survive transplantation to a modern national context.

Furthermore, place-memory has become something of a subfield in memory studies itself, and its investigation has deepened understanding of its role as a mnemonic framework. For philosopher Edward C. Casey, place is an important if not essential conduit of memory. Casey writes, "To be placeless in one's remembering is not only to be disorientated: it is to be decidedly disadvantaged with regard to what a more complete mnemonic experience might deliver."[61] Casey's writing calls to mind the ancient Roman and Greek method of loci, which emphasized that memories could best be retrieved by associating them with particular places. However, what clearly distinguishes Casey's view of place-memory from the chauvinistic Irish "blood and soil" concept is Casey's stress on the role of people in constituting place. This emphasis is important, for it gets beyond a Jungian concept of place possessing its own energetic memory-fields, as suggested in the work of O'Donovan

Rossa, Batt O'Connor, John Montague, and many other Irish nationalist writers from the mid-nineteenth century. "Place is what takes place between body and landscape," Casey affirms succinctly.[62] Likewise, for Yi-Fu Tuan, a key figure in humanistic geography in the twentieth and twenty-first centuries, a sense of place is bound up with feelings: "When space feels thoroughly familiar to us, it becomes place," Tuan writes.[63] Tuan's words suggest that it is the sense of emotional belonging that emerges from place that influences its foregrounding in memory. The love of place in this sense can be understood as a proxy for other emotional attachments, such as love of family, neighbors, or community. In the fervency of late nineteenth-century Irish nationalism, which focused so much attention on the ownership of the land, this metaphorical role of place was evidently forgotten, mutating instead to a literal and quasi-fanatic obsession with land as object rather than subject.

Research by Angela K. Martin and Catherine Nash on place and identity in Ireland highlight both its reductive and politicized conceptualization, as well as its highly gendered evocation as a masculine space.[64] Nash's pathbreaking work strives to expand the traditional Irish conceptualization of place as exclusively connoting a pastoral Irish landscape. Nash writes that "the idea of place operates at the abstract level of the Nation."[65] However, she adds, "it also concerns the visual relationship to place associated with the concept of 'landscape' and the sensual, lived experience of the local environment."[66] Nash thus consciously broadens the conceptualization of the Irish sense of place beyond the inanimate canvas of rural landscape to take account of women's experiences within it.

Martin's and Nash's research opens up new ways of engaging with Irish place-memory by counterbalancing the more frequent study of memories in the context of rural landscape with the study of memories located in intimate, domestic spaces. As this book makes clear, such place-memories are abundant throughout Irish immigrant memoirs, hiding in plain sight. Mary O'Mahoney, for example, recalls the family home back in Ballydehob in the evocative detail:

> I still remember quite distinctly where our house was located, and how it looked both outside and inside. It was a tall three-story house with a cellar or basement underneath. It was built of rock and had a slate roof that was quite steep. The shop was in the front and had three large windows. Two were on the east and one on the north. North of the north window was the hall door. This door led into a long hall at the end of which was the kitchen.

A stairway led up to the second floor from this hall. On the second floor were three bedrooms and the parlor. There was a landing outside these rooms and another staircase led from this landing up to the third floor. It was arranged as the second floor with a landing and four more rooms. Behind the shop were the kitchen and dining room. Doors with glass in the upper half opened from the shop into both kitchen and dining room. The ceilings in all the rooms and in the shop also were very high. The walls were plastered and the upstairs rooms were papered. As well as I remember, the rooms were all about fourteen by sixteen.

Such recollections point to the importance of domestic spaces in locating memories and in turn direct attention to another realm of memory: the multilayered sphere of family memory.

Family Memory

The realm of the family reoccurs constantly in Mary's memoir, accessed in the quote above through the window of domestic space. We circle back to the specifics of family memory, then, as the final social framework in this study of Irish immigrant life writing. As I noted earlier, memory studies often spotlight memory acts generated by or related explicitly to the politics of the nation-state. Pierre Nora's iconic *Realms of Memory*, for instance, creates an inventory of French "sites" of memory that in the words of Pim den Boer "were created, invented or reworked to serve the nation-state."[67] Despite or perhaps because of the ideological nationalism of Nora's work—work that thinly veiled Nora's resistance to the replacement of a French national hegemonic memory with a more diverse and multicultural model—a comparative body of research on national *lieux de mémoire* took place across Europe in the 1990s and early 2000s, maintaining the focus on memory as a project of and for the nation-state. This sidelined the study of many other social frameworks of memory, including the family, the local community, and, as I will explore in a subsequent chapter, the realm of intimate friendships.

The foregrounding of the nation-state is unfortunate since, as Halbwachs noted, family is a primary node in the network of collective memory.[68] Indeed, Halbwachs discerned three distinct roles that family plays in the formulation of memory. First, he understood family as a fundamental component of the individual's social framework, constituting for most individuals a first experience of group belonging and thus a formative *lieu de mémoire*.

Second, Halbwachs identified family memory as a specific type of collective memory, distinguished by its focus on relationships, its informal but sustained transmission through face-to-face interaction, and its emphasis on emotions rather than facts. Although Halbwachs did not include gender as a distinguishing feature of family memory, given the research that subsequently emerged through Fentress's work on social memory, it is clear that family memory as a type tends to be orchestrated and mediated by women as much as if not more than by men. In this regard family memory is unique, and the role of women as the primary transmitters of family memory perhaps partially explains why it has been so overlooked in memory studies, which has prioritized male modes of memory.

Third, Halbwachs identified family as a conduit of broader forms of social memory, such as religious, cultural, national, or political. This is obvious in Henry's and Mary's memoirs, which illustrate how the Irish nationalist cause was encoded into Mary's childhood memories through her parents' role in the Ballydehob branch of the Land League. Erll reinforces the importance of this third type of family memory by adding that oral histories and other acts of memory "have shown that official, national and transnational memory is continually refracted through acts of remembrance taking place within small communities such as families."[69]

My focus on family as a social framework of memory in this study is stimulated not just by Halbwachs's sense of its importance but also by three further discoveries I made as I researched this book. First, memoirs in general and women's memoirs in particular reveal that the family life cycle frequently provides a narrative structure for Irish immigrants' written reminiscences. Memoirs often begin by giving the birth dates and birthplaces of the narrator's parents and end with descriptions of events such as the births of the memoirist's own children or the death of their spouse. Arguably, this narrative structure is influenced by the memoirist's exposure to the generic schema of memoir, which foreground narrations of certain elements of family life.[70] However, the structural role of family in memory acts is also apparent in oral histories, which are less restricted by established generic rules yet also tend to "remember" through the architecture of the family, especially when the oral history participants are women.

Second and inextricable from the first point, this book's immigrant memoirs make it clear that it was often the presence of children or grandchildren that inspired individuals to write down their memories. Passing on memories was understood in some cases as a form of social remittance, one that would fortify and unify the family memory. In other cases it was envisioned as a form of inheritance, bound up with the narrator's sense of their own mortality and their attendant desire to leave something behind for their descendants to remember them by. In all cases it confirms the importance of family, both as an architecture and stimulus for the release of personal memory, even in contexts that would seem to be dominated by other experiences, such as emigration.

Third, in the context of post-Famine Irish emigration to the United States, family emerges as a particularly important site of what Beiner refers to as "prememory." For Beiner, prememory signifies the building blocks of memory that predate historical events, such as the emigration of a family member.[71] In the context of emigration, these building blocks are not just cultural but also specifically familial, since by the post-Famine period emigration had become a part of most Irish family's lived experience. Postcards, letters, and other memorabilia family members sent from America back to Ireland thus generated prememories for those who would eventually emigrate themselves: the information that had circulated about America before their departure made their own experiences and "memories" of migration more predictable.[72] As Tom Brick observes in his memoir, "I had a fair knowledge of United States history from a large United States history book that my sister Mary Brick had brought back home on a visit from Salix, Iowa, U.S.A., about 1897 or 1898." Nora O'Connor similarly recalls that her sister Nellie "sent home the latest songs to us from America": "'The shade of the old apple tree' was very popular then and many the summer evening the 'bunch' walked arm in arm down the Quay Road [in Bantry, County Cork,] singing it."

For Irish immigrants, these prememories were not emblematic of a conceptual story of Ireland but part of the intimate stories of their families. They are cultural memories preserved, nested, and embodied in women like Mary Brick and Nellie O'Connor, without whom the songs and books sent back from America may have been forgotten or relocated to the sphere of abstract knowledge. By the mediation of intimates such as family, friends, neighbors, and lovers, that information becomes memory. And if we look to other immigrant groups, we inevitably discover the universal location of memory within close-knit circles. As the historian of memory Peter Burke has concluded, "It is normal for memories to be more vivid at the level of village or family rather than the nation. . . . Take the case of my late mother-in-law, born in Brazil of Italian parents. Her mother came from South Italy, a very Catholic and conservative family. . . . And what she remembered were the stories of the family . . . she did not read histories of migration."[73] This is the way, Burke insists, that people remember the past versus what history books can tell us. And we need the view from both sides.

Conclusion

In this introductory chapter, I have signposted the different frameworks of memory that I have considered most carefully when analyzing Irish immigrants' life writing. For the sake of exposition, I have dealt with each framework separately, but I am not suggesting that any of these *cadres sociaux* can exist independently of the others, nor do I mean to imply their definitiveness as closed concepts. The notion of family, for instance, can include close friends, and indeed it is within friendships that individuals often experience the acceptance and support that is so often associated with family. Furthermore, as Erll reminds us, every individual memory is related to several collective memories because every person belongs to various social groups—not only to family but also to, say, a village community, a political movement, a football club, a work union, and, yes, a nation. All of these realms provide specific experiences and memory systems, which in turn are reconstructed over time in accordance with a particular group's fluctuating needs and aspirations.[74] The specific challenge now lying before us is to apply these shifting, overlapping frames to interpret the memory discourses that emerged among Irish immigrants in the United States from the late nineteenth to the mid-twentieth century. To begin this journey, we turn to popular memory discourses concerning the Irish in the United States at the turn of the twentieth century as channeled through print, parades, and political rhetoric.

Notes

1. Henry O'Mahoney and Mary O'Mahoney Lupton Memoirs, University of Galway Archive, P155/11/2 - P155/32/6.

2. Gregor Feindt et al., "Entangled Memory: Toward a Third Wave in Memory Studies," *History and Theory* 53, no. 1 (2014).

3. Maurice Halbwachs, *On Collective Memory*, trans. Lewis A. Coser (Chicago: University of Chicago Press, 1992).

4. Brian Casey, *Class and Community in Provincial Ireland, 1851–1914* (London: Palgrave, 2018), 125. O'Mahoney's Fenianism is also referenced in Frank Rynne, "The Great Famine in Nationalist and Land League Propaganda, 1879–1882," *Mémoire(s), identité(s), marginalité(s) dans le monde occidental contemporain* 12 (2015), doi.org/10.4000/mimmoc.1864.

5. Jan Assmann, "Communicative and Cultural Memory," in *Cultural Memory Studies: An International and Interdisciplinary Handbook*, ed. Astrid Erll and Ansgar Nünning (Berlin: De Gruyter, 2008), 109.

6. Paul Ricoeur, *Memory, History, Forgetting* (Chicago: University of Chicago Press, 2004), 24.

7. Quoted in Jeffrey K. Olick and Joyce Robbins, "Social Memory Studies: From 'Collective Memory' to the Historical Sociology of Mnemonic Practices," *Annual Review of Sociology* 24 (1998): 111.

8. Astrid Erll, "Locating Family in Cultural Memory Studies," *Journal of Comparative Family Studies* 42, no. 3 (2011): 314.

9. James Fentress and Chris Wickham, *Social Memory* (Oxford: Blackwell, 1992), 96.

10. Guy Beiner, "Probing the Boundaries of Irish Memory: From Postmemory to Prememory and Back," *Irish Historical Studies* 39, no. 154 (2014): 298, 299.

11. Astrid Erll, introduction to *A Companion to. Cultural Memory Studies*, ed. Astrid Erll and Ansgar Nünning (Berlin: De Gruyter, 2010), 2.

12. Assmann, "Communicative and Cultural Memory."

13. Harald Welzer, "Communicative Memory," in *A Companion to Cultural Memory Studies*, ed. Astrid Erll and Ansgar Nünning (Berlin: De Gruyter, 2010), 291.

14. Welzer, "Communicative Memory," 292.

15. J. Olaf Kleist, *Political Memories and Migration: Belonging, Society, and Australia Day* (London: Palgrave Macmillan, 2017), 7.

16. Recent developments include Ayşe Gül Altınay, María José Contreras, Marianne Hirsch, Jean Howard, Banu Karaca, and Alisa Solomon, eds., *Women Mobilizing Memory* (New York: Columbia University Press, 2019). See also Marianne Hirsch and Valerie Smith, "Feminism and Cultural Memory: An Introduction," *Signs*, no. 1 (2002): 1–19.

17. Fentress and Wickham, *Social Memory*, 137.

18. E. J. Hobsbawm and T. O. Ranger, *The Invention of Tradition* (Cambridge: Cambridge University Press, 1983).

19. Silvia Federici, *Witches, Witch-Hunting and Women* (San Francisco: PM, 2018); Joanna Bourke, *Husbandry to Housewifery: Women, Economic Change, and Housework in Ireland, 1890–1914* (Oxford: Clarendon, 1993).

20. Fentress and Wickham, *Social Memory*, 140.

21. Fentress and Wickham, *Social Memory*, 141.

22. Fentress and Wickham, *Social Memory*, 142.

23. Fentress and Wickham, *Social Memory*, 142.

24. Fentress and Wickham, *Social Memory*, 142.

25. Fentress and Wickham, *Social Memory*, 142.

26. Willa Cather, Gertrude Stein, Edith Wharton, and Mary McCarthy were just some of the era's popular authors. It is difficult to imagine that these writers' focus on the female experience did not influence the writing of a self-professed book lover like Mary. See further exploration of Irish immigrant women's engagement with American writing in Geraldine Meaney, Mary O'Dowd, and Bernadette Whelan, *Reading the Irish Woman: Studies in Cultural Encounter and Exchange, 1714–1960* (Liverpool: Liverpool University Press, 2013).

27. Hasia R. Diner, *Erin's Daughters in America* (Baltimore, MD: Johns Hopkins University Press, 1983); Linda Dowling, "A Great Time to Be in America: The Irish in Post-Second World War New York City," in *Ireland in the 1950s: The Lost Decade*, ed. Dermot Keogh, Finbar O'Shea, and Carmel Quinlan (Cork: Mercier, 2004).

28. Ghassan Hage, "Migration, Food, Memory and Home-Building," in *Memory: Histories, Theories, Debates*, ed. Susannah Radstone and Bill Schwarz (New York: Fordham University Press, 2010); Marianne Hirsch, *The Generation of Post-Memory: Writing and Visual Culture after the Holocaust* (New York: Columbia University Press, 2012).

29. Oona Frawley, ed., *Diaspora and Memory Practice*, vol. 2 of *Memory Ireland* (Syracuse, NY: Syracuse University Press, 2011), 4.

30. Simon Schama, *Landscape and Memory* (London: HarperCollins, 1995), 15.

31. Liam Harte notes that concerns about inauthenticity haunt the autobiographical writings of the Irish in Britain. This is less apparent in Irish American autobiographical writing. Liam Harte, "Migrancy, Performativity and Autobiographical Identity," *Irish Studies Review* 14, no. 2 (2006).

32. Frawley, *Diaspora and Memory Practice*, 5.

33. Andreas Huyssen, "Diaspora and Nation: Migration into Other Pasts," *New German Critique*, no. 88 (2003).

34. Huyssen, "Diaspora and Nation," 150.

35. Huyssen, "Diaspora and Nation," 149.

36. Huyssen, "Diaspora and Nation," 150.

37. Yasemin Nuho Flu Soysal, *Transnational Trajectories in East Asia: Nation, Citizenship, and Region* (London: Routledge, 2014), quoted in Huyssen, "Diaspora and Nation," 150.

38. Huyssen, "Diaspora and Nation," 152.

39. Michael Rothberg, *Multidirectional Memory: Remembering the Holocaust in the Age of Decolonization* (Stanford: Stanford University Press, 2009), 3.

40. Rothberg, *Multidirectional Memory*, 5.

41. A rare exception is Kleist, *Political Memories and Migration*, 3.

42. Assmann, "Communicative and Cultural Memory," 111.

43. Assmann, "Communicative and Cultural Memory," 112.

44. Kevin Kenny, *The American Irish: A History* (Harlow, UK: Longman, 2000); Timothy Meagher, *Inventing Irish America: Generation, Class, and Ethnic Identity in a New England City, 1880–1928* (Notre Dame, IN: University of Notre Dame Press, 2000); David Thomas Brundage, *Irish Nationalists in America: The Politics of Exile, 1798–1998* (Oxford: Oxford University Press, 2016); Michael Glazier, ed., *The Encyclopedia of the Irish in America* (Notre Dame, IN: Notre Dame University Press, 1999).

45. Jeremiah O'Donovan Rossa, *Rossa's Recollections, 1838–1898* (Shannon: Irish University Press, 1972).

46. John Creedon, *That Place We Call Home* (Dublin: Gill, 2020), 38.

47. Kevin O Neill, "The Star Spangled Shamrock: Memory and Meaning in Irish America," in *History and Memory in Modern Ireland*, ed. Ian McBride (Cambridge: Cambridge University Press, 2001), 121.

48. Elizabeth Grubgeld, *Anglo Irish Autobiography: Class, Gender and the Forms of Narrative* (Syracuse, NY: Syracuse University Press, 2004), 24.

49. Patrick Sheeran, "Genius Fabulae: The Irish Sense of Place," *Irish University Review* 18, no. 2 (1988), http://www.jstor.org/stable/25484245.

50. Sheeran, "Genius Fabulae," 198.

51. Hastings Donnan, "Material Identities: Fixing Ethnicity in the Irish Borderlands," *Identities: Global Studies in Culture and Power* 12, no. 1 (2005): 96.

52. Donnan, "Material Identities," 75.

53. Ray Cashman, "Visions of Irish Nationalism," *Journal of Folklore Research* 45, no. 3 (2008): 375.

54. Henry Glassie, *The Stars of Ballymenone* (Bloomington: Indiana University Press, 2006); Henry Glassie, *Passing the Time in Ballymenone: Culture and History of an Ulster Community* (Philadelphia: University of Pennsylvania Press, 1982).

55. Angela K. Martin, "The Practice of Identity and an Irish Sense of Place," *Gender, Place and Culture* 4, no. 1 (1997): 89.

56. Benedict Anderson, *Imagined Communities: Reflections on the Origin and Spread of Nationalism* (London: Verso, 1983), 175.

57. Schama, *Landscape and Memory*, 15.

58. James Koranyi and Tricia Cusack, "The Making of Landscape in Modernity," *National Identities* 16, no. 3 (2014): 192.

59. Hobsbawm and Ranger, *The Invention of Tradition*.

60. Guy Beiner, *Forgetful Remembrance: Social Forgetting and Vernacular Historiography of a Rebellion in Ulster* (New York: Oxford University Press, 2018), 29.

61. Edward S. Casey, *Remembering: A Phenomenological Study*, 2nd ed. (Bloomington: Indiana University Press, 2000), 184.

62. Edward S. Casey, *Getting Back into Place: Toward a Renewed Understanding of the Place-World*, 2nd ed. (Bloomington: Indiana University Press, 2009), 29.

63. Quoted in Casey, *Remembering*, 178.

64. Catherine Nash, "Landscape, Body and Nation: Cultural Geographies of Irish Identities," PhD thesis, University of Nottingham, 1995; Angela K. Martin, "The Practice of Identity and an Irish Sense of Place," *Gender Place, and Culture* 4, no. 1 (1997): 89–114.

65. Nash, "Landscape," 228.

66. Nash, "Landscape," 228.

67. Pim Den Boer, "Loci Memoriae—Lieux de mémoire," in *A Companion to Cultural Memory Studies*, ed. Astrid Erll and Ansgar Nünning (Berlin: De Gruyter, 2008), 20; Pierre Nora, *Realms of Memory: The Construction of the French Past*, 3 vols., ed. Lawrence D. Kritzman, trans. Arthur Goldhammer (New York: Columbia University Press, 1996–98).

68. Erll, "Locating Family in Cultural Memory Studies," 305.

69. Erll, "Locating Family in Cultural Memory Studies," 312.

70. Grubgeld, *Anglo Irish Autobiography: Class, Gender and the Forms of Narrative*.

71. Beiner, "Probing the Boundaries of Irish Memory."

72. Meaney, O'Dowd, and Whelan, *Reading the Irish Woman*.

73. Justin Winkler and Peter Burke, "Cultural Displacements and Intellectual Moorings—A Conversation with Peter Burke," *Mobile Cultural Studies*, no. 2 (2016): 143.

74. Erll, "Locating Family in Cultural Memory Studies," 305.

2

Irish American Memory Narratives

In 1905 the leader of Ireland's Gaelic League, Douglas Hyde, embarked on a fundraising tour of the United States organized by John Quinn, a bourgeois Irish émigré. Hyde's reception reflected the dawn of a new era for Irish immigrants in North America. Hyde lunched at the White House and attended dinners hosted by the political, legal, and financial elite of New York, Chicago, Washington, and San Francisco. His lectures across country sold out to audiences of Irish immigrants dressed in the finest formal evening attire.[1] "The genteel, black-tie congregation" that greeted Hyde was, in the words of Liam Mac Mathúna, "a world away from the emaciated, ragged hordes who had flooded into American east coast ports half a century earlier in a desperate bid to escape from the Famine stalking the emerald isle."[2]

The iconography and discourse that framed Hyde's tour and its portrayal as a counterpoint to the conditions of Irish immigrants in the wake of the Great Famine make available the memory narratives that had emerged over the previous century among the Irish in America.[3] In advance of Hyde's arrival, an Irish night held at Manhattan Beach by the Gaelic League of New York "included a pyrotechnic display projecting images of Hyde's face, a multi-colored harp and the features of Robert Emmet." At a dinner in Chicago, Hyde was regaled by tales of wealthy Irish Americans "who were not ashamed to admit" that they had fled the Famine.[4] Rows broke out over the music that Hyde should be entertained with: While some favored the sentimental, commercially successful laments of Thomas Moore's *Irish Melodies*, others preferred traditional songs and melodies originating from Irish-speaking artists in the West of Ireland.[5]

Irish Americans also closely analyzed the discourse of Hyde's speeches. While a newly emerged middle class applauded the intellectual, forward-looking, and apolitical tone of Hyde's speeches, others bemoaned the absence of references to political events that had come to form the centerpiece of Irish American memory. John O'Callaghan of the United Irish League in Boston thus wrote bitterly that Hyde had made no mention of Thomas Davis, the men of '48, Parnell, or the Land League movement.[6] For his part, Hyde fielded protests from some impassioned Irish American nationalists who resented the "tuxedo-wearing brigade" who had come out to greet him, arguing that they were rarely known to have played any role in advancing the Irish "cause."[7]

As Margaret Kelleher notes, these jostles reveal the socioeconomic tensions that had developed among Irish Americans by the turn of the twentieth century.[8] They also highlight the extent to which, for many, Irish nationalism in America hinged on a memory of violent separatist republicanism. To understand the forces that shaped these memories requires a review of the rhetorical and material culture associated with Irish America, as identified by its many scholars. This exercise may point us toward the experiences and the people disregarded during the fashioning of Irish American collective memory.

Emigration as Exile

Perhaps the most iconic scholarship on Irish emigration to the United States remains Kerby Miller's *Emigrants and Exiles*.[9] A formative work of interpretation, Miller's tome reveals that Irish emigration was principally narrated as exile, a trope that flourished in speeches, sermons, popular music, and in emigrants' own correspondence across the nineteenth and twentieth century. The reason for this perceived banishment was overwhelmingly portrayed as Britain's colonial legacy of high rents, eviction, and agricultural mismanagement. For example, a woman in County Meath in 1850 wrote, "Our fine country is abandoned by all the population, the landlords sending them away from the ditch to the cradle."[10] Similarly, an American traveler in 1848 wrote that the Irish set "all their misfortunes and misery ... to the account of English interference—high rents, heavy taxes, potato rot, and all."[11] For Miller, this theme was pervasive to the point of being suspicious. "It must," Miller concludes, "have performed crucial functions in post-Famine Ireland."[12]

This seems all the more probable given that even after the relaxation of tenant right in the 1880s and the foundation of the Irish Free State in 1921, fewer than 10 percent of Irish immigrants in America chose to return to Ireland.

Miller develops two theories to explain the origin of this exilic memory narrative. First, he argues that the beliefs and practices of what he sees as a premodern Catholic peasantry predisposed the Irish to regard emigration fatalistically, imagining and indeed remembering it as involuntary banishment rather than voluntary enterprise or self-improvement.[13] For Miller, this irrational attitude to emigration is also reflected in the simplistic and binary terms in which the Irish perceived the United States. "Especially in the West of Ireland," notes Miller, "the United States was either seen as a halfway stage to heaven or else as an awful forbidding place where most pined and starved their way to early graves."[14]

The second and more convincing of Miller's theories argues that emigration as exile is a narrative popularized by an emergent Irish Catholic bourgeoisie, who realized during the Famine that their own economic prosperity through large-scale agriculture hinged on the continuance of mass migration. Miller premises this argument in the economic conditions that precipitated emigration in post-Famine Ireland, which, unlike the pre-Famine and Famine period, were principally a result of forces wielded by Irish Catholic society itself. The first of these forces concerned the shift across the countryside toward impartible inheritance of land, through which only one (usually male) heir was named as successor to the farm. Although impartible inheritance could be understood as a forced response to the global market, which increasingly demanded dairy and beef and which required farmers to graze ever larger tracts of pasture, it was also inevitably a family decision, and one that forced all but the inheriting son to emigrate. Irish families in the post-Famine years were thus systematically choosing futures that prioritized the productivity of their land over the unity of their families.

The post-Famine shift away from tillage farming and potato cultivation and toward dairy and beef farming had a similarly devastating effect on landless laborers and noninheriting children. Grain and vegetable cultivation before the Famine required substantial human labor and thus provided a means of paid employment for tens of thousands of nonlanded Irish men and women. Dairy and beef, on the other hand, were less labor intensive, leaving those who traditionally relied on farmwork without a viable future. As a result, the percentage of landless laborers in Ireland declined from 73 percent in 1841 to 56.7 percent by 1911.[15] Acreage devoted to potato cultivation fell from 2.1 million acres in the early 1840s to 587,000 in 1902, further depleting the workforce and particularly reducing female employment opportunities.[16]

This increasingly market-driven rural economy had a devastating effect on small landholders. Between 1841 and 1861, farms under fifteen acres decreased from 78 percent to 47 percent of the land; between 1845 and 1861, smallholdings and cottiers' plots between one and five acres declined by 53 percent; and by 1861 they made up just 14 percent of all farms. Meanwhile, land became consolidated by a new class of "strong" farmers. Farms over thirty acres increased both numerically, by 23 percent, and proportionately, from 20 to 28 percent, between the end of the Famine and 1861, with over 15 percent of all holdings exceeding fifty acres in size.[17] It was this latter group that came to dominate the county electorate and that would set the agenda for local nationalist politics, with its hypocritical myths of Irish identity as hinging on exile on the one hand and on a "blood and soil" place-boundedness on the other.

Indeed, for Theodore Hoppen, the post-Famine decades of the nineteenth century were defined by Catholic farmer triumphalism, when the strong farmers and graziers who had benefited most from the Famine leveraged their resources, atomized their families, and encouraged the weakest and most vulnerable to emigrate in droves.[18] Joe Lee puts it more bluntly: "Few people anywhere in the world have been so prepared to scatter their children around the world in order to preserve their own living standards."[19] Kerby Miller sees exile as essentially a "screen memory" for these triumphant farmers, enabling them to deflect personal responsibility for emigration to the English, to obscure social conflicts between cottiers and a new Catholic bourgeoisie and to relieve psychological tensions within a body of Irish immigrants unwilling to recognize that the perpetrators behind their emigration had become their own families and communities.

The evolution of emigration as exile into a memory narrative is evidenced in its reappearance across different times, places, and contexts over the two centuries after the Famine. It exists in 1916, in a personal letter sent from Ireland by Nora Connelly to the Irish American businessman Hugh Daly: "I do hope, Mr. Daly," Nora writes, "that I will be permitted later to get to the United States and tell our exiled children and Americans in general the story of Easter Week."[20] It lingered through the years after the establishment of the Irish republic, when "the near absences of images of Irishness outside the national borders affirmed the notion of the emigrant as an exile," as Mary Trotter notes in her review of Irish theater in the twentieth century.[21] It cropped up in a speech William Halley delivered in Toronto on Saint Patrick's Day 1860, when he called the Irish "the Ishmaelites of the earth."[22] It is inferred in David Lawlor's memoir, *The Life and Struggles of an Irish Boy in America*, which opens with an eviction scene that explains the cause for his family's emigration:

> The landlord came to my grandfather and told him that his second wife, a lady of the nobility of England had found that my grandfather's farm interfered with her view of the road. He offered him a farm of equal or greater value nearby, but this was not acceptable and it led to a lawsuit. . . . On the day that the verdict was given in the high courts, it was in the fall of the year and the crops were all ready to harvest, a regiment of soldiers appeared, ruined the crops, burned the house and put the whole family out on the roadside.[23]

Most beguilingly, exile was a ubiquitous motif in emigrant songs and poems (many of them dating from United Irishman songs of the late eighteenth century), which Irish immigrants frequently turned to in order to come to terms with their own dislocation. Nora O'Connor's memoir, written in the 1940s, thus includes a poem entitled "An Exile's Prayer" inside its front cover.[24] These lines mask the fact that it was Nora's own mother who forced her to emigrate. Similarly, Michael Kilkrane's turn-of-the-century memoir recalls the lines of a poem to situate his own heartbreak in America:

> Oh pity the fate of the poor Irish stranger
> that wanders so far from home[25]

Yet as it turns out, Michael's grief was less about exile than the recent death of his mother. Clearly, the proliferation of the exile motif in songs, poetry, and public rhetoric across the nineteenth century provided individual post-Famine immigrants with an intoxicating myth that they could live by, one that camouflaged the disturbing truths of their own families' and communities' roles in their immigration to America.

The Great Famine

Together with exile, the Great Famine of 1845–50 has come to the fore of Irish American and Irish diasporic examination.[26] Unlike the study of exile, the

Famine earned the label of a memory narrative arguably because the enormous growth in its study from the 1990s—influenced partly by increased interest in Irish diaspora studies and partly because of emergent famines in Africa—also coincided with the boom in memory studies. The theoretical frameworks of this research facilitated memory-based analyses of monuments, commemorative practices, and art dedicated to the Famine. Yet there is no reason to let the Famine overshadow exile as a memory narrative, since both have been demonstratively regenerated and recycled across different contexts and timescapes in Ireland and America, articulated as personal and collective forms of memory alike.

For Joe Lee, "the memory of the Famine became the focal point around which crystallized Irish America's search for historical understanding of why they found themselves where they were."[27] Likewise, Emily Mark-FitzGerald writes that the Famine appears as subject and reference in political rhetoric, popular and literary fiction, drama, art, and visual culture from the nineteenth century to the present day.[28] Kevin O'Neill argues, in one of the first examinations of Irish American memory, that "the Famine provided Irish-Americans with a charter myth—a creation story that both explains our presence in the new land and connects us to the old via a powerful sense of grievance."[29] Kerby Miller agrees that the remembrance of the Famine intensified the narrative of exile and particularly formed Irish American Catholic and nationalist self-image. Marguérite Corporaal reinforces the Famine as a memory narrative, defining the Famine Irish as "iconic figures of memory" in Irish and Irish American fiction in the late nineteenth and twentieth centuries.[30] For Corporaal and Jason King, the portrayal of Famine in fiction served to idealize Ireland as a pastoral utopia, while the sheer magnitude of the calamity "reinforced a sense of social cohesion amongst Irish Catholics well into the twentieth century."[31] As Miller mentions, this social cohesion took place along religious lines, differentiating Irish Catholics from Irish Protestants and Presbyterians. Lee agrees, noting that "Famine memories would feature prominently in the Catholic sense of identity and in the Protestant not at all."[32]

Yet this agreement on the prominence of the Famine as a memory narrative has not always existed. Mary C. Kelly's erudite work proposes the opposite thesis, arguing that the stigma associated with Famine memories were a major threat to American integration and were thus suppressed in the group's collective memory until the 1990s, at which point Irish Americans felt sufficiently confident to engage in Famine commemoration.[33] In line with Kelly's Freudian-inspired inquiry into repressed memory, scholars of Ireland and the Irish diaspora have historically used terms like *amnesia* and *trauma* to explain the apparent absence of memories of the Famine from the Irish archives.[34] In her examination of the national folklore collection, for example, Maura Cronin puzzles over the lack of recorded vernacular memories of the years between 1845 and 1850, leading her to wonder how a period of such intense devastation and change had made so small a dent on Irish folkloric records.[35] Literature scholars, too, note the absence of Famine from the texts of the time. Based on his analysis of the era's most popular books, Christopher Morash writes that "even when the Famine is remembered, it is mostly through shattered narratives, in texts of radical disorder."[36] When Joseph O'Connor published *Star of the Sea*, in 2003, historian Terry Eagleton applauded the belated arrival of a novel that finally dealt with the trauma of the Famine period.[37] Indeed, as Cormac Ó Gráda argues, the use of trauma to interpret the Famine became something of a cultural phenomenon after 1997, suggesting not just a newfound appreciation for the ramifications of the Famine but a fresh conviction in the existence of a collective memory. References to trauma, writes Ó Gráda, "were echoed repeatedly by Minister of State Avril Doyle, by academics such as Kevin Whelan and David Lloyd and by representatives of the third world charities."[38] Ó Gráda quotes Whelan's claim that "the Famine experience burned itself into the Irish character."[39] Ó Gráda also references Tom Hayden's 1997 collection of essays on the Irish Famine, dedicated to "all those who have had to live with their deepest stories denied."[40]

These variations in opinion suggest that the Famine as a memory narrative was deployed in different ways at different times for different purposes. For Irish Catholics in America, however, its recollection became specifically and strategically important, not only because it helped stoke the resentment O'Neill refers to but also because Famine memory was ideally integrated into the highly symbolic genre of modern autobiography, the popularity of which had exploded by the turn of the twentieth century in Ireland and America alike.

The boom in the publication of immigrant autobiographies included well-known literary texts like Mary Antin's *The Promised Land*, Frederick Gehle's *Our Dubbledam Journey*, and Jacob Riis's *The Making of an American*.[41] The function of such texts was, according to Rachel McLennan, to personify the exceptionalism of the white American male and, as Paul de Man says, to track his "move from cognition to resolution and to action, from speculative to political and legal authority."[42] Critically, this sense of movement and progress requires a challenging starting point—usually situated in the immigrant's impoverished home country—for, as Liz Stanley shows, the American memoir's narrative trajectory tends to cover a life from difficult beginning through trials toward a realized self.[43] In the Irish immigrant context, what but the catastrophic Famine could have better fulfilled this purpose for those desperately seeking acceptance into American life?

As Lee and Miller note, for Irish Protestants in the United States the memory of the Famine was hardly perceptible. There are various reasons for this, including the myth that the Famine did not affect Protestant families. But the most likely is that Irish Protestants did not experience the prejudice leveled at Irish Catholics in nineteenth-century America and thus did not need to rally around a charter myth of victimization. Conversely, for Irish Catholics in the United States, the Famine as a memory narrative worked as a distance marker, signposting the strides they had made from the mid-nineteenth century to the turn of the twentieth century. The grittier the Famine memory, the more the well-integrated Irish immigrant authors could claim to have inherited the qualities of the self-made American. Accordingly, in the late nineteenth century visceral Famine narratives began to emerge in Irish immigrant memoir, popularized by immigrant nationalists like John Mitchel and Jeremiah O'Donovan Rossa, whose Famine memoirs "helped to shape the collective memory of the Famine within the Irish diaspora in America."[44]

Of course, for Mitchel and Rossa the Famine served multiple purposes as a memory narrative, not least the creation of a republican Irish nationalist base in America. For Rossa, the Famine validated his Fenian oath, while for Mitchel recollections of what the Irish had suffered during the Famine had a surreptitious white supremacist function. As Peter O'Neill argues, Mitchel's writing appropriated images of the African slave ship to describe the Famine-era Irish coffin ships, and Mitchel's discourse insisted on the white racial purity of the Irish, whose suffering during the Famine was worse, he claimed, than anything experienced by enslaved Africans.[45] For other immigrants, memories of the Famine legitimized the decision to leave Ireland and thus became interwoven with the memory narrative of exile. John Solon's memoir, for example, opens with a scene of people so beleaguered that "no pen could describe" their condition: "Coupled with destitution, a raging fever set in, caused by starvation. The country was overrun with beggars. I often heard my father tell of my mother distributing meal to fourteen beggars while cooking a kettle for breakfast. That was the scene that fixed his determination to leave the country."[46]

Similarly, the autobiography of immigrant Patrick Cudahy opens with a memory, communicated through his mother, of the years 1847–49, when the Famine, brought on by "misgovernment" as well as lack of employment and crop failure, meant that "anybody that could scrape up money enough left there and came to America. As I have heard my mother say, years before the Famine when people were leaving Ireland there was great sadness and sorrowing, but during the Famine, wherever people had means to go away, sorrowing was changed to rejoicing."[47]

Deploying recollections of the Famine helped these Irish immigrant memoirists construct a compelling narrative of progress and incline, the upward arc of which had become a highly anticipated literary form that served to reinforce the exceptionalism of the United States as a place where anyone could succeed, in spite of the conditions from which they had emerged. Of course, for this narrative arc to progress *away* from the Famine and toward social stability required further actions and chapters, iterations and phases. The next of these would come, in some circles, to be understood as the Irish role in the American Civil War and the subsequent emergence of the Irish American nationalist.

The American Civil War

Kevin O'Neill believes that Irish participation in the American Civil War gave Irish Americans a sustaining social memory. "There is no question," writes O'Neill, "that for the Famine Irish of America the Civil War provided an opportunity to transform both their role in American society and their self-image in positive ways. This transformation was, without question, the single most formative force in the re-working of Irish American social memory and Irish American nationalism."[48]

Richard Jensen agrees. He uses the well-trodden historiography of the Irish brigade and the gallant Irish performance for both the North and the South to contradict claims of anti-Irish prejudice in the mid-nineteenth century. Jensen believes this participation validated Irish claims to American citizenship and indeed acted as the force that led to the naturalization of thousands of Irish in the 1860s. Jensen also argues that their role in the Civil

War enabled Irish immigrants to top longtime Yankee citizens' claims as Republicans, since the Irish had not only fought in the war on their adopted continent but also fled from English oppression in their native land. After the Civil War, the Irish became quintessential patriots.[49]

The veracity of these historical claims can be partly corroborated by the frequency with which Irish immigrant men's autobiographies allude to the Civil War. Although Patrick Cudahy was only twelve years old when the war began, it looms large in his autobiography. "The Civil War broke out while we were still living in the old cottage, and what was known in those days as the Fair Grounds was converted into a military camp," he writes, and he goes on: "The southwest corner of the camp ground was within two or three hundred feet of our cottage and I was back and forth among the soldiers during the first years of the war. I have very vivid recollections of the drilling of the men and the punishment of the unruly ones in the guard house, etc."[50]

This particular memory leads Cudahy to recollect another scene from his childhood, when he received a silver dollar from a group of men in a nearby butternut grove, which later became a Civil War camp. "I do not think any sum of money ever looked so big to me as that dollar did," Cudahy writes; "I ran away home as fast as my legs could carry me and gave the dollar to my mother, and I tell you it made me feel happy to do so."[51] Cudahy interprets this episode as a testament to the struggle of the self-made American man:

> Often have I thought of the cause and effect of where people are poor and of the homes from which spring the self-made men of the country. The father and mother of a large family in times such as I have been telling about, sit around the fireside at night and the subject for conversation or discussion is, what are we going to do to provide for the winter; where are we going to get the wherewith? The boys of five or six years and up to fourteen or fifteen are sitting about, drinking in the father's and mother's conversation and feel part of the distress themselves, and if it were possible for them to assist in any way, nothing would give them greater pleasure, that is, if they are made of the right stuff. So as soon as an opportunity presents itself this young barefoot boy is only too glad to take advantage of it to help the family. This is the grinding that we generally speak of, that makes the man.

This narrative structure suggests how an Irish immigrant had learned to sequence memories of the Civil War, poverty, and eventual economic prosperity in his memoir in order to reassert the rags-to-riches narrative of the Irish in America that was by then an expected literary genre.

In contrast to Cudahy's, the Civil War memories of Henry O'Mahoney, who enlisted in 1865 on the Union side, are far more immediate. O'Mahoney does not hold back from evoking the hardship that he suffered on a gunboat in Cairo, Illinois, the details of which illuminate the broader horrors of a war that would claim the lives of more than ten thousand Irish American men:

> There was nothing there for us but hard work, poor rations, and malaria on the river bottoms. We were on every beat from Cairo to New Orleans, and had to sometimes work day and night to coal up ship. . . . Many times we had to stand this work for twenty-four hours at a stretch with no time to rest except while we ate. I often thought, when sick and worn out from work like that, that death by leaping overboard would be preferable. The rations we got were terrible. The beef was blood red when crumbled with the finger. We often got hardtack which when broken open was full of bugs.[52]

Two of the best memoirs of Civil War service written by Irish officers include those of Andrew J. Byrne and William McCarter. Byrne was just nineteen years old when he emigrated from Dublin, and he wrote his memoir at the turn of the twentieth century. Much of it focuses on his experience as a corporal in the Sixty-Fifth New York Volunteer Infantry Regiment. Byrne's writing captures the sense in which enlisting for the North was a natural step for newly arrived Irish immigrants. He writes, for instance, that "thousands of men were idle, yet thousands of emigrants were landing every week in the Castle Garden," in New York, the country's main immigration processing center: "Some of the new regiments had very fanciful names and catching uniforms. The wives and families of soldiers in the city were provided for by the Municipal Council that along with the money sent by their husbands would keep them comfortable if properly laid out."[53] Byrne's memoir also suggests that, as Jensen and O'Neill argue, enlisting provided Irish immigrants with the "title deeds" to American citizenship. In richly descriptive prose, Byrne reflects on his pride upon entering the Union army: "We arrived in New York and were warmly received as we marched down Broadway in [an] open column of companies, our guns at the shoulder and our drums beating a march. The sidewalks were lined with people who clapped their hands and cheered us on our way. I and my friend Jenkins bore our colours aloft and marched as brave as any man. There was many an eye on the colours so we thought ourselves no small potatoes that day."

In turn, the memoir of William McCarter, an Irish Protestant immigrant who enlisted on the Union side in 1862, shines light on the most eulogized chapter of Irish involvement in the Civil War: that of the Irish Brigade and their ultimately disastrous attack on Marye's Heights at the Battle of Fredericksburg, Virginia, on December 13, 1862. Led by the celebrated Thomas Francis Meagher, famed for his Young Ireland activity to win independence and democratic reform in Ireland, the Irish Brigade became the group that Catholic associations like the Ancient Order of Hibernians (AOH) would fix upon in situating memories of Irishness and the Civil War in the century that followed. McCarter, while evidently uninterested in the Irish American nationalism promoted by the AOH, did not shy away from describing Meagher's exemplary character:

> In kindness and thoughtfulness for his men, he was the shining light and bright star of the whole Union Army. Meagher made unceasing efforts to have his soldiers all well provided for and made comfortable. He often brought some poor, sick or perhaps dying soldier into his own private tent in cold weather. Wrapping him up there in blankets, Meagher administered with his own hands such medicine as was prescribed by the brigade head doctor. . . . He was one of the very few military leaders who never required or would ask any of his command to go where he would not go himself. Meagher was first to lead the way. He was a soldier who not only prided in doing his own duty but encouraged and helped all under him to do theirs. Glory, honor and praise to his memory as a soldier, firm and true to his government and his country.[54]

Despite their vividness, it remains questionable whether such first-person accounts of the Civil War ever fully evolved into the kind of unifying social memory O'Neill claims they were. Although the postwar writings of Irish Brigade veterans like McCarter, David Power Cunningham, Father William Corby, and St. Clair A. Mulholland forged a body of literature that worked to mythologize Irish participation in the Civil War, there is a lack of evidence to prove that Civil War recollections were unilaterally reconstituted as part of Irish American collective memory in subsequent generations.[55] Likewise, despite their best efforts, the AOH did not seem to have transformed the Civil War into the positive mnemonic touchstone they aspired to make it, especially among WASP Americans.[56]

There are numerous reasons for this failure. First, the twenty thousand or so Irish men who fought on the Confederate side were effectively erased by the South's "lost cause remembrance," which downplayed Irish involvement in an attempt to portray its side as a racially pure group of Anglo-Saxons, the last bastion of civility in the United States.[57] Second, the "fighting Irish" moniker that emerged from the Irish Brigade arguably reinforced problematic portrayals of the Irish as quarrelsome rather than promoting a more positive image of Irish American patriotism. Indeed, in spite of Jensen's arguments to the contrary, there remains debate as to whether the Irish role in the Civil War actually changed negative opinions of Irish immigrants in any meaningful way. According to David Gleeson, even the heroic efforts of the Irish Brigade did not do enough to counter the belief among many in the North that the Irish had been halfhearted in the Union cause.[58] Gleeson points out that the New York City draft riots, in which Irish immigrants rose up against conscription, occurred after the Irish Brigade's heroic performance at the Battle of Fredericksburg. Gleeson convincingly argues that ultimately these riots cast a long shadow over the Irish sacrifice made for the North and marred the coherence of Irish patriotism in the Civil War as a mnemonic for Irish Americans in the twentieth century.[59] William Kurtz agrees, adding that Irish Catholic leaders' indecisiveness on emancipation neutralized the value of Irish military service in the Civil War for many Northerners, while debates over abolition among Irish nationalists and the violence of the 1863 draft riots perpetuated "Protestant antipathy to a cohort ... seen as incompatible with America's founding principles."[60] The inconsistency of the view of the Irish role in the Civil War irrevocably damaged its success as a memory narrative in later decades.

Yet as Damien Shiels and Peter Quinn convincingly argue, the sheer numbers of first- and second-generation Irish men who enlisted in the Civil War—calculated as between 150,000 and 200,000—necessarily meant that even if their participation in the war was unevenly maintained in public memory, it remained an integral family memory for hundreds of thousands of Irish American families across the next century.[61] This is best evidenced in military pension files, which include a vast archive of letters and testimonials written by Irish mothers and widows to attest to their relatives' services in the war. As Shiels shows, many of these women had carefully stored their husbands' or sons' letters from the battlefield and cherished their memories not only because doing so might produce pensions but also because their men's roles in the Civil War were a deeply significant part of the transition from Ireland to America. Memoirs of the Civil War evidently formed a centerpiece of these families' communicative memory. Many of the women who submitted to the pension bureau battlefield letters from their sons, husbands, or fathers poignantly requested that they be returned—a request the military archives ultimately ignored.

Irish American Nationalism

For many post-Famine Irish emigrants, a sense of familiarity with American life existed even before they ever set foot on the country's fabled shores.[62] Throughout the nineteenth century, prememories of the happiness that life in the United States entailed were implanted by the letters and packages family members sent back to Ireland. For Manny Steen, who emigrated relatively late, in 1921, the information from his siblings in the United States had inculcated in him a sense of America's exceptionalism and greatness: "What we knew about America then was cowboys and Indians and that the streets were paved with gold.... We knew you could do terrific over here."[63] This prememory was evidently shared by other passengers on the ship Steen eventually took to the United States. As they came within sight of land, Steen recalled that "everybody was excited and cheering, 'America!'": "They were yelling and crying and kissing. As we came in further, Manhattan started coming up. Then we saw the Statue of Liberty coming up out of the ocean. Everybody knew about the Statue of Liberty and here it was. Here was America."[64]

Even on the Blasket Islands, remotely situated off the west coast of Ireland, information circulated about the exciting prospects in America. The main well at the top of the village was known as the American Well (*Tobar an Phuncáin*) because, according to Michael Carney's immigrant memoir, "the women used to talk about America up there all the time."[65] In Muiris Ó Súileabháin's *Twenty Years A-Growing*, also set on the Blasket Islands, captures great anticipation predated arrival in America: "Kate Peg was constantly coming to the house and she and Maura talking about nothing but America. They would run across to the wall where pictures from Springfield were hanging. 'Oh,' Kate would say, 'we will go into that big building the first day, Maura.'"[66]

This expectation of a new and better life in America was underwritten by historic admiration in Ireland for US political values. Irish nationalists since the United Irishmen had expressed open admiration for Thomas Jefferson and the American founders' principles of liberty, equality, and justice. In the 1840s Daniel O'Connell developed an extensive network of American associations as part of his campaign to repeal the Acts of Union 1800, and he interlocked his repeal campaign with the antislavery movement in the United States.[67] The Young Irelanders, too, found inspiration in iconic figures like George Washington. In a speech delivered at a meeting of the Repeal Association in 1843, Young Irelander Thomas Francis Meagher argued his position on the necessity for revolutionary violence by appealing to Washington's heroic role in the War of Independence. "Abhor the sword? Stigmatize the sword?" he asked. "No, for at its blow, and in the quivering of its crimson light a giant nation sprang up from the waters of the Atlantic, and by its redeeming magic the fettered colony became a daring free Republic."[68] This political admiration for America filtered through the cultural worlds of ordinary Irish people in the nineteenth century via songs, newspapers, and even school curriculum. Tom Brick's memoir, for example, alludes to the teachers in the national school in Ballyferriter, who encouraged their students to learn about Christopher Columbus and to perfect their English language and American geography, "for that's where most of ye will be going."[69] Similarly, Frank Roney, reminiscing about his journey to America, wrote that "in my heart I hailed America as the land of liberty . . . the land which the dear old teacher had taught me to look on as their own final home; the land of Lincoln, that one great, towering human figure. When other memories should have perished his will live and be loved by generations to come."[70]

Because post-Famine immigrants viewed their Irish past and American future as reconcilable and mutually reinforcing, Irish and American nationalism fused into a movement that became, in the words of David Brundage, "a work of political invention and imagination involving multiple generations of men and women."[71] Indeed, says Brundage, American Irish nationalists were "often the main proprietors of collective memory" in Ireland and the United States alike and would remain so across the nineteenth and twentieth centuries.[72]

The memory narratives developed by Irish nationalists in America include the themes of exile and Famine discussed in earlier sections of this chapter. John Mitchel's *Jail Journal,* published in the United States in his newspaper the *Citizen* in 1854, particularly encouraged the Famine as an origin myth for the Irish exodus to America, working a nationalist angle by popularizing its interpretation as a genocide by the British against the Irish people. "The Almighty indeed sent the potato blight," wrote Mitchel, "but the English created the Famine."[73] Mitchel's words would have an incalculable impact on Famine immigrants and inarguably encouraged their mass support of the Fenian Brotherhood, an organization founded in 1858 in the United States by exiled leaders of the Young Irelanders of 1848. Membership of the Fenians grew astronomically in the preceding years, altering the fabric of Irish identity in America. "The Fenians' most important and original legacy," writes Brundage, "was in helping to hone a separate and distinct ethnic identity among the Irish, intensifying their sense of social and cultural difference from mainstream America."[74]

Irish nationalists in America were alert to the power of memory in building support for their movement. After 1848, when several of the leaders of the Young Irelanders fled to the United States after their failed uprising against the Irish government, this support needed to recognize the legitimacy of revolutionary separatism and the pursuit of Irish republicanism through violent resistance.[75] To validate this ideological belief, immigrants like R. R. Madden made a concerted effort to write alternative histories of 1798, creating a pantheon of heroes for Young Irelanders and Fenians to revere. Irish nationalists in America leaned heavily on the memory of the leading eighteenth-century revolutionary Wolfe Tone and the United Irishmen. Matilda Tone's publication of her husband's autobiography became a critical moment in Irish nationalism, making Tone a deeply inspirational figure for later generations of Irish republicans in America.[76] Monuments to Robert Emmet and his brother, Thomas, were erected across the United States, helping to keep alive memories of the 1798 rebellion.[77]

Political rhetoric also maintained 1798 at the center of Irish American memory. In 1904 Chicago's John Finerty, in his acceptance speech as president of the United Irish League of America, repeatedly invoked the memory of the Irish uprising.[78] In New York in 1914, Patrick Pearse paid special tribute to Robert Emmet, saying he was a greater hero than Brian Boru and calling his final speech the most memorable words ever uttered by an Irishman.[79] Even Americans of non-Irish backgrounds were drawn to the memories of the United Irishmen kept alive by Irish American nationalists. Such was the case for journalist Charles Edward Russell, who joined the Irish republican movement in 1923, expressing admiration for "Ireland's long memory of its own resistance and its distinctive tradition of self-sacrifice."[80] Russell himself helped to regenerate memories of 1798 and the Easter Rising of 1916 with his poems in honor of Wolfe Tone, Patrick Pearse, and Mary MacSwiney.[81]

The influence these memory narratives had on ordinary Irish immigrants is made plain in their life writing. Tim Cashman, who emigrated from Cork in 1893, remembered that the rhymes recited on the ship from Ireland to America included Emmet's "Speech from the Dock," the exilic "The Banks of My Own Lovely Lee," and "fine Fenian songs."[82] Cashman himself frequently quoted the poetry of Young Irelander Thomas Davis in his memoir. George Pepper, a Methodist minister who emigrated from Down to Ohio in 1854, also frequently drew on the memories of the United Irishmen. He even recalled how during the Civil War, in which he served as a minister, a young English solider "set audiences on fire" with his recitation of Emmet's "immortal vindication."[83]

Irish nationalists in the United States relied on symbols, traditions, and rituals derived from Celtic legends to forge an image of themselves as a brotherhood of patriotic warriors. This was particularly true of the Fenians, whose name itself was an anglicization of the Irish word *Fianna*, the hunter-warriors of Fionn Mac Cumhaill, a hero in Irish mythology. Invoking the military identity of the Fianna justified the Fenian's construction of a highly gendered political organization that severely limited women's participation.[84]

This masculinization of Irish nationalist memory continued even after support for the Fenians had dwindled, consistently taking the form of male iconic national heroes. From 1878 these figures most consistently included Charles Stewart Parnell, Michael Davitt, and John Redmond, each of whom were deeply involved in the political affairs of the Irish in both Ireland and America. Images of these men featured regularly in newspapers like the *Irish World*, the most widely circulated Irish American newspaper in the early twentieth century, with a readership of about 125,000 in 1904.[85] The *Irish World* countered "memories" of the drunken, simian Irish Celt of Thomas Nast's political cartoons in the 1870s with images of heroes that occasionally drew from Greek mythology and that promoted a sophisticated image of Irish and Irish American political engagement.[86] Through the *Irish World* and the more anarchic *Gaelic American*, figures of Irish male nationalist heroism were pushed to the fore of the Irish American consciousness and became seared into the memories of the newspapers' readership. As a result, autobiographies written by Irish American nationalists in the twentieth century would intermingle narratives about the monster meetings held by O'Connell and the fallen heroes of 1798 with the more current betrayal of Parnell and the debates around Redmond's leadership. In turn, these Irish role models were favorably compared with American icons as memoirists continued to balance American and Irish patriotism. So it is that Hugh Daly, an Irish

American businessman and socialite, mistily compared the qualities of Parnell and Theodore Roosevelt in his memoir, while Irish nationalist Francis Hackett sighed over the admirable characteristics of Abraham Lincoln in one paragraph and in the next added a comparable reflection on Charles Stewart Parnell. By the mid-twentieth century, the male political patriot was the embodiment of Irish American collective memory.

There was an important racial dimension to the development of Irish American nationalist collective memory. From the 1880s, Chinese as well as Italians and other Europeans began to arrive in the United States en masse. Irish immigrants leveraged their perceived whiteness over these newer immigrants, emphasizing it and their experience (however contentious) in the Civil War as part of a shared American identity. In his 1936 memoir, Frank Roney provides insight into the nature of this evolving racially based identity politics and its impact on Irish integration into American society:

> The Irish immigrant, driven to America by Famine and landlord oppression, had at first worked as a cheap laborer on the railroads and wherever work was hardest and most menial. The native Americans regarded him as a menace, treating him with contempt, varied by assaults with rocks and brickbats. In a few years the Irishman became a citizen. No longer a cheap laborer, he became interested in politics, held office, conducted businesses of various kinds, entered the professions and developed into a good American with the vested right of jeering at the cheap laboring German who succeeded him, whom he in turn treated as he had been treated. This then continued until the German had asserted himself as a business man and politician. Then both pitched into the Italian for the same reasons that they had been assailed, and then all of them concentrated upon the Chinaman. To assail and assault and oppress one portion of humanity seems to be the delight, inherent right, and practice of another portion.

Interwoven with this racial collective memory of "becoming" white was a popular memory narrative of anti-Irish discrimination in the United States, captured in an 1862 song by John Poole, "No Irish Need Apply." According to Richard Jensen, within a matter of months the song (which had originally featured an Irish woman's experience of prejudice in England) was widely sung by Irish immigrants in the United States, especially Irish men, who connected with the now male protagonist of the song. "By 1863," writes Jensen, "every Irishman knew and resented the slogan" "No Irish need apply."[87] Jensen argues that the stimulus for this resentment was mainly aural and helped Irish people explain their poverty and validate their social defiance during episodes like the draft riots.[88]

Oddly, rather than unifying Irish immigrants with other racialized populations such as African Americans and Chinese immigrants, their "memory" of anti-Irish prejudice, whether grounded in reality or not, frequently crystallized into racial hostility.[89] Noel Ignatiev's *How the Irish Became White* chronicles the heightened resentment and antipathy fostered by Irish immigrants toward people of color in the mid- and late nineteenth century.[90] Numerous reasons have been given for this animosity. First, asserting their difference from and antipathy to their Black neighbors may have been a survival strategy for Famine-era Irish immigrants who remembered and still chafed at the cartoons in *Harper's Weekly* that compared them to enslaved Black peoples. Second, labor competition in the postbellum United States may have stoked resentment against Black and Asian workforces, groups that the Irish feared would undercut their wages. Third, many Irish immigrants in the late nineteenth century harbored the same racist ideologies that then contaminated mainstream American and European culture.

Steadfast beliefs in social Darwinism are peppered across many Irish immigrant memoirs, including the crude 1885 memoir of Scotch Irish immigrant Thomas Mellon, who wrote aggressively of the inferiority of both African Americans and Irish Catholics alike.[91] For Mellon, North American Indian tribes and "the tribes of interior Africa" exemplified "the savage state" and produced "a sparsity of population and a state of degradation approaching the nature of the predatory animal." "These bad qualities," according to Mellon, "were so long and thoroughly cultivated among the Irish, and so perfectly ingrained into their nature, that modern civilization has as yet been unable to extract the virus." While less overtly racist, the Irish Catholic immigrant Henry O'Mahoney expressed his suspicion of the African Americans who worked by his side in the South after the Civil War. O'Mahoney begrudged the former enslaved men who complained about bad treatment to the officials of the Reconstruction: "The negro's evidence was accepted in preference to that of the white man's. The offender was fined by the 'Carpet Bagger' in proportion to his ability to pay. If he had not money enough on his person with which to pay the fine he was locked up until the fine was paid by his relatives or friends. I suppose such cases were numerous all over the South at the time. As the negroes were so numerous in the South they together with the Carpet Baggers controlled the state governments." O'Mahoney neglected to mention in his memoir that his own fortune in Texas was made in part by acting as a loan shark to African American workers, whom he exploited with illegally high interest rates. This information emerged in the memoir of his observant daughter, Mary. Suffice to say that Irish immigrants' creation of a collective memory hinged on racist defensiveness and a concerted effort to "remember" their white European origins.

From Patrick to Columbus: Catholic and Middle-Class Respectability

By the turn of the twentieth century, a sector of Irish American nationalists became increasingly interested in entering the circle of American political elites and set about to refine Irish American associational culture.[92] Popular groups like Clan na nGael and the Ancient Order of Hibernians began to compete, rhetorically and socially, with more moderate associations like the Knights of Columbus and the United Irish League of America. As Timothy Meagher describes it, the "belligerent ethno-centrism" discourse of mid- to late nineteenth-century Irish American nationalism shifted to more moderate discursive practices focusing on Catholic respectability and constitutional nationalism.[93] This in turn diversified the memory narratives of Irish America. For example, according to Meagher, the Irish in Worcester, Massachusetts, at the turn of the twentieth century began to embrace mnemonic rituals that prioritized the commemoration of Christopher Columbus over that of Saint Patrick. "Columbus served Worcester Irish well in a way Patrick could not," Meagher notes in *Inventing America,* for "Columbus was an American, indeed the first American if you dismissed the Native peoples, as the Worcester Irish did. His holiday was thus a perfect opportunity to demonstrate the power and solidarity of a new group, a Catholic American group—militantly Catholic and patriotically American."[94]

For class-conscious Irish Americans, the Gaelic revival of the late nineteenth century provided an alternative bank of cultural memories that distanced them from the republican and victim-led motifs favored by Fenian enthusiasts of the mid-nineteenth century. The "lecture tours" of the United States undertaken by poet W. B. Yeats (1903, 1911, 1914, and 1920), actor Maud Gonne, and writer Lady Augusta Gregory (1911 to 1912) helped to fuel this appetite for alternative portrayals of Irish identity, featuring as they did memory narratives of a rich heritage of Gaelic literature and folklore that was apolitical, intellectual, and aesthetically sophisticated.[95]

Equally, the Irish-language revival spurred by the US visit of Gaelic League president Douglas Hyde regenerated "memories" of a culturally unique homeland, redolent of a pure, vibrant, linguistically complex Gaelic community. The impact of Hyde's rhetoric on immigrants is reflected in the memoir of Francis Hackett, a James Joyce obsessive and office clerk, who attended Hyde's talk at the Chicago auditorium and who was moved irrevocably by it. "I was so carried away," writes Hackett, "that I could hear lugubrious primitive wails emitted from me as from an animal in pain. I had never known I was so Celtic."[96] Hackett continued to write that "the departure of the Hydes left me in a state; to call it confusion would be too mild. Everything Irish in me was stirred." Hyde's lecture tour also had an enormous effect on the young immigrant James F. Kenney. After hearing Hyde's talk in Toronto, Kenney went on to become a librarian who foregrounded Irish material and produced the monumental, 880-page *Sources for the Early History of Ireland: An Introduction and Guide*. By looking back through the memory narratives woven by the Gaelic revivalists, Irish immigrants learned to move forward—and upward—in American society.

Stage Irishry versus Fine Irish Lace: Competing Memory Narratives

The memory narratives explored above did not emerge in a rigid linear order. Although the rise of a middle-class American Irish community at the turn of the twentieth century influenced a change in memory traditions, the others—Famine, exile, blood sacrifice—remained and indeed may have gained strength from the Celtic-inspired tone of Yeats's and other revivalists' plays and poems. Nonetheless, tensions over the authenticity of certain memory narratives inevitably emerged, especially as these came to be understood as reflections of Irish American class status.

One contested memory tradition was that constructed through the popular theatrical experience of Tin Pan Alley and vaudeville. Arising out of mid-nineteenth-century minstrelsy, these shows were despised by the middle class for their hyperbolic vulgarity but remained important group mediators of memory for working-class urban Irish Americans through the early twentieth century. These audiences may have related the jocular, defiant forms of

Irishness they saw on stage with the narratives that Irish republican nationalists in the US had promoted from the Famine era. E. P. Quinn argues that the
pugilistic songs of Tin Pan Alley resonated with working-class Irish Americans because they were abstractions of the oral and musical traditions of an
Irish peasant culture specifically adapted to show how an Irish masculine
persona might survive in the United States.[97] For Quinn, the performances
of the Irish actor and playwright Dion Boucicault were particularly influential in this regard, as they showcased comical and patriotic caricatures of the
Irish "Paddy." In Boucicault's plays, Quinn argues, the Irish Paddy embodied
a number of Irish American memory narratives: the defiant opponent of
English aristocracy; the sentimental, place-bound Irish peasant; and the
economically and politically progressive nationalist. There is little doubting
the resonance of Boucicault's productions, which became so popular that his
song "The Wearing of the Green" became a kind of national anthem for Irish
Americans.[98] The lyrics pay special homage to the 1798 rebellion, confirming the endurance of Fenian-era memory narratives of Wolfe Tone and the
United Irishmen.

But if the memory narratives evoked through vaudeville Irishry were
pleasing and familiar to urban working-class Irish Americans, they were
puzzling to other Irish. These included Gaelic revivalists in the homeland
itself, who were embarrassed by the hokey commercialism of vaudeville.
Stage Irishry was also alienating to members of the Irish diaspora who had
settled in different locations. Such was the case for Lucy Farr, a fiddler from
Ballynakill in Galway who emigrated to England in the 1930s while her elder
sister emigrated to the United States. When Lucy visited her sister in Boston
some later years, she was taken aback by the Boston Irish appetite for what
she dismissed as "a weird sort of music." "I'd play a few tunes," she wrote,
"but it went over their heads. The crowd there weren't interested in what you
and I would call traditional music. They wanted rebel songs. That would be
wonderful if you played as many rebel songs as you could. I didn't like that.
I couldn't associate with rebel songs."[99]

Stage Irishry was offensive as well to bourgeois Irish Americans like Francis O'Neill, once a police chief in Chicago and a famed collector of Irish
traditional music from the West of Ireland. O'Neill was outraged when he
discovered that the repertoire played for Douglas Hyde during his January 1906 visit to Chicago included Thomas Moore's "The Harp That Once
through Tara's Halls" and "The Minstrel Boy."[100] O'Neill did not elucidate

the reasons for his disappointment, but it may have had something to do with the highly commercial nature of Moore's *Irish Melodies*, which portrayed Irishness as chronologically distant, idealized, ancient, and abounding in romantic images of Irish castles and shamrock-covered pastures.[101] In spite or perhaps because of these sentimental abstractions, Moore's *Irish Melodies* remained widely popular in the United States well into the twentieth century, the Celtic symbolism in his lyrics chiming with those espoused by the Fenian Brotherhood a half a century earlier. That Moore was a friend of Robert Emmet and wrote "O Breathe Not His Name" in his honor is also notable, though probably less significant than the goal of transatlantic mass appeal that Moore envisioned when producing his *Irish Melodies*.

Another window onto what Charles Fanning calls the "dueling" nature of Irish American cultural memory is evident in two deeply contrastive Irish exhibits at the 1933 Chicago World's Fair. One, known as the Irish Village, was the hasty brainchild of American Irish entrepreneurs who sought to cash in on popular Irish tropes derived from vaudeville and Tin Pan Alley. The village featured "a battering array of ersatz Irish artifacts," including "a leaning round tower, the well of saint Bride, a bit of Blarney Castle, thatched cottages, a Colleen Bawn Rock and a couple of pubs christened Mooney's and Dirty Moore's."[102] Widespread criticism of the exhibit was voiced across the United States, especially by Catholic figureheads, who were horrified by the racy "colleen" dancers who entertained the crowds, their legs suggestively clad in shamrock-patterned stockings. The Irish Village was, according to one Catholic commentator, nothing short of "a travesty on the Irish race."[103]

The other Irish exhibition at the Chicago Fair was the antithesis of the Irish Village, underpinned by a transatlantic aspiration toward credibility as a sophisticated culture.[104] Sponsored by the Irish Free State, the exhibit promoted a genteel, region-specific, cottage-industry image of Ireland by featuring fine linen, lace, and cloth from different parts of the island. The exhibit also re-endorsed the Irish pastoral as an appropriate memory narrative by featuring landscape paintings by Sean Keating, Sean O'Sullivan, George Russell, Paul Henry, and Jack Yeats. It emphasized the ancientness and complexity of Ireland's Gaelic past through a widely circulated booklet, *A Century of Progress in Irish Archaeology*. The booklet stated that "archaeology is a great force in the shaping of a sound self-consciousness in a nation," adding that "knowledge of its own past and of the achievements of former generations adds to a proper appreciation of national growth." Finally, the exhibition showcased Irish- and English-language literature emerging from the Free State, thus building on the memory narratives earlier pressed by the literary and Gaelic revivalists in the United States.

Through its careful curation, the Free State's exhibition attempted to cast a new mold for twentieth-century Irish American social memory by providing tangible examples of the arts and intellectual life of contemporary Ireland. It remains to be debated whether this effort succeeded in challenging "the old moth eaten baloney about the Blarney Stone and the conception of the Irish as a people who spend their time rapping each other's skulls with shillelaghs and dancing jigs" remains to be debated.[105]

The Irish Pastoral

Perhaps the most ubiquitous of all memory narratives for Irish immigrants in the United States was that of the idyllic pastoral homeland. According to Oona Frawley, the origins of this memory narrative date to precolonial Gaelic literature, which focused on nature, place, and landscape as sources of self-representation. During the colonial period, the Irish pastoral became a site of nostalgia in Irish literature, a site "from which to express longing for lost culture."[106] With the emergence of the Land League in the early 1880s, the Irish pastoral took on new meaning, as land (and its ownership) became a metaphor for nationality.[107] Subsequently, after the foundation of the Irish Free state, treatments of the Irish pastoral reflected a shift in gender norms, with landscape symbolizing a masculine "blood and soil chauvinism" developed in response to Irish statesman Éamon de Valera's rural nation building.[108] Given the close transatlantic relationship between Ireland and the United States, the heightened nostalgia and rural origins of many Irish immigrants, and the potent symbolic function that the Irish pastoral had come to fill in political and cultural discourse, it is hardly surprising that the Irish in America so readily engaged memory narratives of the Irish pastoral as a way of dealing with the psychological consequences of emigration.

Corporaal remarks on the ubiquity of the rural Irish landscape in Irish American fiction from the Famine period, noting several functions of these pastoral narratives.[109] First, the pastoral "becomes a point of ethnic identification" through which Irish immigrants could recollect and reconstruct a sense of Irishness in exile.[110] Second, shared memories of a pastoral homeland were deployed to remind Irish immigrants of their innate difference from urban Americans. According to Corporaal's textual analysis, this search for differentiation stemmed from authors' religious anxieties—specifically, from a fear that Irish girls would be absorbed by Protestant Anglo-American urban culture and abandon their Catholicism along the way. Irish American novels that emphasized memories of an Irish pastoral homeland, then, also "conveyed the idea that immigrant girls should avoid the public area of the American city, especially the streets, if they wish to safeguard their honour."[111] Third, descriptions of Erin as a *locus amoenus* (literally, "pleasant place") served an ethnic purpose insofar as they presented "a strong, coherent Irish American ethnic identity in the face of opposition."[112] Corporaal concludes that "pastoral representations of motherland Erin play an essential role in the construction of diasporic Irishness."[113]

While Corporaal stresses the religious and ethnic function of the Irish pastoral in Irish America, the memoirs of prominent Irish American figures suggest its potency as a metaphor for Irish nationalist politics. Batt O'Connor, who fought in the war of independence alongside Michael Collins, wrote of his heartbreak at leaving the landscape of North Kerry when he emigrated to the United States in 1892. Like O'Donovan Rossa before him, O'Connor wrote of the Irish pastoral in curiously anthropomorphic terms. "To leave Ireland," he said, "does not make one love Ireland more, but it does make one aware of the strength of that love. While we are at home, Ireland is a part of ourselves. Its landscape is as familiar as the face of father or mother."[114] This tendency in Irish men's memoirs to reimagine the landscape as a human entity, capable of begetting and generating affection, is indicative of the effect of Irish nationalism's focus on land as the foundation of identity and the extent to which place as a mnemonic had been pushed beyond its reasonable limit.[115]

The political symbolism of the Irish pastoral memory narrative is also reflected in the abstracted terms in which it came to be used in America. Instead of evoking specific memories of their town or village or farm, Irish nationalists in America drew on general pastoral recollections to represent a national idea of Ireland rather than a subjectively intimate one. In his memoir, *A Summer in Ireland*, published in 1931, Michael Pathe writes: "When I stood on the deck of the Lusitania and saw the form I loved fading, ever fading back into the hazy distance, I tasted for the first time a sorrow as bitter as it was real."[116] Years later, when Pathe returned for a visit to Ireland, he again drew on the Irish pastoral to represent a national territory: "There was a streak of light far over the ocean.... And there in her green and golden loveliness lay the Emerald Gem of the Western World, the queen of the waters, the Ireland of all our dreams." By "remembering" landscape through a national lens, Irish American immigrants like O'Donovan Rossa, O'Connor, and Pathe were attempting to fashion through their words the nation that they had psychologically invested in so heavily.

Like many of the other memory narratives, the Irish pastoral was a trope that many of Ireland's dispossessed must have had difficulties relating to. After all, most of the three million immigrants that arrived in the United States from Ireland after the Famine had effectively been refused a place within the mythologized Irish pastoral by their families, through the enactment of impartible inheritance. While Irish American social memory emphasized an idyllic, benevolent pastoral, immigrants' private memories of the land were more likely to be bound up with shame, humiliation, and rejection.

The foregrounding of the Irish pastoral as a unifying memory narrative was especially ironic for Irish immigrant women, given that their place in the Irish landscape was deeply contested by Irish male hierarchies.[117] This was particularly true after the Famine, when women retreated or were removed from the countryside with the dramatic reduction in both farm-based employment and rural-based marriage opportunities. This period also coincided with the Young Ireland movement, whose nostalgic poetry and prose reimagined the land as a feminized entity, a place to be owned, mapped, and fertilized by Irish men.[118] The accent on landownership through the 1880s raised men's suspicions of women's competing sense of land entitlement. Women were thus banned from becoming members of the National League from 1882, despite their having played an active role in the Land League since 1879.[119]

What is more, Catholic and Victorian values repeatedly emphasized that a woman's place was in the home. Whereas working the land alongside brothers, fathers, and husbands was normal for women in the pre-Famine era, in its aftermath it was understood as a form of social and moral transgression.[120] As Silvia Federici argues, enclosure was the defining experience of rural women in the late nineteenth century, as their bodies and actions were subjected to increased surveillance and censorship.[121] Given these conditions, it seems unlikely that Irish immigrant women would have looked back to the Irish pastoral with the same sense of nostalgia as their male compatriots. What we must consider, then, is how linking the Irish pastoral to a masculine mentality of working of the land in the post-Famine period may have influenced

Irish women in the United States to develop and procure an alternative sense of place, independent of the freighted, masculinized symbolism of the Irish landscape.

Conclusion: Narratives of Incline

By the mid-twentieth century, the American Irish had developed a confident public narrative of incline, in which memories of exile, Famine, patriotism, and anti-Irish prejudice were strategically sequenced to evoke Irish immigrant social and economic progress. Memory narratives of Ireland as an Edenic motherland presented a wholesome image of Catholicism that contrasted starkly with Protestant urbanity. As well as discouraging Irish girls from embracing Protestant urban American culture, the Irish pastoral narrative was deployed to legitimize Irish Americans' claims for a separate Irish republic. Collectively, these popular Irish American memory narratives broadly satisfied the American expectation for progress while retaining a shared ethnic identity.

This chapter's preliminary excavation of historical scholarship suggests that Irish American memory narratives were based almost entirely on the triptych of masculinity, motherland, and militarism. From high-cross monuments dedicated to the Irish Brigade to the political cartoons of the *Irish World* to the characters of the vaudeville stage, male figures were front and center of American Irish memory making between the mid-nineteenth and mid-twentieth centuries. Frequently, these men were lauded for their republican separatist politics, their personas layered onto the memories of the United Irishmen on one hand and the founding fathers of the American republic on the other. This political emphasis shifted slightly at the turn of the twentieth century to embrace more apolitical cultural forms, with the emergence of a middle-class American Irish community that looked to male icons like Douglas Hyde and W. B. Yeats as the embodiment of a sophisticated Gaelic culture. At the turn of the twentieth century, Irish memory narratives expanded to include male icons of American as well as Irish Catholicism. Thus, while recollections of Protestant Irishmen like Wolfe Tone were partially kept alive through frequent commemorations of 1798, the memory narratives of Irish America were overwhelmingly based on a fiercely Catholic and nationalist worldview, erasing the experiences of those who did not ascribe to these belief systems.

Despite the formidable work of women like Matilda Tone, Anna Parnell, Mother Jones, Augusta Gregory, and Maud Gonne there is little evidence that Irish women's narratives were incorporated into the design of American Irish collective memory.[122] The result is not just erasure from the immigrant ethnic record but also a perceived "failure" of Irish women to fulfill the idealized image of the Irish American. Tim Cashman, for instance, looks askance at the Irish women who accompanied him on his voyage to the United States: "The Irish girl described by Thomas Davis in his fine piece of poetry cannot be applied in a single instance aboard *The Scythia* among the Irish emigrant girls," Cashman writes, in a sentence that reveals both the influence of Young Ireland rhetoric over Irish immigrant men as well as the Young Irelander's abject failure to represent the reality of Irish women's lives.[123]

In one of the first studies to examine Irish women's experiences in the United States, Hasia Diner discusses the flip side: Irish women's inability to relate to the male-dominated memory narratives of Irish America.[124] Diner identifies Irish American men's pervasive frustration at the women's disinterest in fulfilling the images of Irishness that had been set for them. "Irish men believed that in America their women had become altogether too self-involved, too self-centered and too imitative of the Yankee Protestant women around them," writes Diner.[125] In particular, Irish men were disgusted by women's interest in American styles and fashions, which they interpreted as a betrayal of their pastoral Catholic origins. Again, this suggests the inability or refusal of Irish women to relate to the popular memory narratives that Irish American nationalist leaders had prescribed for them.

As well as sidelining the experiences of women and non-Catholic immigrants, the nationalist-focused memory narratives of the American Irish also overlooked linguistic and cultural traditions that gave coherence to groups of people at parochial and regional levels.[126] This is particularly true of Irish-language speakers from the West of Ireland, who, as Kevin Kenny points out, were historically impervious to the Irish nationalist cause.[127] Unable to relate to the overt nationalism of a Fenian-inspired American Irish identity, many of these immigrants continued to rely on their own Irish-language speaking narratives and memories to restore and regenerate their ethnic identity. If this left them out in the cold in terms of national or transnational representation, it may also have allowed them to independently explore and develop different memory narratives, derived from their subjective experiences in a modern American landscape.

Our challenge, then, is to retrace, recover, and recenter these occluded memory narratives by investigating the writings of Irish immigrants who fell outside of the heteronormative worldview of the male Irish American nationalist. Fortunately, the United States in the twentieth century had developed an encouraging culture of immigrant self-reflection and life writing, providing flexible, self-sustaining, and inclusive memory frameworks for Irish immigrants left out of their ethnic community's memory record. It is toward these realms that we now turn our attention.

Notes

1. Hyde's lecture in Carnegie Hall was attended by four state supreme court justices, prominent lawyers and district attorneys, leaders of large-scale state construction projects, and many of the main actors of the Tammany Hall political engine. See Margaret Kelleher, "Ambassadors of Irish Taste': The Irish Lecture in America," Newberry Library Scholarly Series, Irish Studies Seminar (online), 19 March 2021.

2. Douglas Hyde, *My American Journey*, ed. Liam Mac Mathúna, Brian Ó Conchubhair, Niall Comer, Cuan Ó Seireadáin, and Máire Nic an Bhaird (Dublin: University College Dublin Press, 2019), xliii.

3. In comparable studies the concept of *lieux de mémoire* rather than memory narrative is often used. The schema developed by Pierre Nora reflects, like memory narratives, on the imaginative ways that identity has been represented through the ages. However, where the term *memory narratives* focuses on concepts addressed in oral and written language, Nora's *lieux* engendered enormously diverse concepts, ranging from symbols to pedagogy to countermemories. Apart from wanting to avoid conceptual vagueness, my reticence in deploying the term *lieux de mémoire* primarily derives from Nora's tendency to locate memories within specific national territories. Emigrant memory, by its nature, will always be transnational and dislocated, while the accent on "places" of memory in Nora' work ideologically reinforces the relationship between motherland and memory. Lauren Gervereau affirms this criticism, contending that "Nora's map of history as a mnemonic landscape rendered history vulnerable to identity politics. Far from making history the master of memory," Gervereau goes on, Nora's *lieux* made history "become prey to the biased interpretations generated at the topical reference points on his maps of memory." Quoted in Patrick Hutton, "Pierre Nora's *Les Lieux*," in *Routledge International Handbook of Memory Studies*, ed. Anna Lisa Tota and Trever Hagen (New York: Routledge, 2016), 38.

4. Hyde, *My American Journey*, 76.

5. Hyde, *My American Journey*, xl.

6. Hyde, *My American Journey*, xlviii.

7. In his diary Hyde writes how "one evening six or seven men called to the hotel to see me with a long list of complaints. From their appearance, it seemed the end of the world was nigh. Looking as worried as could be, they informed me that the 'welcome' was not in the hands of the right people, that the tuxedo brigade never did anything worthwhile for Ireland." Quoted in Kelleher, "'Ambassadors of Irish Taste.'"

8. Kelleher, "'Ambassadors of Irish Taste.'"

9. Kerby Miller, *Emigrants and Exiles: Ireland and the Irish Exodus to North America* (New York: Oxford University Press, 1985).

10. Miller, *Emigrants and Exiles*, 299.

11. Miller, *Emigrants and Exiles*, 305.

12. Kerby Miller, *Ireland and Irish America: Culture, Class, and Transatlantic Migration* (Dublin: Field Day, 2008), 108.

13. Kevin Kenny, "Diaspora and Comparison: The Global Irish as a Case Study," *Journal of American History* 90, no. 1 (June 2003): 137.

14. Miller, *Ireland and Irish America*, 102.

15. K. Theodore Hoppen, *Ireland since 1800: Conflict and Conformity*, 2nd ed. (London: Longman, 1999), 92.

16. Hoppen, *Ireland*, 93.

17. Miller, *Emigrants and Exiles*, 380–81.

18. Hoppen, *Ireland*, 93.

19. J. J. Lee, *Ireland, 1912–1985: Politics and Society* (Cambridge: Cambridge University Press, 1989).

20. Hugh O'Daly's unpublished memoir was written in the 1940s. O'Daly emigrated from Monaghan to Montana in 1888, subsequently making it as an Irish American tycoon in California. Hugh Daly Memoir, Monaghan/Montana, California, University of Galway Archive, P155/7/1.

21. Mary Trotter, "Re-Imagining the Emigrant/Exile in Contemporary Irish Drama," *Modern Drama* 46, no. 1 (2003): 39.

22. Marguerite Corporaal, *Relocated Memories: The Great Famine in Irish and Diaspora Fiction, 1846–1870* (Syracuse: Syracuse University Press, 2017), 183.

23. David S. Lawlor, *The Life and Struggles of an Irish Boy in America: An Autobiography* (1936; repr., Whitefish, MT: Kessinger, 2008).

24. Nora O'Connor, unpublished memoir, 1947. O'Connor was born in 1886 and emigrated in 1906. Nora O'Connor Stine Memoir, Cork/New York City, Michigan, University of Galway Archive, P155/14/2.

25. Kilkrane was born in 1862, emigrated in 1880 and wrote his memoir in 1912. Michael Kilcran Memoir, Leitrem/ Chicago, University of Galway Archive, P155/108/19.

26. Arnold Schrier, *Ireland and the American Emigration, 1850–1900* (Dublin: University College Dublin Press, 1997); Arthur Gribben, ed., *The Great Famine and the Irish Diaspora in America* (Amherst: University of Massachusetts Press, 1999); Gerard Moran, *Sending Out Ireland's Poor: Assisted Emigration to North America in the Nineteenth Century*, 2d ed. (Dublin: Four Courts, 2013); Timothy J. Hatton and Jeffrey Williamson, "After the Famine: Emigration from Ireland, 1850–1913," *Journal of Economic History* 53, no. 3 (1993).

27. Joseph Lee and Marion R. Casey, eds., introduction to *Making the Irish American: History and Heritage of the Irish in the United States* (New York: New York University Press, 2006).

28. Emily Mark-FitzGerald, *Commemorating the Irish Famine: Memory and the Monument* (Liverpool: Liverpool University Press, 2013).

29. Kevin O'Neill, "The Star-Spangled Shamrock: Memory and Meaning in Irish America," in *History and Memory in Modern Ireland*, ed. Ian McBride (Cambridge: Cambridge University Press, 2001), 118.

30. Marguérite Corporaal and Jason King, ed., *Irish Global Migration and Memory: Transatlantic Perspectives of Ireland's Famine Exodus* (London: Routledge, 2017), 303.

31. Corporaal and King, *Irish Global Migration*, 308.

32. Lee and Casey, *Making the Irish American*.

33. Mary C. Kelly, *Ireland's Great Famine in Irish American History: Enshrining a Fateful Memory* (Lanham, MD: Rowman and Littlefield, 2014).

34. For a particular focus on trauma, memory, and the Famine, see Cormac Ó Gráda, "Famine, Trauma and Memory," *Béaloideas* 69 (2001), doi.org/10.2307/20520760. For a complete overview of the topic of the Famine and memory, see Cormac Ó Gráda, *Black '47 and Beyond: The Great Irish Famine in History, Economy, and Memory* (Princeton, NJ: Princeton University Press, 1999).

35. As well as addressing the absence of oral narratives of the Famine, Maura Cronin's work speaks compellingly to the use of Famine folklore and the development of the national folklore archive as a strategy for postindependence nation building: Maura Cronin, "Oral History, Oral Tradition and the Great Famine," in *Holodomor and Gorta Mór: Histories, Memories and Representation of Famine in Ukraine and Ireland*, ed. Lindsay Janssen Christian Noack, and Vincent Comerford (London: Anthem, 2014).

36. Christopher Morash, *Writing the Irish Famine* (Oxford: Clarendon, 1995), 176. Morash's quote from Asenath Nicholson's overview of Irish literature in the 1850s marks the depths of this puzzling lack of literary engagement with the Great Famine: Nicholson writes that "the Famine changed [Irish writers'] poetical romance into such fearful realities that no time was left to bestow on imagination." Asenath Nicholson, *Lights and Shades of Ireland* (London, 1850).

37. Sinead O'Connor, *Universal Mother* (London: Ensign, 1995); Terry Eagleton, "Another Country," *Guardian*, January 25, 2003.

38. Ó Gráda, "Famine, Trauma and Memory," 136.

39. Ó Gráda, "Famine, Trauma and Memory," 137.

40. Ó Gráda, "Famine, Trauma and Memory," 137.

41. Mary Antin, *The Promised Land* (Boston: Houghton Mifflin, 1912); Jacob A. Riis, *The Making of an American* (New York: Macmillan, 1901); Frederick W. Gehle, *Our Dubbledam Journey: An Account of How a Family Came to America 1891–1941* (New York: Costello and sons, 1941). For an overview of this genre, see William William Boelhower, "The Brave New World of Immigrant Autobiography," *Multi-Ethnic Literature of the United States (MELUS)* 9, no. 2 (1982). Also Robert Sayre, "Autobiography and the Making of America," *Iowa Review* 9, no. 2 (1978).

42. Paul de Man, "Autobiography as De-facement," *Comparative Literature* 94, no. 5 (1979): 922. Rachel McLennan in turn interprets American autobiography as originating in American exceptionalism and as being especially contingent on the political dominance of the Western white male, the character of whom conditions the figurative outcomes of most US autobiographies: Rachel McLennan, *American Autobiography* (Edinburgh: Edinburgh University Press, 2013).

43. Liz Stanley, *The Autobiographical I: The Theory and Practice of Feminist Autobiography* (Manchester: Manchester University Press, 1995), 11. See also Andrew William Palmer, "The Autobiographical Pact and the Selection of Self in Memoir" (PhD diss., University of Lincoln, 2016), 9.

44. Peter O'Neill, "Memory and John Mitchel's Appropriation of the Slave Narrative," *Atlantic Studies* 11, no. 3 (2014): 322.

45. O'Neill, "Memory," 338.

46. John Solon Memoir, Mayo/Wisconsin, University of Galway Archive, P155/11/3.

47. Patrick Cudahy Memoir, Kilkenny/Milwaukee, University of Galway Archive, P155/10/3.

48. O Neill, "The Star-Spangled Shamrock," 122.

49. Richard Jensen, "'No Irish Need Apply': A Myth of Victimization," *Journal of Social History* 36, no. 2 (2002): 406.

50. Patrick Cudahy Memoir.

51. Patrick Cudahy Memoir.

52. Henry O'Mahoney and Mary O'Mahoney Lupton Memoirs, University of Galway Archive, P155/11/2–P155/32/6.

53. Andrew J. Byrne Memoir, University of Galway Archive, P155/18/1.

54. William McCarter, *My Life in the Irish Brigade: The Civil War Memoirs of Private William Mccarter, 116th Pennsylvania Infantry.* (Savas: California, 1996).

55. Craig A. Warren, "'Oh, God, What a Pity!': The Irish Brigade at Fredericksburg and the Creation of Myth," *Civil War History* 47, no. 3 (2001).

56. One extraordinary keeper of Civil War memory was Ellen Ryan Jolly, who campaigned for the erection of the Nuns of the Battlefield Memorial to commemorate the role of the Catholic religious who aided the Union cause in the American Civil War, 93 percent of whom Jolly estimated to have been Irish. As president of the Ladies Auxiliary of the Ancient Order of Hibernians, Jolly declared, "As Catholic women, women of Irish Blood, women connected by the closest ties with those brave soldiers living and dead who were the recipients of the tender care of the Catholic nuns, we have a duty to perform. We must not allow the deeds of our Catholic nuns to be ignored." Kathleen Szpila, "Lest We Forget: Ellen Ryan Jolly and the Nuns of the Battlefield Monument," *American Catholic Studies* 123, no. 4 (2012): 32. Szpila also notes (p. 29) that Jolly was frequently invited by Irish organizations "to speak on topics combining ancestral Irish pride with loyal American patriotism," as she did in her talks "Patriotic Irish in America" to the Rhode Island Historical Association in 1909 and "Patriotic Irish in the American Civil War" to the Knights of Columbus in Providence in 1908.

57. E. Moore Quinn, "Introduction: The Irish in the American Civil War," *Irish Studies Review* 18, no. 2 (2010).

58. David T. Gleeson, *The Green and the Gray: The Irish in the Confederate States of America.* (Chapel Hill: University of North Carolina Press, 2013), 208.

59. Gleeson, 209. See also David T. Gleeson, "'Faugh a Ballagh!' (Clear the Way): The Irish and the American Civil War," in *Reconfiguring the Union. Studies of the Americas,* ed. I. W. Morgan and P. J. Davies (New York: Palgrave Macmillan, 2013).

60. William Burton Kurtz, *Excommunicated from the Union: How the Civil War Created a Separate Catholic America* (New York: Fordham University Press, 2016).

61. Damian Shiels, *The Irish in the American Civil War* (Dublin: History Press Ireland, 2014). See also Quinn, "Introduction."

62. Geraldine Meaney, Mary O'Dowd, and Bernadette Whelan, *Reading the Irish Woman: Studies in Cultural Encounter and Exchange, 1714–1960* (Liverpool: Liverpool University Press, 2013), 90.

63. Manny Steen Memoir, Dublin, Sligo / New York City, University of Galway Archive, P155/14/3. Note: This document is Steen's authorized summary of an oral interview he gave to Arnold Schrier.

64. Manny Steen Memoir, P155/14/3.

65. Michael Carney and Gerard Hayes, *From the Great Blasket to America: The Last Memoir by an Islander* (Cork: Collins, 2013), 30.

66. Muiris Ó Súileabháin, *Twenty Years A-Growing* (New York: Viking, 1933), 216, 217.

67. David Thomas Brundage, *Irish Nationalists in America: The Politics of Exile, 1798–1998* (New York: Oxford University Press, 2016), 3.

68. Brundage, *Irish Nationalists*, 89.

69. Tom Brick memoir, Kerry / Iowa / South Dakota, University of Galway Archive, P155/106/11.

70. Ira B. Cross, ed., *Frank Roney: Irish Rebel and California Labor Leader* (1931). See also Frank Roney Journal, San Francisco, University of Galway Archive, P155/31/12.

71. Brundage, *Irish Nationalists*, 221.

72. David Brundage, "Matilda Tone in America: Exile, Gender, and Memory in the Making of Irish Republican Nationalism," *New Hibernia Review / Iris Éireannach Nua* 14, no. 1 (2010): 98.

73. John Mitchel, *Jail Journal*, published in the *Citizen* (New York, 1854).

74. Brundage, *Irish Nationalists*, 90.

75. "The result of the abortive insurrection of 1848 was to change the base of Irish revolution from Ireland to America." Brundage, *Irish Nationalists*, 94.

76. Brundage, "Matilda Tone in America," 106.

77. Thomas Emmet's 1829 monument was inscribed in Irish as well as English and Latin. According to Brundage, the monument, which featured a sculpted image of an eagle holding an Irish harp in its talons, illustrated "the synthesis of Irish and American republicanism that United Irish exiles labored to effect." Brundage, *Irish Nationalists in America*, 53.

78. Brundage, *Irish Nationalists in America*, 137.

79. Donald Akenson, "Remember Emmet," *Irish Studies Review* 12, no. 3 (2004): 343.

80. Brundage, *Irish Nationalists in America*, 168

81. Brundage, *Irish Nationalists in America*, 170.

82. Tim and Dan Cashman, Memoirs, Letters, Poems, Essays, Cork / Massachusetts, Montana, University of Galway Archive, P155/16/1.

83. George Pepper Memoir, Down/Ohio, University of Galway Archive, P155/22/1.

84. Brundage, *Irish Nationalists in America*, 103.

85. Kevin Kenny, *The American Irish: A History* (Harlow, UK: Longman, 2000), 175.

86. Úna Ní Bhroiméil, "Political Cartoons as Visual Opinion Discourse: The Rise and Fall of John Redmond in the Irish World," in *Ireland and the New Journalism*, ed. Karen Steele and Michael de Nie (New York: Palgrave, 2014), 120.

87. Jensen, "'No Irish Need Apply,'" 408.

88. Jensen, "'No Irish Need Apply,'" 410.

89. E. Moore Quinn, "The Irish Rent . . . and Mended: Transitional Textual Communities in Nineteenth-Century America," *Irish Studies Review* 23, no. 2 (2015): 213.

90. Noel Ignatiev, *How the Irish Became White* (New York: Routledge, 1995).

91. Thomas Mellon Memoir, Tyrone/Pittsburgh, University of Galway Archive P155/9/1.

92. Kenny, *The American Irish*, 171.

93. Timothy Meaghar, *Inventing Irish America: Generation, Class and Ethnic Identity in a New England City, 1880–1928* (Notre Dame, IN: Notre Dame University Press, 2001), 3.

94. Meaghar, *Inventing Irish America*, 377.

95. Kelleher, "'Ambassadors of Irish Taste,'" 3.

96. Francis Hackett, *American Rainbow: Early Reminiscences* (New York: Liveright, 1971), 51

97. Quinn, "The Irish Rent," 218.

98. Quinn, "The Irish Rent," 215.

99. Lucy Farr, interview by Reg Hall, no. 2CDR0007585 1988, British Sound Archives, https://sounds.bl.uk/sounds/lucy-farr-interview-10071987 -1001219923290x000007.

100. Hyde, *My American Journey*, xl.

101. Sarah Rebecca Gerk, "Away o'er the Ocean Go Journeymen, Cowboys and Fiddlers: The Irish in Nineteenth Century American Music" (PhD diss., University of Michigan, 2014), 40, 48.

102. Charles Fanning, "Dueling Cultures: Ireland and Irish America at the Chicago World's Fairs of 1933 and 1934," *New Hibernia Review* 15, no. 3 (2011): 100.

103. Fanning, "Dueling Cultures," 95.

104. Fanning, "Dueling Cultures," 109, 110.

105. Fanning, "Dueling Cultures," 102–3.

106. Oona Frawley, *Irish Pastoral: Nostalgia and Twentieth-Century Irish Literature* (Dublin: Irish Academic Press, 2005), 3.

107. Philip Bull, *Land, Politics and Nationalism: A Study of the Irish Land Question* (Dublin: Gill and Macmillan, 1996), 95.

108. Tricia Cusack, "A 'Countryside Bright with Cosy Homesteads': Irish Nationalism and the Cottage Landscape," *National Identities* 3, no. 3 (2001): 230.

109. Marguérite Corporaal, "From Golden Hills to Sycamore Trees: Pastoral Homelands and Ethnic Identity in Irish Immigrant Fiction, 1860–75," *Irish Studies Review* 18, no. 3 (2010).

110. Corporaal, "From Golden Hills to Sycamore Trees," 342.

111. Corporaal, "From Golden Hills to Sycamore Trees," 338.

112. Corporaal, "From Golden Hills to Sycamore Trees," 336.

113. Corporaal, "From Golden Hills to Sycamore Trees," 333.

114. Batt O'Connor Memoir, Kerry/New Hampshire, University of Galway Archive, P155/15/9; Batt O'Connor, *With Michael Collins in the Fight for Irish Independence* (London: Peter Davies, 1929).

115. Elizabeth Grubgeld sees this tendency in Anglo-Irish as well as indigenous Irish writing, noting that in both forms "it is place which locates memory and gives language its referential significance." Elizabeth Grubgeld, "Topography, Memory, and John Montague's 'The Rough Field,'" *Canadian Journal of Irish Studies* 14, no. 2 (1989): 25.

116. Michael Pathe, *A Summer in Ireland* (Madison, WI: Cantwell, 1931).

117. Bernadette Whelan, *Women and Paid Work in Ireland, 1500–1930* (Portland, OR: Four Courts, 2000).

118. Katie Barclay, "Place and Power in Irish Farms at the End of the Nineteenth Century," *Womens History Review* 21, no. 4 (2012); Cara Delay, ""Deposited Everywhere': The Sexualized Female Body and Modern Irish Landscape," *Études-Irlandaises* 37, no. 1 (2012).

119. Janet TeBrake, "Irish Peasant Women in Revolt: The Land League Years," *Irish Historical Studies* 28, no. 1 (1992).

120. Joanna Bourke, *Husbandry to Housewifery: Women, Economic Change, and Housework in Ireland, 1890–1914* (Oxford: Clarendon, 1993) ; Barclay, "Place and Power."

121. Silvia Federici, *Witches, Witch-Hunting and Women* (San Francisco: PM, 2018).

122. Sally Barr Ebest, "Agency and Activism in Irish American Women's Memoirs," *Multi-Ethnic Literature of the United States (MELUS)* 44, no. 4 (2019).

123. Tim Cashman, Journal of a return visit to Ireland, University of Galway Archive, P155/30/2.

124. Hasia R. Diner, *Erin's Daughters in America* (Baltimore, MD: Johns Hopkins University Press, 1983).

125. Diner, *Erin's Daughters*, 142.

126. John McGahern's *Memoir* observes that in England's Irish emigrant communities "the local and the individual were more powerful than any national identity." Liam Harte, ed., *A History of Irish Autobiography* (Cambridge: Cambridge University Press, 2018), 211.

127. Kenny, "Diaspora and Comparison."

3

Life Writing and the Irish Immigrant

Twenty-six hours after arriving in the United States, a nineteen-year-old Gaeilgeoir named Tom Brick sat on a train, moving westward. For a time, the train had been occupied by Irish and Lithuanian and Swedish immigrants, their talk constant across the journey's first hours. But each had descended at different points along the route, and Tom was now left alone, looking through the window at the darkening northern plains.[1]

The silence in the railcar was broken by a trolley pushed by a news-seller. On the trolley's trays were loose oranges, apples, and bananas; magazines; and a stack of paperback books. Pressed by the boy, Tom reluctantly drew out a coin and pointed to the oranges. He said little, shy of his limited English. While the boy searched for a bag for the fruit Tom's eyes rested on a book atop the first shelf. Tom read English better than he spoke it. Sensing an opportunity, the salesboy took the volume from the pile and thrust it into the traveler's hands. The book, published in 1899, was by William Drannan (1832–1913), an immigrant from France who had settled in the American plains. This was the story of his life, spent chasing "Indians" and selling beaver pelts. Tom paused. He had less than a dollar left and did not know how much longer it would take to reach his destination, Salix, Iowa. If his sister was not at the station, he would need to find a boarding house. Reluctantly, he returned the book to the boy, dipping his head by way of regret. An hour passed, then another. Tom regarded the black night, and he imagined Drannan's Indians on horseback, racing alongside the train, awaiting his descent. In time, he heard again the rattle of the sales trolley as it crossed the metal gutter from the neighboring car. He beckoned the boy over and pointed toward Drannan's memoir. Noiselessly, he produced a coin from an inside breast pocket.[2]

Immigrant memoirs were, from the turn of the twentieth century, an integral form of American popular culture.[3] In the first twenty years of that century, autobiographies by immigrants including Edward Bok, Mary Antin, Constantine M. Panunzio, Abraham Cahan, Michael Pupin, Edward Alfred Steiner, and Marcus E. Ravage topped the literary market, their work applauded for its documentation of the journey from ethnic "other" to incorporated American.[4] President Theodore Roosevelt called the popular immigrant autobiographer Jacob Riis an "ideal" American citizen.[5] Both Bok's and Pupin's memoirs received the Pulitzer Prize, in 1921 and 1924, respectively. Americanization brochures from the 1910s included references to American immigrant memoirs, recommending them for teaching English and civics.[6] Immigrant memoirs featured in school curricula, giving immigrants "a voice in contemporary debates about Americanization."[7]

As well as being published in paperback, the memoirs were serialized in magazines and periodicals, from the *Atlantic Monthly* to ethnic newspapers, making them both affordable and widely accessible.[8] American fiction took up the theme: Upton Sinclair's *The Jungle* (1906) and Willa Cather's *O Pioneers* (1913) and *My Ántonia* (1918) each dealt with immigrants' daily lives. As the interest in the immigrant experience held steady across the twentieth century, more and more immigrants tried their hand at the genre of life writing. After World War II, these memoirs joined with the writings of people of color to represent the lives of the dispossessed, subverting the idealization of the American dream threaded through earlier autobiographies. Canonical life writings of this period include Maxine Hong Kingston's *The Woman Warrior* (1976), which shone light on the experience of Chinese American women; Angela Davis's *An Autobiography* (1974), which used Davis's trial on charges of terrorism to analyze race and class in America; and Mexican labor rights organizer Ernesto Galarza's *Barrio Boy* (1971), documenting its author's migration from Mexico to the United and his subsequent involvement in California's farm labor movement.[9]

In 1970, by then close to ninety years old, Tom Brick was in the depths of writing his own immigrant life story from his home in South Dakota. He began by describing his childhood in Ballyferriter, County Kerry, recounting folk stories from the Slea Head peninsula, then went on to describe the first year after his emigration to the American northern plains. He recalled with particular clarity that first train ride west and the book he bought to pass the journey. "I still have the book here at my home with no price marked on it," Brick writes. "The name and title of the book is *Thirty-One Years on the Plains and in the Mountains* by Capt. William F. Drannan." That the memory of Drannan's book loomed large in Brick's memoir fifty years later seems to confirm the widespread scholarly conviction of the influence that such autobiographies had over newly arriving immigrants. What is less clear is the nature, intention, and consistency of this literary influence. Some claim that immigrant autobiographies were tools of the American assimilation process, acting as veritable handbooks for new immigrants on the values and behaviors expected of them in their new country.[10] In contrast, others argue that autobiographies were immigrants' way of critiquing and resisting Americanization.[11] Still others insist that the genre of immigrant autobiography was simply a frame that allowed individual authors to explore issues that transcended the immigrant experience, such as spirituality, abolitionism, labor rights, and women's suffrage.[12] Increasingly, readings of autobiography argue that they must be interpreted not from the stubborn stance of American generic conventions but from the perspective of authors' subjectivities and by considering their gender, race, or ethnicity.[13]

In this chapter, with these various positions in mind, I explore the possible lives that were expressed in different Irish and American autobiographies as well as their draw for Irish immigrants. I examine canonical life narratives from both nations and establish how the "inherited forms of imagining a life" in these narratives may have inspired and given design to ordinary Irish immigrants' life writing in the United States.[14] Along the way, I suggest the alternative Irish immigrant memory narratives that the dynamic culture of American autobiography may have helped to evoke and preserve, while also grappling with the ways that the genre's conventions mediated and conventionalized immigrants' memories. The journey begins with a review of the emergence of life writing as a genre before going on to explore key features of the Irish and American autobiographical tradition.

Life Writing: From Pilgrimage of Place to Pilgrimage of the Self

Between the tenth and twelfth centuries, pilgrimage was central to the devotional practice of Christians in Europe and Euro-Asia.[15] Walking in the footsteps of Jesus and the saints was a form of embodied remembrance, fueling knowledge of and communion with God. After the Reformation, however, this practice came into question. If God was everywhere, Luther's followers argued, how could he be more present in some places than others? Protestantism thus activated a shift in mindset, turning worshippers away from place as a site of memory and toward an interior relationship with God.

To track development through this mental space, Christians embraced a genre of writing first deployed by Saint Augustine and subsequently defined as spiritual autobiography.[16] This form of life writing was designed to communicate authors' movement from a place of doubt and uncertainty to a place of enlightenment and self-understanding, akin to a mapping of the soul's journey toward God. As such, it formed a foundation for life writing that was based on the logic of progress, centered around the self and resistant to the gravitational pull of place.[17] With the settlement of the Puritans in North America beginning in the seventeenth century, spiritual autobiography's popularity strengthened and its form expanded; it came to function not just as a chronicle of spirituality but also of the colonization of place and people. William Bradford's *Of Plymouth Plantation* (1630–51), John Winthrop's journals (1630–49), and Captain John Smith's diaries of colonizing Virginia (1608–30) were signature texts of this era, prescribing in Udo Hebel's words "a formula for U.S.-American commemoration of an Anglo-centric myth of origin."[18] This trend continued into the nineteenth century, when, according to Susan Balée, American cultural identity resonated with Nathaniel Hawthorne's Puritan characters and Augustus Baldwin Longstreet's *Georgian Scenes* as clearly as it emanated from the bales of cotton, barrels of whale blubber, and crates of cranberries returning to Europe from the New World.[19] The 1868 publication of the complete and definitive autobiography of Benjamin Franklin (parts of which first appeared in the 1790s) confirmed the centrality of autobiography as an American form of consciousness, with one crucial adjustment: Franklin substituted the former focus on God with a focus on America. Franklin's rags-to-riches autobiography set the framework for modern American identity, remaining a bestseller for nearly a century after its widespread release in the United States.[20]

During the nineteenth century, as readers became more diverse and Western society more liberal, autobiography followed Franklin's example, discarding the religious focus of spiritual narrative and replacing it with a new secular subject—the sacredness of the examined self. Leigh Gilmore observes that modern autobiography became a "monument" to the idea of personhood: "To write a memoir," Gilmore argues, is "to create the person you discover yourself to be. . . . The self [comes] into being as a distinctive entity in memoir."[21] Diane Bjorklund agrees, saying that autobiography has two authorial functions: to understand the self and to impress as wide a readership as possible that the author is to be admired by contemporary standards.[22] Eamonn Hughes likewise stresses the centrality of self in modern autobiography, writing that more than any other genre autobiography concerns itself with identity, while Liam Harte defines the genre as a means through which to compose, proclaim, and perform multifaceted senses of belonging.[23] Critically, and as these scholars suggest, rather than being grounded in realism, autobiography is a method of artful self-invention, a genre through which to achieve or at least express desire for an ideal self. These various understandings of the form lead Philippe Lejeune to define autobiography as a retrospective text focused on an individual life, in particular the story of one's personality.[24]

Lejeune's definition of autobiography, while seemingly simplistic, becomes more applicable when we are faced with the innovative forms of life writing that emerged across the nineteenth century. This change was accelerated by political and social transformations in the latter part of the century, which saw a diversity of narrators turn to life writing to address the issues that affected them. The *Narrative of the Life of Frederick Douglass, an American Slave* (1845) was a key text in this movement, raising awareness of the evils of slavery and necessity of abolition through Douglass's description of his personal story.[25] In this era life writing was increasingly a political act, bound up with assertions of agency and demands for a fairer society.[26] Harriet Jacobs's *Incidents in the Life of a Slave Girl* (1861) and Elizabeth Cady Stanton's *Eighty Years and More* (1898) are further examples of texts that addressed questions of women's suffrage, labor rights, colonization, nation, and race through the genre of life writing, shifting focus away from the story of the author's personality. For Lejeune, the form that emerged from this political struggle was *memoir*, defined in contrast to autobiography as principally concerned with a chronicle of social or political issues through the vectors of personal history.[27]

Lejeune's differentiation of memoir and autobiography has been contested, and the terms continue to be used interchangeably.[28] Lejeune's classification nevertheless proves helpful to readers of the genre, since it channels attention to the most pressing intentions of the narrator. Also integral to Lejeune's interpretation of the autobiographical space is his sense that the life writings of known authors (a richly populated field of the genre) must be read differently from those of unknown writers. For Lejeune, there exists an "autobiographical pact" between reader and writer that is calibrated by whether or not the writer is known to the reader as an "author." Indispensable to the reading of autobiography, Lejeune insists, is "that sign of reality which is the previous production of other texts."[29]

Unfortunately, literary scholars have also overlooked this dimension of Lejeune's work, continually conflating the features of vernacular life writing with the autobiographies of well-known authors, politicians, and other public figures. The result is a field of study that is dominated by reviews of elite autobiographies that disproportionately reflect a singular "making of the great man/woman" narrative. In contrast, the forms and functions of vernacular, private life writing remain misunderstood as amateur derivatives of professional autobiographical writing rather than having their own narrative logic and functions.[30]

Self-Narrativity in Early Modern Ireland

In comparison to the United States, autobiography in Ireland has a relatively short history. This relates in part to early modern preferences for oral and folkloric traditions, especially among the indigenous Catholic population. For this group, song, storytelling, and poetry were dominant cultural forms, and these were conceived as communal crafts, culturally rather than individually authored.[31] For instance, the names of storytellers, poets, singers, and musicians were rarely recorded, and the choreography of their performances was also carefully arranged to avoid an emphasis on the self. This folk-based narrative convention dates back to at least the late Irish medieval period. E. C. Quiggin's research in the early 1900s on Irish poetry from the thirteenth through to the sixteenth centuries noted the tendency for Irish bards to avoid reciting their own work in public. The following lines describe how the poet ("rymer") would sit aside while a "rakry" recited his compositions: "Now comes the Rymer that made the Ryme, with his Rakry. . . . The Rakry is he that shall utter the ryme; and the Rymer himself sits by with the Captain verie proudlye. He brings with him also his harper."[32]

The scholarship on nineteenth-century Irish music and songs suggests streams of continuity between bardic and modern conventions. Sorcha Nic Lochlainn's examination of Irish emigrant songs notes that it was unusual for composers themselves to sing the songs that they had written, as was it atypical to ascribe the composition of a song to any particular author.[33] Henry Glassie recognizes the continuity of this self-erasing pattern in 1970s storytelling conventions. Listening to the old men talk around the fireplaces and pubs of County Fermanagh, Glassie notes their aversion to autobiographical narration and concludes that "the old people are not drawn to self-centered life review, and autobiographical anecdotes, with their glint of the bright, do not fit in the ceili where people tell anecdotes about others."[34]

However, transnationalism, emigration, colonialism, and formalized education in the nineteenth century inevitably shifted attention from oral and folkloric to written and authored forms. This change was accelerated by the introduction of the Irish national school system in 1831, which focused on increasing Irish literacy rates and expanding the use of English as a lingua franca. Regarded as an agent of "civilisation, socialisation, assimilation, politicisation and the reproduction of colonial values," the national school system prioritized pedagogical and curricular input that offered alternatives to Irish, peasant-centered worldviews and communication methods through Anglo-centric textbooks and narratives.[35] The nationalized education system had a profound and immediate influence on literacy rates in Ireland, so that by 1900 illiteracy had decreased from 52.8 to 18.4 percent.[36] According to David Fitzpatrick, girls in particular benefited from the system, as economic crisis in the post-Famine decades made employment as an alternative to schooling less accessible.[37] Thus, at the dawn of the twentieth century, a new generation of "peasant sophisticates" had emerged in Ireland, and many of them would set off for America. If and when these immigrants encountered autobiographies in the streets or train carriages of the United States, they would be in a better position to engage with them.

Irish Nationalist Autobiography

The flow of autobiography into Ireland's literary bloodstream can be traced to significant moments in the Irish republican movement. As noted in chapter 2, the posthumous publication in 1826 of *The Life of Theobold Wolfe Tone* was a cultural milestone for Irish nationalists, breathing life into their Famine

and post-Famine political campaigns.[38] Tone's memoir was particularly influential for Young Irelanders and arguably influenced its members to deploy
autobiography themselves so as to broaden the range of heroes, symbols, and
narratives available to future Irish republicans. John Mitchel's *Jail Journey*
(1854) and Jeremiah O'Donovan's Rossa's *Six Years in Six English Prisons*
(1874) were two of the memoirs that emerged as a result, the latter published
in sections in *The United Irishman*. Other political memoirs followed, including Michael Davitt's *Leaves from a Prison Diary* (1885), T. D. Sullivan's
Recollections of Troubled Times in Irish Politics (1905), and William O'Brien's
Recollections (1905). According to Liam Harte, these political literary productions were "so persuasive and voluminous that they inaugurated a cultural
tradition of Irish autobiography that conceived the responsibility of literature
to be the production and mediation of a sense of national identity."[39] Declan
Kiberd concurs, writing that "autobiography in Ireland becomes, in effect,
the autobiography of Ireland."[40]

There is near unanimous acknowledgment of the apathy with which Irish
women writers related to these questions of nationhood in the nineteenth
century. Harte has commented that far from offering a sense of completion,
nationalism severely limited women's apprehension of a full identity.[41] Taura
Napier agrees, showing through her analysis of Irish women's literary autobiographies that women took particular care in their autobiographies to separate
the ideas of nation and self.[42] Hughes also understands that women autobiographers were "compromised by the paradigmatic narrative of the dissolution
of self into nation."[43] Similarly, Elizabeth Grubgeld, writing on Anglo-Irish
autobiography, notes that "those autobiographers who deemphasize ethnic or
national identity tend to be women."[44] Michael Kenneally, too, recognizes Irish
women autobiographers' refusal to "explore and define themselves in terms of
patriotic values and national goals."[45] In essence, memoir, in the masculinist
and nationalistic paradigm through which it was written in nineteenth-century
Ireland, was almost universally unappealing to Irish women.

Owing to the importance of male readers in the Irish literary market as
well as the heightened Irish nationalist fervor of the early twentieth century,
the publication of nationalist memoirs prevailed as Irish writers learned to
satisfy demand for life writing that paralleled the life of the individual against
the life cycle of the newly emergent Irish nation. Prominent memoirs that
emerged from this milieu include Dan Breen's *My Fight for Irish Freedom*
(1924), Douglas Hyde's *Mise agus an Conradh* (1931), and Ernie O'Malley's

On Another Man's Wound (1936). According to Eamonn Hughes, the vectors of Irish independence and Irish autobiography remained so entwined during this period that "to tell the story of the self [was] to write the narrative of Ireland."[46] Irish women also began to contribute to this corpus of life writing. Nora Connolly's *The Unbroken Tradition* (1918) shared her firsthand experiences of the events leading up to the 1916 Easter Rising, with a subsequent book, *Portrait of a Rebel Father* (1935), focusing on the republican exploits of her father. Maud Gonne's 1938 memoir, *A Servant of the Queen*, chronicled her nationalist pursuits, including her role in founding Inghinidhe na hEireann (Daughters of Ireland) in 1900. Máire Nic Shiublhaigh's *The Splendid Years* (1955), Lil Conlon's *Cumann na mBan and the Women of Ireland, 1913–23* (1969), and Kathleen Keys McDonnell's *There Is a Bridge at Bandon* (1972) were later editions to the corpus of nationalist Irish women's autobiographical writing. Although their presence on the bookshelves indicates an expansion in women's roles in public life, the containment of their life narratives within a strict nationalist framework is a reminder of the rigid conventions of the genre in Ireland, as well as the restrictive nature of women's lives. Indeed, as Margaret O'Callaghan writes, the fact that most Irish women could not write about the self except in the most limited terms is in itself a political and cultural story.[47] O'Callaghan adds that until at least the 1980s, "confessional writing that revealed the story of Irish female subjectivity as anything other than a virtuous one could have socially ruinous consequences for its authors."[48]

Mary Carbery's *The Farm by Lough Gur* (1937) is a more atypical example of women's Irish autobiography in the early twentieth century, in that it focuses on the everyday agricultural life and attachment to land of a middle-class Catholic family in Limerick. Beautifully written, Carbery's book *is* conventional insofar as it reflects the tendency in twentieth-century Ireland to corelate the concepts of place and nationhood.[49] Additionally, Carbery's romanticism and cheerful review of the relationship between the people of the house and their poorer Catholic servants was surely influenced by another of Ireland's nineteenth- and twentieth-century autobiographical tropes: the Anglo-Irish "Big House" memoir.

The Anglo-Irish Memoir

From Katherine Tynan's five autobiographical volumes (1913–24) to Elizabeth Bowen's *Bowen's Court* (1942), Anglo-Irish autobiographies mark a distinct counterpoint to the male and nationalistic dominated canon discussed in previous paragraphs. Perhaps best known for their romantic portrayal of life in the Big House, Anglo-Irish autobiographies provided a melancholic perspective on Ireland before World War I, wistfully recording Anglo-Irish families' claims to and affection for the Irish landscape. Grubgeld summarizes the canon as collectively articulating a "narrative of decline," as Anglo-Irish families faded from social and financial grace with the foundation of the Irish Free State. According to Grubgeld, Anglo-Irish authors, male and female alike, "uniformly express their sense of having lived in a world apart from the majority population and having now reached the end of that era."[50] Grubgeld's erudite analysis of Anglo-Irish autobiographies also highlights the canonical stances that its authors adopted, suggesting in turn the narrative conventions that had come to be associated with the genre of memoir in Ireland, at least among the Anglo-Irish. In the first instance, autobiographers generally had a strong sense of the historical significance of their life writing. This implies a sense of self-regard that is absent in contemporaneous Irish peasant and working-class memoirs, in which narrators struggle to perceive their import and distinctiveness in the world.[51]

Second, Anglo-Irish memoirs, like their nationalist counterparts, took on the responsibility of representing their culture through their personal life writing. "I am ruled by a continuity I cannot see," wrote Elizabeth Bowen in 1942, indicating the influence of her background both on how she told her life story as well as what she chose to write about. In effect, Bowen and her contemporaries saw themselves as translators of their culture, a position that required the cool eye of the distant observer. Again, this distinguished them from Irish Catholic autobiographers, who appeared to perceive the world with less detachment than their Anglo-Irish contemporaries. Indeed, George O'Brien has commented on the struggles of rural peasant Irish memoirists at large to see themselves as distinct from their environment, writing that "the primacy of place limited the ability to narrate an interplay between self and world."[52] An obvious exception to this rule was the corpus of Irish-language and Irish emigrant navvy memoirs that emerged among peasant Irish Catholics from the early twentieth century. In both cases, writing was precipitated by the authors' awareness of the exceptionality of their life experiences: the uniqueness of life on the Blaskets, for instance, or the alterity of life as an emigrant worker in Britain.[53]

Third, and perhaps most insightfully, the coverage of Anglo-Irish women's autobiographies was severely limited by middle-class taboos and social etiquette. Literary gatekeepers of the late Victorian period disapproved of the narration of female experiences such as pregnancy, childbirth, nursing, or infant loss, subjects that were deemed inappropriate for public discussion.[54] And yet the private communications of women across the class spectrum in late-nineteenth-century and twentieth-century Ireland reveal that it was precisely these themes that most occupied women's minds. Middle-class women's unpublished letters and diaries from this period reflect their preoccupation with maternal desires, anxieties, and heartbreaks, even as their public writing focused on more sanitized subjects, such as their roles in vocational and professional worlds.[55] These same maternal interests fill the written and oral literature of working-class women, who, owing to their "compromised" class status, were even less sought after as autobiographers.[56] Given the absence of published material that represented their domestic, maternal, romantic, and professional concerns, women in Ireland and Britain thus relied on information gathered through informal and formal networks to respond to their questions about childbirth, family planning, nursing, childcare, and nutrition. This is to say, for most women in twentieth-century Britain and Ireland, the formal modes of autobiography as they had come to know it remained alien and inappropriate.[57]

American Autobiography in the Twentieth Century

The same was not true of the United States. There, popular culture had evolved by the early twentieth century to promote multiple representations of American womanhood, communicated through a booming film, advertising, and literary scene.[58] So where women who stayed in Ireland were culturally insulated by censorship, clerical dominance, legislation governing sexual behavior, masculine nationalism, and an underdeveloped economy, their counterparts in the US were freely exposed to the values of "the American way" through cinema, advertisements, magazines, mass-produced fiction, and autobiographies. These values incorporated materialism, godlessness, divorce, and danger, as well as progress, high standards of living, independence for women, birth control, and loving marriages.[59] The golden era of Hollywood particularly affected women, as movie stars from Marilyn Monroe to Grace Kelly defined new standards of beauty and allowed women to "indulge in dreams of escape from everyday life and to express interest in sexual power, the exotic, presence and influence."[60]

Adjacent to these glamorous images of womanhood were published life narratives that evoked American women's rebellious, political, sexualized, and disruptive roles in society.[61] From the close of the nineteenth century, suffragists such as Abigail Scott Duniway and Elizabeth Cady Stanton used their personal life histories to document American women's fight for the vote.[62] In the words of Ann Gordon, these memoirists portrayed new possibilities for women that included mothers as lobbyists, wives as political campaigners, and housewives as authors, making these roles appear both humanly possible and politically desirable.[63] The twentieth century saw this kind of feminist writing come of age, as women from all walks of life asserted their independence, contesting the gender norms that limited their participation in social and political life. Key texts of this era include the autobiography of Jane Addams, which illustrated her commitment to improving the plight of the working class in Chicago.[64] Other major works were the writings of "frontier feminists" like Elinore Stewart, Hilda Rose, and Annie Pike Greenwood, each of whom exemplified the ability of women to succeed as homesteaders on the harsh American frontier.[65] For their part, Gertrude Stein's *The Autobiography of Alice B. Toklas* and her subsequent *Everybody's Autobiography* presented playful, ironic, and sexually beguiling images of a bourgeois woman's inner world.[66]

It did not take long for women of Irish descent to join this burgeoning style of writing. Canonical life narratives that represented such women include Mary McCarthy's critically acclaimed *Memories of a Catholic Childhood* (1957). A target of much derision from American Catholics, McCarthy deliberately shirks Irish ethnic claims of identification, instead exploring her sexual awakening from her teenage years.[67] McCarthy's is one of some seventy-five Irish American women's memoirs published in the twentieth century, with notables including Mary Harris Jones's *The Autobiography of Mother Jones* (1925), Margaret Higgins Sanger's *The Autobiography of Margaret Sanger* (1938), Elizabeth Flynn's *The Rebel Girl* (1973), and Margaret A. Haley's *Battleground: The Autobiography of Margaret A. Haley* (1982). According to Mary Mason, these writings were highly influential and paved the way for a distinct stream of Catholic and radical female activist literature in North America.[68] Sally Ebest notes that these autobiographies collectively index Irish women's leading roles in the labor movement, women's suffrage, and efforts to legalize contraception.[69] They also illustrate Irish immigrant women's embrace and mastery of a style of life writing that would have been impossible to pursue had they or their families remained in Ireland.

Critically, as well as promoting different versions of womanhood, American life writing welcomed working-class and ethnic voices into a genre that in Britain and Ireland remained the preserve of social and political elites. Although the American vogue for "undistinguished" memoirists began in patronizing fashion with the 1906 publication of Hamilton Holt's *The Life Stories of Undistinguished Americans, as Told by Themselves*, it grew into a highly regarded literary field.[70] As we saw at the beginning of this chapter, in the acclaim Antin, Bok, Riis, and others received, the genre reflected the American promise of opportunity for all and altered the country's conceptualization and expectations of its immigrants.[71]

And yet against these increasingly liberal life narratives, a current of conservative tropes derived from the colonizer's mindset of the seventeenth century continued to irrigate the modern American mind. These included life narratives that documented the taming of American wilderness and its native population, which were now visually supplemented by popular Western movies.[72] There was as well a vogue for spiritual conversion narratives, such as those by the journalist and social activist Dorothy Day.[73] Modern American literature also upheld white supremacist belief systems and demonstrated, in the words of Amy Kaplan, the "racial underpinnings" shared by domestic and imperialist discourses in the first part of the twentieth century.[74] Margaret Mitchell's widely popular *Gone with the Wind* (1936) exemplifies such a text, though the majority of books borrowed from public libraries in the early decades of the twentieth century were written by white male writers.[75] Perhaps most pervasively, the American prerogative for the accumulation of capital at the time fueled a demand for a life writing that illustrated economic progress and idealized the self-made man, as did autobiographies by Andrew Carnegie (1920) and Lee Iacocca (1984).[76]

With all of these generic styles and shifts, Irish immigrants in the United States who felt compelled to write their life stories were hardly lacking in inspiration or choice. The popular culture of twentieth-century America provided ready access to life narrative frames that included firsthand immigrant testimonies, radical feminist treatises, spiritual parables, romantic love stories, self-made-man narratives, and much more. Irish immigrants could also draw from an established pool of Irish autobiography, which, while more rigid in terms of convention, nonetheless offered templates for those who wished to claim space on the map of Irish nationalist cultural memory. Realizing the depth and range of Irish and US autobiographical conventions is important, for it enables us to appreciate the authorial control involved in the production of Irish immigrants' life writing. Part 2 of this book further develops this conversation, providing portraits of four individual Irish immigrant memoirs read in light of the conventions of memory and life writing identified in part 1. Before departing on this journey, however, we return for a last glimpse at the man we met at the beginning of this chapter, to see how he fared with the autobiography thrust into his hands on his maiden voyage across America.

It took Tom Brick a long time to settle down. In rural Iowa, where he worked as a farmhand on his brother-in-law's farm, he confessed to finding himself disturbed by the new environment and especially by the treatment of the Native Americans by white settlers. "I am very unhappy with my lot," grumbles Brick, recollecting that first year in America. Significantly, he linked his unhappiness to all the "Indian fighting and killing" he had read about in Drannan's autobiography, a text he ultimately rejects as gory and crude.[77] "After completing reading that book that I bought from the newsboy on the train coming from Chicago, with all its Indian fighting and killing, I was getting homesick and telling my sister I wanted to go back to my old haunts in Ireland," Brick writes. It is a tantalizing window onto the power of literature in shaping immigrants' thought processes as well as evidencing their resistance to certain cultural norms that they were exposed to in the United States.

Luckily for Brick, other literary models had become available. He abandoned the tradition of western autobiography represented by Drannan's *Thirty-One Years on the Plains and in the Mountains* and adopted a style of writing that had exploded in popularity by the mid-twentieth century and expressed a way of life that surely resonated with his own childhood experiences: the Gaeltacht memoir.

While Brick was making his way across the Great Plains, his neighbors back in West Kerry were beginning to write themselves into history.[78] The years between 1900 and 1940 saw the publication of several West Kerry autobiographies by famed storytellers from the Blasket Islands, including Tomás Ó Crohan, Peig Sayers, Muiris Ó Súileabháin, and Micháel O'Guibheen.[79] Evidently, the characteristic aversion to self-directed review had begun to disintegrate, if indeed it had ever truly existed at all. For, as John Eastlake writes, texts such as that of Tomás Ó Crohan's pulse with their authors' search for self-understanding and indicate a deep need in the Irish "peasant" psyche to come to terms with their lives through concentrated self-reflection.[80] At the same time, and unlike their American counterparts, these texts were highly prized for their descriptions of a distinctly communal way of life on Ireland's western fringes. The poet and critic Seán Ó Tuama, for instance, summed up Ó Crohan's effort as "more the biography of an island community than of a single islander and lauded it as 'a majestic social document.'"[81] A comparative analysis of Brick's writing makes it clear that this commitment to community and the communication of a life narrative through language that reflected West Kerry oral storytelling conventions was fiercely appealing. Through repetitive, rhythmic language, written in the dialect of West Kerry, Brick forsakes the narrative conventions of American western memoir, portraying himself instead as a wanderer, a gatherer of tales for the entertainment of those back home. In so doing, he manages to fulfill the duty of the Irish *seanchaí*, transcribing to print the stories that he might have told by the fireplace, had he been able to stay on the Slea Head peninsula. Through writing, Brick psychologically transported himself to his old haunts.

Brick's response is unique, a conglomerate of his personal memories, immigrant experiences, artistic preferences, and cultural habitus. As part 2 of this book will show, other immigrants responded differently to the art of life writing, drawing on an impossibly diverse array of both direct experiences and canonical conventions. This variety of responses illuminates a much-neglected feature of the Irish immigrant experience: the richly textured nature of their cultural worlds and the variety of literary forms that were available to them when reflecting on their own life trajectories. It points, too, to the artistic ways in which Irish immigrants in America grafted memory narratives and storytelling practices from Ireland onto generic American autobiographical conventions, and vice versa. Finally, the range of narrative styles that will be reviewed through part 2 reminds us of the gravitational pull of time when conceiving of the self. As Maria Stepanova writes in her iconic *In Memory of Memory*, "It is as if every age produces its own particular dust that settles on every surface and in every corner."[82] Through their writings, the signs of time and modes of thought in which these Irish immigrants imperceptibly moved become momentarily visible. Like tufts of dandelion floating in sunlight, they begin to shimmer.

Notes

1. This description is based on Tom Brick's memoir, Kerry/ Iowa/ South Dakota, University of Galway Archive, P155/106/11.

2. William F. Drannan, *Thirty-One Years on the Plains and in the Mountains; or, The Last Voice from the Plains: An Authentic Record of a Life Time of Hunting, Trapping, Scouting and Indian Fighting in the Far West* (Chicago: Rhodes and McClure, 1900). According to Clay Coppedge, Drannan's book "helped satisfy the American public's seemingly insatiable appetite for stories about the frontier. Young boys were especially keen on the books, as they described a life full of adventure that was the fundamental stuff of their dreams." Clay Coppedge, "William F. Drannan Told It Like It Wasn't," *Texas Escapes.com*, accessed April 4, 2023. For further exploration of Drannan's memoir, see Sarah O'Brien, "Tom Brick of South Dakota, Irish Emigrant Life Writing, and the Dynamics of Storytelling," *New Hibernia Review* 22, no. 4 (2018).

3. Susan Balée, "From the Outside In: A History of American Autobiography,"*Hudson Review* 51, no. 1 (1998). See also Geraldine Meaney, Mary O'Dowd, and Bernadette Whelan, *Reading the Irish Woman: Studies in Cultural Encounter and Exchange, 1714–1960* (Liverpool: Liverpool University Press, 2013).

4. Thomas Ferraro, "Ethnicity and the Marketplace," in *The Columbia History of the American Novel*, ed. Emery Elliot (New York: Columbia University Press, 1991); Edward Alfred Steiner, *From Alien to Citizen: The Story of My Life in America* (New York: Fleming H. Revell, 1914); Mary Antin, *The Promised Land* (Boston: Houghton, 1912); Marcus Eli Ravage, *An American in the Making: The Life Story of an Immigrant* (1917; repr., New Brunswick, NJ: Rutgers University Press, 2009); Mihajlo Idvorsky Pupin, *From Immigrant to Inventor* (New York: Scribner, 1923); Edward Bok, *The Americanization of Edward Bok* (New York: Scribner, 1920); Constantine M. Panunzio, *The Soul of an Immigrant* (1921; repr., Whitefish, Montana: Kessinger, 2010); Jacob A. Riis, *The Making of an American* (New York: Macmillan, 1902).

5. Cristina Stanciu, "Marcus E. Ravage's *An American in the Making*, Americanization, and New Immigrant Representation," *Multi-Ethnic Literature of the United States (MELUS)* 40, no. 2 (2015): 14.

6. Stanciu, "Marcus E. Ravage's *An American in the Making*," 11.

7. Stanciu notes that Ravage's memoir was widely used in New York schools. Ravage was also "involved in selecting and awarding scholarships to promising young men and women of foreign parentage." Stanciu, "Marcus E. Ravage's *An American in the Making*," 11–12.

8. For instance, Ravage's autobiography was serialized in *Harper's Bazaar*. Excerpts from Riis's memoir were featured in the *Outlook*, the *Churchman*, and *Century*. Mary Antin's memoir was published in part in the *Atlantic*

Monthly. Jeremiah O'Donovan Rossa's memoir appeared in the *United Irishman* newspaper. See Aneka Pavlenko, "The Making of an American: Negotiaton of Identities at the Turn of the Twentieth Century," in *Negotiation of Identities in Multilingual Contexts,* ed. Aneka Pavlenko and Adrian Blackledge (Cevendon, UK: Multilingual Matters, 2004). Julia Watson and Sidonie Smith add that "at the turn of the twentieth century, many narratives appeared originally in national magazines or newspapers, among them *The Independent, The Atlantic Monthly,* and *The Boston Globe,* and in local newspapers such as *The Butte Evening News.*" See Sidonie Smith and Julia Watson, *Life Writing in the Long Run* (Ann Arbor: Michigan Publishing Services, 2016).

9. Angela Davis, *An Autobiography* (New York: Knopf, 1971); Ernesto Galarza, *Barrio Boy: The Story of a Boy's Acculturation* (Notre Dame, IN: University of Notre Dame Press, 1971); Maxine Hong Kingston, *The Woman Warrior: Memoirs of a Girlhood among Ghosts* (New York: Knopf, 1976).

10. William Boelhower, "The Brave New World of Immigrant Autobiography," *Multi-Ethnic Literature of the United States (MELUS)* 9, no. 2 (1982); Maria Lauret, "When Is an Immigrant's Autobiography Not an Immigrant Autobiography? The Amerianization of Edward Bok," *Multi-Ethnic Literature of the United States (MELUS)* 38, no. 3 (2013).

11. Sidonie Smith and Julia Watson, *Reading Autobiography: A Guide for Interpreting Life Narratives,* 2d ed. (Minneapolis: University of Minnesota Press, 2010).

12. Sally Barr Ebest, "Agency and Activism in Irish American Women's Memoirs," *Multi Ethnic Literature of the United States (MELUS)* 44, no. 4 (2019).

13. Sau-Ling Cynthia Wong, "Immigrant Autobiography: Some Questions of Definition and Approach," in *American Autobiography: Retrospect and Prospect,* ed. Paul John Eakin (Madison: University of Wisconsin Press, 1991).

14. Elizabeth Grubgeld, *Anglo Irish Autobiography: Class, Gender and the Forms of Narrative* (Syracuse, NY: Syracuse University Press, 2004), 1.

15. Kathryn Rudy, *Virtual Pilgrimages in the Convent: Imagining Jerusalem in the Late Middle Ages* (London: Brepols, 2011); Ian Reader, *Pilgrimage: A Very Short Introduction* (Oxford: Oxford University Press, 2015).

16. Paul Ricoeur, *Memory, History, Forgetting* (Chicago: University of Chicago Press, 2004).

17. Smith and Watson write, for instance, that spiritual autobiography typically unfolds as a journey through sin and damnation to a sense of spiritual fulfillment and place of sustaining belief. Smith and Watson, *Reading Autobiography,* 47–48. Andrew Palmer's convincing thesis also confirms that spiritual autobiography was the beginning of all autobiographical writing in the West. Andrew William Palmer, "The Autobiographical Pact and the Selection of Self in Memoir" (PhD thesis, University of Lincoln, 2016), 8. According to

Liz Stanley, narrative trajectories of the modern memoir tend, like the novel, to cover a life from difficult beginnings through trials toward a realized self. Liz Stanley, *The Autobiographical I: The Theory and Practice of Feminist Autobiography* (Manchester: Manchester University Press, 1995), 9.

18. Udo Hebel, "Sites of Memory in U.S.-American Histories and Cultures," in *A Companion to Cultural Memory Studies*, ed. Astrid Erll and Ansgar Nünning (Berlin: De Gruyter, 2010), 48.

19. Susan Balée, "From the Outside In: A History of American Autobiography," *Hudson Review* 51, no. 1 (1998): 41.

20. Note that Franklin started his autobiography in 1771, and it appeared in portions beginning in 1791 but was not published as a complete work until 1868. See Smith and Watson, *Life Writing in the Long Run*; Balée, "From the Outside In."

21. Leigh Gilmore, *The Limits of Autobiography: Trauma and Testimony* (Ithaca, NY: Cornell University Press, 2001), 36.

22. Diane Bjorklund, *Interpreting the Self: Two Hundred Years of American Autobiography* (Chicago: University of Chicago Press, 1998).

23. Eamonn Hughes, "'The Fact of Me-Ness': Autobiographical Writing in the Revival Period," *Irish University Review* 33, no. 1 (2003): 30; Liam Harte, "Migrancy, Performativity and Autobiographical Identity," *Irish Studies Review* 14, no. 2 (2006): 235.

24. Philippe Lejeune, *On Autobiography* (Minneapolis: University of Minnesota Press, 1989), 5.

25. Comparable texts from and about Ireland in this period include Asenath Nicholson's *Annals of the Famine in Ireland* (1847–49) and Elizabeth Owens Blackburne Casey's autobiographical novel *Molly Carew* (1879).

26. Harte, "Migrancy, Performativity and Autobiographical Identity," 226.

27. Lejeune, *On Autobiography*.

28. Boelhower is a particular critic of Lejeune's autobiographical pact, though his reasons are unclear. William Boelhower, "The Brave New World of Immigrant Autobiography," *Multi-Ethnic Literature of the United States (MELUS)* 9, no. 2 (1982): 5–23.

29. Lejeune, *On Autobiography*, 12.

30. O'Brien, "Tom Brick of South Dakota."

31. Walter Ong, *Orality and Literacy: The Technologising of the Word* (London: Routledge, 1982).

32. I am indebted to Liam Mac Mathúna for drawing my attention to E. C. Quiggin, "Prolegomena to the Study of the Later Irish Bards, 1200–1500," *Proceedings of the British Academy* 5 (1911).

33. Sorcha Nic Lochlainn, "'Bear My Greetings across the Sea': Emigrant Experiences and the Gaelic Song Tradition," *Béaloideas* 82 (2014): 26.

34. Henry Glassie, *The Stars of Ballymenone* (Bloomington: Indiana University Press, 2006), 70. Glassie was evidently familiar with E. C. Quiggin's discoveries. He notes in *The Stars*, "The solution—with firm precedent in the bardic practice of the Middle Ages—is to divide the task: one to compose, one to sing." Glassie, *The Stars*, 70.

35. Tom Walsh, "The National System of Education, 1831–2000," in *Essays in the History of Irish Education*, ed. Brendan Walsh (London: Palgrave, 2016), 8.

36. Walsh, "The National System of Education," 11. For an excellent review of reading habits in nineteenth-century Ireland, see Meaney, O'Dowd, and Whelan, *Reading the Irish Woman*.

37. David Fitzpatrick, "'A Share of the Honeycomb': Education, Emigration and Irishwomen," *Continuity and Change* 1, no. 2 (1986).

38. David Brundage, "Matilda Tone in America: Exile, Gender, and Memory in the Making of Irish Republican Nationalism," *New Hibernia Review / Iris Éireannach Nua* 14, no. 1 (2010).

39. Liam Harte, ed., *A History of Irish Autobiography* (Cambridge: Cambridge University Press, 2018).

40. Declan Kiberd, *Inventing Ireland: The Literature of a Modern Nation* (London: Jonathan Cape, 1995), 119.

41. Harte, *A History of Irish Autobiography*, 160.

42. Taura Napier, *Seeking a Country: Literary Autobiographies of Twentieth-Century Irishwomen* (Lanham, MD: University Press of America, 2001).

43. Hughes, "'The Fact of Me-Ness,'" 39.

44. Grubgeld, *Anglo Irish Autobiography*, 30.

45. Michael Kenneally, "The Autobiographical Imagination and Irish Literary Autobiographies," in *Critical Approaches to Anglo Irish Literature*, ed. Michael Allen and Angela Wilcox (Gerrards Cross, UK: Colin Smythe, 1989), quoted in Liam Harte, ed., *A History of Irish Autobiography* (Cambridge: Cambridge University Press, 2018), 5.

46. Hughes, "'The Fact of Me-Ness.'"

47. Margaret O'Callaghan, "Women's Political Autobiography in Independent Ireland," in *A History of Irish Autobiography*, ed. Liam Harte (Cambridge: Cambridge University Press, 2018), 135.

48. O'Callaghan, "Women's Political Autobiography in Independent Ireland," 135.

49. Place and landscape remained important themes in twentieth-century Irish autobiography. Michael Kenneally writes that "historical and mythic place" are to the fore of the genre, while Kevin P. Reilly's examination of male Irish autobiographies "posited a direct link between male writers' persistent but ultimately unfillable desire for intimacy with an archetypal national goddess." Quoted in Harte, *A History of Irish Autobiography*, 4.

50. Grubgeld, *Anglo Irish Autobiography*, xii.

51. George O'Brien, "Memoirs of Irish Rural Life," in *A History of Irish Autobiography*, ed. Liam Harte (Cambridge: Cambridge University Press, 2018).

52. O'Brien, "Memoirs of Irish Rural Life," 194.

53. O'Brien, "Tom Brick of South Dakota"; Emmet O'Connor, "The Autobiography of the Irish Working Class," in *A History of Irish Autobiography*, ed. Liam Harte (Cambridge: Cambridge University Press, 2018); Briona Nic Dhiarmada, "Irish Language Autobiography," in *A History of Irish Autobiography*, ed. Liam Harte (Cambridge: Cambridge University Press, 2018).

54. For instance, Grubgeld notes that "many Anglo Irish autobiographers were also mothers but none discussed birth, only a handful mentioned nursing or the physical care of children and few write at all about their children during infancy." She also writes that "the terms for writing about one's family (in Victorian England) were so sentimentally circumscribed that they did not allow for the greater realism sought by later writers." Grubgeld, *Anglo Irish Autobiography*, 67, 64.

55. Grubgeld observes that Lady Augusta Gregory's private letters and diaries reflected emotionally on her role as a mother and her concern for her son. This theme was entirely absent in her public correspondence.

56. Elizabeth Roberts, *A Woman's Place: An Oral History of Working-Class Women, 1890–1940* (London: John Wiley and Sons, 1995).

57. Valerie Sanders, *The Private Lives of Victorian Women* (New York: Saint Martin's, 1989).

58. Film attendance in 1939 in the United States was eighty million, and women made up most of the cinema attendees. See Meaney, O'Dowd, and Whelan, *Reading the Irish Woman*, 158. From the 1920s, mass-produced American fiction by authors like Sophie Kerr (1916–53) documented changing attitudes toward working women. These built on nineteenth-century feminist literature by writers such as Louisa May Alcott and Willa Cather. See Meaney, O'Dowd, and Whelan, *Reading the Irish Woman*, 143.

59. Meaney, O'Dowd, and Whelan, *Reading the Irish Woman*, 174.

60. Meaney, O'Dowd, and Whelan, *Reading the Irish Woman*, 150.

61. Smith and Watson, *Life Writing in the Long Run*.

62. Abigail Scott Duniway, *Path Breaking: An Autobiographical History of the Equal Suffrage Movement in Pacific Coast States* (Portland, OR: James, Kerns and Abbott, 1914); Elizabeth Cady Stanton, *Eighty Years and More: Reminiscences, 1815–1897* (1898; repr., New York: Schocken, 1971).

63. Ann Gordon, "The Political Is the Personal: Two Autobiographies of Woman Suffragists," in *Fea(s)ts of Memory*, ed. Margo Culley (Madison: University of Wisconsin Press, 1992); Duniway, *Path Breaking*; Stanton, *Eighty Years and More*.

64. Jane Addams, *Twenty Years at Hull-House* (1910; repr., Champaign: University of Illinois Press, 1990).

65. Annie Pike Greenwood, *We Sagebrush Folks* (New York: Appleton, 1934); Elinore Pruitt Stewart, *Letters of a Woman Homesteader* (Boston: Houghton Mifflin, 1914); Cristiana Holmes Tillson, *A Woman's Story of Pioneer Illinois* (Chicago: Donnelly, 1919); Hilda Rose, *The Stump Farm: A Chronicle of Pioneering* (Boston: Little, Brown, 1931).

66. Gertrude Stein, *The Autobiography of Alice B. Toklas* (New York: Harcourt Brace, 1933); Gertrude Stein, *Everybody's Autobiography* (1937; repr., New York: Cooper Square, 1971).

67. Mary McCarthy, *Memories of a Catholic Girlhood* (1947; repr., New York: Harcourt Brace Jovanovich, 1981); Ellen McWilliams, "Looking for Irish America in the Memoirs of Mary McCarthy," *Women's Studies* 49, no. 4 (2020).

68. For instance, the American activist Dorothy Day described her awe at first meeting Elizabeth Gurley Flynn. Day wrote of Flynn's "warmth, her equanimity, her humor and above all the purpose of her life—her aim to help bring about the society where each would work according to their ability and receive according to his needs." Dorothy Day, *By Little and Little* (New York: Knopf, 1984), 145. See also Mary G. Mason, "Dorothy Day and Women's Spiritual Autobiography," in *American Women's Autobiography: Fea(s)ts of Memory*, ed. Margo Culley (Madison: University of Wisconsin Press, 1992).

69. Ebest, "Agency and Activism," 177.

70. Hamilton Holt, *The Life Stories of Undistinguished Americans, as Told by Themselves* (New York: James Pott, 1906).

71. Stanciu insists that immigrant autobiographies humanized the experience of immigration and allowed writers to counter the nativist and racist discourses that operated in the early decades of the twentieth century. Stanciu, "Marcus E. Ravage's *An American in the Making.*"

72. Elizabeth Bacon Custer, *Tenting on the Plains: General Custer in Kansas and Texas* (New York: Charles L. Webster, 1887); J. F. Finerty, *War-Path and Bivouac; or, The Conquest of the Sioux: A Narrative of Stirring Personal Experiences and Adventures in the Big Horn and Yellowstone Expedition of 1876, and in the Campaign on the British Border, in 1879* (New York: Donohue Brothers, 1890).

73. Mason, "Dorothy Day and Women's Spiritual Autobiography"; Clifford J. Clarke, "The Bible Belt Thesis: An Empirical Test of the Hypothesis of Clergy Overrepresentation," *Journal for the Scientific Study of Religion* 29, no. 2 (1990).

74. Amy Kaplan, "Manifest Domesticity," *American Literature* 70, no. 3 (1998): 584.

75. Meaney, O'Dowd, and Whelan note that the American fiction writers most borrowed in the 1930s from public libraries were Lucille Papin Borden, Isabel C. Clare, Mary Theresa Waggaman, Elizabeth Garver Jordan, Mary

Johnson, Elizabeth Madox, May Stanley, Stewart Edward White, Ruth Comfort Mitchell, and Sophie Kerr. Meaney, O'Dowd, and Whelan, *Reading the Irish Woman*.

76. Andrew Carnegie, *Autobiography of Andrew Carnegie* (New York and Boston: Houghton Mifflin, 1920); Lee Iacocca with William Novak, *Iacocca: An Autobiography* (New York: Bantam, 1984).

77. Drannan, *Thirty-One Years on the Plains*. For a description of Drannan as an old man, see H. P. Lovecraft, *A Means to Freedom: The Letters of H. P. Lovecraft & Robert E. Howard*, vol. 2, *1933–36*, ed. S. T. Joshi, David E. Schultz, and Robert E. Howard (New York: Hippocampus, 2009). Clay Coppedge's *Letters from Central Texas* also hint at the influence of Drannan's autobiography in early-twentieth-century Texas. Clay Coppedge, *Letters from Central Texas*, accessed April 4, 2023, http://www.texasescapes.com/ClayCoppedge/Clay-Coppedge .htm.

78. As Carolina P. Amador Moreno lucidly discusses, the "Gaeltacht peasant memoir" of West Kerry became one of the dominant genres in Irish literature at the turn of the twentieth century. Moreno also calls attention to the lesser-known Donegal corpus of Irish-language memoirs by Mícheál MacGabhan (1865–1948), Patrick MacGill (1891–1963), and Seamus Ó Grianna (1889–1969). Carolina P. Amador Moreno, "Remembering Language: Bilingualism, Hiberno-English and the Gaeltacht Peasant Memoir," *Irish University Review* 39, no. 1 (2009): 76.

79. Tomás Ó Crohan, *The Islander*, trans. Garry Bannister and David Sowby (Dublin: Gill and Macmillan, 2012); Peig Sayers, *Peig: The Autobiography of Peig Sayrs of the Great Blasket Island*, trans. Bryan MacMahon (Syracuse: Syracuse University Press, 1974); Muiris Ó Súileabháin, *Fiche Blian Ag Fás*, 4th ed. (Maynooth: An Sagart, 2008). Note that Tomás Ó Crohan's *An tOileánach* (*The Islander*) was first published in 1928 and documented the years 1919–23. Muiris Ó Súileabháin's *Fiche Bliain ag fás* appeared in 1933, while Peig's first autobiography, entitled simply *Peig*, was published in 1936. For an insightful reflection on the Blasket Island memoirs, see Lillis Ó Laoire, review of *Róise Rua: An Island Memoir*, by Pádraig Ua Cnáimhsí, in Lillis Ó Laoire, "Augmenting Memory, Dispelling Amnesia," *Dublin Review of Books*, September 2017.

80. John Eastlake, "Orality and Agency: Reading an Irish Autobiography from the Great Blasket Island," *Oral Tradition* 24, no. 1 (2009), doi.org/10.1353 /ort.0.0035.

81. Significantly, the historian John Eastlake bemoans Ó Tuama's critical lens, arguing that such a review denies the search for self-understanding that throbs at the heart of Ó Crohan's writing. See Eastlake, "Orality and Agency."

82. Maria Stepanova, *In Memory of Memory*, trans. Sasha Dugdale (London: Fitzcarraldo, 2020).

PART II
Life Writing

Note of Introduction

Part 2 explores in detail the life writing of four immigrants who left Ireland for the United States in the post-Famine period. Three of these narratives are authored by women—Mary Jane Hill Anderson, Nora O'Connor, and Margaret McGuinness—and one by a man, Edmond (known as Ned) Ronayne. Ronayne's is the only memoir of the four to have been published, under the title *Ronayne's Reminiscences: A History of His Life and Renunciation of Romanism and Freemasonry* (1900). Two of the writers are Catholic, one Presbyterian, and one a convert from Catholicism to Protestant evangelicalism. The writers were born in various parts of Ireland (Counties Cork, Cavan, and Sligo), and they settled all over the United States (New York City, Texas, Chicago, Colorado, and Michigan). Their reasons for emigrating and their experiences in the United States were very different. It could be argued that the only commonality between all four immigrants was their determination to create a record of their lives: to leave traces of their thoughts, feelings, and memories through written self-reflection.

To illustrate transformations in the style and tone of Irish immigrant life writing, I have arranged the memoirs according to the order in which they were written. We begin in 1900 with the memoir of Ned Ronayne, progress to 1922 and the life writing of Mary Jane Hill Anderson, proceed to 1947 and the life story of Nora O'Connor, and end in 1973 with the life writing of Margaret McGuinness.

Three distinct questions guide my interpretation. First, I seek to understand the cultural influences, historical and literary, that gave design to the production of these autobiographical texts. Second, I consider how these private life narratives map on to the popular memory narratives of Irish America explored in part 1. And finally, I wonder what these manuscripts might reveal about the operations of Irish cultural memory in general and Irish emigrant memory in particular.

The microscopic examination of life narratives in part 2 is counterbalanced in part 3 by a telescopic view of all thirty-two memoirs surveyed throughout this book. In part 3 I summarize the patterns and themes of memory shared by all writers, in a bid to show universalities in the memory practices of the Irish in the twentieth-century United States.

4

Edmond Ronayne's Memoir (1899–1900)

Before preparing me for bed they led me to the bedside of my father and, standing me on a chair that he might see me better, they said to him as sooth-ingly as they could, "Oh, John, look at poor little Neddy; what shall we do with him?" . . . I have never forgotten that night or those scenes which I have mentioned. They are as fresh in my memory today as though they had transpired only yesterday. I was too young then to realize what this meant to me—absolutely alone, a little, delicate child without brother or sister, and now fatherless and motherless.[1]

One of the strangest features of the Irish Famine is said to be the silence that surrounds it.[2] Studying the literature that emerged during the Famine period, Chris Morash notes the inability of Irish writers to reckon with the loss of human life and the scale of human suffering between 1845 and 1850. Likewise, a survey circulated by University College Dublin's folklore archive in the 1930s returned scant memories of the Famine among Irish families.[3] Language fails before the enormity of the fact, Morash concludes, creat-ing a collective amnesia around this cataclysmic event.[4] "Trauma" has been alighted upon as an explanation for this elision of Famine memory.[5] The term refers to victims' struggles to process appalling images from their past in predictable and resolvable ways. Psychiatrists believe that "traumatic" memories are stored in a different location from banal recollections, in a part of the brain called the hypothalamus, allowing them to be overlooked most of the time.[6] This atypical storage can in turn produce contemporary effects for the victim, as traumatic memories act as a foreign body, continu-ally stimulating the victim in increasingly distressing ways.[7] "The victim of recurrent traumatic memories," writes Edward C. Casey, "is in the anomalous position of wanting to forget—but being unable to do so."[8] According to George Bonanno and Sharon Dekel, the intensity of a traumatic experience creates a "crisis of truth," the force of the event so powerful that it disables any coherent knowledge or memory of its origin.[9]

Ronayne's early years included many appalling images. He was born on November 5, 1832, the only child of Irish-speaking farm laborers in Gortaroo, Killeagh, East Cork. Ronayne wrote of his family as a happy unit, and yet between the 1830s and 1850s an impossible amount of tragedy was visited upon them. In 1833 Ronayne's mother died of overwork, having overstrained herself while reaping grain in the fields.[10] His father died four years afterwards, during an outbreak of cholera. Ronayne's memories of his father's funeral are particularly vivid: "I well remember the cry of the *ban keena* as my father's funeral passed along down the road toward Killeagh, on the way to the burying-ground at Clonpriest, some nine miles away. . . . My father was buried on the 17th of March, and just one week thereafter, on the 25th of March, his brother William was borne over the same road and in the same manner and buried by his side!"

Having become an orphan, Ronayne was placed in the care of his aunts Margaret and Mary. "No mother," he writes, "could more tenderly care for and cherish her child than these two devoted women loved and cared for me." A decade later, further tragedy was to strike the family: the Famine. While East Cork was initially insulated through its access to fishing stocks, the population eventually felt the effects of the Famine. In 1847 typhus became rampant in Killeagh. Ronayne describes the death of the first of his aunts (the sister-in-law of Margaret and Mary) and three of his cousins by the disease:

> It was about the beginning of February, if my memory serves me right, that the black fever broke out in Killeagh and vicinity, and very soon its deadly havoc became widespread. . . . The pestilence raged with uncontrollable fury in the neighborhood of Killeagh, and the first we heard it broke out in the uncle's family, carrying off the three youngest children in a few days. My aunts made inquiry from day to day as well as they could, in order to learn if any more of the family were sick, and very soon word was brought that the mother herself was taken down. . . . There she lay, having no care, no medical attendance, not even a neighbor to lend a hand, moaning and tossing in the delirium of that awful pestilence, and her condition was the condition of all. The next we heard she was dead. She died on Friday evening and was buried the following Sunday.

Within a day, Ronayne's beloved aunts Mary and Margaret had also contracted typhus. "Monday morning came, and my poor aunt was unable to rise," he writes. "I was sent that morning to Ballymacoda with a message to my Uncle David, and when I returned that afternoon she was gone, and I never saw her again alive." Hereafter Ronayne's memoir focuses on the horror-tinged events that proceeded from Margaret's death. The narrative is particularly attuned to the emotional impact of the deaths on the remaining members of the family. "My Aunt Mary was fairly beside herself with grief," Ronayne writes:

> They had always been together and loved each other devotedly, and now Margaret had been conveyed in a little donkey cart to the hospital possibly never to return. . . . We received word of her death, and Sunday morning I was sent up to Tom Hickey, our old friend at Glenawn, with the request that he send a horse and cart to take her body to the burying-ground. . . . The coffin was brought out and put into the cart. My Aunt Mary sat at one side and I at the other, and thus we passed through Killeagh and out by the Youghal road to Clonpriest, where we buried her beside my father and Uncle William.

Perhaps the most harrowing part of Ronayne's memoir is his description of his second aunt's death. At this point, both nephew and aunt had contracted typhus. The two lay together in bed "without a soul to help us or hand us so much as a drink of water." Ronayne describes the moment that he realized his aunt had passed away: "On Friday morning at about nine o'clock, as I was leaning on my right arm looking down upon her, her life went out peacefully and quietly, and I was left alone with my dead."

Ronayne's life writing conveys what Cormac Ó Gráda labels "the disarticulation of value systems" during the Famine, as the normal rituals of comfort and support during bereavement were stripped from a population focused on self-survival.[11] Ronayne recalls that his uncle "dreaded the fever" and "made himself quite drunk" in order to remove his sister's body. One can imagine the additional trauma that this caused the young boy: "He lifted my aunt out of the bed and laid her on the floor. He then went out and procured some rough boards to make a coffin, as he had done for his other sisters, and on Sunday forenoon they carried my Aunt Mary off in the same cart which was used for my Aunt Margaret and buried her beside all the others."

Further travails followed. Ronayne eventually recovered from typhus, which he battled alone in the family cottage. When he finally arose from bed, he discovered that theirs was the only house left standing at the bottom of the village. All others had been razed, under the orders of Killeagh's absentee landlord, Sir Arthur Brooke. Between the beginning and end of February 1847, then, almost everyone that the boy knew had died of typhus or been permanently displaced.

Ronayne portrays this particular moment in his life as a turning point, when his conversion to Protestantism began. He writes that during the socially imposed quarantine that followed his aunt's death he encountered a Bible, thrown prophetically at him from over the wall of the cottage by a neighboring boy:

> I picked up the book and turning to the title page to see what it was I read there, "The New Testament of our Lord and saviour Jesus Christ." I had never heard of such a book, much less seen it. . . . I became interested almost from the first. I read about the visitation of the angel to Mary and to Zechariah, of the births of John the Baptist and of Jesus, of the flight into Egypt, of the baptism, temptation and wonderful miracles of our blessed Lord. . . . I was positively delighted and being entirely alone I made my new testament my daily companion, finding especial delight in reading over and over again the simple holy life, the parables and the extraordinary miracles of Jesus Christ.

The deliberate orchestration of this scene is one of several early passages that suggest the designs that Ronayne may have had on his reader.[12] We realize here that this may not in fact be an unmediated firsthand account of the Famine but rather a narrative defined by what Culley identifies as a rigid canonicity.[13] The title of Ronayne's memoir—*Ronayne's Reminiscences: A History of His Life and Renunciation of Romanism and Freemasonry*—begins to bear down on the contents of the page. Evidently, Ronayne chose to record memories that fit the shape of what is ultimately a spiritual conversion narrative, the literary form responsible for the emergence of modern American autobiography.[14]

The character of religious practice in Ireland palpably changed after the Famine, influenced in no small part by the existential fear that the catastrophe had wrought on the poorest of Irish Catholic society.[15] In most cases this change manifested in a rejection of cultlike Gaelic rituals and the cultivation of a more disciplined form of devotional church-based practice—a change long desired by the Irish Catholic hierarchy. A minority of others, like Ronayne, converted to Protestantism, influenced perhaps by rumors of the Famine as evidence of God's retribution for the blasphemous beliefs of

Ireland's "papists." That Ronayne's description above emphasizes the comfort he derived from reading the Bible also hints at another highly subjective reason for his eventual conversion to a religion that encouraged Bible study. Given all that he had experienced, together with his continued isolation in the solitary cottage, it is plausible that Bible stories of angels' visitations and wonderful miracles offered Ronayne welcome respite from the horrific realities of the surrounding world.

Conversion was to have a fundamental effect on Ronayne's life trajectory, leading him down a path that became increasingly erratic and obsessive. At sixteen years old, Ronayne moved to Cappamore, County Limerick, and then to Kilrush, Country Clare, where he taught the Irish language in Protestant schools. In 1856 he emigrated to Quebec, Canada, passing himself off as a staunch Orangeman while continuing to teach in Protestant school settings. From Quebec, Ronayne moved onward to Chicago, where he became an enthusiastic member of the Freemasons. After the Great Chicago Fire, Ronayne took another religious turn, this time following the evangelist Dwight L. Moody. Ronayne described these many spiritual twists and turns in a memoir published by an obscure Methodist press in 1900 and followed that in 1917 with his *Handbook of Freemasonry*. The latter text, like much of Ronayne's first memoir, quotes liberally from scripture and is a turgid, esoteric treatise on the evils of freemasonry and the salvation of evangelism.

Yet Ronayne also left behind a description of the Irish Famine unique in its lucid descriptions, which seem to defy trauma. Indeed, compared to the "texts of radical disorder" Chris Morash identifies in his study of Famine-era literature, Ronayne's account of his family's dissolution in 1847 seems calm and steady, every possible filament of information offered up for inspection. It stands up, too, to historical scrutiny: every contextual detail Ronayne mentions can be corroborated by "official" history.[16] But as we go between text and theory, testing the facts of Ronayne's memoir against symptoms of trauma, a question arises, niggling at first but soon deafening in its urgency: How can it be that Ronayne managed to write, systematically and with cool, historical accuracy, about an experience that horrified into silence even the most accomplished of Irish writers?

"All memories," argues Halbwachs, "however personal are linked to ideas we share with many others."[17] According to the sociologist, it is impossible to retrieve memories qua memories if they do not first have historical, cultural, or geographical reference points in the surrounding society. What is important in one group may well be unimportant in another, Halbwachs points out, so that individual memory must adjust to the demands of its affiliated social groups. In coming to this discovery, Halbwachs also concludes that the expression of personal memories hinges on the existence of an emotional community that can facilitate their storage and retrieval rather than their repression and forgetting. Expanding on this theory, Erika Apfelbaum writes that "interpersonal proximity, in particular emotional proximity, is a necessary condition to make communication possible, to establish meaningful dialogue, one that helps subjects to process their experiences into living memory."[18] Ronayne, then, could have recovered and expressed his memories of the Famine only with the support of a community that comprehended their meaning and encouraged their discussion.[19] Of whom could this community have consisted?

Ronayne came of age into an era not just of Famine but of intense political violence and animosity. Prior to and during the Famine, secret nationalist societies like the Molly Maguires, the White Boys, and the Irish Republican Brotherhood flourished.[20] In Cork alone there existed at least thirty confederate or Fenian clubs, while in West Cork it was claimed that "in the cellars, in the woods and on the hillsides we had men drilling in the night time and war and rumors of war were on the wings of the wind."[21] In 1848 and 1849, the Young Irelanders staged two separate risings, mobilizing some two thousand men.[22] Both rebellions were short-lived, but it is notable that the second took place just a few miles away from Ronayne's home village of Killeagh and led to widespread arrests in the area. One set of circumstances that thus shaped Ronayne's early sociocultural world was that of militant Irish nationalism, the success of which relied on communal remembrance of Ireland's suffering.

Evidence of Ronayne's proximity to such groups exists in the pattern of his teenage years. When Ronayne was fifteen, he left his uncle's house and was employed in one of Killeagh's taverns, then owned by James Hayes. As Toby Joyce and Kerby Miller show, pubs and taverns were noted locations for secret-society activity, and Hayes's tavern emerged as a well-known center for East Cork Fenianism in the 1860s.[23] Further, according to R. V. Comerford, secret societies like the Irish Republican Brotherhood (whose US affiliate was the Fenian Brotherhood) had a particular gravitational pull for young Irish men after the Famine, providing them with cohesion and a sense of intimacy through tavern oath-swearing and nighttime drilling.[24] Given his tragic past and increasingly lonely present, it is not difficult to imagine the appeal that such fraternity would have offered the orphaned Ned Ronayne in his teenage years. On writing about Hayes's "dram shop" in 1900, the newly evangelized Ronayne hints at its sinful and corrupting atmosphere, thought, notably, he avoids any overt references to political activity: "Looking back upon the time I spent in that dram shop, with all its accompanying temptations, the associates I was constantly with, the obscenity and blasphemy I daily listened to, and the scenes of reckless violence and drunken folly to be witnessed on every hand I have many a time wondered that I did not sink so low as to be utterly beyond the reach of recovery."

The influence of an Irish nationalist community did not recede after Ronayne's emigration to North America. Indeed, it may have intensified, given that his migration in 1856 coincided with the formation of the Fenian Brotherhood in New York City, the legacy of which palpably shaped late-nineteenth-century Irish American culture.[25] Fenian ranks were drawn mostly from Irish immigrants—many of them ex-soldiers of the American Civil War—radicalized into a justice-seeking campaign against England in the wake of the Irish Famine.[26] Kerby Miller argues that the Fenians were defined as much by a Famine-tinged hatred of England as by a love of Ireland, and their expressed desire was the repatriation of thousands of Irish soldiers in America to their original lands in Ireland. Miller, Ellen Skerrett, and Bridget Kelly also make a compelling case, based on an examination of membership records in Quebec City, that one Ned Ronayne was himself a subscriber to the *Irish People*, the Fenian Brotherhood newspaper—a dizzying discovery, given that Ronayne was simultaneously a member of Quebec's Loyal Orange Order, a group dedicated to the destruction of Fenianism.[27]

Over the course of its 1858–71 campaign, the Fenians developed a transatlantic strategy with the Irish Republican Brotherhood aimed at exacting revenge on England. To recruit support among the Irish in America, it employed vernacular cultural forms such as music, ballads, and print media to highlight Ireland's suffering under British rule.[28] One of this effort's most enigmatic ballads was "Revenge for Skibbereen," a song attributed to the poet Patrick Carpenter that detailed the tragic fate of a town in West Cork during the Famine.[29] The ballad was based on descriptions of Skibbereen by its horrified absentee landlord, Nicholas Cummins, who discovered "famished and ghastly skeletons" living in the cottages on his estate. Who but Ned Ronayne could have identified so closely with such a scene?[30]

It's well I do remember on a bleak November's day,
The landlord and the sheriff came to drive us all away;
they set my house on fire with their cursed English spleen
And that's another reason why I left Old Skibbereen.

"Revenge for Skibbereen" plays host to two strains of memory. One emerges
from the pathos of an immigrant's eviction experience. It behaves as a personal memory, naturally evoked, framed in a particular time, in a particular
space: "a bleak November day." The other, conversely, shifts in tone from a
lone reflection to a choral outcry:

Oh father dear, the day will come when in answer to the call
Each Irishman with feelings stern will answer one and all,
I'll be the man to lead the van, beneath our flag of green,
And loud and high we'll raise the cry, "Remember Skibbereen!"

Here, the balladeer's personal memory is projected onto the masses, mutating into a secondary-source public "memory" of what happened at Skibbereen. By abstracting from an individual to a collective memory, "Revenge for
Skibbereen" makes the listening audience complicit in a mutual experience
of Famine and British oppression. "Remember Skibbereen!" is no longer an
involuntary memory but instead becomes a coordinated effort, poised for a
future political purpose rather than an accurately evoked past. In the context
of such memory popularization, we can come to see how Ronayne may have
encountered the social reference points he needed, first, to reconstitute his
experiences of the Famine as a legitimate personal memory and, second, to
recognize this memory as having significant cultural capital.

Additional details of Ronayne's life in the US reinforce the notion that
Fenianism played a role in the emergence and articulation of his Famine
memories. In April 1865 the Fenian Brotherhood, armed with hurleys and
decommissioned arms from the American Civil War, invaded Canada. At the
outbreak of the invasion, Ronayne was living in Chicago, a city that seethed
with anti-Irish animosity and political corruption. He was penniless, un-
employed, and in such deteriorated health because of physical work that he
developed pneumonia, again falling close to death. When he rose, dazed,
from his sickbed, he had just fifty cents in his pocket. Outside, rumors of the
scandalous Fenian invasion of Canada were gaining ground. His memoir

tells how, in a final bid for survival, he decided to invest his last fifty cents in postcards of the Fenian leaders John O'Mahony. Ronayne peddled the postcards at Chicago's many Irish bars and saloons, with significant financial success. Within a year he had one hundred dollars, enough to rent his own home. Ronayne had been quite literally saved from financial ruin by the public's desire for Fenian memorabilia.

Ronayne must have heard strains of songs like "Revenge for Skibbereen" sung through the streets of his neighborhood. After all, from 1865 to 1900, he lived at the edge of Kilbuggin, a poor, working-class district in Chicago with a rapidly growing Irish Catholic population.[31] It may also be significant that the publication of his memoir, in 1900, took place just two years after the appearance of the autobiography of Fenian leader Jeremiah O'Donovan Rossa, which was excerpted in the Irish American newspaper the *United Irishman*. Many of O'Donovan Rossa's descriptions of the Famine years in Rosscarbery, County Cork, bear striking resemblance to Ronayne's account. O'Donovan Rossa's account of the burial of a neighbor, for example, echoes the visual realism of Ronayne's scenes in the Clonpriest graveyard: "I dug the grave for her; she was buried without a coffin, and I straightened out her head on a stone, around which Jack McCart, the tailor of Beulnaglochdubh, had rolled his white-spotted red handkerchief."[32]

The purpose of the publication of O'Donovan Rossa's memoir in the *United Irishman* was clear: Here was further proof for the necessary Fenian rising against the British Crown. Famine memory as political ammunition henceforth gained popularity in Irish American neighborhoods, offering a layer of preservation, if not prestige, to those willing to invest in a repository of Irish cultural memory that furthered the Irish nationalist cause. Weighing all of this up, it seems increasingly plausible that the Fenian fervency Ronayne directly encountered in Chicago (to his economic benefit) had the potential to play a pivotal role in his reconstitution of his appalling experiences of the Famine from a fragmented mental form to a coherent written one.

A second set of circumstances that defined Ronayne's sociocultural world, and by consequence his memory making, involved religious fervor. According to Ronayne's memoir, he was from his earliest years steeped in a blended culture of Catholic and pagan ritual, the experiences of which he says were seared forever into his memory, as was apparent in his accounts of his father's and aunts' burials. The following paragraph, during which Ned recalls his first mass in Killeagh, testifies to this same magnetic mnemonic effect:

> I shall never forget the solemn feeling of awe and reverential fear that came over me as I witnessed the first mass I ever listened to. There was the glare of lighted candles on the altar, the priest dressed in embroidered surplice and richly ornamented vestments, the snow white covering of the altar itself, the Latin so holy (as I was told) and so high above the comprehension of any except the priest, the chiming of the little bell, and above all the moment when the whole congregation knelt on the bare floor, and bowing their heads beat upon their breasts as if they felt the deepest sorrow and contrition.

If such passages attest to Ronayne's religious formation, they also betray the motive of his "remembering." The distaste that undergirds Ronayne's descriptions of his Irish Catholic upbringing is a necessary part of a memoir that ultimately serves as an evangelical conversion narrative. As previously noted, Ronayne converted to Protestantism around the year 1851.[33] Thereafter, he devoted his life to Protestant evangelism, intensifying to the point where he eventually spent his days walking the streets of Chicago carrying banners painted with gospel texts such as "He that believeth not shall be condemned."[34] As W. Clark Gilpin notes, evangelicalism from the eighteenth century onwards emphasized that conversion—the new birth—was the defining event of true religion: "Consequently, personal conversion narratives telling individual stories of descent into sin and redemption by divine power proliferated as oral and literary forms throughout the various churches that participated in this transatlantic evangelical awakening."[35]

To encourage the emergence of such vernacular literature, evangelical pastors molded a strict "grammar of conversion" for their religious communities. "In spiritual conversion narratives," writes Jeffrey Barbeau, "there is a turning about of the mind as from one belief to its opposite, and a turning about *ad se ipsum*. . . . There is an inner necessity to cast out nature, to extirpate everything apparently external to salvation, everything that might stand between the naked self and God."[36] Notably, conversion narratives also cherish the testimony of the common man or woman "because every individual could attest to the transformed life."[37] Given Ronayne's humble origins and his construction of a narrative that traces his journey from sinful papist to awakened evangelical, it becomes apparent that the mode of recollection in his memoir strictly aligns with the demands of the burgeoning, Moody-led evangelical community. The reliance on memory as a path to salvation can in turn be directly related to the influence of deeply rooted Christian memory practices originating in the autobiography of Saint Augustine. In Augustine's *Confessions*, the very act of remembering oneself is honored and celebrated. From the early saint's perspective, God was first sought in memory and could be accessed only through a concentrated interior journey. Ricoeur point out that this premise allows for the saint's release of extraordinary personal "confessions."[38] Augustine could talk freely of desire and sex, of sin and suffering, because each revealed secret brought him closer to his greatest wish: to know God fully. "The heights and the depths—these are the same things," concludes Ricoeur in his reading of Augustine. Every memory, no matter how shameful or traumatic, was in the eyes of Augustine a gift to God. Indeed, in this Christian tradition, one way to overcome the "trauma" of past experiences is to launder their memory through the grammar of confession and conversion. Thus, bolstered by the incongruous influences of Fenian rhetoric and evangelical conversion narratives, Ronayne immersed himself in a memory project through which he ultimately sought his own salvation.[39]

Yet doubt and inconsistency leak through the cracks of his autobiography. Despite the armor provided by tell-all conversion narratives, his own memoir never fully reconciles his losses with his gains. On the one hand, he frames his departure from Gortaroo to the United States as the first step in a providential journey toward Jesus Christ, writing, "I look upon that removal as the initial step in that mysterious and providential journey through which God has led me, in bringing me out from the thralldom and superstition of popery, to a knowledge of himself and to precious fellowship from the Lord Jesus."

On the other, Ronayne's reminiscence frequently lapses into nationalist-style recollections of his homeland in East Cork, locating his memory by wrapping it around old place-names—Youghal, Ballymacoda, Killeagh, Castlemartyr, and Clonpriest. Thus he opens his memoir with a careful description of the place of his birth: "Between two and three miles from this once famous place, and almost on the very verge of the Atlantic Ocean, is a little hamlet called Gortaroo an Irish name signifying a brown field or rather a brown cornfield."

Indeed, in spite of his best efforts to distance himself from his Catholic upbringing, Ronayne admitted at the end of his life that his deepest desire was to return to visit the site of his family's burial in Clonpriest graveyard. "I have always revered their memory," Ronayne wrote of his aunts, "and nothing would give me greater pleasure could I afford it than to go back to Ireland to visit their graves." Such was the pull of place, and of people, for an immigrant who survived but never psychologically recovered from the toll of the Irish Famine.

Notes

1. Edmond Ronayne Memoir, Cork/Quebec/Chicago, University of Galway Archive, P155/15/9.

2. For a particular focus on trauma, memory, and the Famine, see Cormac Ó Gráda, "Famine, Trauma and Memory," *Béaloideas* 69 (2001), doi.org/10.2307/20520760. For a complete overview of the topic of the Famine and memory, see Cormac Ó Gráda, *Black '47 and Beyond: The Great Irish Famine in History, Economy, and Memory* (Princeton, NJ: Princeton University Press, 1999).

3. Maura Cronin, "Oral History, Oral Tradition and the Great Famine," in *Holodomor and Gorta Mór: Histories, Memories and Representation of Famine in Ukraine and Ireland,* ed. Lindsay Janssen, Christian Noack, and Vincent Comerford (London: Anthem, 2014).

4. Christopher Morash, *Writing the Irish Famine* (Oxford: Clarendon, 1995).

5. Ó Gráda warns against the tendency in contemporary Irish studies to diagnose post-Famine Irish society with collective or individual post-traumatic stress disorder (PTSD). For one thing, Ó Gráda argues, the Famine was not experienced evenly. By examining the disparate geographical and psychological effects of famine in Ireland and elsewhere, Ó Gráda makes the point that the creation of an identikit Irish Famine "memory" glosses over and filters out much of the history of the period and ignores the divisions that it created— psychological, social, and economic—among those who witnessed it. He observes that "it was not 'society' but the very poor in that society who were unable to bury their dead. Nor were the better-off forced to confront the sheer horror of the Famine first-hand like the poor. Nor had they the same need for fatalism" (Ó Gráda, "Famine, Trauma and Memory," 131). For another, Ó Gráda points out, the life span of trauma, individual or collective, remains abstract and ill defined. Ó Gráda asks the following (presumably rhetorical) question to drive home his argument: "Were Irishmen and Irishwomen in the mid 1840s still emotionally affected by the massive Famine that struck the country in 1740–1?" (Ó Gráda, "Famine, Trauma and Memory," 141).

6. Catherine Merridale, "Soviet Memories: Patriotism and Trauma," in *Memory: Histories, Theories, Debates,* ed. Susannah Radstone and Bill Schwarz (New York: Fordham University Press, 2010), 379.

7. Roger Kennedy, quoting Josef Breuer and Sigmund Freud, *Studies in Hysteria* (1895), in Roger Kennedy, "Memory and the Unconscious,'" in *Memory: Histories, Theories, Debates,* ed. Susannah Radstone and Bill Schwarz (New York: Fordham University Press, 2010), 179.

8. Edward S. Casey, *Remembering: A Phenomenological Study,* 2d ed. (Bloomington: Indiana University Press, 2000), xiv.

9. The literature on trauma and posttraumatic stress disorder is intimidatingly vast. I am indebted to the Irish Memory Studies Network's Memory Cloud archive for initially guiding me toward current scholarship in this area. Podcasts from this series were accessed online through University College Dublin's Irish Memory Studies website: http://irishmemorystudies .com/index.php/memory-cloud. Particularly illuminating in relation to PTSD is Martijn Meeter, "Cognitive Models of Memory, Trauma and Truth," Irish Memory Studies Network Distinguished Lecture Series, Dublin, 2 December 2015; accessible at http://irishmemorystudies.com/index.php/memory -cloud/#meeter. Sharon Dekel and George A. Bonanno's longitudinal research also makes interesting references to resilience and the plasticity of memory even in survivors of traumatic events, disproving the theory that memory for potential trauma remains fixed and unnegotiable: George A. Bonanno and Sharon Dekel, "Changes in Trauma Memory and Patterns of Posttraumatic Stress," *Pyschological Trauma: Theory, Research, Practice and Policy* 5, no. 1 (2013).

10. This is how Ronayne wrote about his mother's death:

> The women invariably did the binding after the men, and as there was a rivalry among the men to see who could reap the fastest, there was a similar, or even keener rivalry among the women to see which could bind the fastest. My mother was considered a good hand at binding any kind of grain. Being one day in such a contest as I speak of she took a pain in her left side, having possibly over strained herself, and, as I was many a time informed afterward, she never recovered from that strain, whatever it was, and died a few months thereafter.

11. Ó Gráda, "Famine, Trauma and Memory."

12. For an insightful discussion of a writer's design on the reader of the autobiography, see Margo Culley, ed., *American Women's Autobiography: Fea(s)ts of Memory* (Madison: University of Wisconsin Press, 1992), 9–11.

13. Culley, *American Women's Autobiography.*

14. W. Clark Gilpin, review of *The Evangelical Conversion Narrative: Spiritual Autobiography in Early Modern England,* by D. Bruce Hindmarsh, *Spiritus: A Journal of Christian Spirituality* 6, no. 2 (2006), doi.org/10.1353/scs.2006.0056; Andrew William Palmer, "The Autobiographical Pact and the Selection of Self in Memoir" (PhD thesis, University of Lincoln, 2016).

15. According to M. P. Carroll, the Famine corroded Irish peasants' belief in Gaelic providence, the strength of which had hitherto sustained popular

nature-based practices of Catholicism, such as making rounds of the well. After the Famine, writes Carroll, guilt-ridden Catholics turned toward a more formal and fervent worship of God, adhering belatedly to the calls of the clergy for a more disciplined approach to saving their souls. M. P. Carroll, "Rethinking Popular Catholicism in Pre-Famine Ireland," *Journal for the Scientific Study of Religion* 34, no. 4 (1995): 354. Emmet Larkin favors a more economic explanation to account for the "devotional shift" in Catholic practice after the Famine, arguing that lack of money and personnel on the part of the Catholic Church prior to the Famine was what perpetuated folk religious practice. Emmet Larkin, "The Devotional Revolution in Ireland 1850–75," *American Historical Review* 77, no. 3 (1972): 625–52, 648.

16. The veracity of Ronayne's memoir as well as other "forgotten" features of his life are proven in Kerby Miller, Ellen Skerrett, and Bridget Kelly, "Walking Backward to Heaven?: Edmond Ronayne's Pilgrimage in Famine Ireland and Gilded Age America," in *Ireland's Great Famine and Popular Politics*, ed. Enda Delaney and Breandán Mac Suibhne (New York: Routledge, 2015).

17. Maurice Halbwachs, *On Collective Memory*, trans. Lewis A. Coser (Chicago: University of Chicago Press, 1992).

18. Erika Apfelbaum, "Halbwachs and the Social Properties of Memory," in *Memory: Histories, Theories, Debates*, ed. Susannah Radstone and Bill Schwarz (New York: Fordham University Press, 2010), 88.

19. Apfelbaum, "Halbwachs and the Social Properties of Memory," 88.

20. Toby Joyce, "'Ireland's Trained and Marshalled Manhood': The Fenians in the Mid-1860s," in *Gender Perspectives in Nineteenth-Century Ireland: Public and Private Spheres*, ed. Margaret Kelleher and James H. Murphy (Dublin: Irish Academic Press, 1997).

21. Jeremiah O'Donovan Rossa, *Rossa's Recollections 1838–1898* (New York, 1898), 99, quoted in Toby Joyce, "'Ireland's Trained and Marshalled Manhood': The Fenians in the Mid-1860s," in Margaret Kelleher and James H. Murphy, eds., *Gender Perspectives in Nineteenth-Century Ireland: Public and Private Spheres*, Society for the Study of Nineteenth Century Ireland 2 (Dublin: Irish Academic Press, 1997), 70–80.

22. Miller, Skerrett, and Kelly, "Walking Backwards toward Heaven?," 112, 113.

23. Toby Joyce, "'Ireland's Trained and Marshalled Manhood': The Fenians in the Mid-1860s"; Gary Owens, "Popular Mobilization and the Rising of 1848: The Clubs of the Irish Confederation," in Laurence M. Geary, ed., *Rebellion and Remembrance in Modern Ireland* (Dublin, 2001), 51–63; cited in Miller, Skerrett, and Kelly, "Walking Backwards toward Heaven?," 113. See also Henchion, "Gravestone Inscriptions of Co. Cork—IX: Killeagh," pt. 2, (1973), 63; and Killeagh-Inch Historical Group, "Killeagh Parish through the Ages," 285.

24. R. V. Comerford, "Patriotism as Pastime: The Appeal of Fenianism in the Mid-1860s," *Irish Historical Studies* 22, no. 87 (1981): 239–50.

25. Kerby Miller, *Ireland and Irish America: Culture, Class, and Transatlantic Migration* (Dublin: Field Day, 2008), 67.

26. Miller, *Ireland and Irish America*, 66.

27. Miller, Skerrett, and Kelly write that "sometime before mid-1865, when he lived in Quebec City, Ronayne joined the Fenian Brotherhood and subscribed to the *Irish People*, the Fenians' revolutionary-republican newspaper, which was published in Dublin and edited by O'Donovan Rossa himself. . . . Astonishingly, then, Ronayne in Quebec was simultaneously—or at least sequentially—an evangelical Protestant, a member of the Loyal Orange and Masonic orders, and a member of a secret revolutionary organization that was dedicated to the violent overthrow of all the institutions and symbols that Orangemen, Masons, and Anglo-Protestants most revered." Miller, Skerrett, and Kelly, "Walking Backwards Toward Heaven?," 111.

28. It is noteworthy that the use of lyrical balladry as a social force can be linked to the English romantic poets Samuel Taylor Coleridge and William Wordsworth, who copublished their lyrical ballads in 1797. This inevitably influenced the ballads that would emerge in Ireland soon after, especially those written to commemorate the 1798 rebellion. See Rosemary Ashton, *The Life of Samuel Taylor Coleridge: A Critical Biography* (London: John Wiley and Sons, 1996).

29. Carpenter's poem was published in *The Irish Singer's Own Book* (Boston, 1880). An insightful essay about family memory as political ammunition is Dan Milner, "'Old Skibbereen': Fenian Anthem or Famine Lament?," *History Ireland* 24, no. 5 (2016).

30. Lyrics retrieved from http://www.irishsongs.com on August 17, 2019.

31. Miller, Skerrett, and Kelly, "Walking Backwards toward Heaven?"

32. Jeremiah O'Donovan Rossa, *Rossa's Recollections 1838–1898* (New York, 1898), 202.

33. It is outside the remit of this book to explore the pretext for Ronayne's conversion. Miller Skerrett, and Kelly have hypothesized that it may have been stimulated by an ideological fracture between Ronayne and the parish priests in Killeagh, whose disapproval of his Fenian activity may have sent him searching for alternative spiritual solace. My sense is that as a youth Ronayne may have internalized the popular belief that the Famine was proof of God's anger with Catholics for their misguided pagan and Roman practices. These beliefs were compounded by (false) rumors that only Catholic regions of Irish land were affected by potato blight. An extract from the memoir of Thomas Mellon, an Irish American autobiographer of Ulster Protestant descent, provides a flavor of the popular thought patterns through which these rumors circulated: "A

singular peculiarity exists in the Celtic nature, consisting in a periodic overflow of temper, moving in cycles, and terminating in outbreaks. . . . I incline to the opinion that this feature of their character has grown out of the continued irritation and consequent exercise of the evil passions from generation to generation, in a people naturally emotional and excitable, and involved in gross ignorance and superstition." Additionally, the 1856 writing of an R. MacMullan overtly opine the discrepancy between Catholic and Protestant experiences of the Famine: "Four-fifths of the paupers are, in most of these houses, the mere Irish and these priests' glory in their shame. In the Carrickmacross poorhouse there are but few Protestants; and it is a singular fact, that not one Presbyterian family is to be found an inmate. Such is the abhorrence entertained by the poor of the Presbyterian Church, that nothing but dire necessity could induce any of these honest and high-spirited people, how poor soever, to demean themselves to become a burthen on the industry and means of their richer neighbours." R. MacMullan, *Sketches of the Highlands of Cavan, and of Shirley Castle, in Farney, Taken During the Irish Famine* (1856).

34. Ronayne writes with candor about this phase of his conversion under the heading "The Silent Evangelist," Ronayne's Memoir, University of Galway Archive, 158.

35. Gilpin, review of *The Evangelical Conversion Narrative*, 257.

36. J. W. Barbeau, "Romantic Religion, Life Writing, and Conversion Narratives," *Wordsworth Circle* 47, no. 1 (2016): 33.

37. Barbeau, "Romantic Religion," 32.

38. Paul Ricoeur, *Memory, History, Forgetting* (Chicago: University of Chicago Press, 2004).

39. Sidonie Smith and Julia Watson write that "spiritual autobiography typically unfolds through sin and damnation to a sense of spiritual fulfillment . . . and place of sustaining belief." Sidonie Smith and Julia Watson, *Reading Autobiography: A Guide for Interpreting Life Narratives*, 2d ed. (Minneapolis: University of Minnesota Press, 2010), 47–48.

5

Mary Jane Hill Anderson's Memoir (1922)

It was here that our first great sorrow came to us. The house was on the edge of a meadow, and there was a little stream which at this time of the year overflowed. John and Robert wandered down to it and fell in. John somehow scrambled out, catching hold of the grass on the edge of the stream. His cries brought the men, who were home for dinner, but it was too late to save little Robert. I have always thought he might have been saved if we had known what to do, he was in the water such a short time.

There was no church or graveyard, so we buried him in a field of McCoy's, under a tree, until we could move his body. We made a little box of rough boards, and marked the place with a rail fence, to keep out the cattle. Several years went by, and we hoped to have a graveyard, but the tree was cut down and the fence taken away and we could never find the little grave.[1]

Perhaps the most interesting example of "forgetting" within the Irish American diaspora relates to the amnesia assumed by non-Catholic Irish immigrants regarding their Irish origins.[2] An estimated one hundred thousand Protestant Irish crossed the ocean to North America between 1783 and 1814.[3] Between 1814 and the beginning of the Famine, another 125,000 followed,[4] while the years spanning 1856 and 1900 saw almost nine hundred thousand further Protestants in Ulster, a large majority of whom were Presbyterian, follow their forebears to North America. Nonetheless, Irish emigration remains conceptualized as a largely Catholic phenomenon.[5]

This *mémoire d'oubli* (memory of forgetting)[6] relates in part to the formative nature of Irish American Catholic institutions, which permitted little variation when it came to Irish American collective memory. Equally, Irish

Protestant, Presbyterian, and Anglican groups from the eighteenth century carefully avoided claims of Irishness in the US.[7] In the face of the xenophobic, anti-Catholic Know Nothing party in North America as well as historic class and religious animosity between Protestants and Catholics in Ireland, Protestant Irish immigrants in the US had little to gain through Irish identification and much to benefit by WASP assimilation.[8] They achieved this, as Kerby Miller shows, through careful political and cultural rhetoric that promoted memories of a "timeless and respectable 'Scotch Irish' ancestry."[9] For some a myth, for others a meaningful coordinate in the British Isles, ethnic claims to Scotch Irish identity was a vital mode of differentiation in America, enabling Protestants and other non-Catholic denominations born in Ireland to become more proximate to their new nations' political and cultural elite. If this may have served them well socially, it also contributed to a lack of historical understanding around the particular migrant experience of Irish Protestants in North America. Luckily, this elision is partly remedied by the private life writing of these immigrants, one of whom was Mary Jane Hill Anderson. At the formidable age of ninety-five, Mary Jane collated her life narrative into a detailed 13,300-word manuscript. Although conceived as a conscious act of memory, it is also a beguiling window onto the imperatives of forgetting and selective recollection amongst Irish Protestants in the United States.

Mary Jane was born into a Church of Ireland family in Bailieborough, County Cavan, in 1827. Her father was a strong farmer with several subtenants, and the family kept servants, at least for a time. "While there were plenty of servants," Anderson recalls, "they were so deceitful and immoral that [Mother] could not bear to have them in the house." The animosity between these (Catholic) servants and Protestant employers intensified during the Famine, which decimated Cavan yet which Mary Jane, quite significantly, never mentions or strategically forgets.[10] Rather, her descriptions evoke an Edenic childhood. Her father, Mary Jane writes, was hardworking and "lived his religion," while her mother had admirable "business judgement" and "thriftiness." This choice of language is important, for these attributes were highly prized in Protestant communities, who considered them systematically lacking amid the Irish Catholic majority.[11]

Religious identity is at the fore of Mary Jane's sense of self. Her earliest recollections are of Bible stories told within the polished dark wood of the Episcopalian church in Bailieborough. She treasures the memory of sitting alongside her mother through religious services, trying to remember each word spoken by the rector. She recalls, too, the days she spent at the school in the neighboring castle, learning needlework and even embroidering clothes for Queen Victoria. "I was proud to be permitted to do part of the work on the handkerchiefs," she writes, in a clear assertion of her loyalty to the British Crown. By mentioning these aspects of her childhood in the beginning pages of her memoir, Mary Jane clarifies her political, class, and religious allegiances, ensuring that the signal of her Irishness did not shine too brightly.

In 1850 Mary Jane married a neighbor, Robert Anderson, the Presbyterian son of a grist-mill owner. Soon after their marriage, the couple emigrated to the US, where they joined Robert's aunts and uncles in rural Illinois. They settled into a classic life of frontier homesteading, moving in 1854 to a 160-acre farm in Eden Prairie, Minnesota. Mary Jane chronicles the family's progress with care, creating a text that leaves vital clues regarding the memory narratives and cultural influences that most resonated for an Irish Protestant woman at the turn of the twentieth century. The title of Mary's memoir—*Autobiography of Mary Jane Hill Anderson, Wife of Robert Anderson*—offers immediate insight: Unlike the contemporaneous life writings of Irish Catholics, this title does not signal an emigrant or Irish background. It does, however, contain what Margo Culley terms a "gendered signature" that places an accent on Mary Jane's sense of self as wife and woman. In this regard Mary Jane's text aligns with the modern American autobiographical canon, which saw one in five white women either repeating her name or using some other sign of gender in the title of her work. Well-known examples include *Unfinished Woman, Wyoming Wife,* and *Memories of a Catholic Girlhood.*[12] "White American women," concludes Culley, "represent themselves in the titles of their autobiographies by their relationship to others."[13]

The same is not true of male-authored texts. A key feature of nineteenth-century male American autobiographies is the assuredness with which they represent their sense of an *I*. As Sidonie Smith argues, the *I* of autobiography is depicted as unitary, bold, and indivisible, creating what she terms a "metaphysical self" that perceives the world through an assumed objectivity and rationality derived from the philosophies of the Enlightenment. This *I*, continues Smith, is unabashedly white, Eurocentric, colonizing, and male. Traditional male autobiography "reaffirmed, reproduced and celebrated the agentive autonomy of metaphysical selfhood, valorizing individuality and separateness while erasing personal and communal interdependence."[14]

Yet Mary Jane Hill Anderson's memoir raises the shortcomings of such a sharply gendered distinction. To be sure, Mary Jane's sense of self is "encumbered" by her role as mother and wife, and her writing consistently uses *we* rather than *I* as a point of self-reference. She also portrays herself in her writing as timid and irrational, contrasting her emotional frailty against her husband's strength and courage. In one paragraph, for example, she describes a night on the frontier when Indians were "on the prowl": "I think I know how it is possible for one to die of fear. They bathed my feet, as my teeth still chattered, and Mrs. Brewster made a cup of tea, but I was still deathly sick. Realizing that my condition needed to be dealt with gently but firmly, Father shook me and said, 'Mary Jane, *where* is your faith? They can't do anything but what the Lord permits them to do. Brace up now and take this tea and you will feel better.'"

However, this evocation of female fragility belies the tone of Mary Jane's words, which is at all times self-assured. For example, reflecting on their settlement on the frontier, Mary Jane writes unapologetically of the ecocide and genocide that facilitated her family's resettlement. She celebrates the "blazing of 160 acres of trees" on which the family built their farm and notes the family's seizing of a field of cranberry bushes that they knew were crucial to nearby Native Americans' survival. She also blithely describes the widespread murder of Native Americans who resisted removal from the lands occupied by the Hill family. Indeed, Mary Jane's narrative exhibits the characteristics of "metaphysical selfhood" far more successfully than, say, the narrative of Tom Brick. Where Brick's encounters with Native Americans on the frontier led him to question his sense of self and his decision to emigrate, Mary Jane's memoir bears no such signs of reflexivity or self-division.

Even the memory of her son Robert's death by drowning does not provoke a perceptible crisis of truth in Mary Jane's writing. Noting that she was never able to recover her son's body, she writes, "But the little body is in His safe-keeping; it will rise from there, for the Lord does not forget where we lie." This resonates with what Dean Ebner recognizes as a Puritan autobiographical tradition, which "superimposed onto the welter of remembered facts the unity and order of a present mental attitude."[15] Her treatment of what must have been a deeply traumatic experience for Mary Jane also reflects the tropes of nineteenth-century American religious autobiographers. As Ann Taves and Joanna Gillespie observe, the form required a submissive response from women regarding affliction.[16] "It was not," notes Gillespie, "for followers to say what trouble God should send."[17]

The moral certitude evident in her writing inevitably relates to Mary Jane's internalization of a particular cultural ideology fostered in white Christian colonizer communities on the North American frontier from the mid-nineteenth century. *American exceptionalism* and *Manifest Destiny* are terms commonly associated with these groups, who display a virtuous sense of the inevitability and entitlement to expand west as part of God's and America's rightful destiny.[18] Mary Jane's acceptance of these tropes is further refracted in the memories she gives precedence to in her life writing, which coalesce around four main themes: the American Civil War, her family's acquisition of frontier land, the building of a United Presbyterian community, and the world of her intimate relationships. All illustrate the writer's determination to contribute to a traditional, white, nineteenth-century American autobiographical tradition of individualism, conquest, and progress.

For immigrants at the turn of the twentieth century, the American Civil War was a formative collective memory. Enlisting in the war allowed immigrant families the "title deeds" to American citizenship, and claiming a direct memory of the war in later life brought them into the mainstream of modern US cultural memory.[19] It was also, of course, a fraught period for families, as husbands, fathers, and sons were cast into the battlefield. As Mary Jane writes:

> These were gloomy days for the North. The men of Eden Prairie were volunteering and there were several drafts. The young men were all gone. We had seven small children. John, the oldest, was only fourteen, and small for his age. He had to stand on the manger to put the collar on a horse. We discussed what was our duty; should Father enlist? It seemed that until there was a shortage of men he ought to stay with his family. And so he decided to wait for the next draft. We felt that if he was then disabled or killed there could be no doubt that it was the Lord's will. The last draft came, and it took about all the able-bodied men who were left, including Father.

Mary Jane carefully details the emotional toll her husband's departure took on the family. "The morning he went away," she writes, "Grandmother Anderson came to be with us. We were all in tears. Mary wept on Grandmother's knee." Mary Jane goes on to list the names of the other members of their community who left for war in the last draft: "Uncle Archie, Mr. Lougee, William Stinson, both the Brewsters, John Clark, John Logan, and others." Given what would quickly unfold, this writing seems somewhat melodramatic. Within hours of the men's reaching the army recruitment camp, word arrived that the South had surrendered, and the men of Eden Prairie were back home with their families that night. Nevertheless, her husband kept his Union uniform and musket, and Mary Jane proudly maintained the memory of her husband's brief role in the Civil War into the next generation.

Mary Jane's memories of the war were colored by the threat she perceived from Native Americans. The Civil War, she claims, emboldened "savages" in Minnesota to attack white settlers. Her treatment of this period highlights her highly racist attitudes and reinforces her community's sense of entitlement to the indigenous lands they had colonized.[20] She describes the army's capture in 1862 of three hundred Native Americans, thirty-nine of whom were hanged. "This put an end to the trouble," she writes, without any sign of remorse. She also recounts many "thrilling" episodes of the murder of indigenous people by white settlers. In one such story, she admiringly recalls a woman who had spied Native Americans near her house and quickly mounted a self-defense that led to the horrific deaths of eleven indigenous:

> Hastily dragging a feather-bed down into the cellar, and getting her daughter and the baby down, she closed the trap door in the floor, but not before she had left a jug of whiskey where the Indians could find it, as whiskey was the first thing they looked for. She took time to put strychnine, which they kept in the house for rat poison, into the jug, and had barely time to close the door when the savages were upon them.
>
> She could hear them rattling dishes and moving around above her. It was not very long before they began to fall on the floor and groan and writhe and kick, and she knew that the poison was doing its work. At last everything was quiet and so she tried to lift up the trap door. But one of the Indians was lying across it, so they had to stay in the cellar until her son-in-law came home. He found eleven Indians lying dead on the floor.

While disregard for the lives of indigenous was not unusual in the 1800s, it does become less common in the twentieth century, when frontier literature became more utopian, conciliatory, and idealistic about the relationship between white settlers and Native Americans.[21] It is therefore evident that Mary Jane, writing in 1922, resisted shifts in American generic convention that in any way challenged a Puritan origin myth of European superiority and divine providence in North America.

Mary Jane's life writing scrupulously details how the Anderson family acquired and expanded their landholdings. As though her memoir were also an accounting log, she records the price the Andersons paid for each acre and the means by which they acquired the title deeds. This section of her narrative is propelled by a sense of progression and competitiveness, commensurate with the "discourse of improvement" associated with nineteenth-century Protestantism.[22] Indeed at times Mary Jane's writing seems almost to strain to prove her family's value by enumerating an endless list of their achievements. Her efforts may be indicative of the pressure placed on women after the Reformation to adhere to the norms demanded by "the Protestant way of life" as determined by those with the greatest resources and power:[23]

> Father was the first in the neighborhood to adopt new improvements. We had the first sewing machine, a "Grover and Baker", and what a wonderful thing it was. The neighbors came from everywhere to have me stitch for them, and it seemed so easy compared with the slow hand sewing. We had the first reaper. It was a "McCormack Self-Rake". There was a big red wooden arm that went round and round, and to balance it there had to be a large iron ball on a long iron rod, as a sort of counter-weight. When the big red wooden arm came up over the reaper it looked as though it would come down on the horses' backs as it revolved. The horses were frightened and it was a hard task to get them used to it so they wouldn't shy at it and run away. We had the first orchard—ours was bearing apples before the others began to plant orchards.

Unusually for this period of American autobiography, there is an absence of sentimentality with regard to the rural landscape in Mary Jane's writing. Whereas frontierswomen like Hilda Rose and Elinore Pruitt wrote at length in their autobiographies about the beauty of their pastoral surroundings, Mary Jane engaged with the farm in Eden Prairie purely in terms of its utility.[24] This, too, reflects the commitment of her writing to a particularly Protestant expectation of progress and expansion. As geographer Tricia Cusack writes, "Cultural and social identities are expressed and maintained partly through the shaping and use of landscape."[25] As a member of a nineteenth-century "enlightened Protestant" community, Mary Jane was very likely primed through improvement discourses to think about landscapes in scientific and commodified terms as opposed to the bemoaned "instincts of nature" favored by the indigenous peoples and, later, feminist pioneers of the twentieth century.

Adjacent to Mary Jane's narrative of her family's advancement in the US was a chronicle of their creation of a United Presbyterian community. She provides granular details regarding the building of a school and church in

Eden Prairie, consistently casting light on the leading role she and her husband played in these community innovations. She records the price of the church pulpit and notes the lodging her family provided to visiting pastors and schoolteachers across the decades. Mary Jane is quite transparent in explaining the purpose of her writing: "I want to leave some of my memories of the efforts of the early settlers of Eden Prairie to spread the gospel," she explains. "The present generation has no idea of the untiring zeal and self-denial the early settlers practiced to leave the two churches—Methodist and Presbyterian—a heritage to their descendants in the community." Her tone again reveals the Puritan-inspired nature of Mary Jane's memoir. As Kathleen Swain notes, Puritan autobiographers enjoyed telling and hearing tell of the details of their own and each other's achievements. Like Mary Jane, Puritans valued their life histories as texts inscribing divine doctrine and imperatives.[26]

Yet Mary Jane's effort to emphasize her family's role in developing both a successful homestead and a religious community may also be indicative of her compulsion to forget as opposed to remember. According to Herman Parret, the work of forgetting is one of selection: In order for memory to blossom, some reminiscences have to be eliminated. "Forgetting a reminiscence," Parret explains, "is not yet forgetting a fact but rather a certain treatment: a certain interpretation of the fact."[27] And there are quite a few memory treatments in Mary Jane's memoir that seem to serve as screens for more challenging and irreconcilable experiences. This is especially true of her relationship with her husband, Robert Anderson. In the following paragraph, Mary Jane describes an interlude with her sweetheart, which opens an interesting window onto the dynamics of their relationship:

> One day Mother and Father had to drive in to Sherkuk, the nearest village, to do some marketing, and before leaving, Mother said to me, "Mary Jane, I want you to sack up those goose-feathers in the feather house, so they will be ready to take the next time we go to town." ... The children and I were working industriously on our task, when I heard a familiar whistle at the gate. It was Robert, for you may be sure he lost no time in coming down when Mother and Father drove out of sight. They passed the Anderson house on the way to town. I went down to the gate to meet him. The little girls, who soon grew tired of working alone, ran out to play, and when I next thought of the feathers, and looked back, such a sight as met my eyes! Clouds of feathers were floating on the breeze, and the whole countryside seemed covered

with them. . . . When Mother and Father drove into the yard that evening there were still plenty of them flying around. Mother said not a word, but made her way to the feather house and opened the door. When her sharp eyes discovered the empty room and unfilled sacks she said, "Mary Jane, has Robert been here today?" I will spare you the details of her wrath and will only say that I was confined to my room for a week, with plenty of time for thought, enough hand-work to keep me busy, for Mother was thrifty, and only bread and water for my meals.

In recollecting the day of Robert's visit, Mary Jane selects a certain treatment of her memory. She focuses on the loss of feathers and associates her mother's wrath with this waste. Her treatment makes sense: thrift was an essential part of the Protestant mentality, so her selected interpretation imbues the narrative with a larger coherence, an authentic familiarity. The treatment that Mary Jane *avoided* selecting was the less explicable fact that her mother immediately associated the wasted feathers with Robert Anderson.

As previously mentioned, Robert Anderson was a member of a Presbyterian family. Though the divide was not as pronounced as that between Protestants and Catholics, Presbyterians in Ulster in the pre-Famine years were significantly disadvantaged, and Anglicans and Episcopalians looked down upon them. More Presbyterians emigrated from pre-Famine Ulster and its border regions than any other religious group, their departure motivated in part by their discrimination by Protestant ruling elites.[28] Presbyterian migrants who wrote back to Ireland from America spoke in anger of the unfair treatment that had precipitated their exile, the silent signals of the Protestant bourgeoisie that had forced them from their homes. In America they continued to traverse a precarious path, alienated as they were from the Anglo-Saxon Protestants but equally fearful of association with the even more despised ranks of the Irish Catholic.[29] Also, despite the Irish Unionist myth that the Famine did not affect Ulster—that it, its Protestant inhabitants—Presbyterians in particular suffered from poverty, hunger, and disease during the Famine, the very time when Mary Jane and Robert began their relationship.[30] She does not explicitly say so, but it becomes clear: marrying Robert signified, for Mary Jane Hill's family, a process of social deviation, if not outright decline. It constituted the opposite of the Protestant commitment to progress.

In several anecdotes in her writing, Mary Jane alludes to the pressures to marry she faced during her upbringing in Cavan. Though she consistently tries to underplay the social differences between herself and her beloved husband, she admits that "I had other, and from a financial standpoint, more desirable suitors." She continues: "One man in particular was encouraged by Mother and my aunts because they thought it would be such a suitable match. My aunts lavished affection on me at this time, and often invited me to visit them. This man, whose name was John McIlwain, was forever under my feet. He was respectable, rich, and middle aged. Oh, how I hated the dour old face of him!"

According to the historian Marilyn Cohen, a wave of evangelical Protestantism from the 1820s embedded in Ulster's upper classes a renewed social and political conservatism.[31] A special feature of this reformation, Cohen continues, was the focus on Protestant women as pivotal actors in sanctifying bourgeois family relationships and in guarding the norms of "respectability" through industry, cleanliness, piety, sobriety, and chastity. Mary Jane came into womanhood during this exact climate and evidently received these cultural expectations through the vectors of her mother and aunts. In re-reading her line "my aunts lavished attention on me at this time, and often invited me to visit them," we become ever aware of the intensity of emotion that she must have experienced during this time in her life, torn between the social aspirations of her surrounding community and a deep attachment to her sweetheart. In turn, we recognize the dialectic of intimacy at the center of Mary Jane's predicament. Just as in her earliest childhood memory, where her prize for sitting silently through Sunday service was the gift of proximity to her mother, the bait evidently used by her aunts to coerce her into marrying "up" was the promise of their intimacy.[32]

After describing her marriage to Robert, Mary Jane makes no further mention of her own Irish-based family in the rest of her memoir, nor does she reminisce about her birthplace of Cavan. Conspicuously absent in her writing is any reference to the death of her parents, an event that for many other migrants was a critical moment of self-reflection. Instead, Mary Jane's memoir devotes full attention to her relationships within the Presbyterian community of Eden Prairie, largely made up by her husband's family and acquaintances. She also highlights female friendships. She describes, for instance, a friend named Martha who assisted her through her first labor:

> All the way I was suffering, and when we reached Martha's I was helped out of the wagon. She sent for a neighbor woman and that night John was born. . . . I shall never forget Martha's kindness. . . . She brought my baby to

me and said, "Here's a dear little son to comfort you." . . . Right here I want to say that I can look back and see the Lord's hand leading us and raising up friends in our times of need. I had not even a few hours to spare at the end of a three month's journey until my time of delivery. I had no definite plans and no money; but I firmly believe it was His loving care that directed Martha to Galena. She, of all others, would have been my choice to be with me in my distress.

Mary Jane also details the fundraising work that she and the other women undertook to establish the community church and school, and the friendships she cultivated as a result. Taves comments on the expanded opportunities that Christian associationalism provided for nineteenth-century women, which provided initial steps for the feminist activism of the twentieth century.[33] However, although she wrote in 1922, when feminist texts were growing in popularity, Mary Jane's memoir is careful to uphold the structured hierarchy of her relationships, portraying female dependence and subordination as proper and decent. It could also be argued that the sense of proximity and intimacy she creates through her accounts of female friendships serve a vital exclusionary purpose. By creating a tightly bound religious, racial, and gendered world within her life narrative, Mary Jane is arguably able to sustain the perceived contrast of outsider and insider, colonized and colonizer, heathen and Christian that gave order to her community's expansionist regime on the US frontier.

Through the production of her life writing, Mary Jane reveals the sense of orientation and fulfillment with which a Protestant Irish woman faced her life on the American plains. Far from the alienation and homesickness experienced by Irish Catholics in urban America at the same moment, Mary Jane's memoir is ultimately a celebration of a realized divine destiny. We can only imagine the many recollections she buries in order to sustain this sense of progress.

Notes

1. Mary Jane Hill Anderson Memoir, University of Galway Archive, P155/10/1 and P155/35/5.

2. William Kelly and John Young, eds., *Ulster and Scotland, 1600–2000: History, Language and Identity* (Dublin: Four Courts, 2004).

3. Kerby Miller, *Emigrants and Exiles: Ireland and the Irish Exodus to North America* (New York: Oxford University Press, 1985), 169.

4. Kerby Miller, *Ireland and Irish America: Culture, Class, and Transatlantic Migration* (Dublin: Field Day, 2008), 190.

5. Miller, *Emigrants and Exiles*, 169–170; Maldwyn A. Jones, "Scotch-Irish," in *Harvard Encyclopedia of American Ethnic Groups*, ed. Stephan Thernstrom (Cambridge, MA: Harvard University Press, 1980); Jay P. Dolan, *The Irish Americans: A History* (New York: Bloomsbury, 2008).

6. Guy Beiner, *Forgetful Remembrance: Social Forgetting and Vernacular Historiography of a Rebellion in Ulster* (Oxford: Oxford University Press, 2018), 41.

7. Miller, *Ireland and Irish America*, 137.

8. Curtis Wood and Tyler Blethen, *Ulster and North America: Transatlantic Perspectives on the Scotch-Irish* (Tuscaloosa: University of Alabama Press, 1997).

9. Miller, *Ireland and Irish America*, 138.

10. Mary Jane was eighteen years old (a period of particular mnemonic sensitivity) when the Famine struck, decimating County Cavan's poorest populations. When traveling through Bailieborough, County Cavan, in 1856, one R. MacMullan gaped in horror (and open disgust) at the "hunger-bitten population," at the beggars "squatted down in cabins"; R. MacMullan, *Sketches of the Highlands of Cavan, and of Shirley Castle, in Farney, Taken During the Irish Famine* (Belfast: J. Reed, 1856). MacMullan bemoaned in particular the decline of Bailieborough, which he remembered before the Famine as a thriving market town and which he now found in a state of social ruin. From the writer's perspective, fault for this ruin lay in the cost of supporting Irish beggars: "The resources of the kingdom were a good deal exhausted by the moneys advanced by the treasury, and lavished away on 'relief works.'" Indifference to the sufferings of the Irish Catholic majority during the Famine and the belief that the blight was a validation of the Anglican Church and the British establishment are also captured in MacMullan's sketches of Cavan. He writes: "We know that nothing happens without a cause; and it follows as a matter of course that the potato blight, which appeared so suddenly and so destructively, at the very time Ireland was threatened with an insurrection of the lower orders against the higher, was sent as an arrest to prevent a greater evil, by the infliction of a lesser evil; and the facility with which God put a stop to the Repeal Movement and the revolutionary schemes of the 'Young Irelanders,' should make survivors to feel the truth of that pithy saying, 'Man's extremity is God's opportunity.'"

11. For an insightful illustration of the perceived social differences between Protestant and Catholics in Ulster and its environs prior to the Famine, see Marilyn Cohen, "Religion and Social Inequality in Ireland," *Journal of Interdisciplinary History* 25, no. 1 (1994): 1–21. See also Miller, *Ireland and Irish America*.

12. Lillian Hellman, *An Unfinished Woman* (New York: Little, Brown, 1969); Rodello Hunter, *Wyoming Wife* (New York: Knopf, 1969); Mary McCarthy, *Memories of a Catholic Girlhood* (New York: Harcourt Brace Jovanovich, 1957).

13. Margo Culley, ed., *American Women's Autobiography: Fea(s)ts of Memory* (Madison: University of Wisconsin Press, 1992), 7.

14. Sidonie Smith, "Resisting the Gaze of Embodiment: Women's Autobiographies in the Nineteenth Century," in *American Women's Autobiography: Fea(s)ts of Memory*, ed. Margo Culley (Madison: University of Wisconsin Press, 1992), 79–81.

15. Dean Ebner, *Autobiography in Seventeenth Century England* (The Hague: Mouton, 1971), 19.

16. Ann Taves, "Self and God in the Early Memoirs of New England Women," in *American Women's Autobiography: Fea(s)ts of Memory*, ed. Margo Culley (Madison: University of Wisconsin Press, 1992), 61.

17. Joanna Bowen Gillespie, "'The Clear Leadings of Providence': Pious Memoirs and the Problems of Self-Realization for Women in the Early Nineteenth Century," *Journal of the Early Republic* 5, no. 2 (1985).

18. Manifest Destiny is related to the initial generations of settlers who saw the colonies as constituting a divinely ordained "errand into the wilderness," which has come to be called the mythology of American exceptionalism. The nature of this destiny, Perry Miller and Deborah Madsen show, was interpreted both as the purification of the Anglican Church and the perfection of a new political system of democratic republicanism. "What remained constant was the vision of this destiny as a matric of political, religious, economic, social and above all territorial relations," writes Madsen; Deborah Madsen, "The West and Manifest Destiny," in *A Concise Companion to American Studies*, ed. John C. Rowe (Oxford: Wiley-Blackwell, 2010), 371. See also Tanfer Tunc, "Manifest Destiny's Child: Mary Hazelton Blanchard Wade and the Literature of American Empire," *Children's Literature in Education* 48, no. 3 (2017). Memoirs that documented the expansionism of white Americans include Solomon Nunes Carvalho's 1857 *Incidents of Travel and Adventure in the Far West: With Colonel Fremont's Last Expedition across the Rocky Mountains, Including Three Months' Residence in Utah, and a Perilous Trip across the Great American Desert to the Pacific*, ed. Ava F. Kahn (Lincoln: University of Nebraska Press, 2004); John Benton Frémont, *Memoirs of My Life* (Belford: Clarke, 1887). For an authoritative text on Manifest Destiny, see Perry Miller, *Errand into the Wilderness* (Cambridge, MA: Harvard University Press, 1956).

19. William Burton Kurtz, *Excommunicated from the Union: How the Civil War Created a Separate Catholic America* (New York: Fordham University Press, 2016).

20. Reginald Horsman makes the racism of US expansion abundantly clear, showing that by 1850 the expansion was located within a powerful discourse of

Anglo-Saxon superiority and inevitable racial destiny. Reginald Horsman, *Race and Manifest Destiny* (Cambridge, MA: Harvard University Press, 1986).

21. Lynn Z. Bloom, "Utopia and Anti-Utopia in Twentieth Century Women's Frontier Autobiographies," in *American Women's Autobiography: Fea(s)ts of Memory*, ed. Margo Culley (Madison: University of Wisconsin Press, 1992).

22. Tricia Cusack, "'Enlightened Protestants': The Improved Shorescape, Order and Liminality at Early Seaside Resorts in Victorian Ireland," *Journal of Tourism History* 2, no. 3 (2010), doi.org/10.1080/1755182X.2010.523146.

23. Miller, *Ireland and Irish America*, 188.

24. Hilda Rose, *The Stump Farm: A Chronicle of Pioneering* (Boston: Little Brown, 1928); Elinore Pruitt Stewart, *Letters of a Woman Homesteader* (Boston: Houghton Mifflin, 1914).

25. Cusack, "'Enlightened Protestants,'" 166.

26. Kathleen Swain, "'Come and Hear': Women's Puritan Evidences," in *American Women's Autobiography: Fea(s)ts of Memory*, ed. Margo Culley (Madison: University of Wisconsin Press, 1992), 34.

27. Herman Parret, "The Communicative Value of Forgetting," *Empedocles: European Journal for the Philosophy of Communication* 2, no. 1 (2010): 98.

28. According to Miller, "Between the end of the American Revolution and the beginning of the Great Famine, at least one quarter of a million and probably much closer to half a million Protestants left an Ulster which, near its demographic peak in 1831, contained less than 1.1 million Protestants. Both denominational and social class factors heavily determined which Protestants would emigrate and which would not. Modern analysis of census data show that they were overwhelmingly Presbyterian as well as predominantly cottage artisans (principally weavers) and small to middling tenant farmers or their children." Miller, *Ireland and Irish America*, 190.

29. MacMullan provides insight into the social distinctions made between Protestant, Presbyterian, and "mere Irish" Catholic in the following passage: "Four-fifths of the paupers are, in most of these houses, 'the mere Irish,' and these priests 'glory in their shame.' In the Carrickmacross poorhouse there are but few Protestants; and it is a singular fact, that not one Presbyterian family is to be found an inmate. Such is the abhorrence entertained by the poor of the Presbyterian Church, that nothing but dire necessity could induce any of these honest and high-spirited people, how poor soever, to demean themselves to become a burthen on the industry and means of their richer neighbours." MacMullan, *Sketches of the Highlands of Cavan*.

30. Miller writes that "even in the predominantly Catholic 'outer' Ulster counties of Cavan, Donegal and Monaghan, proportional losses among Presbyterians in 1831–61 exceeded those among Anglicans and Catholics alike." Miller, *Ireland and Irish America*, 221.

31. Marilyn Cohen, *Linen, Family and Community in Tullylish, County Down, 1690–1914* (Dublin: Four Courts, 1997); Marilyn Cohen, "Religion and Social Inequality in Ireland," *Journal of Interdisciplinary History* 25, no. 1 (1994): 1–21.

32. Regarding this early childhood memory, the exact words Mary Jane uses are: "It could not have been long after that when she told me I could go to church with her if I'd sit very still, and if I could tell her something of what the minister said, she would take me again."

33. Taves, "Self and God in the Early Memoirs of New England Women," 58.

6

Nora O'Connor's Memoir (1947)

> I remember the very last evening Jim and I walked together. We had reached what we called the Brittius mine and on turning back a lark flew past us and soared high, high up in the sky singing like mad! We stood and watched it fly out of sight. In the morning we were to leave and I said to Jim "I shall never forget that lark.

In 1947, from her silent house in Michigan, an elderly Irish woman named Nora sat to write her memoir. A request from her daughter began the process:

> "Mom, why don't you write the story of your life so we could have it and read it later?"
>
> I laughed at her and said "Oh yes I guess I could write a wonderful story at that!". But why not?" The children will know then what kind of mother they had. The real me.

The task took her two years. When she had finished, Nora had crafted a manuscript that exceeded one hundred pages, revealing through the soft prose of an unrealized author the texture of emotional remembrance.[1] Unwittingly, Nora's writing also opens a window onto an eclectic and sensitively recalled immigrant's world, suggesting the influences, cultural and historical, that framed the writing of her narrative and gave cadence to her memories.

The literary tropes that may have shaped Nora's writing are initially apparent in the title she selected for her life writing: "The Life of a Young Irish Girl from Bantry, County Cork, Ireland to America 1885–1918." In deciding on this title, Nora committed to a signature that accented her Irishness and her status as an American immigrant. These are features of identity that Mary Jane Hill Anderson in 1900 had attempted to subvert and that other immigrant writers like Margaret McGuinness and Mary McCarthy would also subsequently reject.[2] This immediately places Nora's memoir within the milieu of turn-of-the-twentieth-century American immigrant autobiography, which celebrates self-consciously "ethnic" tales like Mary Antin's *The Promised Land* and Maxine Hong Kingston's *The Woman Warrior*. Whether or not she was aware of it, Nora was unequivocally writing herself into an American cultural tradition that had momentarily embraced intermediary, female immigrant experiences as an essential part of US collective memory.

Nora fulfills the pact of the immigrant autobiographer with great skill. She describes her severe seasickness on the voyage to New York and lingers over the cultural shock that she felt upon arriving in America. She emphasizes the way she and her younger brother Dennis were teased on account of their Irish accents, portraying a classic picture of the bewildered, ill-at-ease "greenhorn." Nora also reflects with precision on the homesickness she experienced her first months in New York, suggesting the coordinates to which her sense of home and place were fixed:[3]

> Week after week went by and my heart was breaking to go home to the family. I knew I was homesick and it can make you sick. *Real sick*, I was that. Sometimes I'd walk all the way home to either Auntie's place or Jerry's with the news "No luck today". Yes, I'd walk all those blocks, all alone. Dennie of course was working every day and feeling good, but I was sick, heartsick. I didn't like America. The heat was bad by this time and those awful thunderstorms really put terror into my heart. I wasn't used to them and I cringed at every streak of lightening. Mary Ellen did her best to cheer me up. I had found where Maggie Finnegan lived with an old Aunt and called on her. She was going to be married anyway to her Irish sweetheart who had preceded her out here. I also found Mae McGann and visited her, but nothing cheered me.

This depiction of a listless, lonely, and disorientated life in urban America stands out in contrast to the first part of Nora's memoir, where she recounts her years in the Edenic environs of Bantry House, an Anglo-Irish manor house in West Cork. Nora became a domestic servant there at seventeen, soon after leaving school. Her recollection of her first interview at the house is a magical scene centered on Mrs. Leigh-White, an Englishwoman whom Nora would come to adore: "One of the footmen conducted us to Mrs. Leigh-White's private sitting room and I'll never forget how beautiful she was. Not much older than myself, a little past 18 she was, and as she said a few years later as she bid me goodbye, that she fell in love with me. 'You are just what I want,' she said in her crisp English accent. 'Someone that can be trained, and some-one from Bantry.'"

Nora's memoir evokes an inspiring, soft, and sensual space. "A large Conservatory opened off the dining room," she recalls, "and also off the Ballroom," and "each had a fountain of water playing in them all the time. Sometimes I think if Heaven will be anything like Bantry House, I'll be satisfied! All my life I've dreamed of being back there. I wonder if I'll see it and the little town where I was born and spent so many happy days on my way when my soul is flitting from this old World!"

Interestingly, Nora describes Bantry House not so much as a hierarchically structured place of employment but as a home in which she was free to roam, (while the family was away) surrounded by people to whom she felt deeply attached, as suggested by her use of *we*: "We spent many a happy evening sewing, crocheting, darning or reading," Nora wrote of those years: "We had evenings off whenever we wanted and many the walk the 'bunch' took along the Quay road. We all had sweethearts, of course. . . . Oh, we were kept busy, but had a chance also to enjoy the beautiful grounds. . . . You could stand on the Terraces and see far off the little island of Whiddy, with its small population of a few families, sitting right in the middle."

Although rooted in Nora's personal experiences, this part of her narrative bears a striking similarity to the classic Irish Big House novel, the most enduring subgenre within Irish literature and one that enjoyed considerable popularity around the time Nora was writing her memoir. For more than two centuries, the Big House served as a setting, subject matter, symbol, motif, and theme in Irish fiction.[4] Countless authors contributed to the genre, including Elizabeth Bowen, George Moore, and Molly Keane, collectively providing a cultural window onto Anglo-Irish life in Ireland.[5] Invariably, the Irish Big House was portrayed as a cosseted, timeless, and idyllic place. J. R. Henn's *Five Arches*, for instance, eulogizes his open-air existence on his mother's County Clare estate, appropriately called Paradise. Similarly, Joseph Hone, writing of his upbringing in Kilkenny, remarks: "The world with its larger obligations, impositions and uncertainties was elsewhere. High on the hill between the two white gates we were a world and law onto ourselves."

According to Grubgeld, this nostalgic depiction of the Big House was framed by its rapid cultural decline. James Calahan similarly notes that the

Big House novel was inherently retrospective, earning its name only long after the invention of the genre. Its popularity grew as the power of the Protestant Ascendency was waning. "Big House literature," writes Calahan, "has persisted throughout the twentieth century while the Big Houses themselves have largely been abandoned."[6] Declan Kiberd attributes this nostalgia to a sense of colonial privilege. "In their subsequent autobiographies," he writes of the Anglo-Irish revivalists, "childhood was identified as a kind of privileged zone, peopled with engaging eccentrics, doting grandmothers and natural landscapes. What they were describing, of course, was childhood in a colony.... They sought relief amidst the scenes of childhood memory, only to discover that the very act of dreaming that dream was itself tainted with the politics of Anglo Irish relations."[7]

Nora's depiction of Bantry House complicates Kiberd's hypothesis. Her tone makes it clear that the Big House at Bantry was not just a site of historical or cultural importance that gave coherence to her Irish past: it was a place that was as Edenic for Nora and the other Catholic domestic servants as it was for their employers. In fact, for Nora, the hallways and gardens of Bantry House firmly anchored a sense of home. As Nora's memoir develops, it becomes evident that her detailed and loving exposition of her time at Bantry House serves a critical narrative function, allowing her to challenge an enduring myth of Irish emigration—the allegation that the mass emigration of people like Nora was an exile enforced by the English gentry such as those at Bantry House.

In *Emigrants and Exiles,* Kerby Miller has argued that deep within the Irish migrant psyche was a collective delusion about the factors that forced their emigration.[8] Blame was popularly heaped on the British and Anglo-Irish, whose colonial legacy was imagined to have forced millions of Irish immigrants to flee to America. Nora tackles this memory narrative head on by explicitly recounting the events that precipitated her own departure to America. She begins by confirming the sense of financial stability that her work in Bantry House had secured her, adding that her relationship with her beau, Jim Hazel, had also imbued her life in Bantry with quiet joy. "In the time that I had been at Bantry House," she writes, "I had grown and gained confidence in myself. I helped my mother by giving her a certain amount of my wages, putting the rest in a post office savings account.... Life went on dreamily. It was nice to be young and to be loved by someone."

This peace is shattered when Dennis, her younger brother, mentions his desire to go to New York—and his wish for Nora to take him there. One night

Dennis meets Nora on her way home from work and announces his intentions, adding a loaded question to his nervous chatter: "He said as he got in step to walk me home 'Why don't you come to America with me?' I stopped and stared at him for a moment in amazement. 'Go to America?' I said 'not me boy, get that nonsense out of your head'. 'Gee' he said, 'it would be nice if we could go there together.'"

"I hated the mention of America," Nora says of those months. And yet her personal aversion to leaving her life in Bantry House is undermined by her family, most specifically her mother, Ellen, who sees it as Nora's duty to accompany her brother to North America.[9] Nora writes that the pressure from her family mounted until her visits home from Bantry House to see her family became almost unbearable:[10] "The winter passed and every time I went home I was approached about America. Mother began by saying I didn't want to be the only one of the family left home and I should go with my brother. On and on it went until I hated to go home. Finally, Dennis' passage money came the first part of May."

This excerpt reveals a significantly gendered family dynamic. Even though Nora had a job and (we suppose) a future spouse in Jim Hazel, her mother evidently considered her lifestyle and happiness as more disposable than her less-established younger brother's. The excerpt also eludes to the mentality of progress that was baked into Ireland's early-twentieth-century culture of migration. In the post-Famine years, a common belief was that the Irish who chose to stay at home rather than emigrate represented the outliers of Irish society. For instance, in 1864 William Wilde described the Irish who had not gone to Britain or America as "the poor, the weak, the old, the lame, the sick, the blind, the dumb, the imbecile and insane."[11] The persistence of this belief is evident in comments made much later, in 1956, by Ireland's Commission on Emigration and Other Population Problems. Those overseeing the commission lamented that over the course of the previous hundred-year cycle of emigration, the country had lost a disproportionate number of its more "gifted" population.[12]

Ellen O'Connor was clearly caught up in this mode of thought and willing to use the stigma of the place-bound Irish youth to coerce her daughter into emigrating. Heartbroken but incapable of disobeying her mother's wishes, Nora eventually relented. She goes to Bantry House to hand in her notice, severing her relationship with home:

> Mrs. Leigh-White was astounded when she heard it. God, how I hated to leave. Annie and Agnes sobbed the day I left and there were tears in Miss

King's eyes. She, Annie and Agnes gave me a beautiful little traveling clock as a fare well gift and a prayer book. Mrs. Leigh-White sent for me. I went to her boudoir and she took my two hands in hers and made me promise her if I didn't like America I was to write her right away and she'd send my passage money to come home. "Will you promise me, Nora?" I promised but didn't keep that promise. I could hardly say goodbye, my throat seemed choked and my eyes were full of tears. So I left Bantry House and Happiness.

Nora's sorrowful goodbye brings the historical irony of her emigration to a crescendo. Through a swell of personal memory, Nora inverts the symbolic national and political roles of the Irish mother and the English gentry of the Big House, at the same time subverting the classic cultural memory of exile. It is Nora's mother who becomes the indifferent colonizer, forcing her daughter out of Ireland, while the Englishwoman Mrs. Leigh-White embodies the role of protective mother, actively attempting to prevent Nora's departure.

As well as challenging a popular memory narrative, Nora's life writing also emphasizes the ways in which gender and motherhood channel and influence the memories that she goes on to recount. In the opening page of her memoir, she signs her name "Mom" and clarifies that the purpose of her writing is to satisfy a request from her daughter. "I'm getting ahead of that story my children want, and they are all so kind and wonderful to me," she comments in her book's prologue, betraying the familial audience that occupies her thoughts as she writes her life story. The gendered nature of her life narrative is also indexed in a phrase within its title: it is the story of a "young Irish girl." Nora thus participates in a common naming practice that saw women autobiographers doubly inscribe their gender so as to shape the reading experience in a particular way.[13] Nora understood her autobiography to be a female immigrant story and sought for it to be interpreted as such. Moreover, Nora mentions that she wants her children to know "the real me." Evidently, this sense of a true or real self is intimately bound up with her Irish past as well as her life before motherhood, for it is ultimately these parts of her history that Nora focuses on in her manuscript. Through her writing, she tells her children about her many admirers in Bantry, her slim waist and cascading black curls, and her love for her sweetheart. At one point she pauses to note: "I want to impress on you children that maybe I was just as giddy, wanting to impress the boys, as you were in your youth." Through this narrative gesture, Nora reveals that a prerogative in writing her memoir is to recall memories that illustrate the streams of continuity she feels exist between her life and that of her daughters. Nora signals the shared hopes and expectations of mothers and daughters across vast tracts of time and space.

The genre of American immigrant autobiography in the first half the twentieth century hinged on an expectation of assimilation. The documentation of a journey toward Americanization was an inescapable plotline in Roosevelt's America, one to which Nora was evidently attuned.[14] For, in spite of expressing her initial resistance to American life, her memoir gradually falls into a linear plot that travels from disoriented greenhorn to integrated American. But for Nora this process of Americanization was registered not through the standard American measure of individual success or capitalistic accumulation but rather through the vectors of family.

The melancholy that defines the first part of Nora's memoir begin to recede once she describes meeting Jim Stine, an American soldier who would become her husband. Her marriage to Jim and the subsequent birth of her children create a sense of cultural symmetry between herself and the outside world, imbuing her recollections with a sense of contemporary relevance. In the following passage Nora explores the specific rituals of family life that gave coherence to her daily life in the United States:

> We enjoyed all the birthdays, Christmases, holidays, anniversaries in our small way. Halloween with the kids bobbing for apples. We had nuts, candy and pumpkin lanterns (real ones), but we never allowed them to "beg" as they call it here. We always put on a party with Jim and Mother just like kids too. Of course, I engineered the plans (leave it to me). Birthdays, the fairy Godmother hid in the flowers and bushes and brought birthday gifts. On Christmas, Santa Claus came; every Christmas Eve without fail and I'll never forget the face on my first born when she saw him for the first time. The second hid as usual behind Mother's skirts, but Brave! Oh Boy! I, of course, had run to the neighbors while Santa made his appearance. When I came back I was met with "Oh Mama, Santa was here and look what he brought me" Such childish trust, and I enjoyed it too with them. I lived for them and wanted them happy above all! A happy childhood is something to remember.

The last line of this excerpt is noteworthy: "A happy childhood is something to remember." This again signals the degree to which Nora's writing was motivated by her desire to bring happiness to her children.

Nora's devotion to her children might have been influenced by her own sense of rejection at the hands of her mother. Although her memoir carefully balances her regret at leaving Bantry with her joy at her children's entry into her life, it leaves a gnawing sense of the possibility of a life in Bantry that was sabotaged by her own mother's aspirations. This is brought to full effect in a final narrative gesture that reveals in compelling, heart-wrenching symbolism the scar that persisted in the wake of her emigration. Inside the cover of her writing pad overflowing with words of love, with happy family memories of her youth and her children's births, Nora pasted a poem—no comment, no addendum. It sits on its own page, an epigraph to her life story:

An Exile's Prayer
Sometimes, Lord, O let me see
Blossoms on a hawthorne tree.

Let me wander once again
Down a little crooked lane.

Let me hear the linnet sing
On some glittering day in spring.

Grant my heart its deep desire
An evening by a bright turf fire.

Lord, O Lord, before I die
Let me see an Irish sky.

Here, we come to see the mode through which a personal, implicitly gendered experience of exile reached out to make sense of itself, searching for an echo in the broader repositories of print culture. Irish America in 1947—the year Nora completed her memoir—was awash in place-based nostalgia, in myths of collective political exile cultivated for a nationalist cause. It would do. Here was some shelter for Nora's own pain, a version of her familial banishment, inexact but adequate: the memory of a daughter's loss invisibly mapped onto the landscape of a nation.

Notes

1. Nora O'Connor Stine Memoir, Cork / New York City, Michigan, University of Galway Archive, P155/14/2.
2. Ellen McWilliams, "Looking for Irish America in the Memoirs of Mary McCarthy," *Women's Studies* 49, no. 4 (2020).

3. Ghassan Hage provides an insightful taxonomy of the qualities that he perceived as making up the migrant's sense of home in the Lebanese Australian context. See Ghassan Hage, "Migration, Food, Memory and Home-Building," in *Memory: Histories, Theories, Debates*, ed. Susannah Radstone and Bill Schwarz (New York: Fordham University Press, 2010).

4. Claire Norris, "The Big House: Space, Place, and Identity in Irish Fiction," *New Hibernia Review / Iris Éireannach Nua* 8, no. 1 (2004): 107; Otto Rauchbauer, "The Big House in Irish History: An Introductory Sketch," in *Ancestral Voices: The Big House in Anglo-Irish Literature*, ed. Otto Rauchbauer (Hildesheim, Germany: Georg Olms, 1992); James M. Cahalan, review of Paul Hyland and Neil Sammells, eds., *Irish Writing: Exile and Subversion*; Otto Rauchbauer, ed., *Ancestral Voices: The Big House in Anglo-Irish Literature*; Jacqueline Gened, ed., *The Big House in Ireland: Reality and Representation*; and John W. Purser, *The Literary Works of Jack B. Yeats, Modern Fiction Studies* 38, no. 4 (1992).

5. Elizabeth Bowen, *Bowen's Court* (New York: Knopf, 1942); Molly Keane, *Two Days in Aragon* (1941; repr., Virago, 1993); George Moore, *A Drama in Muslin* (London: Walter Scott, 1886).

6. Cahalan, review, 968.

7. Declan Kiberd, *Inventing Ireland: The Literature of a Modern Nation* (London: Jonathan Cape, 1995), 101, 105.

8. Kerby Miller, *Emigrants and Exiles: Ireland and the Irish Exodus to North America* (New York: Oxford University Press, 1985).

9. David Fitzpatrick has written that between 1802 and 1921, "The decision to emigrate was made in a family rather than an individual way. Post famine emigration was integrated into the life cycle of both sexes, tending to occur soon after [sexual] maturity or never." David Fitzpatrick, *Irish Emigration, 1801–1921* (Dublin: Economic and Social History Society of Ireland, 1984), 8.

10. The family pressure placed on Nora to emigrate to the US resonates with the contemporary experiences of some Mexican migrants. According to Andrew Halpern-Manners's study of twentieth-century emigration from Mexico—the rates and scale of which compare to those of Ireland in the nineteenth century—a culture of migration develops as the advantages of having a family member anchored in the "new world" become apparent. Halpern-Manners found that migrant children in the US positively transformed the lives of their families back in Mexico, not just through economic remittances but also through the sociocultural materials, values, and belief systems they transmitted back to their home country, which collectively raised the status of the remaining family. Andrew Halpern-Manners, "The Effect of Family Member Migration on Education and Work Among Nonmigrant Youth in Mexico," *Demography* 48, no. 1 (2011). See also Alejandra Núñez Asomoza, "Transnational Youth and the Role of

Social and Sociocultural Remittances in Identity Construction," *Trabalhos em Linguística Aplicada* 58, no. 1 (2019): 118–38.

11. William R. Wills Wilde, *Ireland, Past and Present: The Land and People* (Dublin: McGlashan and Gill, 1864), 40.

12. C. F. Carter, G. A. Duncan, Donal Nevin, and Liam Ó Buachalla, "Symposium on the Report of the Commission on Emigration and Other Population Problems," *Journal of the Statistical and Social Inquiry Society of Ireland*, Dublin 19 (1952–57): 104–21; paper read before the society January 27, 1956. The commission's belief that emigration of younger family members was necessary for the survival of the remaining family is also made evident in the following comment: "The fact that emigration is possible should be a matter for rejoicing. It may not always be possible. Britain and the United States . . . may both have their future problems of excess population. . . . Emigration is necessary to secure for those remaining at home a stable or rising standard of living" (105).

13. Margo Culley, ed., *American Women's Autobiography: Fea(s)ts of Memory* (Madison: University of Wisconsin Press, 1992), 7; Philippe Lejeune, *On Autobiography* (Minneapolis: University of Minnesota Press, 1989).

14. Susan Balée, "From the Outside In: A History of American Autobiography," *Hudson Review* 51, no. 1 (1998).

7

Margaret McGuinness's Memoir (1973)

It was an exciting summer for Gertrude and me. Months were flying by and the lovely summer was drawing to a close. We were very happy that summer and perhaps that is why we didn't want it to end. I wonder if we had a feeling that we might never be that happy again. I wonder.

In 1975 the historian Carroll Smith-Rosenberg wrote in her pathbreaking article "The Female World of Love and Ritual" that "the long-lived, intimate, loving friendship between two women is the type of historical phenomenon that virtually no one has written about."[1] According to Rosenberg's study of eighteenth- and nineteenth-century American society, middle-class women enjoyed markedly intimate relationships with their female peers, the emotional richness becoming one of the most treasured qualities of women's day-to-day lives. Far from confirming the widely perceive notion of its emotional repression, Rosenberg concluded that life in America until the end of the nineteenth century provided a liberal spectrum of opportunities for love and affection, specifically between and among women.

At the same time that Rosenberg wrote her article, an elderly Irish emigrant woman named Margaret McGuinness (born in Sligo, 1887) began to write her life history from her home in Long Island. With what seems like total indifference to the sentiment that has become synonymous with Irish American print culture—that is, nostalgic homages to Eire's distant shores—Margaret's writing conveys an intimate world of female friendships in New York City, where she immigrated in 1905. By highlighting these relationships above others, Margaret's memoir suggests that the importance of women's friendships continued to resonate into the twentieth century. Further, it hints at a realm of Irish migrant experience previously hidden from view: the unlikely role of nonfamilial, nonethnic, same-sex friendships in shaping Irish women's lives in twentieth-century America.

To provide an initial sense of the nature of these relationships, let us consider excerpts from Margaret's memoir in which she describes her lifelong friendship with a young American woman. "I'll never forget how kindly her voice sounded," Margaret writes, recalling the first time the girls met, when both were eighteen years old and working as cashiers in a department store in New York: "Immediately I knew that I had found a friend. Her name was Gertrude Cant. She was dressed in black and looked very pretty. Later I found out she was in mourning for her father who had just recently passed away. We arranged to have lunch together every day and got to know each other quite well."

From this moment onward, Margaret's memoir focuses on her shared life with Gertrude Cant. Rather than other family members, such as her parents and even her husband, it is Gertrude Cant who appears in almost every page of Margaret's memoir. In one particular passage, Margaret describes a vacation that she, Gertrude, and some other girls from work took to the countryside: "There were only two allowed in a room but Gertrude pleaded and she arranged to have a cot put in our room so that we could be together."

When Gertrude had to stay away from work for a week to care for her sick mother, Margaret became depressed and lonely. Indeed, within the first year of their meeting Margaret's and Gertrude's lives evidently became so interwoven that Margaret eventually suggested that she move out of her brother and sister-in-law's house to live with the Cant family. To the reader of today, this may seem outlandish, but for both Margaret's and Gertrude's family, the arrangement was acceptable, even though the Cants were Protestant while Margaret was devoutly Catholic. Within a few days, Margaret thus found herself a fully integrated member of Gertrude's family. She writes that during those days of sharing a room with her beloved friend in Brooklyn, she and Gertrude "talked of many things before going to bed. . . . We nearly always had those heart to heart talks at that time. It must have been a time of consultation, which I know now we had many times during the years. It was a friendship, which meant implicit confidence in each other, and neither of us was ever disappointed."

The longevity and significance of the friendship is encoded into the fabric of the memoir itself. Margaret writes at one point, "I had become so fond of my friends, Gertrude and Anna [another work friend, who features occasionally but less systematically than Gertrude in Margaret's memoir], that the thought of parting and never being so close to them again was frightening. How little I knew what God had planned for me: that Gertrude was to be my close friend for life and that now at eighty-five, her children and grandchildren are calling me 'Aunt Margie.'"

The endurance of Margaret's attachment to Gertrude is confirmed in a memoir subsequently written by Margaret's niece, Alice McGuinness.[2] Alice reveals that some years after Gertrude married and moved to Canada, her aunt Margaret went missing from New York. Later, the family discovered that Margaret had mysteriously reappeared in Toronto and was with Gertrude. Three days after arriving in Canada, Alice wrote, Aunt Margaret met a man named Ed Elliot, whom she subsequently married, conveniently allowing her to live close to Gertrude. Notably, Margaret herself did not write about this sudden trip to Canada, nor did she reflect on her own marriage to Ed, nor the years thereafter. In what feels like a deeply significant ending, her autobiography finishes with a poem dedicated to Gertrude. "As I think of her now," writes Margaret, "these words come to me . . . from a poem we both knew years ago:

> And when memory seeks a pleasant trip
> And the choice of a pathway comes
> I'll choose the bridge of yesterday
> To the days when we were chums.

Given the intense love and attachment expressed in these excerpts, it would be tempting to interpret Margaret's relationship with Gertrude by focusing on her sexuality. To do so, however, may fail to fully account for the sociocultural world in which Margaret and Gertrude moved, a world that, as Smith-Rosenberg has shown, traditionally nurtured and supported intense bonds between women. To speculate on Margaret's sexual orientation would also distract from the broader sociocultural insights that can be gleaned from her memoir, as I discuss in greater detail below. Far from presenting a deviant case of the Irish migrant experience, Margaret McGuinness's memoir seems to open a particularly revelatory door, showing the intimate, interpersonal mechanisms that powered Irish migrant memory.

One of the most remarked-upon features of Irish emigration is its release of millions of young, unaccompanied girls into an unprotected world in which women were still traditionally viewed as vulnerable and dependent. According to David Fitzpatrick, this disproportionately high level of female Irish emigrants suggests both the refusal of Irish women to accept less than their male peers and their desire for a standard of living that surpassed that of their mothers. This latter point requires further examination, deviating as it does from Rosenberg's conviction that the strong emotional bonds between female friends in the nineteenth century extended in harmonious continuity from the relationships between mothers and daughters. Mothers were a young women's primary role models, writes Rosenberg, preparing their daughters for marriage and domestic life through a system of apprenticeship that sought to help daughters attain the status of their female forebears. How, then, can we explain Irish girls' apparently contradictory attitudes, both wanting to emulate their mothers' lives yet supposedly determined to go beyond the worlds into which they had been maternally acculturated?

An answer presents itself in the dismal conditions of Irish women's lives in the late nineteenth century.[3] Even before the disastrous years of the Famine, Irish society had spiraled into pauperization because of explosive population growth and restricted access to land.[4] For women, this had the particular effect of restricting their opportunities for marriage, at the time the only means by which a woman could achieve a stable position in society.[5] The Famine further exasperated these marital limitations, while economic restructuring in the post-Famine years also decreased women's already diminished opportunities for employment.[6] Fitzpatrick suggests that another effect of the Famine was the reduction, albeit in the short term, of the value of women as producers of life, as limited resources imperiled weakened families.[7] Cormac Ó Gráda has noted the disarticulation of cultural systems during the Famine as a potential driver of cultural trauma. It is then worth considering whether a rupture occurred between mothers and their daughters during this period, as their daily lives became increasingly precarious.

In late-nineteenth-century Ireland, two further factors combined to accelerate the difference between the life trajectories of mothers and their daughter. The first was education. After the Famine, literacy among Irish females rose exponentially, propelled by increased participation in the national education system. According to Fitzpatrick, this was partly due to the decreased demand for girls in the local agricultural economy, but it also reflects, in Akenson's view, the "impoverished sophisticate" society of nineteenth-century Ireland and the desire for education in spite of or perhaps because of grinding poverty.[8] Through the classroom and its attendant colonial values of progression and enlightenment, Irish girls' worldviews were directed away from that of their mothers, rendering obsolete the latter's skills, knowledge, and values.

The second disruptive factor between mothers' and daughters' lives was the readily available option of emigration. With the steady stream of letters from former neighbors and older siblings living in America, Britain, and Australia, the possibility of a better life outside of Ireland became unquestionably clear and increasingly attainable. That statistically more young women than men chose to take up this option in the late nineteenth and early twentieth century is perhaps the best indicator of the particular disenchantment with which girls perceived their future options in Ireland.

However, it would be a mistake to conflate young Irish women's disavowal of life in Ireland with a disavowal of their mothers' way of life. As we have seen, younger women overwhelmingly sought out emigration as a way of increasing their chances of marriage and motherhood, thus facilitating the possibility of realigning their experiences and duties with those of their mothers. Furthermore, as Fitzpatrick observes, the emigration of young girls was a decision infrequently arrived at by women alone and influenced by the insistence of stronger members of society, especially the family matriarchs.[9] The memoirs of Nora O'Connor and Ann McNabb (a pseudonym) forcefully attest to this factor, as both women were encouraged to emigrate by their mothers as a strategy to improve the social and economic capital of the family as a whole.[10] Notably, both Nora and Ann subsequently acted as family anchors in America for their mothers, who followed them to the US several years later, settling close to their daughters' new family homes. Suggesting the degree to which her singular journey to America was made in a spirit of filial devotion, Margaret McGuinness writes, "I wanted to become a Yankee and buy my mother silk dresses and a home where she and my sisters could live." Margaret also hints at her mother's collusion in Margaret's emigration, noting that the last words her mother said to the group of friends gathered for Margaret's farewell party was, "I may never see her again but I always have this to remember—Margaret never said *no* to me." We might, then, come to think of emigration as an act that, counterintuitively, brought increased emotional proximity and continuity to Irish mothers and daughters, in spite of the physical distances it entailed.

It is a common assumption that young Irish emigrants who arrived in the US were safely absorbed into the folds of the family networks that preceded them. Yet much of the autobiographical writing of Irish immigrants reveals that after older siblings providing the newcomers with some initial orientation, their hospitality soon wore thin, as the more settled immigrants still struggled to support and establish their own expanding families.[11] For Margaret, the realization that she could not remain with her elder brother and sister-in-law was raised soon after her arrival, when her brother explained that a baby was on the way. "One day," Margaret wrote, "when I got home from work, my brother told me I would have to go to my friends, the Duffs, for a few days as there was a baby coming to the house and when it arrived I could not come back."

The importance of having support networks outside of the family unit thus comes to the fore, and Margaret's subsequent suggestion that she move in with Gertrude Cant's family makes more sense. Replacing her own family with the Cants was not just a symptom of her attachment to her friend but a vital survival mechanism for Margaret as she sought stability and protection in New York City within an environment that simulated that of the nuclear family. The degree to which the Cant family filled the roles that would have been carried out by Margaret's own mother and siblings is confirmed in Margaret's memoir. She writes that Mrs. Cant monitored Margaret's suitors, provided guidance on how she should handle men's attentions, and oversaw the girls' friendship and courtship rituals. In turn, Margaret carried out duties in the Cant home typical of those of a daughter, nurturing the younger Cant children, carrying out household tasks, and caring for Mrs. Cant when she was ill. Just as Margaret was heartbroken when she received the news of her own mother's death, she mourned equally over the death of Mrs. Cant, feeling the loss for years afterwards.

This is not to say that family receded altogether as a mode of emotional support for Irish immigrants but rather casts light on the particular importance of female role models in directing the lives of newly arrived immigrants. As well as Gertrude and Mrs. Cant, Margaret depended on her sister-in-law, Alice, who came to play a much more prominent role in Margaret's life than did her brother. Among other forms of support, Alice provided guidance on the clothes she should wear in society so as to attract the right kind of people. Margaret recalls, for instance, that Alice "bought me the most beautiful red suit and a white velvet hat. I thought it was the loveliest outfit I had ever seen.

With the suit I wore a white blouse with a lace jabot, which I kept for years."
Margaret's memories of her shopping expeditions with Alice, along with her
careful recollection of the people she was introduced to through her sister-
in-law, indicate the long-reaching effect that this female apprenticeship had
on her adaption to American life.[12] Years later Margaret would write with
affection and dazzling clarity of the moment she was introduced to Alice and
the impression she had on her: "My brother said, 'Now you must meet my
wife', so I met Alice, who from then on I was to know as my sister-in-law. I
thought she looked lovely—she was dressed beautifully. Her hat, especially,
must have been very becoming as that was the one thing I remembered so
well. It had two different shades of ostrich plumes, which matched so well
with the rest of her costume."

Besides material support, female friendships also provided newly arrived
immigrants like Margaret a critical bridge between the cultures of the new
world and the old. Margaret's memoir is unambiguous about her desire to
fully assimilate into American society and transcend the limitations of her
Irish ethnic background (the title of her memoir, "My Life—An Adventure," suggests a certain resistance to being identified as an Irish immigrant).
Her dream, she writes, is to become a Yankee, and through the subsequent
writing of Margaret's niece Alice, we gain particular insight into Margaret's
efforts to achieve this aim. "Somehow," Alice writes after her aunt's death,
"she acquired a perfect accent. Not accidently, as she explained, but through
practice. When she first came from Ireland, she would sit down and practice
a New York pronunciation three times and master it. Laughingly, she said
that she even mastered 'Ain't' the same way."[13]

Margaret's determination to rebuff any association with Irish ethnicity is
clear in her reminiscence of Jim Duff, a potential suitor. Margaret is quick
to put the boy in his place, pointedly writing that he "became quite interested in me, not because I was a girl but because I was an Irish immigrant.
I wasn't too interested in him because I didn't like the way he combed his
hair." Margaret's writing casts light on a mindset most frequently captured
in quantitative data showing that Irish women migrants in the twentieth
century were more likely than their male counterparts to marry non-Irish
partner, to live in a non-Irish neighborhoods, and to achieve, over the process of several decades, "lace-curtain" (middle-class) status that for them
symbolized American identity. Far from portraying an atypical or subjective
worldview, Margaret's memoir displays the eagerness for assimilation that

ran through the psyche of millions of Irish migrant women at the beginning of the twentieth century.

Less recognized until now has been the specific role that female friendship networks may have played in supporting this metamorphosis from Irish immigrant to American citizen. As Margaret's memoir shows, spending time with Gertrude Cant and their friend Ann Mueller, both full-fledged, working-class Americans, enabled her to absorb the rituals of an American society that increasingly sought a share of the middle-class lifestyle. Margaret's recollections are replete with details of the cafes the girls frequented in 1905, the food they ate (with a focus on decadent cakes, ice cream, and lemon pies), the places where they went for strolls on the weekend, and the boroughs they would walk through on their way to and from work. "Gertrude, Ann and I would meet on Sunday afternoons and take trolley rides to different parks," Margaret writes.

> I remember Gertrude suggesting Pelham Bay Park, which in those days was in the country. I remember so well how wonderful it was to be out in the country. Gertrude told me that her father was a coachman for Knox the Hatter and the Knox family that lived in a beautiful home near the park. And that her family lived over the stable in a lovely apartment and she as a child played with the Knox children. Gertrude lived on 117th Street east and on some Sundays Ann and I would meet her there and since she lived near Central Park we very often took walks in the park and then to her house for tea.

After moving in with the Cant family, Margaret became even more accustomed to middle-class American life, as she learned through their upwardly mobile household how to entertain friends and attract potential suitors. Despite their different cultural backgrounds, Gertrude and Margaret shared a similar social orientation, both striving to enter the American middle class through methods beguilingly revealed in the following passage: "It was the custom in Brooklyn that the girls on New Year's Day had to have a reception for their favorite boyfriends," Margaret wrote:

> A table was set up in the living room with fancy sandwiches and cookies (which you were supposed to make yourself) and a bottle of wine. We saved our pennies for a couple of weeks to get all the things together, and the table did look very nice. The reception was from 3:00 o'clock until 5:00. The boys we knew in the neighborhood brought some friends whom we had not met before. They were boys on vacation from college. They were very nice boys

and for the moment very entertaining. One of them was from Yale and as he was a great big fellow, we surmised that he was a football player. So from then on, we were avid football fans, and the sports page of the morning paper was thoroughly scanned for reports of the football games of Yale, Princeton, Columbia and Harvard, which were the most popular colleges at that time.

Margaret's friendship network not only expanded through her relationship with Gertrude, then, but also increasingly encompassed both genders, reflecting the shifting norms of early-twentieth-century America. Her writing takes note of daily conversations she and Gertrude had with men on their way to and from work, revealing interactions that would have been alien in the sex-segregated world of the nineteenth century:

> We were liking Brooklyn more all the time and we used to look forward to going to work in the mornings as the trip on the elevated train was always so exciting. We would meet the same people nearly every day and would usually have some of the boys get up and give us their seats, which meant conversation all the way to the Bridge. Once in a while, some of them would express a remark about our dresses, always a compliment. I remember I had a hat with a bird on it, and that brought the remark from one of the boys, "Oh, the saucy little bird on Nellie's hat." I didn't mind his saying it because I was flattered to know that someone even noticed it."

Of interest in this passage is the consistent use of first-person plural to denote Margaret's interactions with these admiring men and in turn its revelation of yet another function of her friendship with Gertrude. In spite of the apparent liberty of their urban world, it becomes clear that Margaret and Gertrude physically and emotionally relied on each other more than ever as they navigated the precarious path of mixed-sex relationships, requiring each other's company so as to make the contacts that would have been impossible to broach as single women. Thus, Margaret wrote that the two were almost always together when they were at social events, that they advised each other on what they should wear on dates, and that one was at a loss in the occasional moments when she found herself without the other. Indeed, the intense empathy and interdependence that Margaret shared with Gertrude through their courtships contrasted markedly with her often whimsical and disparaging treatment of male suitors. Just as Smith-Rosenberg notes the emotional closeness of nineteenth-century women in comparison to the stifled nature of their interactions with men, Margaret makes clear that the company of men, no matter how novel and desired, was rarely as rewarding as time spent with Gertrude.

The eidetic nature of Margaret's reminiscences of the moments she and Gertrude shared from 1905 aligns with my earlier point that immigrant memory strongly favors past experiences of emotional intimacy. That the sound of Gertrude's voice, the color of her dress, and the words she spoke continued to reverberate in Margaret's memory some seventy years after they first met is reflective of a more general desire in migrants' life writing: to immobilize those specific moments in which their emotional trajectories conjoined with those of another. Margaret's memoir proves that such emotional affection was not limited to heterosocial relations between men and women, nor to the bond between parents and children, but was also enjoyed and embraced outside of the family, in the oft-overlooked realm of female friendship.

The overwhelming focus on remembering friends and acquaintances in Margaret's memoir in turn requires a reappraisal of the prioritization of place in Irish migrant memory. As I have suggested, place—specifically, the fixed coordinates of a native landscape—does not have the mnemonic hold over migrant women that it seemed to exert over their male contemporaries in the twentieth century. That said, reflections on landscape are not altogether absent from Margaret's memoir, and the elderly woman's treatment of landscape presents an opportunity to more deeply probe its role in irrigating migrant memory.

First, let us consider the following sequence, in which Margaret recalls a pastoral scene from her youth. "In those days," Margaret writes, "I longed for Ireland—to be able to go out in the lovely green fields and see the colorful wild flowers":

> May was such a beautiful month. I remember telling Gertrude how I always put daisies and buttercups on the doorsteps of the people I liked on May Day in honor of Mary. I remembered the tradition when I came to live in Buffalo, as I found a friend of whom I was very fond and, from walking home from Mass on May Day morning, if I happened to pass a lawn that had daisies on it, I would pick a few to put on her doorstep. Her name was Ethyl Hendryx and she was a very dear friend and one I miss very much.

Here we glimpse how Margaret's memory of the Irish landscape serves not so much to transport her to the past as to enrich the interpersonal relationships of her present. By sharing her memory of May Day with Gertrude and later with Ethyl Hendryx, Margaret uses her idealized cultural capital to maintain and strengthen her female friendships in America.

And although the extract opens with a classic note of immigrant longing, there is, according to Ghassan Hage, an important mnemonic distinction to be made between nostalgia and homesickness. Hage writes that "homesickness . . . is a state where one's memory of back home plays a debilitating function and produces a state of passivity." Nostalgia, on the other hand, "can readily be conceived in a far more positive light as an enabling memory."[14] When we note that Margaret's writing about the Irish landscape is shoehorned into a memoir that ultimately celebrates her transition to life in America, it seems most likely that Margaret's regard for place was firmly rooted in the realm of nostalgia. Indeed, as Margaret's laying of flowers on Ethyl's doorstep indicates, Margaret seemed remarkably adept at transplanting from her memories of Ireland habits and qualities that supported her long-term settlement in America.

Further investigation of place-based sequences in Margaret's memoir suggests that her memories of the Irish landscape largely functioned to call back precious memories of the family members she had left behind—and especially to return to her a full rendering of the character of her mother. In the following sequence, Margaret lapses into a long description of the Sligo landscape, the environment evidently working to evoke the harmony and closeness that existed between mother and daughter:

> Even after 67 years I have that longing for my mother and the lovely walks we used to take in the fields which were close to our house and the hedges filled with primroses and buttercups and little hills covered with bluebells, which at a distance looked like a beautiful blue carpet. After a long walk we would sit on the grass, which felt so cool because there is so much moss in the grass in Ireland. It felt as if you were sitting on a soft rug. In the distance one could see the mountains covered with heather, and once in a while we would come across a little brook where we would pick watercress to take home for dinner. Oh, if I could only describe the beauty of the crab-apples and sloe blossoms in the hedges. How beautiful it all was! No wonder the Irish immigrant wrote these words, of which I will now try to sing the chorus:

> Ireland, Ireland, though I am over the sea,
> Erin, my country, at night I am dreaming of thee.
> Dear little isle of the west, sweet spot of memories blest,
> Land of the bog and the shamrock, oh, how I long to be there.

Margaret's reminiscence supports the philosopher Edward Casey's insistence that "there is no memory without a bodily basis."[15] Intuitive as Casey's notion sounds, this is not readily apparent in Irish cultural portrayals of place, which tend to be shorn of all human influence and reduced to a primordial conceptualization of landscape that predates and subverts human presence. In contrast, the tone of Margaret's memoir evokes a decidedly sensual and embodied relationship to landscape that is constituted above all by people.[16]

In this sense Margaret's memoir articulates a vernacular understanding of place that Irish women writers have been alluding to for some time. Certainly since the 1980s, the poetry of Paula Meehan, Eileen Ní Chuilleanáin, and Eavan Boland has substituted the "inherited myths of the motherland" with the poets' own perceptions of landscape.[17] For Meehan, this has meant a turning away from physical landscapes toward a meditation on inner-scapes: toward what she terms "her emotional or psychic wilderness." Boland in turn shows that it is not place qua place but rather experiences like motherhood and aging that give form to her memories of place. In the following poem from *The Lost Land*, Boland inverts the usual metaphors of landscape, showing how memory is not inspired by land but rather by the bonds of maternal love:

> Now they are grown up and far away
> And memory itself
> has become an emigrant
> where love dissembles itself as a landscape
>
> where the hills are the colours of a child's eyes
> where my children are distances, horizons[18]

Despite the myriad differences between them, it seems that Margaret's American life writing is carried out in the same spirit as that of Boland's. But while Boland's evocations of intimacy are contained within the traditional realm of family, Margaret's writing breaks past the cultural taboos of the twentieth century to consecrate the intimacy experienced between two young women at the dawn of the twentieth century.

Notes

1. Carroll Smith-Rosenberg, "The Female World of Love and Ritual: Relations between Women in Nineteenth-Century America," *Signs* 1, no. 1 (1975).

2. Margaret McGuiness Eliott Memoir, Connolly letters, Alice McGuiness Memoir, Sligo & Monaghan / New York City, University of Galway Archive, P155/13/2.

3. David Fitzpatrick, "'A Share of the Honeycomb': Education, Emigration and Irishwomen," *Continuity and Change* 1, no. 2 (1986).

4. For a detailed discussion of Ireland before the Famine, see Kerby Miller, *Emigrants and Exiles: Ireland and the Irish Exodus to North America* (Oxford: Oxford University Press, 1985), 58–61.

5. Timothy Foley comments that marriage was the only desirable, if not readily accessible, outlet for women in nineteenth-century Ireland. Timothy P. Foley, "Public Sphere and Domestic Circle: Gender and Political Economy in Nineteenth-Century Ireland," in *Gender Perspectives in Nineteenth-Century Ireland: Public and Private Spheres*, ed. Margaret Kelleher and James J. Murphy (Newbridge: Irish Academic Press, 1997).

6. In her overview of Irish women's role in the workforce, Mary Daly concludes that between 1850 and 1950 there was no perceptible improvement in Irish women's lives. Mary E. Daly, "Women in the Irish Workforce from Pre-Industrial to Modern Times," *Saothar* 7 (1981): 82.

7. Fitzpatrick, "'A Share of the Honeycomb.'"

8. Donald Akenson, *The Irish Education Experiment—The National System of Education in the Nineteenth Century* (London: Routledge & Kegan Paul, 1970), 17; Joel Mokyr and Cormac Ó Gráda, "Poor and Getting Poorer?: Living Standards in Ireland before the Famine," *The Economic History Review* 41, no. 2 (May 1988): 209–35.

9. David Fitzpatrick, *Irish Emigration, 1801–1921* (Dublin: Economic and Social History Society of Ireland, 1984).

10. "Ann McNabb" Memoir, Derry/Philadelphia, University of Galway Archive, P155/11/1–P155/30/10.

11. Nora O'Connor hints at her discomfort in her elder brother's house in New York, especially in light of his heavy drinking. Mícheál Ruiseal speaks of a girl he meets on the dockside in New York who asks him for money because "she was expecting a relative who didn't meet up with her." Ruiseal also indicates the transactional nature of the newly arrived migrant's stay with family members, as when he describes his first day in New York: "I got off the train and was met by somebody who took me to the house of a relative I was to go to. Well, I spent the night there and got up the next morning. I wanted to get a job. The next Saturday I had to give 17 shillings for my board and pay for getting my shirts washed. On Sunday I looked at my money and found that I hadn't gained anything." Michael Ruiseal, Kerry/Massachusetts, University of Galway Archive, P155/13/3; Tom Brick writes of his anxiety when he arrives at the station of his sister's new hometown to find that no one is there. Once work dries up on his brother-in-law's

farm, he takes to the road for a living. Relying indefinitely on the hospitality of family members was generally not an option for immigrants. Tom Brick memoir, Kerry/ Iowa/ South Dakota, University of Galway Archive, P155/106/11.

12. Margaret writes, for instance, "My sister-in-law, being very anxious for me to get over being lonely, introduced me to many more nice friends. One family I remember quite well, the Barry family, who consisted of Mrs. Barry, a widow, whose husband was a very dear friend of my brother and who came from Ireland also. The family consisted of four children who were quite young when I met them. May was the oldest, then Kathleen, Francis and Madeline."

13. Margaret McGuiness Eliott Memoir, Connolly letters, Alice McGuiness Memoir, Sligo & Monaghan / New York City, University of Galway Archive, P155/13/2.

14. Ghassan Hage, "Migration, Food, Memory and Home Building," in *Memory: Histories, Theories, Debates*, ed. Susannah Radstone and Bill Schwarz (New York: Fordham University Press, 2010), 416.

15. Edward S. Casey, *Remembering: A Phenomenological Study*, 2d ed. (Bloomington: Indiana University Press, 2000), 182.

16. Angela K. Martin, "The Practice of Identity and an Irish Sense of Place," *Gender, Place and Culture* 4, no. 1 (1997): 228.

17. Carmen Zamorano Llena, "Overcoming Double Exile: (Re)construction of 'Inner-Scapes' in Contemporary Irish Women's Poetry," *Nordic Irish Studies* 3 (2004): 163, http://www.jstor.org/stable/30001512.

18. Eavan Boland, *The Lost Land: Poems* (New York: W. W. Norton, 1998), 40.

PART III
Narratives of Proximity

Note of Introduction

If Irish American popular memory depicted a narrative of incline, the life writing of the less "distinguished" migrants surveyed through these pages can best be defined as narratives of proximity. Rather than constructing rags-to-riches chronologies, these disparate writers draw upon memories of beloved people and places to establish a sense of connection, to pull the past closer to their present, and to ease the pain of separation induced by emigration and the deaths of loved ones. As well as fostering emotional closeness, these immigrants' life writings attempt to make the cultures of Ireland and the United States more geographically proximate. By writing, these immigrants hoped to familiarize family members born in North America with the sights and sounds of Ireland. Their writings also demonstrate their adoption of modern American writing conventions, tapping into a deeper sense of belonging in the United States. Although they are subjective, these immigrant memoirs illustrate the existence of shared memory narratives previously hidden from view. I summarize these narratives in this concluding chapter.

The Written Mother

Mothers make varied appearances in nineteenth- and twentieth-century Irish autobiography. In the Anglo-Irish life writing tradition, they are distant figures, ghostly and often emotionally inaccessible to their children.[1] Irish Catholic life writing includes more intimate portraits of mothers, though they are inevitably overshadowed by the nationalist and religious themes that dominate the genre from the late nineteenth through the mid-twentieth century. As Elizabeth Grubgeld shows, it was not until the end of the twentieth century that the memoirs of John McGahern, Christy Brown, Seamus Deane, and Frank McCourt presented mothers as central figures of childhood memoirs.[2]

Conversely, in Irish migrants' life writing in the US, mothers and motherhood are so pervasively patterned through immigrants' recollections that they are best understood as distinctive realms of memory.[3] Such a perspective resonates with collective memory theory, which shows that family memories were mediated mostly by mothers or maternal figures.[4] Further, cognitive memory theorists understand such memories to play a formative role in the development of personal identity, outshining other cultural memories in terms of clarity and endurance across a lifespan.[5] The variety of ways in which mothers and motherhood are portrayed in immigrants' life writing in turn speaks to the richness of this particular realm of memory.

For male life writers in particular, mothers are vectors of intimate memories and portals into the often elusive emotional worlds of the late-nineteenth-century Irishman. For instance, David Lawlor's 1930s memoir opens with the following lines, which appear to draw from the form of the Freudian family romance: "The first time my mother kissed me was in the little town of Carrick-on-Suir, County Tipperary. This is in the South of Ireland. I assume that she kissed me because of the wonderful love that existed between us all through her life."[6] Love for mothers was frequently expressed in physical terms, with several male memoirists commenting on their mothers' beauty and the admiration that their physical appearance drew in public.[7] Male memoirists also wrote about treasured private moments with their mothers. In the context of emigration, these memories take on a tragic note and are frequently linked to the trauma of departure from Ireland. For instance, Andrew Leary O'Brien writes, "I was overly dear as a child to my Mother." He continues:

> For several years before I left home she was in bad health, and I believe consumption. She could not rest well at night, and consequently used to sit up till late in the night. I also used to sit up studying my lessons, and when my lessons were studied, as I then was learning to play on the violin, I would frequently, when all the family except my Mother & self were asleep, play for an hour at a time these good and lively old Irish jigs and reels. I believe from these circumstances my good Mother loved me if it be possible better or more than the other of my brothers & hated to part with me.

Mothers are portrayed as more accessible than fathers and as confidantes to their sons. Hugh O'Daly's memoir reveals that every week he wrote to his mother from the United States, whereas he "could not muster up courage to write my father." In turn Thomas Mellon describes how "my mother had been from the beginning let into the secret of my aspirations, and shared my hopes and fears. She was my most confidential adviser at all times." In the case of Ned Ronayne, it was his aunts Margaret and Mary who played the role of mother figure. As we saw earlier, his affectionate memories of these women survived Ronayne's fierce rejection of Irish Catholicism and its adherents. He wrote that "no mother could more tenderly care for and cherish her child than these two devoted women loved and cared for me. I have always revered their memory, and nothing would give me greater pleasure, could I afford it, than to go back to Ireland to visit their graves."

Recollecting the death of a mother gave Irish men an opportunity to express their strength of feeling toward her. Lawlor writes movingly of one of the last nights his mother was alive, when he sat at her bedside to tend to her: "When I woke after a deep sleep I found my head in my mother's lap. She found me asleep, got out of bed, put my head in her lap and she and my guardian angel watched over me. She died a few days after, and seven of us boys marched after the hearse to the cemetery. When the stones from the first shovel struck my mother's coffin, I thought it was the most terrible thing that had come to me in my whole life."

The death of a mother intensified the sense of emigration as a personal tragedy. George Pepper's life writing juxtaposes memories of his departure for America with the memory of his mother's subsequent death:

> As the hour drew near when I was to leave the haunts of my childhood: what a sorrowful hour it was! What a struggle agitated the good heart of my dear mother, between her grief at the parting and her hopes for my future! Though over fifty years have passed, it seems but yesterday, so swiftly does memory recall our early days. She accompanied me a part of the way, and when the time came for us to separate, she embraced me fervently, saying: "Be a good boy, be a good student, be a good Christian; and if we never meet again on earth, we shall meet in heaven." I see her as she stood upon the hill, waving a farewell adieu to me with a white handkerchief. It was a farewell, indeed; for when I returned in less than a month, there was no one on the hill; but, instead, a little group of people waiting about the gate. My mother was dead! . . . We laid her away to sleep in the beauty of eternal peace in the Ballinagarrick Presbyterian Cemetery. May the grass be ever green upon the sod that covers the remains of the best of mothers!

Patrick Cudahy writes in similarly tragic terms about the death of his mother, at "just about the time that her sons began to prosper": "Each of them loved her so much, that, had she lived, she would certainly have had something to live for. I was away from home, at Oshkosh, at the time of her death and came home to the funeral. Do not think I ever grieved so much about anything before or since, as I did over my mother's death."

Male authors also remember their mothers as the glue of the family unit, often keeping the family afloat, especially in the face of feckless, violent, or drunken fathers. Peter Murphy, for instance, writes that his mother is "the heroine of these annals," in particular when compared to his father, whose alcoholism led to the family's social disgrace, ultimately forcing their emigration to America. Murphy portrays his mother as the embodiment of Victorian gentility and believes she was debased by the experience of emigration: "When she had to face unpleasant duties, she did not flinch. She dragged us up—and got very little help from her husband. She used to pray a lot and that certainly helped her to bear her burdens; she cried a lot. She was flagrantly 'good' in the Victorian sense; never did I hear her say a vulgar word."

Owen Peter Mangan describes his mother as a tragic heroine, forced to part from her son because of his jealous and violent stepfather.[8] Similarly, John Logan Power's *Memoir of an Irish Pauper* remembers his mother as a powerless but heroic figure who had to leave her son behind in Callan to accompany her new husband to America.[9] Literary scholars have linked this adoration of mothers by their Irish Catholic sons to the centrality of the Virgin Mary in Irish cultural and religious life.[10] Yet in the case of Irish immigrant life writing, the idealized mothers is present in Protestant and Catholic life narratives alike.

Sons did not forget the economic role that mothers played in the family. Hugh O'Daly recollects that his mother "was a wonderful woman" who "worked hard, cared for us children, never had a doctor, lived to the age of 85": "She never had more than one maid, yet she washed, sewed, cooked for us and our farm workers. She milked the cows, fed the pigs and chickens, did the marketing, besides baked all the bread. She never missed a Sunday or holiday from Mass nor refused aid to a beggar or neighbor who was in want of milk, butter or food of any kind. She had a wonderful sense of humor. I can still see her smile and in fancy hear her cheerful laughter."[11]

Manny Steen, too, reflects on his mother's thriftiness and her efforts to keep the family fed in a tenement house in Dublin at the turn of the twentieth century. Steen recalls his mother sending him, surreptitiously, to the butcher for "meat for the cat and the dog": "The butcher would take a big knife and cut off maybe half a cow's liver, throw in a heart, a couple of lungs, and some soup bones. We'd put it all in newspaper, and I'd have an armful of stuff for about two, three pennies. My mother would make a stew, a kidney stew, put the whole thing in and cook it up. You could feed our whole family for two or three days."[12] Patrick Cudahy remarks that his mother was "the financial manager of the family. . . . All of us boys turned over our wages to our mother until we were twenty-one years and six months of age."[13] Michael Ruiseál remembers how his mother sewed money into his suit pocket before his voyage to the US, evoking the image of a prudent, economically astute mother.[14] Mary O'Mahoney tells how her mother oversaw the shop and pub in West Cork while her husband was in the US.[15] For her part, Ann McNabb proudly recalls that her mother roofed the family's thatched cottage in Derry and was the main breadwinner of the family owing to her father's despondence and alcoholism.[16] The trope of the docile, passive, subservient mother so common in Victorian literature was all but absent from the life writing of Irish immigrants.

Mothers frequently embody discourses of improvement and are remembered for encouraging their children to advance their social positions. Alexander Irvine writes that "my mother was the only one in the house who could read, and she used to read aloud from a story paper called *The Weekly Budget*."[17] Thomas Mellon remembers that "in the stress of farm work and farm payments and family cares, my mother did not neglect my education. There was no school within reach during the first summer, but she drilled me pretty well at home in the spelling book."[18] Mothers are also portrayed as conduits of historical memory, through the stories they tell their children in the family home. These stories often appear to be preparatory narratives, orienting their children toward the possibility of life in America. For instance, George Pepper recalls the following maternal scene, the details inevitably colored by cultural memories of Famine relief from America:

> My mother was a great admirer of the United States. During the famine year, we were visiting in Belfast, when an American ship—I believe it was the *Macedonia*—filled with provisions for the starving, dropped its anchor in the harbor. It was a rare and beautiful sight to see that old warship, freighted with Indian meal for the suffering. My mother was deeply moved, and, taking my hand, she raised it towards heaven, and made me register a vow to God that, if any calamity should ever overtake the generous American people, I would never forget the Stars and Stripes, which that day I beheld for the first time. Though years have passed since that thrilling hour, I can feel at this moment the warm tears of a revered woman falling upon my head. Yes, like all Irish women of honor and of principle, she was a republican, and the names of Washington and Jackson were always on her lips, like a litany.[19]

Mothers also appear as patriotic figures in migrants' memoirs. Lawlor mentions political stories his mother told him, especially those about the heroic Young Irelanders and the rising of 1867. George Pepper recalls his mother's insistence that they attend a gathering of the Young Irelanders in the north of Ireland, and Mary O'Mahoney reflects at length on her mother's role in the Ballydehob Land League. Thus, if mothers in some life narratives are tragic and powerless, in others they appear as ballasts for the cultural memories promoted by Irish nationalists in America.

Although mothers are central figures in the life writing of their daughters as well, women's narratives tend to treat mothers with more complexity and realism than do men's memoirs. As we've seen in the writing of Margaret McGuinness, daughters may have viewed emigration to the United States as a way of maintaining continuity between their own life experiences and those of their mothers. In the US immigrant daughters had a greater chance of marrying, having children, and running their own households, thus maintaining the relevance of the wisdom and knowledge their mothers had handed down to them. By emigrating, daughters could satisfy their mothers' desires for a better quality of life, both for their daughters and for the family as a whole.

It was not unusual for mothers to follow their daughters to America once they had become established there, suggesting that daughters were often placed as anchors for their parents in the new land. This also implies that mothers expected more from their daughters than their sons following their emigration. This burden of responsibility arguably tempers the sentimentality with which daughters reflect on their mothers in their life writing. Indeed, as we saw with Nora O'Connor, the life narrative could communicate the suffering mothers imposed on their daughters. Nora's memoir documents how her mother coerced Nora into emigrating to the United States. But it also illustrates how life writing can subvert popular memory tropes: Defying the anti-British timbre of Irish American memory narratives, Nora portrays her English employer as a sensitive, maternal figure who fights for Nora to remain at home in Cork, significantly weeping the tears of loss that Nora's own mother refuses to shed.

An enduring theme in Irish women's memoirs is the sense to which their own status as mothers and grandmothers encourages the completion of their life writing. Nora O'Connor, Mary O'Mahoney, and Mary Jane Hill Anderson directly address their children or grandchildren in their memoirs and clearly envision these family members as the main audience for their writing. As

immigrants, these female writers evidently saw themselves as cultural translators for their children and grandchildren, responsible for demystifying Ireland for members of the family that would be born and raised in the United
States. In most cases these women writers portray Ireland in a positive light,
drawing from bucolic memory narratives of Irish America to shade in their
own life writing. Mary Jane Hill Anderson, however, was influenced less by
the Irish pastoral than the American Protestant Pilgrim life narrative. Mary
Jane's 1922 memoir thus evokes a life of maternal and spiritual sacrifice on the
American frontier, replete with ecocide and indigenous genocide. Fifty years
later this tone had all but vanished from women's migrant memoirs. Shaped
by the liberal models of womanhood promoted in twentieth-century American popular culture, life writers like Margaret McGuinness openly celebrate
their independence in the US, female relationships, sexual exploits, and the
pleasure of an urban consumer lifestyle. There was a gradual shift, then, from
a mindset in which mothers loomed large toward a more ambivalent sense of
motherhood as a mode of self-identification.

The Irish Sense of Place: From Pastoral to Domestic Memory-Scapes

In 1933 the Irish exhibitions at the Chicago World's Fair featured a gallery of
works by contemporary Irish artists, including Sean Keating, Paul Henry,
and Jack B. Yeats, who portrayed Ireland as a pastoral utopia, in keeping with
the political and social imperatives of the young Irish Free State.[20] The Irish
pastoral remained an enduring memory narrative across the nineteenth and
twentieth centuries, fueled by the political and cultural agenda promoted by
the Young Ireland movement and later by Gaelic revivalism on both sides of
the Atlantic.[21] During these two centuries, the Irish sense of place resonated
with images of open fields, wild coastlines, thatched roofs, and rugged cliffs,
creating a shared cultural memory of the distinctiveness of Irish identity.
Significantly, the juxtaposition of landscape and Irish identity coincided with
a society that fetishized landownership as the ultimate expression of Irish
identity.[22] As explored in chapters 1 and 2, ownership and control of land
were also highly gendered, as women's place on the land became increasingly
contested after the Famine and into the 1980s.

In contrast to public memory narratives, which focus on the Irish pastoral, the life writing of Irish immigrants tends to relate an Irish sense of

place within the closed, solid, and intimate sphere of the domestic. This is especially true of women writers. For instance, in the opening paragraph of her memoir, Margaret McGuinness recounts an early childhood memory centered in her family's living room: "Being alone this evening my memory takes me back to a Christmas Eve in Ireland with my mother and sister. It must have been my last one there as it stands out so vividly in my mind. My mother made a fire of turf and coal, which burned brightly in our living room upstairs. We sat on the floor and enjoyed the warmth of the fire and then my mother made us a large pitcher of orangeade, which was so good I have never tasted anything like it since."[23]

Likewise, the images that come back to Mary O'Mahoney with the greatest intensity are those that encircle the interior of her family's home in West Cork. One space in particular stands out in Mary's memory: the room occupied by her grandmother. Mary was ten years old when, in 1889, the family emigrated from West Cork to America. Her grandmother was left behind. "I was then only a child but I remember her quite vividly," Mary writes:

> Grandmother had her own room separate from the rest of the house, a large room with a huge four-poster bed with curtains that closed it in completely from drafts. There was a large clothes press or wardrobe, a large clock with weights and pendulum hanging almost to the floor. There was also a large table. These articles of furniture and the picture Uncle Jerry made are the chief things I remember about Grandmother's room. It had a window from which one could look down on the street. There was also a fireplace with a grate in which a peat fire always burned. On the mantelpiece were pictures of various members of the family and a pair of brass candlesticks. Grandmother always used candles to light her room.

As we have observed of Margaret McGuinness's memoir, the intense recollection of a childhood memory is made possible for Mary through the material richness of a room. Physical elements such as a turf fire, brass candlesticks, a pendulum clock, and a curtained bed become mementos that help Mary and Margaret move closer to the nexus of their memory: that is, to the people—Margaret's mother, Mary's grandmother—left behind after their emigration. As the objects of the domestic space coalesce into an ordered picture of the past, both writers reconstitute the presence of missing women at the centers of their recollections.

The life narrative of Ann McNabb, who emigrated to the US around the year 1855, provides another example of the domestic orientation of an Irish migrant's sense of place.[24] The McNabb family grew up in extreme poverty and lived close to destitution in a cabin made of peat in Derry. Yet the scene from the past best preserved in Ann's memory relates to the night her mother and father joined her in Philadelphia, several years after she and her siblings had emigrated. Ann's memory of her parents' arrival is electrified, charged by the materiality of the space from which the memory emerges:

> Me and Tilly saved till we brought Joseph and Phil over, and they went into Mr. Bent's mills as weaver and spool boy and then they saved, and we all brought out my mother and father. We rented a little house in Kensington for them. There was a parlor in it and kitchen and two bedrooms and bathroom and marble door step and a bell. That was in '66, and we paid nine dollars a month rent. You'd pay double that now. It took all our savings to furnish it, but Mrs. Bent and Mrs. Carr gave us lots of things to go in. To think of mother having a parlor and marble steps and a bell! They came on the old steamer "Indiana" and got here at night, and we had supper for them and the house all lighted up. Well, you ought to have seen mother's old face! I'll never forget that night if I live to be a hundred.

For Ann, this memory is significant not just for its heightened emotion but also for its demarcation of a shift in her family's social identity. The materiality of the family's new home—the bell, the parlor, the marble stoop, and the bathroom—helped displace Ann's previous memories of her family's destitution in Ireland. Hard-won physical objects restore a sense of hope and possibility to the McNabb family.

Cultural theorists validate this kind of location of a sense of place in the domestic realm. In *Wanderlust: A History of Walking*, Rebecca Solnit advises that to approach a subject fully, we have to localize it in memory. "Memory, like the mind and time, is unimaginable without physical dimensions," Solnit writes.[25] Gaston Bachelard agrees, writing that localization in the spaces of our memory is more important than their temporal categorization. Significantly, Bachelard also stresses that it is not landscape that best emplaces memory but rather the intimate interiority of the domestic. "Memories of the outside world," he writes, "will never have the same tonality as those of home and, by recalling those memories, we add to our store of dreams."[26] This insight has been largely absent from Irish historiography and may account for the continued tendency to associate the Irish sense of place with the outside, natural world. It is also the case that the focus on the Irish landscape as emblematic of "place" emerged from historiography's foregrounding of the male experience of the past, which tended to be located on Irish farms. Women's memories, removed as they were from the landscape because of gendered roles, were not culturally valued, and their role as mediators of a different Irish sense of place remains underappreciated.

To a large degree, immigrant men's life narratives perpetuate the tropes of Irish nationalist autobiography, recycling traditional pastoral images of Ireland to convey their sense of place. A review of thirty-two male-authored texts found that the vast majority systematically avoided domestic-themed memories. Often the authors made no references whatsoever to their family lives at the time of writing, and evocations of their childhood homes were overwhelmingly based on descriptions of the physical landscapes rather than the interiors of the homes. In this regard their life writing rejects the generic conventions of American autobiography, which promotes self-reflection. Irish immigrant men's resistance to these new styles of life writing and Irish women's comparative embrace of it may reflect the role of gender in mediating the immigrants' adaption to their new environment, as well as the appeal to Irish women of the conventions of the intimate and personal American autobiography.

However, there were exceptions to this rule. The life writing of Michael Kilkrane, born in County Leitrim in 1862, is an emotional reckoning with a domestically centered memory of home.[27] It begins with a touching description of Kilkran's heartache after arriving in Chicago in 1880. He writes of the tears that flowed down his cheeks as he wrote a letter home to his father and of the grief that he felt when he thought of his mother, who died just before Michael's emigration (among the few possessions Michael had brought with him from Ireland was a fistful of earth from his mother's grave). Michael's homesickness is amplified by the discomfort of his living situation: he had rented a room in a boardinghouse run by a pair of unpleasant landlords. The pillows and bedsheets, Michael writes, were stuffed with sharp, dried reeds rather than feathers, and the "boarding boss," as Michael was forced to call him, regularly chastised Michael for his perceived inability to cope with the brutal working conditions in Chicago's slaughterhouses. In the context of this cruel and uncaring home in Chicago, Michael's original home in County Leitrim comes to hold even greater value in his memory. In the following evocative passage, Michael describes his loneliness as he walks through the still unfamiliar streets of Chicago, having posted a letter back home to his father. In the rhyme that comes into his mind during the walk home, personal and cultural memory coalesce as Michael attempts to get a bearing on his strange new surroundings:

> On my way back, at the corner of 38th Street, I stopped a while and looked around. Night was coming on and the shops and stores were being lighted. I was very lonely. Memory recalled a few lines I heard so often sung in my native land . . . though they had never before impressed me as they did then. I only remembered two lines of it and I here add some more of my own composition.

> Oh pity the fate of the poor Irish stranger—
> that wanders so far from his home—
> No one to protect him from want, woe or danger—
> not knowing which pathway to roam—
> **But had I the power to fly from that spot**
> **I never would stop 'til I reached the old cot**
> **I never would leave it, though humble it be**
> **The house mother died in far over the sea.**

> Myself and my sad heart then went back to my lodging house. I met the housekeeper at the door and she asked where I was.

The lines that Michael adds to the poem (reprinted here in bold) stand out in stark contrast to its opening because they move the subject away from a general longing for home to a particular desire to be back in his childhood house, with his mother. They show, in short, the need to add specificity and intimacy to a generic form of Irish cultural memory.

If Michael's memoir suggests that a sense of place can coalesce around an embodied domestic memory for an Irish man as well as an Irish woman, it also reveals the limitations placed on men of this epoch in expressing such intimate memories. For despite its initial emotional openness, the remainder of Michael's memoir documents the barbarity of his life as a slaughterhouse worker in Chicago, where men were pitted against each other in fierce and often bloody competition for low-paid and degrading work.[28] Indeed, in many ways Michael's writing traces the evolution of a softhearted greenhorn into a hardened Irish American worker whose survival has become contingent on the suppression of human attachments, personal loyalties, and displays of emotion. More specifically, Michael's writing also infers the insensitivity with which expressions of loss are met in his new social world. Where gendered behavior norms may have accepted and even anticipated female migrants' articulation of homesickness, the same may not have been the case for workingmen in Chicago.[29]

In one passage of Michael's memoir, for example, he describes the negative attention his heartbreak attracts in the boardinghouse. Having seen Michael walking down the street with tears flowing down his cheeks the housekeeper "told all who called that evening how long I remained in my room writing a love letter to the girl I left in Ireland": "So the evening was spent making fun of the Greenhorn. But I was not in a funny mood, and did not care for all the girls in Ireland, nor any one of them for that matter, to the manner the housekeeper had intimated . . . 'a love affair'. No, not so soon for me. The only woman I ever loved was my mother and she was dead. That left me none to love me, but I love her memory still." In the face of the housekeeper's taunts, we sense how Michael's relationship with his mother changes form, as she fades from the present and instead comes to reside in the remembered past. The last line, "The only woman I ever loved was my mother and she was dead. That left me none to love me, but I love her memory still," is particularly stirring. In the depths of Michael's grief, then, memory has taken on a life of its own, capable of begetting tenderness. This moment demonstrates how, in contexts of emigration, memories can abstract away from their source to become their own story.

As well as reconstituting a sense of proximity to family members, emigrants' life writing worked to reestablish connections with old neighbors and local communities in Ireland. This is particularly true of the writing of Tom Brick, which evokes the intimacy of life in a small Irish-speaking village in West Kerry.[30] Brick takes pains to include the names of his old teachers, neighbors, and friends in his memoir, as well as the names of places of note in and around Ballyferriter. The location of Brick's sense of place within shared community life is brought into sharp focus during a corn harvest in South Dakota, when Tom is suddenly struck by a bout of homesickness. Unlike in Ballyferriter, where harvests were carried out through *meitheal* (cooperative) style social gatherings of neighbors, the harvest in South Dakota was a mechanized affair, driven by dangerous machines and completed at great speed by paid teams of workers brought in from afar. Something in this ritualistic decay, in the roar of the thrashers or the irredeemable difference of the landscape to his native Ballyferriter, seems to trigger an intense wave of longing for Brick, whose memories otherwise skirt playfully across the pages of his memoir. The recollection begins with a technical description of corn cutting in South Dakota before dipping into a sober moment of introspection:

> With hay all put up now, we start the second process of corn cultivating again, only with those discs on the cultivator reversed, [which,] when in operation . . . will systematically throw the soil around the growing corn plants now about eight or ten inches in height. Yes, I must say these were very lonesome days for me out in the cornfield. Some days it was hard for me to keep from crying. . . . Mary, my sister, did a lot to persuade me to stay, otherwise I might have gone back to Ireland and to my old haunts: the summer and Sunday afternoon crossroad dancing at Ballyferriter and an occasional Sunday afternoon rowing about in the curragh across the harbour to Ballydavid, to take in the dancing on that side of the harbour; being bona fide travelers now we [were] entitled to two drinks at Peg Carty's bar. With all this on my mind, it is a wonder that I did not go back, but there was always that spirit of adventure and travel characteristic of the Brick family. And [when] I thought of going back to see the girl I loved, married to a farmer and raising a family, that put a crimp in my idea of ever going back, whatever the future had in store for me.

Dancing at the crossroads, racing curraghs across the harbor, and the rite of passage of two drinks each at the local bar: For Tom, a sense of place manifests in the local community, supported by the rites and rituals that could only be known and understood by its members. In this sense, Tom's vision of home reflects the political aspirations of Éamon de Valera, which drew from a genuine Gaeltacht tradition of rural communalism, the glorification of which arguably maintained the cultural relevance of Tom's own memories into the 1970s. Sociologically, too, Tom's description of home dovetails with Bourdieu's notion of habitus, in which the individual possesses a maximal spatial and social knowledge.[31]

And yet the last line of Tom's reflection intimates a barrier to fully recovering his sense of place in Ireland ("And when I thought of going back to see the girl I loved, married to a farmer and raising a family, that put a crimp in my idea of ever going back, whatever the future had in store for me"). Tom's inability to marry his sweetheart in Ballyferriter was caused by his father's decision to leave the family farm to Tom's brother. This decision precipitated Tom's emigration to America and ultimately marred his claim to a full sense of place in Ireland, despite his deep community attachment to Ballyferriter.

Understandably, for many Irish immigrants memories of home and conceptualizations of place were modulated by their class status. Such was the case for Tim Cashman, the son of a cottier farmer who emigrated from Cork to Boston in 1893. Tim's father was a farm laborer who had to move often to find work during the late 1860s and 1870s. This problematized Tim's memories of home in two main ways. The family's movement from place to place prevented the development of close ties to any one community, which, as we have seen from Tom Brick's memoir, plays an important role in the development of a stable sense of home.[32] Then, too, the Cashmans' poverty forced the family to live in physical environments that were, based on Tim's descriptions, barely fit for humans. In the absence of safe, consistent shelter, Tim began to rely more and more on cultural memories for feelings of intimacy and protection. The popular memory narratives of Young Ireland became particularly intoxicating, their idealization of the Irish landscape filling the void created by the Cashmans' domestic impoverishment:

> The "house" in which we lived was a miserable bothán at the end of a long boreen running northwards from the farmer's house in the low-lying land below. We were situated very nearly at the top of a high hill called the "Báwn-Árds" or "White Heights" in English. From the top of those heights was one of the finest views imaginable. Directly to the South could be seen the faint blue line of the ocean over the land beyond Lisquinlan, Bally Macoda, Knockadoon, Garryroe and in fact, from Youghal eastward to Cove to the westward could be seen the beautiful blue streak of the sea. The sea was about seven miles from us in our new place in Garren-James, and from Youghal to Cove would be about 30 miles or so. A magnificent view presents itself from this height towards the north and northeast.[33]

The rural poor, as Cashman's passage suggests, were tightly bound to the local landscape. Because their work depended on an understanding of the precise location and character of a place, it was the laboring classes who tended to be most familiar with the names of fields and other unmarked spaces in rural Ireland.[34] Such knowledge over time converted into a form of intimacy, and imbued the local landscape with a quality of home that those in more comfortable circumstances may not have required or sought out.[35]

If there is a sense of resolve in this reliance on landscape as an expression of home, there is also underlying tragedy. Emigration in the late nineteenth century was the only means of survival for vast numbers of Ireland's working class. As the following passage from Cashman's memoir indicates, the trauma of leaving places that had come to represent home rivaled the ordeal of saying goodbye to family members: "The matter was suddenly thrust upon me by receiving my passage money from my sister in Boston. I was tortured by conflicting thoughts on the matter as I never had any idea of emigration up to then. Leaving old Ireland never entered into my mind until getting that passage-price.... So, I reluctantly got ready for the ordeal of parting with my parents and my native land. Everybody knows the heartbreak of such experience—I mean those who went through such. Needless to repeat it here."

In the United States Tim became an active member of the Irish nationalist movement. The group's rhetoric about the Irish landscape as a site of renewal, security, and belonging must have resonated with Tim in a very personal way. For Tim, the alignment of landscape and home had taken place many years before, through the indignity of his family's destitution.

Hidden Realms of Love and Intimacy

Irish resettlement in North America has long been read as a family-centered saga. The arrival of a letter from America containing a younger sibling's passage has become iconic, and the enormous remittances Irish families received from their children in the United States confirm the loyalty to kinship networks that were maintained across the first half of the twentieth century. And as we have seen, themes of mothers and domesticity only confirmed the centrality of family life in the psyches of aging Irish American immigrants.

At the same time, immigrants' depictions of family life within their memoirs suggest that the family unit was not always the source of support and continuity that we have been given to understand. For women like Nora O'Connor, familial expectations provoked heartbreaking personal loss, as her desire to remain in Bantry was trumped by her brother's and mother's aspirations for a life in America. In turn, when immigrants joined family members in the United States they sometimes found that their welcome soon wore out. Manny Steen and Michael Kilkrane relate the immediate and brutal pressure their siblings placed on the newly arrived immigrants to find jobs and their own living accommodations. In New York, Nora O'Connor was secretly horrified by her older brother's alcoholism, and Mary O'Mahoney's memoir reflects at length on the horror that she and her mother experienced when they joined her abusive and controlling father in Texas. These themes of disappointment and rejection are noticeably absent from the corpus of letters sent back to Ireland, which tend to gloss over migrants' personal lives in favor of a blithe and recurrent message of "all well and doing well."[36] Migration scholars perceive such sentiments as creating a false picture of life in America for the sake of those back home, masking the realities of life for Irish migrants in the United States.

While writing their memoirs may have liberated migrants from the burden of placating family expectations back in Ireland, they remained aware of the impression their memoirs would have on future generations in America. Nonetheless, immigrant life writing managed to record the existence and importance of relationships outside of the heteronormative family unit. The production of such narratives was inevitably influenced by the liberalism of twentieth-century Irish American literature, which allowed well-known writers like Mary McCarthy to question and rebuke family-centered Catholic value systems.[37]

The best example of this emergence in immigrant writings exists in the writing of Margaret McGuinness, which celebrates the pleasure of her life-long, intimate relationship with Gertrude Cant.[38] Similarly, David Lawlor reflects at length on his close friendship with an unnamed "chum" in America. "We were together every night for nearly seven years," writes Lawlor wistfully: "We walked and talked and talked and walked and discussed most every subject that young men of our age discussed. His mind was pure as the clear water of a spring."[39] Lawlor became so attached to his friend that he began to take on his physical traits. His friend, he explains, "was not prepossessing in appearance and there was something the matter with his arm from childbirth—the shoulder dropped some three or four inches. My tailor asked me what in the name of God happened to my shoulder because it sympathetically dropped the same three or four inches." In time this precious friendship appeared to disintegrate because his friend's father "never seemed to look on me with favor." Such beguiling insights hint at the emotionally rich encounters that textured Irish immigrant life in America, the significance and exact nature of which remained the private preserve of the migrant memoirists.

Conclusion

The unpublished body of life writing by Irish immigrant men and women humanizes and illuminates the post-Famine experience of emigration to the United States. The reflexive style in which immigrants approached their writing as well as the range of subjects they chose to explore suggest the appeal of American autobiography for Irish immigrants born in a country where life writing was tethered to a nationalist cause and was reserved for cultural and class elites. The North American autobiographical genre was particularly appealing to Irish women immigrants, whose life experiences could not be represented by the nationalism and masculinity of the Irish autobiographical convention. This uneven response reflects broader trends in the Irish diaspora that confirm the opportunities of emigration for Irish women in terms of personal freedom, quality of life, and an expanded set of life choices.

The firsthand accounts in immigrants' life writing highlight the gendered and politically rigid nature of popular Irish American memory narratives of the twentieth century. The collective memory of Irish America was inspired and overseen by masculine experience. As Irish American novelist William Kennedy writes, the traits that these memory narratives fostered endure, distorting the experiences of post-Famine immigrants who could not relate to these forms of self-identification.[40] A comparative analysis of immigrants' private life writing helps to shine light on the people who resisted the gravitational pull of traditional Irish American parishes and politics. For these memoirists, personal and subjective themes such as family, motherhood, friendships, personal ambitions, and domestic memories of place were far more relevant than the cultural agenda pursued by Irish American nationalists, Catholic leaders, or the Irish Free State. Rather than recycling the antagonistic memory narratives spearheaded by Irish nationalists from the late nineteenth century, these Irish immigrant writers produced what I have defined as narratives of proximity, highlighting the affection, sense of purpose, and connection that emanated from and survived the experience of emigration. And rather than appropriating the melancholic tones of Irish American nationalists, the life writing of many of these immigrants was angled toward the possibilities of the future, not the desperation of the past. These writers gathered their memories of Ireland in a deliberate and constructive way, so as to create prospects for their American families and friends that would be influenced but not dictated by their Irish past.

Immigrant life writing contributes to a clearer understanding of the operations of Irish cultural memory. The memory narratives discovered in this book exist adjacent to popularized Irish American "memories" of Famine, republican nationalism, exile, and the Irish pastoral, tropes that are peppered across the thirty-two memoirs interpreted in this study. The endurance of such themes confirms the success of Irish American nationalists in curating and promoting memory narratives that resonated years later for at least some Irish immigrants in the United States. At the same time, the life writings also confirm the power of communicative, family-based memories in subverting the narratives deployed by official sources. As Astrid Erll and Katie Barclay have shown, family memory has remained an underresearched arena of cultural memory studies, attracting much less attention than the study of national commemorative processes.[41] This study calls attention to the need for parallel studies of national and pan-national realms of memory as well as intimate portrayals of individual and family memories, searching for the points at which these intersect and abrade. It is only at this axis of the personal and social that we can we begin to fully understand the relevance of the claims of state, citizenship, and nationhood for the smallest actors of Irish America.

Notes

1. Elizabeth Grubgeld, *Anglo-Irish Autobiography: Class, Gender and the Forms of Narrative* (Ithaca, NY: Syracuse University Press, 2004), 62.

2. Grubgeld, *Anglo-Irish Autobiography*, 66.

3. As well as featuring in Irish migrant life writing, mothers are also central figures in the oral and written reminiscences of the elderly who stayed in Ireland. See Mary Ryan, Sean Browne, and Kevin Gilmour, eds., *No Shoes in Summer: Days to Remember* (Dublin: Merlin, 1995).

4. Astrid Erll, "Locating Family in Cultural Memory Studies," *Journal of Comparative Family Studies* 42, no. 3 (2011); Peter Burke, *Varieties of Cultural History* (Ithaca, NY: Cornell University Press, 1997); Maurice Halbwachs, *On Collective Memory*, trans. Lewis A. Coser (Chicago: University of Chicago Press, 1992); James Fentress, *Social Memory* (Oxford: Blackwell, 1992).

5. Harald Welzer, "Communicative Memory," in *A Companion to Cultural Memory Studies*, ed. Astrid Erll and Ansgar Nünning (Berlin: De Gruyter, 2010).

6. David Lawlor Memoir, Waterford/Massachusetts, University of Galway Archive, P155/11/4–P155/88/7. Published as David S. Lawlor, *The Life and Struggles of an Irish Boy in America* (Newtown, MA: Carroll, 1936).

7. For example, David Lawlor writes, "Many of the old people who knew my mother very well said that she was the prettiest girl in all of Ireland. Of course, to me, she was the most beautiful girl in all the world and the only equal she could have is the girl I married and who has been my companion for more than

forty years." David Lawlor Memoir, Waterford/Massachusetts, University of Galway Archive, P155/11/4. The memoirs of Thomas Mellon and Patrick Cudahy similarly celebrate the beauty of their mothers: Patrick Cudahy Memoir, Kilkenny/Milwaukee, University of Galway Archive, P155/10/3; Thomas Mellon Autobiography, Tyrone/Pittsburgh, University of Galway Archive, P155/9/1.

8. Mangan writes of his forced separation from his mother at the hands of his stepfather:

> After a good night's rest on a bed of fresh straw and good breakfast of oat-meal for me and the boys, and Mother refreshed with tea and toast and a fresh egg, we started off for the other leg of our journey five miles more, which we reached about six o' clock in the evening. Mother and the boys got a very warm reception but not so with me. My stepfather asked Mother what on earth did she bring me up for. "I couldn't get here with out him" said she, "he carried your boy on his back nearly all the way." "It don't matter" said he, "there is no room here for him and he will have to go back." "Well where will he go to?" said Mother. "Let him back to the school house and he will get something to do." Mother objected but it was no use. After he and she had debated all night I had to go. . . . Poor Mother was heartbroken, at least she seemed so. She kissed me and gave me all the advice in her power to be good and not forget my Prayers. Six pence she said was all she had between her and death which she gave me.

T. J. Barron, ed., *Memoir of Owen Peter Mangan, 1838–1924* (Heart of Breifne Irish Emigrant Database, 1984), https://www.dippam.ac.uk/ied/records/27203. Also available at Owen Peter Mangan Memoir, Cavan / Preston England, Massachusetts, University of Galway Archive, P155/10/2–P155/30/8.

9. John Logan Power, *Memoir of an Irish Pauper Who Became an American Humanitarian*, edited by Joseph Kennedy (1856; Callan, Ireland: Callan Heritage Society, 2020).

10. Grubgeld, *Anglo-Irish Autobiography*.

11. Hugh Daly Memoir, Monaghan / Montana, California, University of Galway Archive, P155/7/1.

12. Manny Steen Memoir, Dublin, Sligo / New York City, University of Galway Archive, P155/14/3.

13. Patrick Cudahy Memoir, Kilkenny / Milwaukee, University of Galway Archive, P155/10/3.

14. Michael Ruiseal, Kerry/Massachusetts, University of Galway Archive, P155/13/3.

15. Henry O'Mahoney and Mary O'Mahoney Lupton Memoirs, Cork, US Army, Texas, University of Galway Archive, P155/11/2.

16. "Ann McNabb" Memoir, Derry/Philadelphia, University of Galway Archive, P155/11/1–P155/30/10. Note that Ann McNabb is a pseudonym provided by the interviewer. The exact dates of Ann's birth and emigration are not clear. "The Story of an Irish Cook," *Independent* 58, no. 2939 (March 30, 1905): 715–17.

17. Alexander Irvine Memoir, Antrim, England, British Army, USA, University of Galway Archive, P155/12/1.

18. Thomas Mellon Autobiography, Tyrone/Pittsburgh, University of Galway Archive, P155/9/.

19. George Pepper Memoir, Down/Ohio, University of Galway Archive, P155/22/1.

20. The paintings of Paul Henry, one of the painter laureates of the Free State, romanticized Ireland as a rural idyll through portrayals of cottage landscapes that erased any references to poverty and avoided evocations of the intimate dynamics of family life. The nationalist painter Sean Keating also drew on West of Ireland landscapes for inspiration, his paintings focusing on the Irish emigrant experience. Keating sets his *Ulysses of Connemara* (1950) at the edge of an Irish coastline, a young man gazing out to sea at the ship that will take him to America. A woman we can assume to be his mother is huddled to the right, taking shelter in what appears to have once been the family home, now fallen into ruins. In *Economic Pressure* (1949), Keating recreates the same scene, the figure in the painting drawn with the same strong lines as sky and sea and rock. Both paintings portray migration as a male phenomenon, and both make the space of the homestead supplicant to the might of the nationally framed landscape.

21. Oona Frawley, *Irish Pastoral: Nostalgia and Twentieth Century Irish Literature* (Dublin: Irish Academic Press, 2005); Tricia Cusack, "A 'Countryside Bright with Cosy Homesteads': Irish Nationalism and the Cottage Landscape," *National Identities* 3, no. 3 (2001); Angela K. Martin, "The Practice of Identity and an Irish Sense of Place," *Gender, Place and Culture* 4, no. 1 (1997).

22. Philip Bull, *Land, Politics and Nationalism: A Study of the Irish Land Question* (Dublin: Gill and Macmillan, 1996).

23. Margaret McGuiness Eliott Memoir, Connolly letters, Alice McGuiness Memoir, Sligo & Monaghan / New York City, University of Galway Archive, P155/13/2.

24. "Ann McNabb" Memoir, Derry/Philadelphia, University of Galway Archive, P155/11/1–P155/30/10.

25. Rebecca Solnit, *Wanderlust: A History of Walking* (Chicago: University of Chicago Press, 2000).

26. Gaston Bachelard, *The Poetics of Space*, trans. Maria Jolas (Boston: Beacon, 1994), quoted in Brian Dillon, *In the Dark Room* (London: Fitzcarraldo Press, 2018), 63. Grubgeld takes a similar approach in her analysis of John Montague's

The Rough Field, citing not only Bachelard's *The Poetics of Reverie* but also drawing from psychiatrist and philosopher James Phillips's essay "Distance, Absence, Nostalgia": "The nostalgic emotion often disregards specific spaces in favor of a generalized ideal. Upon return to the place with which the past was associated, the nostalgic seeker feels himself alien from that place as an encounterable world. He has betrayed himself into thinking it was place he wanted, whereas it was actually lost time." Elizabeth Grubgeld, "Topography, Memory and John Montague's *The Rough Field*," *Canadian Journal of Irish Studies* 14, no. 2 (1989): 26.

27. Michael Kilcran Memoir, Leitrem/Chicago, University of Galway Archive, P155/108/19.

28. One of the more graphic passages in Michael's memoir tells how a fellow worker advised him to bathe his hands, blistered and bleeding from a morning of relentless shovel work, in a nearby barrel of liquid. He subsequently realizes that the barrel contains "pickle," the acid used to preserve pork.

29. The pressure to be tough appears again in Michael's description of returning from work to the boardinghouse, his hands wrapped in bloody cloths: "The Boarding Boss looked at me and laughed and said, "What the —— have you all rags on your hands for?" I said them rags was put there to save me [*sic*] hands. He laughed again saying, "Quit blowing on your fingers and get ready for supper. Don't be such a calf."

30. Tom Brick Memoir, Kerry / Iowa/ South Dakota, University of Galway Archive, P155/106/11.

31. Ghassan Hage, "Migration, Food, Memory and Home-Building," in *Memory: Histories, Theories, Debates*, ed. Susannah Radstone and Bill Schwarz (New York: Fordham University Press, 2010), 418, 419.

32. Tim himself comments on the effect that the family's internal migration for work had on his childhood sensibilities: "As time went by and I, as a boy, was beginning to get a broader view of the country round me in general, my people decided to leave the place. I was getting fairly well on in school at the time in spite of the savage teachers, and it was a blow to me to be uprooted from the place where we had been for eight years. I was deeply interested in the locality and knew the haunts at night of the Banshee, the fairies and all the other well-established ghosts of the neighborhood."

33. Tim and Dan Cashman, Memoirs, Letters, Poems, Essays, Cork / Massachusetts, Montana, University of Galway Archive, P155/16/1.

34. I am grateful to Liam Mac Mathúna of University College Dublin for pointing out this relationship, which he first identified through his students' investigation of the place-names of Irish fields. These (unpublished, to the best of my knowledge) findings showed that the male laborers who had worked the land best recalled the names of fields.

35. Note, however, that middle-class Anglo-Irish autobiographers also articulate deep attachment to the landscape, suggesting the pervasiveness of this memory narrative across the class spectrum.

36. Geraldine Meaney, Mary O'Dowd, and Bernadette Whelan, *Reading the Irish Woman: Studies in Cultural Encounter and Exchange, 1714–1960* (Liverpool: Liverpool University Press, 2013), 131.

37. Ron Ebest, *Private Histories: The Writing of Irish Americans* (Notre Dame, IN: University of Notre Dame Press, 2005).

38. Likewise, Ann McCabb notes the intimacy of her relationship with her employer, Mrs. Carr. "I was in that house as cook and nurse for twenty-two years," she states. "Mrs. Carr's interests was my interests. I took better care of her things than she did herself, and I loved the childher [*sic*] as if they was my own."

39. David Lawlor Memoir, Waterford/Massachusetts, University of Galway Archive, P155/11/4–P155/88/7.

40. Ebest, *Private Histories*, 237.

41. Katie Barclay and Nina Javette Koefoed, "Family, Memory, and Identity: An Introduction," *Journal of Family History* 46, no. 1 (2021); Erll, "Locating Family in Cultural Memory Studies."

Abridged Memoirs

The following is an excerpt from the memoir of Irish-language speaker Edward (Ned) Ronayne. Born in Killeagh, County Cork, in 1832, Ronayne immigrated to Quebec in 1856 and subsequently relocated to Chicago. He wrote his memoir from Boulder, Colorado, publishing it in 1900 with the Free Methodist Publishing House in Chicago. He gave the memoir the title *Ronayne's Reminiscences: A History of His Life and Renunciation of Romanism and Free-masonry*. The pages below cover the years 1832–47, during which Ronayne details the horrific effects of the Famine on his local community.

The largest and most southern county in Ireland is county Cork, one of the six into which the province of Munster is divided. The largest city in the south of Ireland is the city of Cork (whence the county derives its name), said to have one of the finest and safest harbors in the world, including also that of Queenstown, the well known stopping-place for all the ocean steamers plying between America and Europe. The harbor next to Cork in size and importance is that of Youghal (pronounced Yawl), a town of about 6,000 inhabitants, according to the census of 1871, and situated almost at the very southeastern part of the county. Youghal is from an Irish word, *eochaill*, meaning yew wood, from the yew trees nature planted on the slopes on which the town is built. Sir Walter Raleigh was mayor of this seaport borough in 1588, and his house, Myrtle Grove, remains in nearly its original state. Local tradition has it that Sir Walter here planted the first potato ever grown in Ireland, a portion of the crop at a subsequent period being imported to this country— America—for which reason doubtless it derived the name of Irish potato.

Other buildings I remember were the "clock gate" and parish church. The first was a peculiar structure extending across Main Street, surmounted by a large clock and having an extensive archway underneath for purposes of general traffic. But this "gate" was more than a mere arch—it was really a great stone building reaching from one side of the street to the other, and arched over the street as well as over the sidewalks. Indeed this odd building is one of the curiosities of southern Ireland, and in my boyhood days was used for a town hall. The parish church was antique truly, as it was built out of the old St. Mary's church, first erected in the eleventh century.

Between two and three miles from this once famous place, and almost on the very verge of the Atlantic ocean, is a little hamlet called Gurtrue [now Gortore], an Irish name signifying a brown field, or rather a brown cornfield—*gurt* meaning cornfield, and *ruah* meaning brown. In this little hamlet I was "born on the 5th of November, 1832, and was christened in the parish chapel at Youghal, in the parish of Saint Mary's in the county of Cork, on the same fifth day of November, 1832." I copy this data from a sworn declaration sent to me in 1861, while residing at Quebec, British North America. Both my parents were earnest, devoted Roman Catholics, and this accounts for the haste with which I was christened—the ceremony being performed the same day I was born! There is a deeply rooted belief in the heart of every Catholic, planted there of course by the teaching of his church, that any child dying without baptism "goes to a part of hell where he'll endure the pain of loss, and never see the face of God," or, as it is commonly expressed among Roman Catholics, "he shall be in total darkness, but not suffer the torments of the damned." But the chief reason for such speedy action was that I was a very puny, delicate infant when born. Life in my little body held a doubtful tenure, and it would be a terrible thing if I should die without baptism! . . .

My father's name was John Ronayne, my mother's Elizabeth Cunningham. In my father's family were three brothers and three sisters—John, my father, William, David, Margaret, Mary, and Elizabeth. In my mother's family were four sisters and one brother—Elizabeth, or Betty as they called my mother, Hanora, Johanna, Ellen, and John. My father, John Ronayne, married Elizabeth Cunningham, and John Cunningham married Elizabeth Ronayne, making what is called in Ireland a "cross match;" and there is an old superstition among the Irish peasantry that such marriages are always unlucky.

The reader will please remember that I am writing of the early 30's, almost in the very morning of the century, the evening of which is now rapidly closing around us. In those early days, and indeed for a score or more of years thereafter, there were some very quaint and primitive methods of farming in Ireland as in other countries. Grain of all kinds, whether wheat, barley or oats, was cut down with reaping hooks, and each reaper, taking two and sometimes three ridges as his portion, would try to rival all others in the same gang, and thus a contest was always sure to take place where two or more men were at work together. The women invariably did the binding after the men, and as there was a rivalry among the men to see who could reap the fastest, there was a similar, or even keener rivalry among the women to see which could bind the fastest. My mother was considered a good hand at binding any kind of grain. Being one day in such a contest as I speak of she took a pain in her left side, having possibly over strained herself, and, as I was many a time informed afterward, she never recovered from that strain, whatever it was, and died a few months thereafter. I was quite young, probably not more than fifteen months old, when my mother's death occurred, and thus while an infant I was deprived of a mother's love and care; but my father's unmarried sisters, Margaret and Mary, took me into their immediate charge. No mother could more tenderly care for and cherish her child than these two devoted women loved and cared for me. I have always revered their memory, and nothing would give me greater pleasure, could I afford it, than to go back to Ireland to visit their graves. . . .

Well, when I was between two and three years of age my eyes became so affected from some cause that it was feared I would lose my sight. Aunt Johanna, my mother's youngest sister, used to carry me in her arms or on her back two or three times a week to Father Foley in Youghal, that by his reading some Latin over me and making the sign of the cross on my eyes such a dreadful calamity might be averted. They got well in the course of time, and my aunts never missed an opportunity to impress upon me as a boy what a wonderful miracle Father Foley wrought in my behalf by restoring my sight. . . .

How long we lived in Gurtrue after my mother's death I do not know. My uncle, David Ronayne, married and went to live with his wife's family at a village called Ballymacoda where he was very successful as a carpenter. Two of my mother's sisters also married and moved into Youghal, where their descendants, I believe, are still living, while we—that is my father, his sisters Margaret and Mary, Uncle William Ronayne and "the baby"—took up our residence in an inland country place called Glenawn, about nine miles from Gurtrue....

I could not have been very old when we left Gurtrue, our ocean-beach home, for it is at Glenawn that I have my first recollections of my father. I remember well how he danced me on his knee when he returned home from work in the evening, and how he brought me whistles and other little playthings whenever he went to town. Although the climate of Ireland is very healthful, that portion of the country where we lived being remarkably so, and the water, too, most excellent, yet fevers were often prevalent. Those fevers, I should judge, were somewhat of the nature of our typhoid fevers here. Doctors were few and far between, the people generally poor, and therefore medical assistance was difficult to obtain, especially in country places. The poor sick patient was usually left to some old woman in the neighborhood, who did the best she could. If the sick person got well it was all right, but if not it was thought to be God's will, and nobody was to blame. Every one was very much afraid of "the fever," and so one Sunday afternoon when my father returned home from mass at Killeagh, he played with me for a little while, then complained of not feeling well and thought he would lie down for an hour or two. I well remember how terribly frightened my aunt Margaret became, and how she exclaimed in tones of anguish, "Oh, John, I do hope you are not taking the fever." But poor father had "the fever" sure enough, and he never arose from the bed on which he laid down that Sunday afternoon. It was only a few days until his brother William was also taken down with the same dreaded disease. There they lay in the same bed—those two strong young men, for my father could not have been more than thirty-five and Uncle William was still unmarried—moaning and tossing in the delirium of that terrible fever for days and weeks, with no apparent change for the better but rather growing gradually worse. Wages in Ireland were very low in those days and farm work, which my father followed, was not always to be had, hence there could have been little or nothing "put by for a rainy day." My aunts did everything they could to alleviate the suffering and save the lives of their two brothers, aided by the generous help of kind and willing neighbors.

Killeagh was a town two miles from us. We had passed through it when coming from Gurtrue to Glenawn, and to this place my aunts finally sent for a physician, a Dr. Eames, I believe. He tried the usual remedies and methods then in vogue in such cases, but all to no purpose, and at last the priest was summoned to hear their confessions and to administer the Sacrament of

Extreme Unction, which according to the law of the Catholic church can never be administered except to a person "in danger of death by sickness." ...

The priest having performed his usual function took his departure, leaving my poor aunts alone with their deep sorrow and in constant expectation of the grim tyrant Death entering their peaceful little home to snatch from them not one but two dear brothers at once. He came that very night. As the evening advanced and the candles were lighted, my aunts were in terrible distress—there they were, their noble and beloved brother John on the verge of death, going away from them and leaving no other legacy behind than a poor little puny child to bring up as best they could. Two helpless women, and withal in a poverty-ridden country, what should they—what could they do? And their other brother, just as grand a man and equally beloved—he, too, was about to leave this life! There was nothing to look forward to but hardship and privation! Before preparing me for bed they led me to the bedside of my father and, standing me on a chair that he might see me better, they said to him as soothingly as they could, "Oh, John, look at poor little Neddy; what shall we do with him?" He was lying on his back and, turning his head languidly toward me, he merely replied, "Oh, he's such a little fellow." They then lifted me to the back of the chair, and said again, "Now, John, now see what a big boy he is;" but he made no further reply, and I never again saw my father alive. I had not been feeling very well that day and so, having occasion to be lifted out of bed during the night—about one o'clock—the first object my eyes rested upon was my father stretched out at full length upon the floor dead. They had just removed him from the bed to wash and prepare for his coffin. I have never forgotten that night or those scenes which I have mentioned. They are as fresh in my memory today as though they had transpired only yesterday. I was too young then to realize what this meant to me—absolutely alone, a little, delicate child without brother or sister, and now fatherless and motherless. ...

My father, and indeed all our family, had a very large number of friends and acquaintances, so when he was placed in the coffin he was borne on the shoulders of men to a large new barn about two hundred rods from the house, in order that as many as desired might attend the wake there, for but very few would go to the house for fear of the fever; and then again, Uncle William's death was expected at any moment. An Irish wake is perhaps one of the strangest customs that exists among any civilized people, and is peculiar to the Catholic portion of Ireland alone. In proportion to the esteem in which the deceased is held, his friends and acquaintances from far and near assemble during the evening at the house where the corpse is "laid out," and, regardless of the grief of the family or the loss sustained by the death for the person before them, they indulge in all kinds of hilarious sport, such as games, story telling, practical jokes, and almost every species of noisy fun which the merriest and the most witty of them can devise. Pipes, tobacco, snuff and plenty of spirituous liquors supplied by the family are frequently passed around during the night, and of course as the stimulants are imbibed the fun and frolic and jollity increase until, as it often happens, the house of mourning becomes a veritable pandemonium. In my early days it would be considered a disgrace for the friends of the dead person should there not be plenty of whiskey and tobacco "over him at his wake." . . . I was too young and too small to be allowed at my father's wake, but there must have been a very large gathering since both himself and all the family were very much respected. Another strange custom prevailing among the Catholic Irish in my early days was this: If the family of the deceased wished to show special respect to the dead, they would engage one or more women, old or middle-aged, possessing a good voice, to cry over the dead person during the night of the wake and along the road at the funeral. These women apparently felt the most poignant grief, crying out in the loudest voice, sounding the praises of the dead in a sort of mournful chant, all the time swaying their bodies and making a weird lamentation which must be seen and heard to be rightly understood. These mourners were called *ban keena*, or the crying women—*ban*, being the Irish word for woman, and *keena* for cry or crying. . . . It was a common thing at the time of which I speak—about 1837—and I well remember the cry of the *ban keena* as my father's funeral passed along down the road toward Killeagh, on the way to the burying-ground at Clonpriest, some nine miles away. A funeral in the south and west of Ireland among the peasantry of that period was another strange sight—nothing at all like a funeral in this country today. There was no hearse used except on very rare occasions, and never any carriages, the coffin being borne on men's shoulders, two at the head and two at the foot. After a time these men were relieved by others, and these again by others all along the route till the burying-ground was reached. Mourners and friends walked behind in regular procession so that the march to the grave was necessarily slow and solemn. . . .

My father was buried on the 17th of March, and just one week thereafter, on the 25th of March, his brother William was borne over the same road and in the same manner and buried by his side! And then began the serious battle of life in earnest for my aunts, Mary and Margaret Ronayne. They decided to keep me with them, come what would; they could not think of parting with the little orphan boy of their brother.

The language of the people was Irish, especially in the country places, and even in the inland towns that language was most generally spoken, and every one was a Roman Catholic, with but very few exceptions, and even these exceptions far between. . . . Our house in Glenawn was built by the roadside, on ground belonging to Thomas Hickey, a well-to-do farmer, who was one of our nearest neighbors and a most intimate and devoted friend. Behind the house was a large field stretching along the road for some distance, chiefly used for grazing purposes; and in that field, one beautiful summer afternoon about a year or so after my father's death, I witnessed for the first time, and indeed for the last, one of those brutal exhibitions so common in southern and western Ireland at the beginning of the century, namely, a "faction fight." Those faction fights, as the name indicates, were hand-to-hand combats between two opposing, angry mobs, or factions, who clubbed and fought and battered one another until one side or the other was defeated. They usually arose from the most trifling causes—some unintentional slight, or fancied insult, and were sometimes kept up for years with the most intense hatred and an ever increasing desire for revenge. Each faction had a nickname by which it was distinguished and which it used as a sort of battle cry, for instance, one was called "the three-year-olds," another "the four-year-olds," another "the Caravats," "the Shanavests," and so on; and each was ever ready to annihilate the other whenever they met. Just think of it—men in middle life, fathers of families, and men, too, among the well-to-do farmers, all banded together in opposite brawling, revengeful, fighting mobs, carrying terror and oftentimes death wherever they went, and each hurling angry defiance at its opponent at every opportunity! They fought with short sticks about the length of a walking cane, called shillalahs, but a black thorn stick, cut from the black thorn hedge, with its sharp knots was reckoned the most desirable, because the most effective, weapon. I never learned the result of that faction fight at Glenawn, though next morning, being sent on some errand to Mrs. Leahy's, our nearest neighbor, I saw two men sitting on chairs in the middle of the kitchen floor, having the wounds in their heads dressed by Mary Leahy and another young woman. . . .

Though the climate of Ireland is exceptionally mild, the temperature ranging from 41 degrees in winter to 60 degrees in summer, yet the southern and western coasts are often visited by severe storms, frequently causing great loss of life, and destroying the shipping around the seaboard. During our residence in Glenawn, in the winter of 1838, we experienced one of those terrific storms, succeeded by such a fall of snow as possibly was never known before in that country. It became fastened in my mind from the fact that our low, thatched-roof house was entirely covered by the snowdrift, so that Uncle David, who at that time was working up at Dan Hickey's, had to dig us out. A large number of sheep perished that night, and a man called Thomas Cushion, one of the leaders in that faction fight, also lost his life while going home from Killeagh. A gang of men with shovels had to precede the hearse on the day of his funeral, to clear away the snow, and I may add that was the first hearse I ever saw, and I never saw but one other hearse at a funeral in Ireland. In fixing birthdays and other events the old people, even up to the present time, reckon from the "night of the big wind," just as the old residents of Chicago speak of an incident as having transpired before or after "the great fire.". . .

We were becoming more and more dissatisfied every day with living in Glenawn, it was at least two miles from both school and chapel, which were side by side at Killeagh, and I was now getting to be of an age when they thought I ought to go to school. So at the first opportunity my aunts rented a small house with a garden attached, almost opposite the chapel gate at Killeagh, and we moved to that town, if I remember rightly, in the early spring of 1841, when I was between eight and nine years old.

Killeagh was a very pretty little town at that time, but, now that a railway is running though it, it must be still more attractive. It is surrounded by some of the finest farming land in the county Cork, if not in the entire south of Ireland. The island contains 339,858 acres of wood land, and of these the largest and by far the most picturesque and beautiful is Glenbower wood, about three quarters of a mile northeast of the town, extending northward at least seven miles, and containing in the neighborhood of 15,000 acres. It was part of the estate of Sir Arthur Brooke, one of those absentee landlords who collect money from their Irish tenants to be spent in England or on the continent, and in my time this wood was one of the most celebrated fox preserves in the whole country. The Killeagh river . . . flowed from the north through the entire length of Glenbower, and at about the center of the wood, where the river was widest, it was converted into a beautiful lagoon, having a neatly constructed bridge at one end and a large cascade or waterfall at the other, the whole forming a most charming feature of that popular resort.

Neither my parents nor any of their families on either side could speak a word of English, and until I was old enough to go to school, I never heard any other than the Irish language spoken. It was Irish at home, at church, at play; Irish always and everywhere, and as a consequence it will be readily understood that very, very few of the peasantry could read and write. As in instance: In 1872, even, quite forty years after a regular school system was established, 36 per cent. of the men and 46 per cent. of the women in signing their marriage register were unable to write their names. The people had Romish chapels, Latin masses, Irish sermons, such as they were, but they had no schools, properly so-called. ....

It is true that there was occasionally a sort of so-called school to be met with at very rare intervals, especially in the south, but as they were always of a private character and a tuition fee demanded they could be taken advantage of only by the well-to-do class. They were of an exceedingly primitive character, being generally held in some disused barn or empty hut by the roadside, and as the larger boys in summer sometimes studied their spelling-books or worked their examples in arithmetic by the side of a neighboring hedge-row (hedges of thorn brush were used for fences), these schools went by the name of "hedge schools." Once in a great while one of these schools would be kept by a man who had the reputation of being a good mathematician, and in such a case young men from other counties, farmers' sons, would seek him out, and while pursuing their studies would board around among the wealthier families, in turn teaching their children mornings and evenings, thereby paying their way. These young men went by the name of "poor scholars," and nearly all of them became the future schoolmasters when the regular school system was instituted. You perceive, however, that the great mass of the people had no opportunity for acquiring even the simplest rudiments of an education, and it remained for Protestant England alone to establish the only common school system Ireland ever had before 1833 or since that time. It is known as the National School system, and is under the direct control of commissioners of both faiths. Since I was born in 1832 I came into a fortunate condition of things—the national schools being established one year later.

Killeagh, aside from its picturesqueness and the beauty and fertility of the country round about, was also blessed with a most excellent national school, and to that school I was sent in the summer of 1841, or soon after our removal into town.

It is sometimes said that on going into a new place a boy has to fight his way to prove his mettle, and a girl must "tongue" her way, but in my case, instead of fighting, I avoided the boys as much as possible. I was utterly ignorant of books, perfectly green as we say, and did not know one word of English, never having heard it spoken till we came to Killeagh. I soon learned to use the words "yes" and "no" and was very proud of the fact, and I remember quite well how the other boys used to jibe and make fun at my expense, calling to one another in the Irish language, "'yes' and 'no,' that is the most of English"—I wish this could be given in the old Celtic tongue, for then it would sound better. Despite all their jeers and mocking, however, I enjoyed going to school from the very first. I had to pick my steps it is true, since the double difficulty faced me of learning a new language as well as books, but taking all things into account I made very fair progress. Our teacher's name was Dan Sullivan, a man from the county Kerry, whom I subsequently learned was an excellent mathematician. I liked him from the very beginning, and though he was reckoned cross as that word is commonly used in relation to teachers, yet during all the time he taught in the Killeagh national school I do not remember that he ever reprimanded me so much as once, and from the first day I went to school until I finally left for good I was never punished by the teacher. . . .

During our residence in Glenawn my aunts used to attend mass regularly at Killeagh every Sunday, but now that we were living almost across the street from the chapel they could take me along, too, and thus carry out one of their most cherished projects. I shall never forget the solemn feeling of awe and reverential fear that came over me as I witnessed the first mass I ever listened to. There was the glare of lighted candles on the altar, the priest dressed in embroidered surplice and richly ornamented vestments, the snow white covering of the altar itself, the Latin so holy (as I was told) and so high above the comprehension of any except the priest, the chiming of the little bell, and above all the moment when the whole congregation knelt on the bare floor, and bowing their heads beat upon their breasts as if they felt the deepest sorrow and contrition. . . .

I was now attending school . . . and making tolerable progress. I was never absent from mass on Sundays; and the next most important matter in the line of duty was that I should learn my catechism. The manner of teaching the catechism in those days was quite primitive, and of course altogether different from the method employed to impart the same Catholic instruction today. There were no pews in the Killeagh chapel, nor in fact in any country chapel in the south of Ireland that I ever was in for that matter, simply the bare earthen floor, pews being regarded by us poor, superstitious people as a Protestant luxury, and as much to be abhorred as Protestantism itself. Our religious instruction was entirely in the Irish language. After last mass every Sunday the boys and girls used to sit on the bare floor, the boys in one part of the chapel and the girls in another, and then some man who could read Irish or had the catechism well by heart used to walk up and down in front of each group, proposing the question and also giving the answer, which the whole class repeated after him. That was how I learned my Catholic catechism, and that was how every boy in the parish of Killeagh learned his. We had school in the forenoon on Saturdays, and there used to be a pretense of having a little religious instruction, but as only a few scholars attended it never amounted to very much.

Not only were we diligently instructed in the catechism, but we were also taught our prayers—the Lord's prayer, or "Our Father" as Catholics call it, the Hail Mary, the Creed and the Confiteor. These, however, I had already learned from my aunts a long time before, and never missed an occasion of saying them every night and morning. We had two priests in Killeagh permanently, Father Maurice Power, the parish priest, and his brother, Father Henry, who was nominally the curate. The latter, however, was very much subject to epileptic fits, and hence performed but few pastoral or clerical duties, sometimes celebrating first or eight o'clock mass on Sundays and a mass each morning during the week. I heard it repeated time and again, and it was firmly believed by every Catholic in that whole section of country, myself included, that Father Henry had at one time cured a young woman of epilepsy by his great power as a priest, and that her malady was transferred to himself, which accounted for his terrible affliction.

He soon became very much interested in me, partly because I was an orphan and partly because of the care and fidelity with which my aunts were endeavoring to bring me up, so that before many months I became his especial favorite and I was almost altogether instructed by him in all the doctrines of the church—its origin, its truly sanctified character, the power of its priests, and above and beyond all else he used to impress upon me the solemn and serious duty of cultivating the most fervent love and veneration for the Virgin

Mary, as by her all-powerful intercession with her Son, she could obtain for every one who trusted in her all needed grace and blessing, and finally, at the hour of death, a painless departure and a speedy entrance into heaven....

And thus, while I diligently continued my studies at school under Dan Sullivan, Father Henry Power charged himself with my religious training, and was rewarded for his pains when, in 1842, I passed a most creditable examination preparatory to making my "first communion."... Although I had passed a very satisfactory examination in the catechism, yet it was at first somewhat doubtful whether the parish priest would allow me to go on to my first communion on account of my age, but Father Henry having personally vouched for me, that I fully understood the nature of the communion, and the duties and responsibilities connected therewith, I was permitted to proceed, and with the rest of the class attended daily instruction as to how we were to make our confession and perform the penance imposed by the priest....

All the class having made our confession ... we assembled at the chapel the following morning, fasting, to receive our first communion. Each one carried a blessed candle lighted, and it will be readily seen that when one hundred boys and girls, or perhaps one hundred and fifty, march in procession with lighted candles and assemble thus in front of the altar the outward senses are captivated and an impression produced not easily effaced. We were freed from sin through the sacrament of penance, and now we were to receive the body and blood of Christ whole and entire into our own bodies through the sacrament of the Eucharist, and hence, of course, the communion must be received fasting. It was indeed an imposing scene and well calculated to make a lasting impression on the mind, as most assuredly it did on mine. There was the altar with its snow-white cloths and dazzling lights, the priest with his brilliant robes and gaudy vestments, the solemn monotone of the mass in the Latin tongue, (regarded by me, at least, as being superlatively holy), the ringing of the bell, the elevation of the host, the bowed heads of the congregation smiting upon their breasts, and the bright glare of the lighted candles in the hands of the young communicants, all of this when witnessed at the time, even by elderly people, is sure to captivate the senses and render the occasion one never to be forgotten.

The greater portion of the dwellings of the Irish peasantry are built of mud, with a straw roof, and are usually only one story high. The building material is prepared by mixing water and clay to a certain consistency; and they then lay alternate layers of this thick mud and straw until the walls are of the height required. These are then made smooth and even with the spades and shovels of the builders, and when thoroughly dry and hard the rafters are added and the little building finished. The floors are also made of mud, and are thoroughly puddled, so that when dry they become perfectly smooth and hard. I never saw a board floor in Ireland except occasionally in a school room. The thatching of these dwellings is usually of oat straw, and is frequently quite artistic. Some men engage in thatching as a regular business, and a good thatcher is oftentimes in great demand. The chimney is usually built up from the outside, the fireplace being wide and open.

It was a house like one of these that we occupied in Killeagh, only that ours was possibly smaller than the average, containing but two rooms. There we lived, however, in comparative comfort for a number of years, and while I may say we were poor, our wants were few and easily supplied, so that even during the famine years we suffered far less than many of our neighbors. My aunts were employed at out-door labor when they could procure any, but being thrifty and frugal they managed to keep the wolf from the door even at those times when employment was not to be had. It was quite a common thing in those days, and doubtless is yet, to rent a portion of a field from some neighboring farmer, in which to plant potatoes—"con-acre," we used to call it—and my aunts would put in a quarter or half an acre every spring. If their potato crop turned out well, they always had some to sell the following winter, but if there happened to be a slight failure we had quite enough for our own use.

Mr. Richard Green, the resident agent of the landlord, Sir Arthur Brooke, usually employed a gang of men and women the greater part of the year to work around the demesne and often in Glenbower wood, and on those occasions my aunts were always at work. In the summer the men would chop down the smallest of the oak trees in the wood, and from these the women afterwards stripped the bark, which at the end of the season was shipped to different tanneries. The work of stripping being paid for at the rate of so much per hundred weight, they generally made fair wages for that country and period. Potatoes were the only food of the people, except the few gentry, and even well-to-do farmers seldom had any thing else. We had potatoes three times a day, and with our meals we sometimes had milk, sometimes codfish or a herring, and sometimes only salt, and in saying this I speak of all the peasantry. . . .

Having made my first communion I now had ample time to devote to my studies, and I learned rapidly in spite of many drawbacks. Through the hatefulness and jealousy of some of the townspeople, and especially of a man named Cook, our old teacher, Mr. Sullivan, was obliged to resign, and a Mr. Patrick Heffernan took his place. We scholars knew that some ill-feeling existed toward Sullivan, but we never once supposed that any change was contemplated until one Monday morning on going to school as usual we found the new teacher in charge. Many of the larger boys left at once, Mr. S. being much loved by his pupils. I was among those who remained, however, as I wanted to be at school, and there was no other within many miles that I could attend.

Mr. Heffernan, though possibly not as good a scholar as Sullivan, proved himself a very efficient and capable teacher, so that not only did all the old pupils return, but many from the neighborhood of the school he left followed him to Killeagh, and before long we had a larger and more flourishing school than ever. I was in the Fourth Reader when I began with Heffernan, but was very soon promoted from one study to another, and before many months I was advanced to the study of geometry.... If my memory serves me right, I began the study of geometry in the winter of 1843, in my eleventh year, having been at school up to that time nearly three years.

It was the general rule with us that there should be no cramming or slurring over anything, but that each branch should be thoroughly mastered, and it took us quite a long time to perfect ourselves in the various subjects we were learning. I labored under some disadvantages which the other boys in my class were not subject to, as I had to look after things at home while my aunts were away at work. I was excused every day at eleven o'clock, to get the dinner ready, and take it by a quarter past twelve to where they were. I generally had a coal fire in an open fire-place, over which was suspended the iron pot containing the potatoes. I used a bellows to make the fire blaze up more brightly, and while I worked the bellows with one hand I held my Euclid in the other. In that manner I used to study my problems for our afternoon exercises, and though I say it myself, there was not a boy in the class that knew his propositions any better....

But while I was thus pursuing my secular studies and making good progress under "Paddy" Heffernan, as our teacher was familiarly called, my spiritual studies were by no means dropped. Father Henry Power took special pains to watch over that portion of my training, and this he did by giving me every necessary instruction in all the doctrines and ceremonies of the Romish system. Other boys had their earthly fathers to watch over them and assume responsibility for their faith and conduct, but as I was an orphan, Father Henry took it upon himself to look after not only my spiritual but in a great measure my temporal welfare. I have already explained how he prepared me for my first communion, and now in the spring of 1843 he began to prepare me for confirmation, which took place early the following summer. . . .

Confirmation day at last arrived. The bishop took his seat inside the altar rails, having his mitre on his head and his bishop's crook in his hand, while we were marshaled before him in groups of six or eight at a time. Then, extending his hands over all those to be confirmed, he prayed for us all in general that the Holy Ghost might come upon us; then laying his hand upon each one in particular he anointed his forehead with the holy chrism, concluding by giving each one a slight blow on the cheek. That was how I received confirmation at the hands of Bishop Coppinger in the chapel at Killeagh in the summer of 1843, and I well remember that during all that afternoon and evening I wondered if I was any different from what I was before, or how did I receive the Holy Ghost?. . .

But now that I was thoroughly informed in all the Catholic doctrines and duties, and fairly launched on a career of Catholic usefulness, Father Henry next proposed that I should learn the answering of mass, and take my place on the altar, serving the priest at mass. To "answer mass," as it is termed, or to serve the priest on the altar, is one of the highest marks of honor that can be conferred upon a Catholic boy, not alone in Ireland but anywhere else, and I was only too glad therefore to accept with many thanks the very kind offer of Father Henry. . . .

Having completed my course of training for the service of the mass, I was now fairly installed on the altar. I felt quite proud of my position, and especially as I was thus removed from the terrible jam and crush at the second or eleven o'clock mass, when the priest had always something to say about that political agitation which was then so tremendously shaking the entire population of Ireland, Protestant as well as Catholic.

That agitation arose from the strenuous efforts put forth by Daniel O'Connell in the British Parliament, to effect what was commonly referred to as the "Repeal of the Union." The Act of Union passed in 1800 went into force in 1801, by which Ireland became an integral part of the British empire, and because of which Great Britain has been designated ever since as the United Kingdom of Great Britain and Ireland. Yet no Catholic, more especially no Irish Catholic, could hold any office whatever in Ireland under the British crown for a great many years after the union took place, while at the same time they were compelled by law to pay tithes for the support of foreign preachers speaking in a foreign tongue and representing a religion and church which they naturally hated.

It is a curious fact that the Irish language has no distinct word for Protestant. *Sasanah*, derived from the term "Saxony," is the expression for England, and *Sasanach*, derived from "Saxon," is an Englishman. Now notice a bit of adaptation in speech. Protestants came from *Sasanah*—England—bringing their religion with them, and the blundering government of the *Sasanach*, by act of law and oppressive enforcement, tried to compel its acceptance. Englishman and Protestant meant the same thing to all intents and purposes, so the same word came to be applied to both. In the minds of the people an Englishman was only a synonym for a Protestant. They hated the Protestant religion; then they also hated the representative of it—the Englishman—the *Sasanach*. Thus the word seeming to mean one as much as the other was soon in common use, and grew from association to be the strongest term of reproach in the Irish language. The *Sasanach* was hated because of his religion—the religion of Luther as they supposed. That hatred was transferred to the country of *Sasanah*, or to England, and has continued to this very day. How different would have been the condition had England at the time of the Reformation sent the gospel to the Irish people in their own pure, poetic Irish language, instead of sending among them foreigners, speaking a foreign tongue, representing a church they abhorred, while they were compelled by law to give of their little substance for the maintenance of both! England truly sowed the wind, and she has been reaping a whirlwind of rebellions and contentions and strife ever since.

O'Connell had been elected member of the British Parliament from Clare county in 1828, and through his ceaseless persistence the Catholic Emancipation bill was passed under the Duke of Wellington in 1829, thus removing the disability under which the Catholic Irish labored for so many years. After a time the abhorrent tithe system was also abolished, and he was now straining ever nerve to effect the repeal of the Act of Union. His monster gatherings from 1842 to 1845 at Tara, Mullaghmast and other historic places throughout Ireland are matters of history, and had he thought it proper he could have placed 2,000,000 men in the field along in '44 and '45, so great was the national excitement. To prove that he could do this, he caused a bonfire to be lighted at a certain time on the summit of every hill in Ireland.

Money was collected every Sunday at all the Catholic chapels in the country, and the congregations at Killeagh were so large that with all manner of crushing not even one-half the people could find room in the chapel, and the windows were thrown open so that those outside might hear what was said.

Aside from the general excitement an incident of local character happened about this time . . . , which impressed me very much. Sheep stealing was carried on to a most alarming extent throughout the parish of Killeagh. Not alone stolen but mutilated were so many that some rigorous means had to be resorted to in order to stop the destruction and loss. Father Maurice Power, the parish priest, denounced the guilty almost every Sunday from the altar, but in vain, and finally he obtained permission from the bishop to pronounce the severest punishment the church could inflict—the major excommunication. The Church of Rome arrogates to herself the exclusive power of not only expelling from her communion but also of closing and opening heaven itself, thereby admitting or debarring whom she will, and hence Father Power declared the fearful imprecation that Sunday morning, he at the same time closed the mass book, rang the little altar bell, and extinguished the candle, to indicate that the guilty parties, whoever they might be, were from that time forever shut out from any of the joys or glories of the heavenly world. I was on the altar and waited on the priest during the whole solemn ceremony, and I have never forgotten the occasion. It had a terrifying effect, and that was the last of sheep stealing and wanton cruelty to them.

Whenever I am asked what part of Ireland I came from, I almost invariably reply, "From Killeagh in the county Cork." Somehow I have always looked upon that pretty little inland town as my native place. Though I was not born there, and though I have lived in many other parts of the south of Ireland, in the counties of Cork, Limerick and Clare, having many pleasant recollections of nearly all of them, yet my happiest and most cherished memories are all associated with the years I spent in the handsome town of Killeagh. All my schoolboy days were passed there, those pleasant days of books and play and merry, careless boyhood, to which we all love to look back in after years—and there, too, in that little house which I remember so well, my aunts and myself lived for so many years, if not in entire comfort, at least in comparative contentment.

Killeagh is situated on the direct road running east and west between Youghal and Cork, the former being seven miles to the east of it, and the latter twenty-two miles to the west. A fairly large river flowing down from the north, through Glenbower wood, and almost swarming with speckled trout, divides it into two nearly equal parts, that portion of the town west of the river being known as Main Street, and that on the east—the street on which we lived—the Chapel Road, because in it was located the old Catholic chapel, near which also was the national school. Main Street and Chapel Road are connected by a substantial stone bridge, at the western extremity of which in my time was situated the residence of Father Power, and beyond that was the police barracks. I may add that these police barracks are found not only in every town but in every village in Ireland, no matter how few the number of houses.

Beginning near the eastern extremity of the bridge at the end of our street and running northward on a line with the river is a handsome private drive, the entrance to Glenbower wood from the Killeagh side, and as you passed up this drive there was on the right a large field, skirted on one side by evergreens and on the other three sides by a neatly trimmed hedge. One of the most interesting and impressive sights I ever witnessed in Ireland was on a Sunday afternoon along in the summer of 1843, when between two and three thousand men, old and young, were kneeling in rows the entire length of that field, while Father Mathew, passing between, placed his hands on the head of each one on his right and left and administered the temperance pledge, presenting also to each one a medal for which a shilling was charged. I have heard it said, and it was a general belief among the simple peasantry, that any one violating that pledge would be found when dead with his face turned downward in his coffin, as a sure token that he had gone to hell; but in spite of that foolish superstition only a very few kept it for life, while a large majority broke it within a few years.

Father Mathew was doing a great and good work, however, and with Daniel O'Connell was lionized by both priests and people, while both were regarded as the saviors of the country. O'Connell, commonly styled "the Liberator," was becoming more and more aggressive. His agitation, both inside and outside of the House of Commons, was daily becoming more persistent, and as his work was announced each Sunday from every Catholic altar throughout the country, the public excitement was intense. Father Theobald Mathew, the apostle of temperance, was also prosecuting at the same time his powerful crusade on behalf of temperance. Every one, both old and young, was taking the pledge and receiving his medal, and the poor, confiding, superstitious peasantry got it into their heads that surely God, through the means of his servant in making them a sober people, was thus preparing the country for that national uprising which they supposed would be imminent should O'Connell's parliamentary tactics fail and repeal of the Act of Union be finally refused by the British House of Commons.

We come now to the year 1844. There was an unusually large potato crop that year, and the low price at which they were sold was unprecedented, in fact many of the small farmers scarcely considered it worth their while to haul them from the field. In 1845 the people planted their potato crop as usual, but in the fall, when the time for digging came, instead of the fair-skinned tuber of the years previous they found that every potato in the ground was covered with a black crust, and hence 1845 has come to be referred to among the older people as "the year of the black potatoes."

According to their custom, my aunts had half an acre planted, but as was the case everywhere the crop was a total failure. It was all the same whether they were dug and hauled home from the field or left in the ground, they rotted anyhow; and before little more that half that winter was past the famine was upon us, and even as early as that time there was great suffering, especially among the poorer classes.

But now a strange thing happened. Fresh fish was always more or less plentiful in the Youghal market, but in the winter of 1845 they were so abundant all along the southern coast that I have seen scores of donkey carts loaded with fresh herrings and other smaller fish ranged along the Main Street of Killeagh every afternoon, as you may see wagons stand side by side in the public markets in this country.

The multitude of common people in Ireland never peeled potatoes before cooking them, always they were boiled and that, too, with their "jackets on," but now we must peel them first. The heavy black crust once off, a white potato appeared, that had a sweetish taste and was somewhat "soggy" when cooked. For a while the people lived on the fish and these peeled black potatoes, but not for long, as the whole crop so quickly rotted down, the black crust eating deeper and deeper into the potato, until the whole vegetable was black through and through, spoiled and utterly unfit for food for either man or beast. Then every one had to live on the fish that had so unaccountably swarmed to our shores....

But now the famine was upon us, starvation and death were staring us in the face, and the sole aim and object of every one seemed to be how to keep soul and body together. An appeal for help was sent over to the United

States, which was promptly responded to, and ship loads of corn meal were dispatched to the poor suffering Irish people just as speedily as they could be made ready. Relief depots were opened in every town and village and hamlet throughout the entire famine district. Tickets were issued calling for so many pounds of yellow meal, according to the number of persons in each family, but on the days of distribution every member of the household, men, women and children, had to present themselves to receive their little quota of meal, lest any family should draw more that they were allowed by the committee regulations. At first we got our yellow meal dry as it came from the mill, but after a while just as the allowance for each family was weighed and put into the bag it was dipped into a large barrel of water standing near, and you received your portion dripping wet. This was done, as I heard it said, to prevent any one selling his share, for otherwise it might be disposed of to procure tobacco or something else equally worthless.

The various scenes around those relief depots and the suffering among all classes of the people must have been witnessed to be at all appreciated. Everything now appeared to be at an end, and some of us boys did not seem to care whether "school kept or not." I have no recollection whatever as to how much I attended school during that terrible year of 1846, or whether I attended at all. I was quite regular, however, in my attendance on the altar, both on Sundays and during the week, and I remember distinctly that one week-day morning as Father Henry was celebrating mass we heard an angry altercation in the street in front of the chapel gate. Some farmers on their way to Youghal with their loads of grain were attacked by an excited mob for attempting to ship the grain out of the country, and the priest hurrying out without even waiting to remove his robes averted bloodshed by his timely presence, and coaxed the farmers to return home. Something like that occurring almost every day furnished excitement enough, but it was of a different kind from that of previous years, and some of the scenes and incidents witnessed were pitiable and heartrending in the extreme. One afternoon of that same summer of 1846 I saw a pale, emaciated woman, with three half-naked children tugging at her ragged skirt, slowly drag herself along the street, evidently on her way to the relief depot, but before she was anywhere near the place she fell exhausted on the stone pavement, being almost starved to death. She was lifted up and borne into the nearest grocery store, and there because of her weakened condition they had to feed her with a spoon as you would a baby. I heard afterwards that she recovered.

There is always more or less red tape connected with the distribution of relief funds or relief supplies. It was so in the case of the Chicago fire, it was so in the case of the Johnstown flood, and unfortunately it was so to a very large extent in the case of the Irish famine of '46 and '47. Committee meetings were frequent enough, but as a general thing instead of devising the best and most speedy methods of affording the necessary relief, they were very often the cause of delay and consequent suffering. On one occasion a ship load of corn meal was sent from America to the city of Cork, and through some mismanagement on the part of those in authority that vessel had to lie in the harbor for over two weeks before she could land her load of provision! It took nearly two weeks more before that provision was distributed to the various relief depots, and all this time the people of the little town of Skibbereen, some distance west of Cork, were dying of actual hunger, so much so that they killed and ate their donkeys, and it was reported that in one instance several persons were found dead in their little huts, with their faces, feet and hands mutilated by rats.

To add to the general hardship there was no employment anywhere for the people, neither among the neighboring farmers nor among the gentry round about. Every one seemed to feel the awful pressure of the times, and it was to devise some plan by which the hordes of idle men could be profitably set to work that most of those committee meetings were held. Many schemes were proposed, but for a time none seemed to be feasible, until at last a system of public works was projected by which employment was provided on the public highways. Some men were put at work breaking stones, some at digging away the more hilly parts of the roads to make them level, and others at opening up new roads wherever necessary or desirable, and hence 1846 came to be referred to as "the year of the public works."

A meeting was held at one time in the police barracks at Killeagh. The deliberations lasted from ten o'clock in the forenoon to about five o'clock in the afternoon, but nothing was accomplished. The parish priest, Father Power, exasperated no doubt beyond the power of endurance, came out after the meeting adjourned, and standing on a chair in front of the barracks shouted so that all could hear him, "These people, it seems, have nothing better for you than that you go home and eat grass!" The street was crowded all day with hungry men, and when they heard that vehement utterance of the priest they let a most terrific yell of anger and defiance. The cry, "To the mill! To the mill!" was at once responded to; a mad rush was made toward the mill across the river, the iron gate was speedily forced from its fastenings, the door of the mill broken down, and there was not a pound of flour, meal, wheat, or anything else of that kind that they did not bring out and pile up in heaps on the bridge. They wished to show what they could do, and what they would do if driven to desperation. The priest interfered, however, and after a while they carried every grain of the stuff back again, much as their families and themselves were in want, and fastened up the door of the mill. They were promised that the next day something would be done for them, but on the next day when they came they found every shop in the town closed and the street lined with horse dragoons from one end to the other. There was considerable excitement and many angry mutterings were heard, but everything passed off quietly, and no collision between the soldiers and the men took place. That was not the case at Youghal, however, a week or so after, for there a most desperate riot occurred. Men and women, maddened by hunger, attacked the stores, and when the cavalry appeared as they did at Killeagh they were soon driven before that angry mob, many of them, both horses and riders, being hurled over the wharf into the harbor.

Those were indeed times of untold hardship and misery, but times of still greater suffering were approaching. Now all religious differences were hushed, threats or defiances were no longer heard, but one saw everywhere the compressed lip and the tearful eye, and heard the eager questioning as to what measures should be taken for the people. The Protestant clergy in many instances nobly arose to their duty. In almost every parsonage you found the adjunct of a soup kitchen, and beheld the parson's family doling out the daily supplies....

During that never-to-be-forgotten year of 1846 our little family did not seem to share to any great extent in the general suffering around us. We received at stated periods our ordinary allowance of corn meal; sometimes my aunts went for it, and sometimes I did. Occasionally we got the white meal which they made into bread, but more frequently the yellow meal, of which they made mush, or as it was termed in Ireland, "stir-about." They had a little money saved up, and I remember that about the end of autumn they bought some barley flour from the mill, which enabled us to tide over the winter months, at any rate there was no pinching want in our home, as was the case with nearly all our neighbors, and Christmas day ... was passed without unusual anxiety or worry. Little did we think—little did anyone think—of the awful suffering, the fearful distress, the agony, the scenes of woe and death to which we were hastening in the year to come.

It was the beginning of the 1847 and "the famine was sore in the land," but another scourge more to be dreaded, because far more terrible and more destructive in its ravages, was coming upon us. The famine of '46 was surely heartrending enough as to its direful results, but who can adequately picture the awful misery, the suffering and the widespread desolation caused by the black fever of '47! The Rev. Canon Hayman, an honored minister of the church in Ireland, who was at that time an active participant in the work of relief at Glanworth, near Fermoy, in the northern part of the county Cork, thus briefly describes his experience during that time of trial and anguish: "'The famine was sore in the land,' and in its train came the fever that swept away unnumbered victims. Medical men and ministers of different denominations succumbed in numbers to the pestilence; yet none flinched, for the people clung to us as their preservers. The work of relieving distress went on; but after a time the misery outgrew human help. We toiled continually, and when we had done our best were lost in bewilderment. In some instances whole families died, and they lay unsepulchered until we pulled down their homes over them for entombment. I cannot, however, even at this lapse of time, describe these horrors."

It was about the beginning of February, if my memory serves me right, that the black fever broke out in Killeagh and vicinity, and very soon its deadly havoc became widespread. My Uncle John Cunningham's family, consisting of himself, my Aunt Elizabeth and five children, lived at a little place called Ballyverigan, quite close to the Atlantic, and only a short distance from Gurtrue. His chief occupation was gathering sea-weed, which he sold to the neighboring farmers for manure, earning at best only a bare pittance, but since the famine began even that was gone, and the little family had passed through great hardship. The pestilence raged with uncontrollable fury in the neighborhood of Killeagh, and the first we heard it broke out in the uncle's family, carrying off the three youngest children in a few days. My aunts made inquiry from day to day as well as they could, in order to learn if any more of the family were sick, and very soon word was brought that the mother herself was taken down. Ballyverigan was only about five miles from Killeagh, and the day after learning of their sister's illness they sent me out to see her and to take her a little money. There she lay, having no care, no medical attendance, not even a neighbor to lend a hand, moaning and tossing in the delirium of that awful pestilence, and her condition was the condition of all. The next we heard she was dead. She died on Friday evening and was buried the following Sunday.

Both my aunts attended the funeral, and that evening when they returned home my Aunt Margaret said, "Mary, dear, you need not get much meat for supper; I don't think I shall eat any." It was Easter Sunday, and they always managed to have a little meat then and at Christmas. Monday morning came, and my poor aunt was unable to rise. She too was stricken down. Tuesday morning Father Henry Power sent the doctor, Dr. Eames, and he immediately pronounced her sickness to be that malignant scourge, and ordered her to be taken at once to the Infirmary at Castlemartyr, a small town three miles west of us. I was sent that morning to Ballymacoda with a message to my Uncle David, and when I returned that afternoon she was gone, and I never saw her again alive. My Aunt Mary was fairly beside herself with grief. They had always been together and loved each other devotedly, and now Margaret had been conveyed in a little donkey cart to the hospital possibly never to return.

My aunt was taken to the hospital on Tuesday, died the following Friday, and was buried on Sunday. We received word of her death, and Sunday morning I was sent up to Tom Hickey, our old friend at Glenawn, with the request that he send a horse and cart to take her body to the burying-ground. He hitched up at once, and calling on our way for my Aunt Mary we went to Castlemartyr. The coffin was brought out and put into the cart. My Aunt Mary sat at one side and I at the other, and thus we passed through Killeagh and out by the Youghal road to Clonpriest, where we buried her beside my father and Uncle William. While they were filling the grave I fell forward unconscious. I was lifted up into the same cart we came in, and taken home brought down with the same pestilence that was scattering such ruin and desolation and death all around. I cannot tell of the poignant grief of my poor remaining aunt. She must have been distracted.

I was now surely to be the next victim. Aunt Mary laid down for a little while that terrible Sunday night. On Monday she went about the house like one dazed. She laid down again on Monday night, but on Tuesday morning she was unable to rise. We were in the same bed, she lying on the inside and I on the outside, without a soul to help us or hand us so much as a drink of water.

On Friday morning at about nine o'clock, as I was leaning on my right arm looking down upon her, her life went out peacefully and quietly, and I was left alone with my dead. At first I thought she had fainted, and screamed for help as loud as I was able. Our next neighbor, Norry Kelly, hearing my scream came to the door, and I told her my aunt had fainted. She ran to the priest's house a short distance away, and Father Henry came immediately, but when he saw her he pronounced her dead. He at once started a messenger on horseback to tell my Uncle David what had occurred.

That afternoon my uncle arrived. He was always a sober, steady man, but he dreaded the fever, so the better to keep off the disease, as he thought, and at the same time rouse his courage in the face of the terrible scourge, he had made himself quite drunk. With the help of the priest he lifted my aunt out of the bed and laid her on the floor. He then went out and procured some rough boards to make a coffin, as he had done for his other sisters, and on Sunday forenoon they carried my Aunt Mary off in the same cart which was used for my Aunt Margaret and buried her beside all the others.

And there they lie, our once happy little family, my beloved aunts and their two noble brothers, beside the moaning waves of the Atlantic waiting for that glorious morning, which I rejoice to think is now not far off, "when all that are in their graves shall hear his voice and shall come forth." Thus in three short weeks those three loving sisters were taken off, and all who were near and dear on earth to me were gone. . . .

Now I was not only all alone but was also stricken down by the same dread monster that had desolated our peaceful little home, and with no apparent chance of recovery. My Uncle David before leaving for home secured some old woman to take care of me, but I learned afterwards that she did me more harm than good. Father Henry came to see me nearly every day, however, and after a long struggle the fever at last passed away, contrary to all expectation, and I began to get well. The old woman was sent away, and the priest took it upon himself to care for me. When I was able to be about again I inquired after her, and they told me that she had been found dead one day in a neighboring field. It was altogether six weeks before I was strong enough to take any outdoor exercise. . . .

It was now about time that I should leave that little house where we had lived so long! Every house on our side of the street had been long since torn down, most of the people having died and a few managing in some way to go to America, but all were gone—their little homes and gardens were leveled, trees were planted where they once stood and a high stone wall built in front. Our house was the last, and now the landlord was anxious for me to leave. And so Uncle David came one day and took me to his own house in Ballymacoda. He was a carpenter by trade, as I have mentioned, and one of the best in all that section of country, and it was his desire that I should stay with him and learn the trade also. During the summer months of that year of woe (1847) he was engaged with other carpenters in building long low wooden sheds all around a large field about two miles from Ballymacoda, to be used as fever hospitals. I took him his dinner ever day after going to live with him, and felt quite an interest in his work because of my own experience. There were quite a few of those temporary hospitals scattered here and there, and deaths were so numerous in them all that every morning cart-loads of dead bodies were hauled away and buried in trenches dug for the purpose in another field not a great distance off. In 1846 we had only famine, but now in 1847 we had both famine and fever. The population of Ireland was between eight and nine millions in 1845, and when the dark night of death had passed there were only about four and a half millions of people left.

Mary Jane Hill Anderson was a Protestant woman from Bailieborough, County Cavan. She emigrated to the US in 1850 with her Presbyterian husband, Robert Anderson. Her manuscript, written in 1922, details her childhood in Cavan and her family's life in rural Illinois and Minnesota. She entitles her writing, "Autobiography of Mary Jane Hill Anderson, Wife of Robert Anderson." Mary Jane wrote this manuscript when she was ninety-five years old, dedicating it to her children, whom she hoped "may find in it something more than a chronicle of events."

Childhood

I was born in Bailieborough, [County Cavan,] Ireland, September 8, 1827. My earliest recollection of my childhood is of an evening when I was about four years old. My mother was sitting sewing, with a shawl around her shoulders, her sewing basket beside her and the light coming from a candle in a tall stand, somewhat like the modern floor lamp. She was telling me about heaven and hell, and that if I were a good child on earth I would go to heaven and be happy always, but if I were bad I would go to the other place, (she made it plain to my childish mind,) and be with bad people.

I said I wouldn't stay there, and she replied, "Oh, but you would have to. You couldn't leave—you would be there forever and ever."

"But, Mother," I asked, "what is forever and ever?" And she gave me a lasting illustration as follows: "Do you see that high hill over there, dear? Well, if a bird came and carried away a grain of sand every seven years, then when he had carried away the whole hill, it would be only the beginning of forever." I must have understood it, for it startled me so that I jumped up and upset the candlestick.

It could not have been long after that when she told me I could go to church with her if I'd sit very still, and if I could tell her something of what the minister said, she would take me again. Child-like, I wanted to go again, and I tried to grasp a word or two, saying it over and over, but I lost it, so I put the whole time in, trying to catch a word and losing it in the effort to remember another, until I remembered only a part of the benediction. When we were going home Mother asked me what I had heard, and I told her the little word I had tried so hard to remember: "Amen".

And she said, "Well, yes, dear, he did say that, and you were so quiet I believe you may go every Sunday." In spite of the fact that it was a long and tedious service, I was eager to go again.

The little Episcopal church which we attended was within walking distance of our home. It was of gray stone, as I remember it, with a slate roof and a belfry; the seats uncushioned and of dark wood. The morning service was read by the rector, but he was assisted by a clerk, who raised the tunes and led the congregation in responsive reading. After this part of the service the rector went into the vestry, put on a black gown and ascended into a high pulpit, from which he preached a lengthy sermon.

When I was a little older I went to Sunday school before the service and again after the service, which made a pretty long day. There was a stone wall around the church and an iron gate in front. The older boys and girls, who preferred walking home together to staying, hurried out, but I remember one day the minister, however he did it, was waiting at the gate with a cordial but firm invitation, to turn them back.

Mother and Father were very congenial. Mother had good business judgment, and Father always deferred to it. Mother, I think, was more ambitious than Father, and wanted her family to "Be somebody", but Father was always ready to carry out her plans. She was systematic and thrifty, a wonderful woman, really. Father was very quiet, a man of few words, generous, forgiving, always ready to do someone a good turn, even if he had done him a bad one. In fact, he didn't talk much, but he lived his religion.

In the congregation of six hundred, Mother and Father were considered the handsomest couple. Father was tall and broad-shouldered, and carried himself well. Mother was of medium height, with a plump figure, blue eyes and a beautiful complexion.

Father had several farms, of from five to fifteen acres, each having good buildings, which he rented to tenants, in exchange for work. He did what might be called intensive farming. Each tenant had a garden plot large enough to raise his own vegetables and potatoes, and fuel from the peat bog. There was, of course, no wood in Ireland to burn, or even to build with.

School Days

At that time there were no free schools. Therefore, only those who could afford to pay for it had an education. And oh, the old schoolmasters! How they struck terror to our young hearts! The man who was teacher when I was a little bit of a girl never whipped me but once, but I got many a blow with a ruler, on my hands, because in my terror of him I missed a word. One blow for a word, two for two, and so on. The names of all offenders were put on a slate, as there were no blackboards. They had to stay after school and be further dealt with. The upper part of the slate had a list of the names of pupils who had perfect lessons, and each one had the privilege of saving one offender from punishment. Oh, the longing looks that were cast on that slate! Really, there was very little happiness in school days. The children were terrorized and parents were blind enough to submit to it. Terrence Brady, one of the school masters, pulled the ear off William Bannon, who afterwards became my brother-in-law. Then he took his handkerchief and bound it up and sent him home. This was too much, though, and his father had Brady turned out of the school.

There was no recess or noon rest, and we munched on our noon lunches any time we felt like it. We could not leave the room without the "pass", a pig's tooth with a string attached to it, which hung on a nail on the door. Each child must wait until the pass was available. Of course we all took occasion to use it as often as we could, but sometimes, sad to say, nature rebelled at the long wait, and the innocent offender was severely whipped.

Another form of punishment was called putting the head in stocks. The child got down on all fours, with his head between the master's knees, the master using his back for a table. If the child caused the master to make a blot, the time of his punishment was lengthened. The end of our reign of terror came when a drunken schoolmaster whipped ten boys, the oldest of whom was fifteen years of age, for some slight offence, and compelled them to take off all their clothes before the whole school.

Anyone who could hire a house and get enough scholars to pay tuition could teach school. It did not seem to matter much how little he knew.

The first schoolhouse I went to was called the preaching house, and was built by a Mr. Adams, who was wealthy and public-spirited. It was used on Sundays for religious services, and for school on week days. It was a long, narrow building, with a fireplace in one end, which, needless to say, did not give much heat in the back of the room. The children took turns sitting around it to get warm—the teacher keeping track of the time.

My grandfather Gilmore had a large house, and up to this time everyone wove his own linen, but factories were beginning to come in, and fewer of the hand looms were used. So Grandfather conceived the idea of using the weaving room for a schoolroom, and getting a good teacher for his own children and grandchildren, which he did. I went to school there, living in his home as long as I could be spared from helping Mother with the young children. Mr. Hillis, the schoolmaster, was a highly educated man, and in his school my two uncles were prepared for Dublin College. Aunt Margaret afterwards taught Lord Farnham's high school on his estate, and Aunt Mary Ann taught the model school in Bailieborough. Grandfather lived just outside the town.

Lady Young, wife of Sir John Young, whose estate was near our home, had a school in her castle for all the young girls of the neighborhood. There we learned to do all kinds of fancywork; knitting, crocheting, drawn work and embroidery. She let us earn pin money by selling our work for us in London. Queen Victoria was a young woman then, and we made a beautiful white silk cambric dress for her, embroidered in peacocks, and a dozen elaborate drawn work handkerchiefs with embroidered centers. I was proud to be permitted to do part of the work on the handkerchiefs.

Girlhood

My girlhood was spent in quiet homelife as a farmer's daughter. When we were small, Mother kept help, but as soon as we were able to help her, she did without, because, while there were plenty of servants, they were so deceitful and immoral that she could not bear to have them in the house.

We had to take care of the garden, do the housework, sewing and knitting, and work on what girls of the present day would call their hope chests, piecing quilts, making fancywork, embroidering on linens, and so forth. Mother had all this work ready for us in the evening, and one of the family—often Father, who was a beautiful reader—read aloud out of some good book, generally history. We had a bright fire in the grate, put on our prettiest clothes, and this was the time the young men usually dropped in. In winter it grew dark so early that the evenings were long.

We had singing schools, fairs, spelling schools, and occasional parties around the neighborhood, and young people were carefully chaperoned. Parents, brothers or uncles always went with girls to all these places. One of the jolliest occasions for the young people was when the peat was harvested. Just after the crops were in, it had to be cut and piled to dry out for the winter's fuel. It was something like a thick sod, and made a clear, hot, clean fire. The day's work generally ended with a dance, if someone could be found who was clever enough to play on the fiddle.

Courtship and Marriage

Robert Anderson had a grist mill, and his farm joined Father's. He had a family of eleven children, all of whom lived to be men and women. He and my father exchanged work on the farm, and his son Robert often came over to help. He made himself so agreeable that Father grew very fond of him. When it became evident that he was paying some attention to me, Mother was not pleased, although she had no fault to find with him. Several of his brothers and sisters were already in America, "doing well", and she was afraid he would follow and take me away from her, where she would never see me again.

I had other, and from a financial standpoint, more desirable suitors. One man in particular was encouraged by Mother and my aunts because they thought it would be such a suitable match. My aunts lavished affection on me at this time, and often invited me to visit them. This man, whose name was John McIlwain, was forever under my feet. He was respectable, rich, and middle aged. Oh, how I hated the dour old face of him!

On day Mother and Father had to drive in to Sherkuk, the nearest village, to do some marketing, and before leaving, Mother said to me, "Mary Jane, I want you to sack up those goose-feathers in the feather house, so they will be ready to take the next time we go to town. The children can help you, so you will get them done—and be sure to keep the doors closed." The feather house was a small stone building in the orchard, where we plucked the geese and stored and cured the feathers.

The children and I were working industriously on our task, when I heard a familiar whistle at the gate. It was Robert, for you may be sure he lost no time in coming down when Mother and Father drove out of sight. They passed the Anderson house on the way to town. I went down to the gate to meet him. The little girls, who soon grew tired of working alone, ran out to play, and when I next thought of the feathers, and looked back, such a sight as met my eyes! Clouds of feathers were floating on the breeze, and the whole countryside seemed covered with them. I had forgotten Mother's parting word about the doors. "Lord help us, Robert, what shall I do?" I cried. We ran as fast as we could to the feather house, but it was too late. By the time we got the doors closed almost all the feathers had escaped.

When Mother and Father drove into the yard that evening there were still plenty of them flying around. Mother said not a word, but made her way to the feather house and opened the door. When her sharp eyes discovered the empty room and unfilled sacks she said, "Mary Jane, has Robert been here today?" I will spare you the details of her wrath and will only say that I was confined to my room for a week, with plenty of time for thought, enough hand-work to keep me busy, for Mother was thrifty, and only bread and water for my meals.

In my desperation I thought of a plan that seemed to me the only way out of our difficulties, and was sometimes used as a last resort to bring the old folks around; for the young people of Ireland had very little to say about their love affairs in my day. It was not unheard of for young couples to run away together—always going to a friend's house, taking someone along as chaperone, there to await developments. This was considered a most disgraceful episode, and the two families would meet and agree on a suitable dowry for the bride to be, and arrange for a wedding, and usually parental forgiveness and blessing followed.

My week in solitary confinement did not "break my spirit" and fulfill my Mother's hopes, and at the first opportunity Robert and I slipped away to the home of his sister, Ann Jane Brown, who lived near, taking my sister, Ann Eliza, with us. I think I never would have had the courage to go if it had not been for her support and encouragement. She was always on our side.

Well, we had asserted ourselves in a convincing manner. So there was nothing left for our parents to do but meet together and arrange for my dowry and plan a wedding at the little grey stone church. As was the custom, banns were read by the rector at the morning service, three weeks before the wedding. We were married by our rector in February, 1850. The wedding was very simple, with none of the festivities of a wedding of today. We had no attendants. I walked down the aisle on Robert's arm, and my father came in with the minister and gave me away. Only the two families and a few relatives and close friends witnessed the ceremony.

But after the wedding the fun began. Every young Irishman aspired to own a spirited saddle horse, and those of the well-to-do families usually had handsome, blooded animals. When there was a wedding in prospect these horses were fed and groomed with extra care, so that they would be in the best of form for the race to the bride's home, which always followed the ceremony. Attired in immaculate black broadcloth suits and high silk hats, the young men mounted their steeds and galloped to the bride's house, the winner being the first to kiss her.

After we were married Father would gladly have divided his farm with us, as he had no son, but a new rule had come in which deprived him of the privilege. Farms were made larger, instead of smaller. There were several of the Anderson family still to be provided for, and as three of the older ones were already in America and prospering, it was inevitable that we should follow. When I bid Mother goodbye, she said to me, "Mary Jane, if I had all the world to choose a son-in-law from, it would be Robert, except that he is taking you away where I shall never see you again. I want you to tell your children that in all your life you have never said an ugly word to me, and never displeased me except in this one thing. After all, perhaps you had a right to."

For several weeks before we left, my three little sisters, Margaret, Sarah, and Fannie, insisted on sleeping in the sewing room, and Mother, thinking it but a childish whim, allowed them to do it. The night before we left, Robert and I went in to say goodnight and goodbye to them, and he knelt down beside the bed, and oh, how tenderly he prayed, as only he could. When, in the morning, the children found the impressions his elbows had made in the bed they said, "Oh, here are the holes where his elbows were. We will never make the bed, to spoil them." Into my hands that night they had slipped three little samplers, on which they had been working industriously. I have them still, after more than seventy years. "Behind a frowning Providence He hides a smiling face"; "Mizpah" and "Trust in God, for the Lord will provide." They were seven, nine and ten years old.

I wanted to get away before the daylight, so I would not have to see the old home I was leaving forever. But it was a little later than I hoped, when we started. The last thing I saw was Father, Mother and the children standing at the gate. I never saw them again, except Margaret, who came to America after she married John Lucas, and Ellen, who was a widow with five daughters. She came to Sacramento, where I visited her after a lapse of fifty years. There was nothing familiar to me in her looks, but oh, how much we had to talk over!

The Journey

We travelled all day, a distance of about thirty miles, before reaching Dundalk, a small seaport where we took a boat for Liverpool. An old man named Jemmie McGivney, who had been a servant in my father's house since his boyhood, drove the horse and cart which took us and our earthly goods. Jerry, the little horse, was a great pet in the family, and when I left him, knowing that he was the last thing connected with home that I would see, I kissed him on the cheek. As the boat got farther from land I watched the twinkling lights of Dundalk, seeing them dimly through my tears—the last sight of my native land.

We spent the night sitting in a life boat on deck. Everyone around us was in a different state of seasickness, and we found the life boat the cleanest and most comfortable place. By staying out in the open air we were not so sick as most of the others. We reached Liverpool in the morning and went to the house of Robert's cousin, William Breaky, where we stayed several days, waiting to get passage on a boat that was not too crowded. We sailed from Liverpool August eighth, 1850.

Travelling on sea seventy years ago was not what it is in these days. Our boat was a sailing vessel and it took six weeks and three days to reach New Orleans. There were three hundred passengers. The "Forest King", which sailed the week before, carried a thousand passengers, and that wasn't unusual. Often some disease broke out and the ship could not land. We were fortunate in that our journey, from start to finish, was not delayed. We had two bad frights, though.

Once the cookhouse on the deck took fire and it spread to the sails and ropes. The captain was wild, and the sailors in confusion. Sails and ropes were cut and dropped burning into the sea, and the fire was finally put out.

We were sitting on deck one afternoon—this was late in August—and the weather was as calm and beautiful as any day I ever saw, when the captain came out, and with that awful voice of his shouted at the sailors. They scampered, or fairly flew, up the masts like birds. The ship was in full sail, and in an incredibly short time they had the sails all rolled in and tied securely to the masts. Before all the passengers could get below deck the waves were rolling over. The storm raged all night, and until the afternoon of the next day. Oh, I couldn't describe it—it was terrible!

Nobody thought of eating, except a steerage passenger who took his frying pan up to the galley, which was on the first deck. As he was going back with his dinner in the frying pan he passed us and said, all the while holding securely on to the pan, "The ship has sprung a leak. Get to your knees, all of you; it may be at the bottom in twenty minutes. The carpenter is coming down to see if he can mend the hole." Sure enough, in about five minutes, he did appear with his lantern and tools, and disappeared into the lower regions. Everybody believed the man.

All the time the storm was raging, boxes and trunks and various objects were flying back and forth across the decks and endangering the sides of the ship and the passengers. After the great storm was over the sea was rough for a day or two.

My feeling when I thought I was face to face with death, with people praying and crying around me, was like Saint Peter's when he was sinking: "Save, Lord, or I perish." Over and over I said it, and Father sat with his arms around me, holding me tight in silent prayer. Oh, of how little value are the things of the world when death is near. If that ship had been filled with diamonds no one would have cared for them.

The trip was for the most part pleasant. When we reached New Orleans the tide was out and we had to wait for several hours, as the harbor was shallow at low tide. While we were waiting two rowboats came out, filled with winter fruit, to sell to the passengers. There were three negroes in each boat. I had never seen a negro before, and as they looked up with their big eyes and grinning teeth they looked so awful to me! "Oh, Robert," I said, "if these are the people we have come to live amongst, I feel like going home." "Why, you foolish thing," he said, "there are other people here, just like there are anywhere."

When the tide came in, a tugboat came and towed us to the docks. In about an hour a river boat came alongside the ship and took all the passengers who were going to Galena, Illinois, and their belongings. This boat had an engine and a stern wheel. Cordwood was used for fuel. The boat had two decks. There was a kitchen and dining room on the upper deck, and passengers did their own cooking, getting supplied when the boat stopped at the towns. The berths were also on this deck. Freight and engines were on the lower one.

The first day, such a sweet looking woman with gray hair came and sat down beside me, and questioned me about where I came from, and my destination. When she found that I had just come off the ship she said, "Now I want to tell you something you probably do not know. There has been a terrible epidemic of cholera all summer. It is nearly over now, but there are some cases still. If you do as I tell you, I am sure you will reach your friends in Galena safely. Do not eat any kind of uncooked food—fruits or vegetables—and cook only enough for each meal, keeping nothing over. And never sit out on deck in the evening air. Go to bed early after you have a good supper." We followed her advice strictly, and did not get it.

There was a merry party of young people sitting on deck one evening eating fruit and candy. Before morning one of the young men, a fine healthy looking young fellow, was dead, and three others on the trip died just as suddenly and were buried without ceremony at the next landing-place. But the bodies were kept on board until it was convenient to stop, which in one case was two days later. This was a German woman, mother of three children. She borrowed some cooking utensils before supper. Before midnight I saw a light at her berth and the doctor was there. She died about midnight. Her coffin was a dry-goods box and it was placed in front of our berth. I had to climb over it to get in. All the other passengers kept away, (this disease was so very contagious,) but I could not resist the wails of the motherless hungry baby, and I cared for it until we reached St. Louis.

One morning I went down to the pump on the lower deck to get water for our breakfast. It was still dark, and I stumbled over some object, which when I picked myself up I discovered to be the body of another victim, a man about forty years old. Needless to say, I did not wait to get the water. After we passed St. Louis there were no more cases.

While we escaped the cholera, Father had boils on his back, and spent most of the time in his berth. I love to think it over—how the Lord led us, and raised up friends for us all the way. A kind old man waited on him like a nurse. He insisted on buying the food at the villages, and I cooked it for all of us, and made tea. I am sorry that I can't remember his name, but he lived just outside of Galena, and knew Aunt Jane Gray, Father's aunt, to whose house in Galena we went. We were three weeks on the river, just half as long as it took to cross the ocean.

Life in Galena

We were not expected, but Aunt Gray made us more than welcome. Father's two sisters, Martha Ritchie and Sarah Gamble, and his brother John, lived on farms about twelve miles out from Galena, at Beatty's Hollow. Martha lived nearer Hanover. She and I had been school girls together, and great chums. It happened that she was in town doing some trading, when we arrived. She intended to spend a week with friends but decided to go home, so we could go with her, if any of the neighbors were in town. She finally found the next neighbor to James Gamble, who took us with him, promising to take us out to Martha's the next morning. But Father stayed in Galena, intending to follow in a day or two.

Oh, will I ever forget that ride! The roads were frozen and rough. The man had a lumber wagon, and to make it worse, he was drunk. When anyone tried to pass us he whipped up his horses. I thought we would be thrown out, so I got down on the bottom on my knees and clung to the sides. All the way I was suffering, and when we reached Martha's I was helped out of the wagon. She sent for a neighbor woman and that night John was born. Father being in Galena, I went through the ordeal as best I could.

I shall never forget Martha's kindness. When she brought my baby to me and said, "Here's a dear little son to comfort you," I was so worn out that I replied, "Oh, yes, put him in at my back." But when morning came I was glad to have him in my arms. That was November seventh, 1850.

Right here I want to say that I can look back and see the Lord's hand leading us and raising up friends in our times of need. I had not even a few hours to spare at the end of a three month's journey until my time of delivery. I had no definite plans and no money; but I firmly believe it was His loving care that directed Martha to Galena. She, of all others, would have been my choice to be with me in my distress. There was no doctor; my husband was not there; but nature and Providence delivered me.

After I had regained my strength and we had visited around among the families we began to think what we could do to make a living for ourselves. There was nothing to do in the winter except wood cutting—making rails to fence the fields in, as the cattle ran loose—or cutting cordwood for firewood. James Gamble, Father's brother-in-law, offered this work to him, at $25 a month, and board for all of us.

At the end of the first day's chopping, his hands were so swollen and blistered that he could not work for a week. He had never used an axe. There were no trees to cut down in Ireland—all the woods belonging to estates were kept for their beauty. When I saw his hands I burst out crying, and remembering always my father's invitation to come back if we wanted to, I begged him to go. But he said, "Mary Jane, what would we go back with? It would take a lot of money for our passage, and our clothes are getting shabby. I wouldn't go back without new ones. Oh no, we can't go yet, but we will go later if you still feel this way about it." But when we had enough money we didn't want to go.

Adam Ritchie said one day, "Robert, how much money have you?" When he answered that he had eight dollars, Adam replied, "Well, now, I think you had better buy a couple of year-old heifers. They can run with mine, and soon they'll be cows. A man near here is selling out, and I think we can get them for about eight dollars." They cost twelve dollars, but Adam Ritchie put the other four into them himself.

We stayed at James Gamble's for a year and then moved over to Charlie Moore's, where we stayed three years. He had a great big farm, and needed help the year around. We had a little three room house, (for which we paid four dollars a month,) and a piece of ground for a garden where we raised enough vegetables and potatoes, and corn for chickens. We had our fuel, of course, and he gave us meadow land to cut the hay off for our stock, which at the end of four years had increased so that we had two cows and two young heifers.

In the Spring of 1853 John Mitchell, Father's uncle, came down from Minnesota to buy cattle. His was one of four families that had settled about twenty-five miles from St. Paul. By this time all the homesteads in Illinois had been taken up, and it was expensive to buy, so he persuaded Father to go up and look at Minnesota, which he did that fall. He found 160 acres which looked desirable, and left money to start a log cabin, as some improvements were necessary to hold it.

Journey to Minnesota

In the spring of 1854 we started for our final destination with a little money, seven cows, three of which we bought, one sheep, given us by Mr. Steel, a sow with a litter of pigs, presented by Adam Ritchie, plow, harrow, seed oats and corn, and quite a store of provisions—groceries, flour and hams. We had three children now; John, four years old, Robert James, two, and Samuel Gilmore, three weeks old. I was urged not to take the journey with so young a baby, but did not want to stay behind.

We went up the river to St. Paul, and nothing of particular interest happened. At St. Paul we took passage on a very small steamer, called the "Iola", which plied between St. Paul and Bloomington Ferry, on the Minnesota River. Freight had to be distributed carefully, or the boat would tip over. Frequently the passengers ran from side to side to balance it. Several times on the trip the boiler sprang a leak, causing a panic among the passengers. It was patched up as well as possible each time with bags of sand tied around the break, and they filled the boiler with buckets. After many delays we reached Bloomington Ferry, three days and a half after we started. A few hours should have accomplished it. The boat went on as far as Shakopee, and on the return trip it sank, and was never used again. Wasn't that a narrow escape?

Beginning Life in Minnesota

Father drove the stock from St. Paul. At Bloomington Ferry we stayed with William Chambers, who owned the ferry, and was married to Martha Mitchell, Father's cousin. Father got a wagon and took William's oxen and drove us to Billy McCoy's place in Eden Prairie, which was about a mile from our unfinished log cabin. This was in April, and Billy McCoy, with the kind generosity of the early settler, urged us to stay there until we got some crops in, and then we could finish our house.

It was here that our first great sorrow came to us. The house was on the edge of a meadow, and there was a little stream which at this time of the year overflowed. John and Robert wandered down to it and fell in. John somehow scrambled out, catching hold of the grass on the edge of the stream. His cries brought the men, who were home for dinner, but it was too late to save little Robert. I have always thought he might have been saved if we had known what to do, he was in the water such a short time.

There was no church or graveyard, so we buried him in a field of McCoy's, under a tree, until we could move his body. We made a little box of rough boards, and marked the place with a rail fence, to keep out the cattle. Several years went by, and we hoped to have a graveyard, but the tree was cut down and the fence taken away and we could never find the little grave. But the little body is in His safe-keeping; it will rise from there, for the Lord does not forget where we lie.

As Robert's father had died since we left Ireland, his mother sold out the mill and farm and was coming to America with the rest of the family, two girls and three boys. So Father blazed the trees to mark off 160 acres for his mother and brother James, and brother-in-law James Gamble. The others were not of age and could not take homesteads. One day a couple of men named Somers came to our house and asked, "Who lives here?" When Father told them they said, "Oh, you're the Anderson, are you? You aren't going to hold this land. Everywhere we go we see your name. It's Anderson here and Anderson there. Our colony is coming to settle this land." Father said, "No, I've settled this for my relatives and I'll hold it for them until they come in the spring." "Well," said Somers, "we can bring a thousand men and we'll drive off both you and your relatives." "All right," said Father, "bring your thousand men. I'll be ready for them, and I'll promise that you won't take a thousand away!" They never came back, but their colony located across Anderson Lake. The next year relatives came, and they had enough money to pay for the land. Eventually there were three sisters and five brothers living in Eden Prairie.

The Land Sale

The surveyors came the first summer, so we knew where our boundary lines ran and where our hundred sixty acres lay. Father had intended to take the heavily timbered land, but he couldn't do that and have the meadows too, so he gave up part of the heavy woods to his brother James and we took one forty with a big meadow; for he had enough timber. The next year the land sale was held at the land office in the village of Minneapolis. To get our title to the land we had to go to the court house and file our claim to the part we had selected. We had to pay $1.25 an acre, under the pre-emption laws, and to do a certain amount of improvement on each forty acres. After that we could prove up and get title. I had to go with Father so as to sign the application for the claim. Robert the second, named after the other baby, was an infant in arms. It was necessary to leave home in the night, for it was a long, slow trip with oxen. It took till nearly noon, and when we got to the court house there were a great many settlers there, all filing claims to the land they had settled on. There were only a few houses in the village. There was one hotel called the

"Bushnell House", where we had dinner. I went out and looked at the Falls of St. Anthony. They were all natural then—the government hadn't built the apron to preserve them from wearing away. I was impressed by the roaring of the cataract as I stood on the banks near the court house.

Late in the afternoon I was distressed to get home to the baby, but they couldn't get our application made out, there were so many other applicants. Finally Father got to a clerk and explained that I was in distress and must get home to nurse the baby, and the clerk said he would put our application through for ten dollars. Father paid him, but we never quite forgave the injustice. It was nearly dark when we started home. The journey was long and rough. The oxen moved at a snail's pace, and oh, how I suffered with my breasts! No one will ever know what I endured on that trip. It was nearly morning before we got home. But now we had a home! It was our own. There was a sense of ownership, and the feeling that we were free from the necessity of working for others. That feeling bore us through lots of hardships.

Father was the first in the neighborhood to adopt new improvements. We had the first sewing machine, a "Grover and Baker", and what a wonderful thing it was. The neighbors came from everywhere to have me stitch for them, and it seemed so easy compared with the slow hand sewing. We had the first reaper. It was a "McCormack Self-Rake". There was a big red wooden arm that went round and round, and to balance it there had to be a large iron ball on a long iron rod, as a sort of counter-weight. When the big red wooden arm came up over the reaper it looked as though it would come down on the horses' backs as it revolved. The horses were frightened and it was a hard task to get them used to it so they wouldn't shy at it and run away. We had the first orchard—ours was bearing apples before the others began to plant orchards.

There were no seeders in those days. The grain was sown by hand from a sack hung over the shoulder just as you see them in old pictures. Father was taken sick one spring before he finished seeding. There was a little corner of the field not yet seeded. The rest of the field was sprouting and I persuaded him to let the boys finish it. They got the sack hung over John's shoulders and one would hold the sack open while another would scatter the seed. Father got up on his elbow and looked out of the window and said, "Well, thank God for a large family." We never had any cause to change that prayer.

After the crop was in Father sold two cows for one hundred dollars, which was a good price then. With this money he got lumber, windows and doors to finish the log cabin. It had one room, with a loft upstairs reached by a ladder.

Afterward we had a kitchen built on. We made most of our furniture, and with feather beds, dishes and a small cookstove we were quite comfortable. At first we had curtains to divide the rooms, the living room from the bed room, and afterward we built a partition across. We lived in the log cabin for eighteen years, and seven children were born there; Robert James, named after the other baby, Mary Jane, Ann Elizabeth, Joseph McCartney, Josiah Moore, Margaret Ellen and Agnes Emmaline. (In 1872 we built a good frame house and moved into it. We lived there until the fall of 1889.)

Here I think we spent our happiest days. We had a home of our very own, we were young and hopeful, and with our little family and life before us, and always work to do and the strength to accomplish it, what more could we ask?

The second year the land was brought into market, or held for public sale, and you had to pay the $1.25 an acre due, if you wanted to keep it. Nearly everyone had to borrow the money, for they had not raised enough crops to sell much. The money could be borrowed from eastern speculators, but the rate of interest was so high that many were unable to do it. We borrowed the two hundred necessary to pay for the land, paying twenty-five per cent interest.

That fall we picked, with the help of the neighbors, three hundred bushels of cranberries, and sold them for a dollar a bushel. This paid our debt and we had a little over. The marsh where the cranberries grew was very wet—the very thing that made them grow, but we did not know that. Thinking it would be much better to drain it, we did so. The next year we got only thirty bushels, but it grew into a good hay meadow. The thirty bushels were enough to buy a good cook stove, with an elevated oven.

Now, after two years, we had our home paid for, owed no man a cent, and could spend a little as we raised our crops, for comforts and the necessary machinery. What little Fannie had worked on the sampler had come true: "Trust in God, for the Lord will provide." Surely He did provide the cranberries to pay for our home.

Right here, while we are talking about cranberries, I must tell you of my first experience with Indians, and how we came to discover the cranberries. One forenoon in October, Father was cutting some late hay down in what we called the Blind Marsh. He said he would like to have me bring out his supper, so that he would not have to lose any time—the days were getting so short. He said he could finish the piece if I did so, and please to bring lots of tea because he got so thirsty. He told me just how to get there, and about four o'clock I started out with a basket of good things and a large pot of tea.

Before I reached the meadow I had to cross a smaller one with a hillside and a few trees beyond it. Just before I reached this little meadow I saw several squaws picking some kind of berries into baskets. I had heard enough about Indians to make me afraid, but I thought these were only women like myself, and I needn't be afraid of them. My curiosity got the better of me, and I went nearer. The squaws paid no attention to me, but soon five or six men, naked from the waist up, sprang out of the tall grass, clutching their guns. I dropped my basket and pot of tea, and fled, all the while imagining they were after me, and not even turning my head to see. Finally, out of breath, and coming to the shelter of a large tree, I looked back. The whole crowd were sitting around, eating the lunch. I watched them until they had finished the last crumb, after which the squaws shouldered the sacks of berries, and went on their way. I ventured to get the dishes and basket, and looked to see what it was that they were picking. I discovered that it was cranberries. They had picked most of them, but it was the next year that we got the three hundred bushels.

Indian Stories

Many a time my grandchildren have climbed on my knee or into my bed in the morning and begged for Indian stories—"Real Indian stories, Grandma!" And so, although I have told them over and over, I want to leave them on record for those who have not heard them.

Big Indian

One very cold winter morning I was busy about my work. Father had left early with his ox team for St. Paul, and as the trip took two days he had his brother, Archie, come over and stay with me and cut rails in the wood lot. I was washing the breakfast dishes and turned to the stove to get a dipper of hot water, when lo and behold, right in the middle of the floor stood an Indian! Not a sound did he make, and he looked so big and terrible to me. He had a head dress of feathers, and his matted hair hung down his back. He wore a gay blanket around his shoulders, trousers and mocassins [sic] of buckskin, and a belt around his waist made of a snake's skin. From the belt hung all sorts of things—rabbits, squirrels and ducks that he had killed; knives, tomahawks, beads and elk's teeth.

I was so frightened that I was fairly glued to the floor, but I had heard that if you showed fear of an Indian, he would kill you, so gathering my wits together I asked him if he wanted something to eat. By motions and grunts he made it plain that he did, so I made coffee, fried salt pork and gave him some corn bread, which he ate ravenously. I thought I was safe enough while he was eating, but was not sure what he might do when he was through. I decided that if I could only get to Archie, out in the wood lot, before he had finished, he could protect us. But the children—how could I leave them? And I couldn't take them with me.

Hastily throwing a shawl about my shoulders I took the water pail and went out as if I were going to the well, but when I got around the corner of the house I threw the pail down and ran, or tried to, as fast as I could through the deep snow. I could hear the thud of the axe, and finally, panting and exhausted, I somehow got within calling distance. When Archie saw me he grabbed his gun and came to meet me. "Oh, Archie, Indian!" was all I could say. Then, "Save the babies, don't mind me", as he hurried to the house, leaving me to follow as best I could.

When he reached the cabin what a sight met his eyes! There in the middle of the floor sat the Indian, rocking the cradle with one foot, and John, who was about five years old, stood between his knees playing with the trinkets at his belt. When he saw Archie his eyes twinkled and he said, "White squaw heap 'fraid. Big Indian no hurt papooses." He stayed all night, rolling himself up in his blankets, and slipped out as noiselessly as he had come.

Every winter he made a visit to us in the same way, always bringing venison or bear or game of some kind, and sleeping on the floor. Finally his visits ceased, and we knew that he must be dead.

The Log Raising

All the houses and barns at this time and for many years after were made of logs, sometimes just left in the rough, and sometimes barked and squared, and then hauled onto the ground ready for the raising, which was often quite an occasion for festivity. It took all the men in the neighborhood to set the logs in place "up to the square", or ready for the roof. Such baking and brewing as was done by the women to feed the hungry men!

In the spring of 1855 James Anderson had a log raising to build his barn. For some reason I did not go, and as I was timid about staying alone, Mrs. Brewster, a widow who was like a fairy godmother to us all in time of need, stayed with us. About eleven o'clock, Ezra Paine, a boy about eleven years old, came to the door and said, "I was sent to tell the Anderson settlement that the Indians have broken out up on the frontier and are killing the people and burning the houses and villages, and the men were to meet at one o'clock at the Gould schoolhouse to decide whether to build a fort at Eden Prairie, or go to Fort Snelling for protection."

I told him to go over to the log raising to tell the men there, which he did after I had offered to go part way with him to show him the way through the woods. Of course there were very few roads at this time—mostly cow paths. Late in the afternoon we began to look for Father to come home, and we had the table set and the kettle boiling. It grew dark and he did not come. Then we put the children to bed, with their clothes on. We took turns standing outside, listening for his footsteps. At ten o'clock he had not come. Mrs. Brewster came in and said, "Oh, Mary Jane, the Indians are coming. Shakopee is on fire! What shall we do?"

I happened to remember that James Gamble was not very well, and probably was not at the raising, so I said, "Let us take the children and go over to the Gambles." We took them up and started; but before we went Mrs. Brewster, thrifty soul that she was, said, "Maybe after all we better pick up these dishes. The cat might break them." "Oh, never mind," I replied, "we may never be in this house again." And so we went out into the moonlit woods, fear in our hearts lest the Indians should be lurking in the shadows. We heard a footstep, and hid in the bushes, but a familiar cough announced the approach of Father. He took the baby out of my arms, turned its little face up to the moonlight and said, "Thank God, dear, they may kill your body, but they cannot kill your soul."

This was not very reassuring to my already overstrained nerves, and as we went home I had such a bad nervous chill that I could hardly walk. I think I know how it is possible for one to die of fear. When we reached home the singing of the kettle on the stove welcomed us. How many times that old teakettle, (a heavy iron one, by the way,) ministered to our needs. They bathed my feet, as my teeth still chattered, and Mrs. Brewster made a cup of tea, but I was still deathly sick. Realizing that my condition needed to be dealt with gently but firmly, Father shook me and said, "Mary Jane, *where* is your faith? They can't do anything but what the Lord permits them to do. Brace up now and take this tea and you will feel better."

Then he told us why he was so late getting home. It had been decided at the meeting at the schoolhouse to send William and Robert Brewster and William Anderson on horseback in the direction of the trouble to learn the truth about the report. As they had not returned at night it was feared they had been killed, so Father left some of the men at the schoolhouse, hoping against hope for the return of the boys. Late in the night they did return, with the report that there was a little trouble, and several had been killed, both Indians and whites. The story had grown. There was some uneasiness on the part of the settlers because the Indians were beginning to resent their coming, and this particular rumor started in this way:

A white man bought a gun from an Indian and paid for it in counterfeit money. The Indian took the money to the store and when he found it worthless, tried to get the white man to give him back the gun, which he refused to do. This led to an argument, and the white man beat the Indian with a stove-wood stick. Not long afterward a score of Indians came to the white man's farm and shot a steer and took it away for the meat. This led to an attack on the Indians by the whites, and a few were killed on both sides, which led to the story of the up-rising.

In many cases the white settlers were at fault, and the Indians grew more rebellious, but it was not until the Civil War that they gained courage to attack the whites openly, and then they took advantage of the fact that many of the men were at the front. I forgot to say that the fire which Mrs. Brewster thought was Shakopee burning was only a straw stack.

The Outbreak of 1862

Early in the Civil War serious trouble with the Indians developed about fifty miles southwest of Minneapolis. The Indians attacked the settlers, burned and looted their houses and barns, and killed whole families. Stories which were no longer rumors reached us, and women were never left alone if it could be avoided. In August Mrs. Black's first baby was born. (Mr. Black was our minister, and they were living in part of our cabin.) Our stock of groceries was getting low, so the day after the baby's safe arrival Mr. Black and Father decided that they had better go to town and stock up. By this time we had a good team of horses, and they expected to be home before dark. As the day wore on I could hardly conceal my uneasiness from the invalid, and when dark came my anxiety was terrible. I put a shawl up at the window to keep the light from showing out, and made some excuse to Mrs. Black for doing so. Nine, ten and eleven o'clock came, and still no sound of the wagon. But at last, before midnight, I heard the welcome sound in the distance.

During the day, Mrs. McClay, one of the neighbors, came over and said that school had been dismissed and word sent home with the children for everyone to go down to Fort Snelling. The reason Father was so late getting home was that they met so many families with their household goods, and sometimes with their stock, that the road was blocked for miles. Father was always cool-headed, and after questioning a number and finding that no one had actually seen an Indian, or anyone who had seen positive evidence of an attack, he decided that the Indians could not be so very near. And knowing that Mrs. Black was not in a condition to be moved they decided to assume an air of indifference to reassure us. But I had been under such a strain all day that I could not sleep, and during the night I imagined I saw an Indian climbing in the window. I saw his head-dress of feathers and his long matted hair as plainly as if he were really there. But Father slept peacefully through the night.

Many of our neighbors went with their families to Fort Snelling for protection, but after a few days it was found that there was no danger within fifty miles of us and they returned home. That fall (1862) General Sibley, in command of the Sixth Regiment from Fort Snelling, captured three hundred Indians and brought them back to the Fort. They were kept prisoners, tried by court martial, and most of them found guilty. President Lincoln pardoned all but thirty-nine, who were the leaders, and these were hanged, all on one platform, as an example. This put an end to the trouble.

Many thrilling experiences were related by the people who made their escape. One woman told of hearing shots while doing her morning work, and on looking out of the window saw several Indians around a neighbor's house, just down the hill, shooting through the windows. She knew that her turn would come next. Her daughter had a young baby, and her son-in-law had gone to St. Peter, the nearby town, for supplies. Hastily dragging a feather-bed down into the cellar, and getting her daughter and the baby down, she closed the trap door in the floor, but not before she had left a jug of whiskey where the Indians could find it, as whiskey was the first thing they looked for. She took time to put strychnine, which they kept in the house for rat poison, into the jug, and had barely time to close the door when the savages were upon them.

She could hear them rattling dishes and moving around above her. It was not very long before they began to fall on the floor and groan and writhe and kick, and she knew that the poison was doing its work. At last everything was quiet and so she tried to lift up the trap door. But one of the Indians was lying across it, so they had to stay in the cellar until her son-in-law came home. He found eleven Indians lying dead on the floor.

Beginning of the Church

I want to leave some of my memories of the efforts of the early settlers of Eden Prairie to spread the gospel. The present generation has no idea of the untiring zeal and self-denial the early settlers practiced to leave the two churches—Methodist and Presbyterian—a heritage to their descendants in the community.

In 1855 Reverend Hugh McHatten, of Galena, Illinois, was ordered by his doctor to spend the summer in Minnesota in search of health, and he promised the Anderson relatives in Galena that he would see their Minnesota kin folk before he went back. He came to Eden Prairie just after we had built the log schoolhouse on James Anderson's farm. There were only ten children in the school. (Martha Paine, daughter of William B. Paine, was the first teacher. This was the beginning of what in later years was known as School District No. 55.) Well, Mr. McHatten preached in this log schoolhouse for about a month that summer, and before going back to Galena he told us how to go about organizing a church, and promised to write us, giving the address of the General Assembly of the Presbyterian Church, so we could apply for pulpit supplies.

When he was ready to go back he came to Father and said, "Mr. Anderson, I can't get back to Galena. I haven't money to pay my way back." Father didn't know what to do. There was no money; no one had sold anything yet. The settlement was new. We talked it over, and thought of a new neighbor, Richard Neill, who had just come from Canada, and bought out William McCoy, who lived a mile from our cabin. We thought Mr. Neill might have some real money, so Father went over and told him the facts and asked for a loan, for which he would be personally responsible.

Mr. Neill said, "Yes, I have some money put away to pay a note coming due, but money may come from Canada to meet the note. The poor minister must get home. Take the money." And so it happened that Richard Neill gave the first money for Presbyterianism in Eden Prairie.

The next summer, 1856, Reverend Alexander McHatton, a brother of Hugh, came and organized a United Presbyterian Church, with twenty-four members. He stayed three months and preached in the schoolhouse. We had no preaching then until the next summer, but we held Sunday School and prayer meetings during the winter.

The next summer, 1857, a Reverend McCartney came. The Glendale Presbyterian Church, over across the Minnesota River, in Scott county, was organized, and Mr. McCartney preached for us in the morning and in the Glendale Church in the afternoon.

He was followed by Mr. Black. Mr. Black had just been married and was sent with his bride up the Mississippi to look after a church that had been started down on Lake Pepin, and also our church. He was to spend three months at each church, "time about". Well, at the close of the first service at the Lake Pepin church, everyone hurried out and left him and his bride standing there with no place to go. She was heartbroken, and said, "Let us go up to Eden Prairie and see what kind of folks are up there."

Well, when they came, James Gamble went to meet them and the young bride got a warm welcome from everyone. They decided to stay. She couldn't bear to leave. There was no house to give them. We had a lean-to for a kitchen on our log cabin, so we fixed that up for them by putting a partition across. They used the back part for a bedroom and the front to live in.

Father built a shed for our kitchen. I had to go outside to get to this shed, and in stormy weather it was pretty hard to carry food back to the house, but even so we all enjoyed it. Mr. and Mrs. Black stayed there two years, and these were about the happiest years of our lives. That was during the Civil War and the Indian outbreak of 1862.

In 1863 our two babies were born. Mr. Black named his boy Joey and we called ours Josiah. Mr. Black was extremely vain about Joey. It was their first baby. One day when Bob Brewster was visiting us Mr. Black held Joey up admiringly and said, "Now, there's a boy that is a boy!" at which Bob pointed to my baby and said, "Mr. Black, if you had a boy like that one, you'd go crazy."

William Collins, who lived about three miles up on the prairie, had the post office, and Mr. Black went every day to get the latest war news, which came by way of Shakopee. It was sometimes long after night when he came back with the news. He would knock at our door and call, "Are you asleep, Robert?" And then he would sit long into the night talking about the great slavery question and the progress of the war. I remember his bringing the news of the battle of Bull Run. We had gone to bed. He said the retreat was a stampede.

These were gloomy days for the North. The men of Eden Prairie were volunteering and there were several drafts. The young men were all gone. We had seven small children. John, the oldest, was only fourteen, and small for his age. He had to stand on the manger to put the collar on a horse. We discussed what was our duty; should Father enlist? It seemed that until there was a shortage of men he ought to stay with his family. And so he decided to wait for the next draft. We felt that if he was then disabled or killed there could be no doubt that it was the Lord's will. The last draft came, and it took about all the able-bodied men who were left, including Father.

The morning he went away Grandmother Anderson came to be with us. We were all in tears. Mary wept on Grandmother's knee. She tried to comfort her, and pointed to a flock of wild geese flying over the house, in order to divert her, but Mary sobbed, "I don't care for geese, when Father is going to war." Uncle William, earlier in the war, was unable to enter the army, being under weight. He drove our team to Fort Snelling with Father and the neighbors who had been drafted—Uncle Archie, Mr. Lougee, William Stinson, both the Brewsters, John Clark, John Logan, and others.

After they reached Fort Snelling word came that Lee had surrendered, and that no more men were to be taken. Late in the night we heard the wagon coming through the woods. There weren't many wagons passing in those days, and we were anxious to know who could be coming at that hour of the night. As they came down the head of the field, Father couldn't wait, but jumped the fence and came running across the field. What a happy surprise! How thankful Grandmother Anderson was to have him safely home. She was a brave woman.

Father got his discharge, but kept his uniform and arms. The old muzzle-loading musket did good service for many years in hunting wild geese, which were plentiful, until it exploded from an overcharge when Bob was hunting ducks. We had the bayonet made into a breadknife by Whitmore, the blacksmith, and Father made a good wooden handle for it. We never had a better knife, for there was the very best of metal in those bayonets.

The blue "soldier coat" was finally worn out. As I look back at it all now, it seems a pity that some of these things should not have been preserved. We seem to value them after it is too late.

Speaking about hunting, I had an interesting experience soon after we came to Minnesota. My brother-in-law, Sam Anderson, was in the woods, and saw a fine wild goose at the edge of the lake. He came running to our house for a gun. It was a poor old gun we had, without any hammer, but we wanted that goose, for we had been without meat for a long time. He and I crawled down to the shore. He rested the gun across the trunk of a tree. As there was no hammer on the gun, we piled powder on the tube instead of a gun cap, and while he took aim I lit the powder with a match, and we killed the goose. It was a good shot.

Mr. Black, who was pastor of the church during Civil War times, was followed by Reverend A. B. Coleman. The little log schoolhouse was now too small for the growing settlement, and Mr. Coleman went out to secure subscriptions for a church. Everyone seemed ready to help. This was in 1866 or 1867. Jacob Wolff donated the land on which the church was to be built, as his farm was near the center of the settlement.

The building of that church was a work of self denial. Father was treasurer and kept the record, in a pasteboard covered account book. That little book, after nearly three quarters of a century, tells an eloquent story of the faith and love of those founders of a Christian community in the wilderness. It was by such sacrifice that the foundation of a Christian state was laid.

It is interesting to look back from these modern days of luxury to the pinching hardships endured in raising money for the new enterprise. The little account book shows that many contributions were in produce, and the prices at which this produce sold seems [sic] unbelievable in comparison with values of today. Beef brought only four and five cents a pound, and other things were in proportion, but all building materials were high. The front door, which is still in use in the remodeled church, cost $17.00, and the lock and hinges, $6.40. It took 160 pounds of beef to pay for those hinges and that lock. The big cast iron stove cost $36.00. The lamps which hung from the ceiling, sparkling with prism glass, were the pride of the community. How those prisms flashed and glittered in the light of the kerosene flame! No electric lights ever seemed so wonderful. The children were awe-struck with the beauty of them.

The record shows that when the church was finished it had cost $1,057 in cash, with $259 yet to raise before we could feel our church was free of debt. Most of the work had been done without charge by the men of the neighborhood.

A great festival was planned to raise the $259. A supper was prepared and the whole community turned out, including the children. There were games and speeches and good fellowship. In the evening there was what we then called a grab bag. In a later age it would be called a fish pond. The women had brought various contributions of knitted articles, aprons, home-made candies and such things, and these were sold through the grab bag. The festival netted $82.50 toward the debt.

Aunt Jane Brown and I undertook to raise the money to buy the pulpit. We gathered up $354 among the women of the church. This more than paid for a suitable pulpit. Twenty-six years afterward Sam was just beginning in the ministry, and preached his first sermon from that same pulpit. He preached from Luke 5:4, "Launch out into the deep and let down your nets for a draught."

At the time of Father's death, forty-two years after the church was built, a perfectly organized church could have been formed from within his own family circle. His immediate family included a pastor, two elders, and twenty-four members.

Early Schools

The schools of these frontier settlements were very primitive. There was no supervision of public education. Every settlement just ran its own school, and often the trustees were unfit to judge of the merits of the teachers who made application. These trustees, who were elected by the voters of the settlement, examined the applicant, and if satisfied with the results, a contract was made. About $25 a month was paid and in addition the teacher "boarded around", each family furnishing board in proportion to the number of scholars sent to school. This system often provided a teacher who had little or no education. During the Civil War Billy McCoy was chairman of the Board of Trustees, and it fell to him to examine and hire the teachers. I remember one young woman, Nancy Sterret by name, calling at our house on her way to McCoy's to "reply for the school". She said, "Mrs. Anderson, did you know that Sam Clark is coming home from the war on a *furlong*?" And she got the school! It was not until years afterward that the public school system of the state protected the public against this type of service.

The custom of boarding the teacher was a hard experience for the teacher, but it had its advantages, for it brought new life into the home, and in those days few things of interest or profit happened. A young man, named Dave Parker, was engaged to teach during the winter season. He was a good teacher and we all wanted him to have the school, but he had a young wife whom he insisted on bringing with him. Well, we had a "sittingroom" and a spare bedroom adjoining, and it fell to us to let the young schoolmaster set up housekeeping in these two rooms. Soon Joe and the new teacher became fast friends, and they kept up a good tempered bantering and exchange of pranks. Each tried to outdo the other in practical jokes. In those days the woods were full of coon, and coon-hunting was common among the farmer boys. Coon skins were used for coats and robes, but no one ever thought of eating the meat. It was a nauseating mess of fat. Well, Joe, as a special treat, offered to take the teacher coon-hunting, and insisted that the meat should go to the teacher for Thanksgiving dinner. Poor innocent teacher! It sounded all right to him.

They got a coon, and Joe was in hysterics laughing over the joke, while the teacher and his bride carefully roasted and tended the coon. But when dinner was ready they came for Joe and led him to their dinner as a special guest, insisting that he share in the delicious coon meat he had so generously given them. It is more than forty years since that feast of coon's meat, but Joe will change the subject yet if anyone says "coon".

Educating the Family

We were the first to plan to send the children away to school. We decided to send Sam to Minneapolis. (We had never had teachers who could teach much beyond the three R's.) We hadn't means to pay his board, and if he was to go at all it was necessary to find him a place where he could earn his way. A Miss Florence Williams had taught school in the neighborhood during the summer terms. Through her we learned of a Presbyterian minister, Isaiah Faries, in Minneapolis, who wanted a boy to work for his board. We got the place for Sam, and so was begun a friendship which has continued for two generations. Mr. and Mrs. Faries took Sam into their home as a son, and followed him with their prayers and affection through his years of study and on into the ministry.

That was the beginning of a long struggle to educate the family. For fifteen years there was one or more of the children in the Minneapolis schools or the University. To rent rooms and send supplies in from the farm seemed the easiest way. In all the long years, through storms or over impassable roads, Father never failed in his trips to town with the necessary supplies.

I remember one stormy winter. It had snowed till the roads were blocked. Father was out broadening the track to start to town, when one of the neighbors came along and asked why he was starting out on such a day. When Father said he must get supplies to the children in town the neighbor said, "You're a fool. You'll not catch me slaving for mine like that. When you have worn yourself out they'll not thank you for all this slaving."

Long afterward, when Sam was pastor of a church in Toledo, he wrote in gratitude for all the sacrifices we had made, and referred to what this neighbor had said that winter day. In closing his letter he wrote, "I want to testify that the years have not dimmed the memory of those sacrifices, nor shall I ever forget the love that made your hardships a willing service."

We kept up this plan of educating the family for fifteen years, until the time finally came when the children were all grown, and we began to think of the years when we should take things a little easier. None of the family cared to stay on the farm, and in 1889 it seemed that the dear old place had served its purpose and we had done our work for the family, so we decided to rent or sell it.

We rented the place to William Nesbitt, and planned to move to Minneapolis and leave the house vacant for his family. We had sold off everything except the furniture that we might need, and it came time for us to move. The last of our furnishings was to leave the next morning, and Nesbitt's belongings were to be moved in. The girls and Father were in town settling the house we were to live in. It was planned that I should stay over night at Cornwall's, just next door. But when night came I just couldn't leave.

I said to myself, "I've lived here most of my life and reared my family here, and I'm not going to run away the last night." I started up the lonely stairs, but the halls seemed so empty I just couldn't stand it and I grabbed a sunbonnet and fled from the place, and ran over to Uncle Archie's. The next morning the team came and we took the last of our belongings just as the Nesbitts drove into the yard.

And so we left the old life and the scene of many happy years. It was hard for us to give up the old home with all its tender memories, but we built a comfortable house next door to Agnes, and with our grandchildren around us, and in the leisure that we had earned, lived a life of contentment.

It was here that we were again to meet great sorrows, for Anna died, and buried with her baby in her arms. Sam was taken away at the age of 46 at the height of his useful career in the ministry. John and May followed a few years later.

For ten short years we lived in Minneapolis, until Father was called home at the age of seventy-five. When the day came to bear his body to its final resting place, his friends gathered from far and near through drifts of snow and chilling winds, to view once more his peaceful face—the face of one whose faithful life had been a moulding influence in their own.

For twenty-five years I have gone on alone. No, not alone, for I have the memories of nearly half a century of useful and happy life with him, and I am surrounded by loving children, grandchildren and great grandchildren. At the age of ninety-four I am still in perfect health, and able to take an interest in the affairs of the day. With faith and trust in my Divine Redeemer, I am awaiting my summons home—with few regrets for the past, and no fears for the future.

Nora O'Connor completed this memoir in 1947, entitling it "The Life of a Young Irish Girl from Bantry, County Cork, Ireland to America, 1886–1918." Some fifty pages long, the original handwritten manuscript was transcribed in 1995 by Nora's grand-nephew Bill Geoghan and his wife, Mary Ellen. Nora's memoir focuses on her early life as a servant in Bantry House and her adaptation to life in New York and, later, Michigan. It opens with the following prologue, dated March 24, 1947.

I received this book in the mail some time ago. The morning it came, I took it in my hand and for quite a few minutes, my thoughts went back to when my eldest daughter, Eileen said "Mom, why don't you write the story of your life so we could have it and read it later?" I laughed at her and said "Oh yes I guess I could write a wonderful story at that!". She said it would kind of pass away some hours for me. I knew what she meant, lonely hours now. "But why not?" The children will know then what kind of mother they had, the real me.

Time passes very quickly and yet when I was 21 how the years seemed to stretch ahead. Counting the days and months. I had a wonderful, well, simple life. But it ended nearly two years ago when I closed the cover on my sweet love story. I closed it the day the lid closed on the face of the most wonderful man on this earth, to me, anyway.

I'm alone now just where I started before I ever met him, alone and wondering "How long will it be before we'll meet again".

Nobody will ever know the awful heartache I carry around with me. It's bad to love some one like that, to wait for that hour when you hear that beloved step and see that loving smile with the greeting "Hi Pukie" or "what are you doing Mickie?" Oh well, I'm getting ahead of that story my children want and they are all so kind and wonderful to me. God love and keep them.

Mom

Exile's Prayer

Sometimes, Lord, O let me see
Blossoms on a hawthorne tree.

Let me wander once again
Down a little crooked lane.

Let me hear the linnet sing
On some glittering day in spring.

Grant my heart its deep desire
An evening by a bright turf fire.

Lord, O Lord, before I die
Let me see an Irish sky.

Chapter One

I was born in the year 1886 in the dear little town of Bantry, Co. Cork, Ireland on the feast of the Assumption of the Blessed Virgin, 15th of August, the fifth child and the 4th daughter of Michael and Ellen O'Connor.

I really don't know how far back I can go, but I can remember my father's death: the lighted candles at his feet, the long benches and people, lots of people. I also have a faint remembrance of running down a lane with outstretched arms to a very tall person who picked me up and threw me high, laughing and rubbing his beard against my small face. He called me his little black lamb as I had inherited his black hair. The rest were all fair or chestnut; that was my father.

He had spent 21 years serving in India in the British Army, had come home and right away fell in love with my mother who was then 17 years old at the time. I heard people say that she was very pretty.

When my father died due to an accident he was 48 years old and left my mother with 6 children, the youngest just nine months. I myself was a little past two.

From that time on till I was seven or eight seems kind of misty to me but I grew up, I guess like the rest, never having what the children of today have, perhaps tea and bread and butter if we could afford it. God must have looked after us as we were all healthy and we grew up without much sickness.

My youngest brother Dennis and I were great pals in our childhood, in fact, they called us the twins till he got to be 12 and grew taller than I. Poor kid, many the heavy baskets of bread he carried on his shoulders up the long Avenue to the "Big House" as they called Bantry House, the Lord Bantry Estate in our town.

We were both very musical, he had a wonderful voice and as we grew older, sang in the church choir. I remember once a cousin of ours bought him an accordion. I can see him now trying to play it, finally in disgust he said, "here, Sis, you can have it". (I had been itching to get my hands on it.) I took it and in a few hours could play Home Sweet Home and mastered a few more old Irish airs. Oh, Dennis got his hands on that accordion again and mastered it himself and in time proved himself a wonderful accordion player. Was to the day he died and I often think if we had radio in our days how he would shine there as a singer.

My own ambition, I must tell about as it was around this time when I was 13 years old I made up my mind to be an Artist and a Singer. I spent all my spare time out of school drawing. I had very good marks at school in Art. I was attending a Convent school and that was one of the subjects I loved. The Sister that taught me had great hopes for me and helped me along. By the time I was 16 and due to graduate something turned up to spoil my plans. In those days, Ireland was under England's rule and of course so were her schools even though the sisters taught us. And not only should your marks be good but you had to make up a certain number of days in the school year to be able to pass. I had missed quite a few days so I didn't qualify for even an examination. A man from the government examined the classes every year so I didn't pass. I was to take another year.

When school started the next year a very prominent Art teacher arrived at our school and was surprised at my work. She suggested that I should go back to Germany with her and take advanced courses there. There was no expense for my Mother. She called on Mother and actually pleaded with her not to let such talent go to waste. But no, Mother wouldn't think of letting me go so far away. I did want to go. God, how I wanted to be an Artist! But, I guess it wasn't to be.

I left school the next year at the age of 16 and gave up the idea of ever becoming an artist. Took care of children for a few months, and then one day, the whole town was buzzing with news. Bantry House was to be opened. The young heir, Mr. Leigh-White was coming home and bringing an English bride with him. For weeks, the painters and business men of the town were up to their ears in work.

It was a beautiful estate and dated back hundreds of years. The grounds around it were planted with foreign shrubbery of all kinds. Long avenues about two miles long led up to the main house. At intervals around it, lodges were built with beautiful iron gates large enough to let the carriages through with a small passenger gate on the side, and you didn't get through that small gate either without telling your business or being a part of the household.

For years it had been closed, that is since Mr. Leigh White and Mother Lady Leigh White died and once every so often it was thrown open to the public on a Summer Sunday afternoon. The townspeople made a regular holiday as you really couldn't see all the grounds in one day. I remember as a small child visiting it and thinking I was in Paradise with the smell of the foreign flowers and foliage and the beautiful hot houses.

Anyway, it was opened for good this time and of course there would be entertaining galore. I saw some of the servants or "help" as you call them in America, quite classy people in their uniforms and such.

I saw the phaeton with its 4 beautiful horses arriving in town with the coachman and two footmen sitting up so straight and formal. They weren't back only about six weeks and the townspeople were getting used to seeing the ladies in their beautiful finery. One day when Mother and I were in Mr. Warner's big store, (he supplied Bantry House with almost everything except meats), he looked at me and almost shouted "You're the very one!" He had known my Mother as a girl and it was at his place of business my father had his accident which caused his death. Right there he told my mother that Mrs. Leigh-White wanted a girl from the town as 3rd housemaid. I wasn't quite 17 but he said to my Mother, "Ellie, I'll tell her and make an appointment."

A few days later Mother and I walked up that long avenue to see her. It seems funny that I should be maybe going to live there but I was—a little young. I remember my black hair was in braids down my back tied with a ribbon bow on each braid.

One of the footmen conducted us to Mrs. Leigh-White's private sitting room and I'll never forget how beautiful she was. Not much older than myself, a little past 18 she was, and as she said a few years later as she bid me goodbye, that she fell in love with me "you are just what I want" she said in her crisp English accent. "Someone that can be trained, and some one from Bantry." But, she kind of hesitated as she said it "you have to wear your hair up". I was so shy, I could hardly answer her. In those days young girls didn't put their hair up early. When they did they were considered grown up, a young lady. My hair was long, black and shiny, not a bit like it is today. You'd never know by looking at me today (and I don't mean to brag) that I was the same rosy cheeked slim little maid that stood facing Mrs. Leigh-White, with her heart in her mouth, saying "Yes Ma'm" and "No Ma'm." Oh, I was green I guess.

I was to come in a week. In the meantime she gave us a bolt of dress goods to be made up in morning uniforms, tiny small caps and beautiful white aprons that were to tie in a large bow in back. I remember when I first put on an apron, I seemed to be all bow, I was very small and slim in those days. My sister, Margaret, being a dressmaker was to make the uniforms. I also got black to wear in the afternoons. I was so thrilled, I danced instead of walked all the way back that beautiful long avenue. Something I never dreamed would happen, to live at and be part of that beautiful place, Bantry House.

Chapter Two

In a little over a week everything was ready for me to go. Margaret made the dresses and the day came when I returned up that long avenue, again. I was to have an afternoon off a week and every other Sunday. I was introduced to the head housemaid, Miss King. She was a tall, slim English woman of 28 or 30, very strict and efficient in her ways. I was taken to the large room I was to occupy with 3 other maids. Annie, a large jolly girl from another part of Ireland was 2nd housemaid, her sister Agnes joined us in a few months. They were all much older than I and I grew to love them all and they nicknamed me "the little one."

Everything went alright that first day till it came time for dinner, that is, the Servant's dinner. There were ten or eleven of us in the house, 12 counting Miss-Leigh White's lady's maid and the Scotch Housekeeper. I'll never forget that first meal. We ate in what they called the "Servants Hall", a very long room at the end of the long stone passage. All along this passage were the Butler's Pantry, the Silver Room, the lamp room, the kitchen and scullery and a large laundry which never was used. All our laundry went to Cork, a city about 60 miles away and was shipped back by train in large wicker hampers. We gathered in the Servants Hall in answer to a handbell rung by the Scullery maid. Mr. Barton, the butler, sat at the head of the table with Miss Penny, the ladies maid, at his right. Mrs. King, Annie, Mary and myself on the other side. Mr. Martin, the coachman, with Fred, the first footman, and Albert, the second footman, facing us. I know I couldn't eat much that first day. The housekeeper ate in her own sitting room and Jennie, the cook, and the scullery maid ate in the large kitchen. The scullery maid waited on our table. We had no work like that to do. The meals were wonderful with dinner at 12 noon, tea at 4 in the afternoon and supper at six.

I got acquainted quite readily with the rest of the house. I had charge of the long dining room hall and what they called the ante room. You could get all my little Home into one of these places and no fooling, it would take a book in itself to describe these places. Agnes and I together had charge of the Grand Ballroom. There was a marble fireplace at each end and the furniture was antique, very old, but beautiful, so we divided the room, so each would have a fireplace shining brasses and blacking grates, polishing floors, keeping white woodwork clean. We really worked in the mornings. My favorite was the dining room with its beautiful built-in sideboards all round the room carved woodwork laden with mammoth pieces of silver, solid silver platters large enough to hold a small pig. The floor was covered with a green beige carpet. Old Teddy, the gardener, kept the room filled with plants and flowers. He kept me busy taking his footprints off till we got him a pair of house slippers to use!

A large Conservatory opened off the dining room, and also off the Ballroom. Each had a fountain of water playing in them all the time. Sometimes I think if Heaven will be anything like Bantry House, I'll be satisfied! All my life I've dreamed of being back there. I wonder if I'll see it and the little town where I was born and spent so many happy days on my way when my soul is flitting from this old World!

Time passed and the first Sunday that Mrs. Leigh-White insisted we wear our "toques" or little bonnets to Church nearly floored me. I had been wearing sailor straw hats. Well the toques came and I'll never forget that Sunday. I looked at myself in the mirror and saw as I thought, a rosy cheeked old lady. "Annie" I said, "I'll never be seen going through town in this thing". We had to go clear through the town, past the Police Barracks (where we all had admirers), past our boy friends maybe standing on the square. I nearly died and wouldn't look either way with my cheeks flaming till I got home. I had to pass that too on my way, our little house was enclosed in a white picket fence. I rushed in, tore off the bonnet and dashed it almost into the grate fire burning at one side of the room. My grandmother rescued it. I grabbed a sailor hat of my own and just made it in time for Mass. On my way back I stopped to pick up the toque but didn't wear it till I got inside the big gates. Afterwards I really got to love that little head piece and when all three of us Catholic girls went to Mass together, we really did look nice. One friend of my mother's asked her if I had become a nurse, that was what I think made me like it (proud little devil wasn't I?)

Christmas at Bantry House was something to be remembered. Each servant got a nice gift with also a sum of money. We had a wonderful Christmas dinner with champagne for all, (dizzy stuff isn't it?), but it tasted wonderful. The house was always filled with company and of course after the guests left their rooms, it was our duty to take care of them and see that the bath rooms were tidied. I stayed at Bantry House nearly 3 years and in that time waited on a lot of English and Irish nobility. In the second year of my time there, a certain Lady Baltimore visited. She had been there before, but as she had her own maid, I didn't see much of her. This particular visit, she came without her as the maid was planning on getting married. It fell to me to be her waiting maid helping her dress, doing her hair, taking care of her jewels and wardrobe. I liked it but it was extra work for me. She liked me and asked Mrs. Leigh White if she could have me. My lady was planning on letting me go to her when I left Bantry House to come to America. She travelled a lot and I'd go everywhere with her. But I didn't do that either, that's life.

In the Fall of 1904 the glad news spread through the House and town. An heir was expected. Mr. Leigh-White didn't inherit the title of Lord as he descended through the female side of the House. His mother had the title of Lady Elizabeth but she married a common English captain by the name of White. Consequently the name *Leigh-White*, Leigh being the Lady Elizabeth's maiden name and the old family name at Bantry House.

In the main part of the House above there were 30 large rooms, that is outside the large reception Hall and dining room. Besides that, the servants quarters occupied 2 large wings, one for the men, one for the women, on opposite sides of the house with the kitchen and long passages separating them and the long billiard room on the other. There must have been 50 rooms in all in that Big House. There was talk of the West Bow and East Bow rooms being haunted. Each room had its own name like Blue Room, Dressing Room, Step Room and so forth; it would take too long to name them here. In the winter the family went to London for the Social Season, and we were put on Board Wages, that is we were paid to feed ourselves besides our regular wages. That winter we housemaids really enjoyed ourselves. We had our own private sitting room, so we cooked and ate our meals there since it had a large fireplace. We had the all the mending to do and the care of all the bed and table linens. Also a wall safe hidden in the wall contained all the best silver.

We spent many a happy evening sewing, crocheting, darning or reading. We had evenings off whenever we wanted and many the walks the "bunch" took along the Quay road. We all had sweethearts, of course. Annie was the only one that married hers. Also, during the absence of the family, we had all the main rooms to house clean, but the furniture was all covered, shrouded in covers. Oh, we were kept busy, but had a chance also to enjoy the beautiful grounds. Bantry House overlooked the Bay with the Abbey or Quay Road below. You could stand on the Terraces and see far off the little Island of Whiddy with its small population of a few families sitting right in the middle. When the fleet was in (our bay was a naval station also) it was a grand sight to see those stately ships steaming round the islands. I was used to those ships from childhood and they didn't thrill me as they did Annie and Agnes since they had come from inland towns.

As I said earlier in my story, Bantry House had the name of being haunted. Even as a small child I remember hearing my darling grandmother, who we called Mammie, telling ghost stories about it. It seems years ago one of the old Lords had built a kind of track, you would call it, on the estate and was often seen driving his beautiful horses around it. When he died, the old people of the town whispered of hearing him on a stormy midnight cracking his whip and driving his horses. To tell the truth, if I was late getting home to Bantry House at night, my heart would be in my mouth and I'd run like a deer till I saw the lights of the House shining in the distance. One dark night I was halfway up when I heard a terrible crash in the shrubbery and woods on the side of the drive. I ran like all Hades was after me, to find out next day from the lodge keeper that it was a deer that had wandered out of the Deer Park. There were some beautiful specimens kept there and they roamed at will in the woods.

We had one set of rooms called the tapestry rooms. Instead of wallpaper, the walls were hung with the most beautiful tapestries, also the mammoth second landing was covered with them. I remember one scene, with a women giving birth to a child. It wasn't vulgar or anything and in fact I was over a year at Bantry House before I was told by Annie what it meant. After that I kept off that landing if any of the new servants were around (modest wasn't I?)

To get back to the Haunts in the House, I was always afraid when the family was away, to cross that big landing after dark, as of course, there were no lamps lit and no one really in the main body of the house. Instead of going down through the long passages to get to our bedroom in the women's wing, we house maids had a short cut. We could go to the main part of the house, cross this big landing, go up a short open stairs a little higher than the steps to a main altar in Church, then through a suite of rooms which had a secret door and onto the landing outside our bedroom door. I had occasion to go to my room one night for something. It was around 9 at night. Miss King knew of my fears and being English, jeered at them, and I guess was trying to break me of them. She said to go the short way. I told her I'd go through the lower passages. She insisted that I see for myself I had nothing to fear. Annie had gone somewhere before that. We had been working in those same rooms that day and had taken the large feather mattress off the bed and it lay on the floor. Anyway with my heart in my mouth, I took my candlestick in my hand, lighted it, opened the door to the main landing and ran. I had to run down some flights, up another. I bolted into the room I had to cross to get to the secret door when something under the mattress grabbed me by the leg and almost threw me. I screamed and almost fainted. It was Annie hiding under the mattress, so choked with laughter she couldn't get up! Oh, she had quite a time with me for a while, and told Miss King she'd never do that again to break people of being afraid of ghosts.

The West Bow and East Bow Rooms were also supposed to be haunted. It was said a cry was heard outside those windows before a death occurred in the Leigh family. They overlooked the part of the House that faced the bay and now that I don't believe so much, I think maybe it was the wind whistling on stormy nights.

Around that time my youngest brother Dennis had finished school and he went to work for Mr. Warner delivering bread. He came daily to the house while the family was home and two or three times a week when we were on board wages. The girls got to like him and watch for him. He had grown up to be a very good looking young fellow. He'd come up in the evenings sometimes as the lodge keeper knew him of course, and until I started keeping company with Jim Hazel he nearly always saw me home. He was terribly in love with Jim's sister Janie who sang with us in the Church Choir as did Jim. I want to impress on you children that maybe I was just as giddy, wanting to impress the boys as you were in your youth and I had several admirers, but I liked Jim the best, but after all I didn't love him. He was great fun, though if I had really loved him nothing could have enticed me to cross the Atlantic Ocean.

In the time that I had been at Bantry House, I had grown and gained confidence in myself, had helped my mother by giving her a certain amount of my wages, putting the rest in a Post Office Savings Account, buying my own clothes, and sometimes when I could spare it, shoes and clothing for Mammie who I loved dearly. She was a sweet old lady and as pretty as a picture and she loved her twins, as she called Dennis and I. We seemed closer to her as she took charge of us after Father died and my Mother had to go to work. De was the apple of her eye and nothing was too good for him.

Chapter Three

The Leigh-White family came home that fall and we were put to work again. Entertaining went on on a big scale and sometimes all the rooms were occupied. Mrs. Leigh-White wasn't feeling so good but seemed to be on hand all the time. Passing the dining room on my way to and fro in the evening, I could hear a lot of merriment with the footmen and butler busy as bees. Our work in the bedrooms was finished by then except for the job of going around turning down the beds which we did around 9 o'clock since dinner was around 8 in the evening and sometimes the guests came up to their rooms for something after dinner before going down again to the drawing room. Coffee was served there. Sometimes we'd meet some of the gentlemen going around through the passages to play a game of billiards. I had charge of that too and saved Dennis many a cigarette. They were plentiful and laid out in containers so they were never missed. Agnes and I helped ourselves and watched for De when he came with the bread. In the fall we seemed to have more guests as the gentlemen hunted a lot, partridges and quail. There was a lake on the grounds but I never saw anyone on it, fishing I mean, maybe because it was saltwater & part of the Bay. Jim Hazel and I still went together and I also corresponded with a Naval Officer from the H.M.S. Dreadnought.

I had met him a few times and he continued writing, not love letters really, just friendship. He was writing to me yet when I said "yes" to your Dad. As soon as I told him I was to be married I heard no more.

Christmas came. We had the good times as we had before but this time the family and guests had a Ball. An Orchestra from Cork City came. That was the very first time I tasted ice cream, it was brought from Cork, also. Guests from all over came that evening and the dresses of the ladies were something to behold. Jewels sparkling on everyone but none could hold a candle to our mistress even though the stork was due in May.

Then it was our turn, the Servants I mean. Some of the guests had left so the family planned a Ball for us, and it was held in the big Ballroom. We invited our friends and a grand Supper was served. I remember Agnes and I got new dresses for the Occasion. I missed telling you that the summer before, the family gave a big party for the townspeople. Everyone came, they were served on the grounds. The stables had a big kind of courtyard and the people danced there. The coachman and the stable boys kept that place as neat as you keep your kitchen. Over the stable yard gate was a big clock that tolled out the hours, the buildings were dark brick overgrown with ivy.

Mr Martin, the coachman, and Miss Penny, the ladies maid, were engaged by this time. She was a tall, dark, very pretty girl. They were married after I left for America. So were Fred, the first footman and Jessie, the cook, as well as Annie and Mike, the mailman. We had sweethearts all over the place, but Agnes and I didn't bind ourselves to anyone. We were having too good a time, although Jim Hazel and I had a kind of understanding. We were too young, anyway.

By spring everything was "Hustle and Bustle", getting ready to go to London for the Big Event, the birth of the Heir, who was due in May. Mr. and Mrs. wanted to be where they could get the best of doctors. So a "Palace" of an apartment was obtained and lo and behold, I was chosen to be one of the help. Was I thrilled! Miss King & I were to be the housemaids. Fred, the butler, Miss Penny and Mr. Martin came along too and the housekeeper came as cook. Annie, Agnes, Albert, Jessie, and the scullery maid were left behind.

I was allowed to go home and stay overnight to say goodbye to the folks at home and they were to see me off on the train when we left. You'd think I was going to Mars! Of course I was thrilled to be going to live in the big city of London but I missed my pals and although I got so I could find my way around Paddington and around Picadilly Circus and the Park, I never went too far from home. I found Westminster Abbey and the Oratory, the Catholic Church where I went every Sunday. I never thought that a boy of mine from away off America fighting a war would roam the same streets!

Miss King had orders from Mrs. Leigh-White to take me to see a famous play that was on the stage in London that year. I forget the name of it but I did remember a song that was sung in it and used to sing it for my babies when they were little. It was something about a little chimney sweep and I guess I have forgotten that too! We spent a whole afternoon visiting around Windsor Castle and the Towers. The Irish Guards were on Guard that day I remember. I saw the block where Queen Elizabeth lost her head and the tower where the two little Princes starved to death, their handwriting still on the walls. England sure is an old country!

At last came the night when the young heir was born, but it was a little girl, and although they loved her they were disappointed. After a few days each member of the household was invited in to see the baby and given a gift. When my turn came, Mrs. Leigh-White asked me if I heard from home and if the townspeople were disappointed. I had sent the telegram to Bantry House the day the baby came, but in a code of our own so the that folks at the House would know first whether it was a boy or girl.

She presented me with the makings of a beautiful dress from the baby. She was a very nice lady, but no different than anybody else even with all her blue blood. I remember Mrs. Leigh-White said that day "Well better luck next time, Nora". (Funny but I didn't understand her). We were quite busy from then on with 2 nurses in the house, one for the baby and one for Mrs. Leigh-White. The baby was about 3 weeks old when they took her to Westminster Abbey to be christened. All the other servants went too. Mrs. Leigh-White said she wanted me to open the door for them when they came back as Fred had to go on the carriages. Anyway, I think she had something in mind about me being Catholic.

They left for France late in summer and of course gave up the apartment in London. I got a few weeks vacation and came home all alone on a Sunday afternoon. I had bought a whole new outfit while in London and the cat wouldn't know me if he had seen me stepping off the train that Sunday! I had been travelling a day and night so I went straight home to my folks. The first thing Mother said, "Well I hope you did as I told you, not to pick up any of that Cockney twang". Even though living each day with people that used it, I didn't.

I really was glad to get back to Bantry House and work. Miss King arrived after a while and we settled down to the job of fixing up a day and a night nursery. They chose the rooms where Annie had scared the living lights out of me that night, as it was the sunniest. So we lost our short cut across the House. The family didn't come back till fall but we were all ready when they did come. It was funny for awhile to see the nurse with the flowing streamers on her bonnet, pushing a large baby carriage around the grounds. She had full charge of it. They would ring for her if they wanted her to bring the baby to them (nice to be rich).

Chapter Four

Life seemed to go on dreamily as before and I was enjoying it. It was nice to be young, full of fun and loved by someone. Back of the house and skirting the stables were the beautiful rose gardens, rock gardens and fish ponds. Being at the back of the house they were always there, after our work was over, to enjoy. Steep marble steps led up and up till you could almost look out over the house. At intervals were landings with a statue at each corner. It was wonderful to climb up through the roses, sit on the steps and in the moonlight it sure was a little bit of Heaven. We didn't go out on the front while the family was home unless we had business. The front lawn stretched down to a kind of marble Parque overlooking the Quay Road and you could stand there hidden in the shrubbery and watch the sweethearts go by on the road below, and we did that often when the family was away.

Large statues of Venus De Milo and others decorated the front gardens. Agnes and I used to snap pictures of Jim Hazel and her boy friend hugging and kissing the statues and I wonder whatever became of those pictures.

The family had a large yacht which was kept anchored in the Bay, manned by a Captain and Crew. I saw a few of them once when they came to the house for orders, but was on the yacht only once and that of course while the family was away. Mr. Leigh-White was quite a yachtsman and had small flags or something to signal the yacht from the Terraces. The Union Jack (the english flag) was always hoisted every day when they were home, in that way the townspeople knew.

There is one incident I would like to relate here which I know will interest you. At the extreme end of the men's wing was a large room which had been closed for years—twenty-five or fifty some said. On her tour through the house one day Mrs. Leigh-White unlocked it. Miss King was with her that day. Three windows on the outside had been bricked in and ivy grew thick on the outside of them. That left two windows open, one facing the bay and the other the rose garden. Agnes and I often wondered as we sat on the steps what secret that room really contained and why everyone avoided it. The old story finally came out. A son of the House years and years ago had lost his mind through women and wine and had been kept in that room for years. Finally he had been put to death by smothering him between two large feather beds: I had heard my grandmother mention something like that and I asked her about it. She said the story was true as my grandfather had worked on the estate at one time and he had heard it from an old gardener although it was before his time too. It has been used after that as a bedroom for an old butler who had been with Lord Bantry for years and he had died in it also.

Anyway, Mrs. Leigh-White ordered it cleaned out so we started it one day and I never saw anything like it since or before. The dust of ages was everywhere, the bed was just like it was when the old Butler died. The old ornaments on the mantle and the rug or carpet on the floor fell to dust as we touched it. The bed was a large four poster, it still had the curtains around it of red and sprigged calico and believe it or not, the material was good yet, but dirty. Mrs. King gave me those to take home and my mother cleaned them all up and had a quilt made of them which I remember she brought to this country when she came. The curtains were the only things good in that room except the little knick knack ornaments. How I wish I had kept those too. They would be worth a lot to me now.

The day we cleaned that room you couldn't get me to stay in that room alone for one minute. I had heard too many ghost stories about it. Miss King must have felt sorry for me as she gave the care of it to Agnes. It was used as a visiting single gentlemen's room, but being in the men's wing it should have been mine as I had charge of the men's rooms. Agnes had the Women's. Imagine me going up at night to turn down the bed in that room, when it was occupied. "Goosepimples!!!"

The large front hall was a huge place. The floor was made of large tiles with a black and white design on the white coat of arms of the family. We had to scrub that on our hands and knees and it took all four of us to do it. A shallow wide staircase opened off it and in the niche of the staircase hung a large gong which the butler rang with a kind of drum stick when meals were ready in the evening. One gong was called "the dressing gong" and a half hour later it rang for the dinner. That sound penetrated through the whole house and into every room. The double drawing rooms and two ante rooms opened off the main hall, also, and were those drawing rooms beautiful! Miss King had charge of those. Some of the fixtures and ornaments in these rooms were priceless. Glass cases with articles from all over the world stood around the main hall.

Around the year 1902 (actually 1897) my eldest brother Jerry had gone to America. We had 4 uncles living in New York City. I couldn't even remember them as I wasn't even born yet when they left home. So Jerry landed at their house and stayed there until he married around 1904 (1905). He sent for my second eldest sister Nellie, a very pretty girl. I sure hated to see her leave home, she was also a dressmaker by trade. Mother had seen that we girls got to learn dressmaking although I didn't stick with it.

Mary my third eldest sister finally got the bug to leave Ireland around 1905, I believe, and I remember she came to Bantry House to spend a day with me before she left and as we were so close together in age we had a good time. My sister Nellie sent home the latest songs to us from America. "The shade of the old apple tree" was very popular then and many the summer evening the "bunch" walked arm in arm down the Quay Road singing it and we could make music too as we all had good voices.

Around the Fall of 1905 Lady Baltimore again visited and finally asked Mrs. Leigh-White if I could come to her. Her maid had left and she was using one of her house maids until she knew for sure. Dennis was doing a lot of talk about going to America in the Spring, and wanted me to go with him. But I liked and loved Bantry House so much I couldn't say yes yet. He would be 18 and I was a year and a half older, maybe not that much, I can't say for sure.

I hated the mention of America, I wanted to go to London again. No America for me. Mary had, of course, left in the spring of 1905 and her letters gave Dennis the bug alright. He met me one night as I was going through town on my way home. He said as he got in step to walk me home "Why don't you come to America with me?" I stopped and stared at him for a moment in amazement. "Go to America"? I said "not me boy, get that nonsense out of your head". "Gee" he said, "it would be nice if we could go there together. Sis, we have never been apart yet." I told him then "and we needn't be. You are needed here at home, you are leaving the folks with no man to look after them, and it will break Mammie's heart".

"No De", I told him, "I can't go, I wouldn't like it. I'd want to come back again if I ever went there." I had a good clean job. I was saving my money besides helping out at home and why should I go so far away, it all seemed so useless to me. Dennie, of course, thought his future was there. He was young and getting to be a darn good looking fellow. In a way, I didn't blame him, but he could wait till he was 20 anyway. But nothing I said did any good, even his love for Janie Hazel didn't seem to stop his eagerness to leave Ireland. He was going, and that was it. Nell was going to send him his fare. If I went I'd pay my own and kind of help him, too.

The winter passed and every time I went home I was approached about America. Mother began by saying I didn't want to be the only one of the family left home and I should go with my brother. On and on it went till I hated to go home and finally Dennis' Passage money came the first part of May. I had finally gone and given notice at Bantry House. Mrs. Leigh-White was astounded when she heard it. God, how I hated to leave. Annie and Agnes sobbed the day I left and there were tears in Miss King's eyes. She, Annie and Agnes gave me a beautiful little traveling clock as a fare well gift and a prayer book. Mrs. Leigh-White sent for me. I went to her boudoir and she took my two hands in hers and made me promise her if I didn't like America I was to write her right away and she'd send my passage money to come home. "Will you promise me, Nora?" I promised but didn't keep that promise. She wished me God Speed and Good Luck and slipped an envelope with a sum of money into my hand. I could hardly say goodbye, my throat seemed choked and my eyes were full of tears. So I left Bantry House and Happiness.

Chapter Five

From the first of May to the 17th I spent at home visiting old friends and schoolmates, buying and packing the necessary things for our journey across the Atlantic Ocean and trying to cheer the lonely hearts we were leaving behind, some of whom we would never see again in this world. I mean our darling grandmother (Mammie) and Aunt Mag. Tears were in their eyes every day. The weather was nice and evenings, after the evening devotion at the church which was only a few doors away, Dennis and Janie, Jim and I wandered through the countryside which is beautiful at that time of year in Ireland. With the furze in blossom it seemed like the hedges are built of gold. We four made great plans for the future then. We'd be true to each other and

so forth and so on. I was to come back soon. I remember the very last evening
Jim and I walked together. We had reached what we called the Brittius mine
and on turning back a lark flew past us and soared high, high up in the sky
singing like mad! We stood and watched it fly out of sight. In the morning
we were to leave and I said to Jim "I shall never forget that lark." Dennis and
Janie were quite a ways ahead of us on the road. Janie was taking Dennis' going quite hard by this time. As Dennis strolled past the convent she told him
I had been to see my old teachers, the Sisters, that day. They had given me a
crucifix blessed for the happy death (and some Irish lace to give some friend
of theirs which nearly caused my undoing.)

As we came near home we heard the music of the town band and wondered
what celebration was going on. We found the Band assembled at our gate
giving us a farewell concert. They played "Come Back to Erin" and all the old
Irish tunes and quite a crowd of friends were there to bid us God Speed. It
was wonderful, but kind of sad, too. Dennis and I had to sing "just one more
for the old crowd" which we did. I think if I remember right the songs were
"Danny Boy" and the new one "In the Shade of the Old Apple Tree".

Our poor Mammie didn't sleep much that night. I could hear her several
times saying the rosary to herself for her beloved "twins" who were leaving
in the morning. It was Dennis' going that hurt her most, he was her pride
and joy and in her passing the next year I do believe it broke her heart.
Mother often said "she was never the same". Mother and Margaret and
my Aunt Mag felt pretty bad too. In fact by morning when we had to catch
the 10 o'clock train to Cork, we were all feeling so heartsick that not much
breakfast was eaten.

In those days when someone went to America, the whole family went to
the depot or station with them and in my childhood I had witnessed many
a sad scene when a friend left for the U.S.A. Heartbreaking sobs and they
couldn't seem to let them go. It was just like putting a dear one in their grave
and in fact it was just that as some of those boys and girls never saw their
parents again.

Mammie could hardly let us go. She was the worst with her blue eyes
streaming with tears. Jim Hazel came to the house in the morning and
walked with us across the Square to the train. The station was full of our
friends bidding us God Speed. They hardly ever say goodbye in Ireland, it's always "Godspeed" or "God be with you". Achicch Mammie kissed and kissed
me and her last words were "God be with you Agellee, I'll pray for you. Take

care of yourself now". We got our seats on the train and we were still waving our handkerchiefs and throwing kisses till they were out of sight!

Jim Hazel had said his goodbyes to me the night before but there were tears in his eyes when he kissed me at the station. I remember his father met us halfway across the Square and walked the rest of the way with us.

I imagine the folks at home spent a bad day the *17th of May 1906*. Settling themselves down to wait for the first letter from Dennie and Nora from America. They little knew how close they were to having us back with them that evening. We had to change trains at Cork and catch the train to Queenstown, as that was the port we were to sail from. There were several boarding houses right by the pier that we were to leave from and De and I were assigned to one. After a pretty slim supper around 6 that evening we went walking. There was a Catholic Cathedral a few blocks away. You had to climb steps to get up to it. We finally made it and stood leaning on the wall overlooking Queenstown Harbor. The Steamer Teutonic, the sister ship of the Titanic that went down some years ago, was anchored in the harbor. "Look De" I said, "there she is, that's the Teutonic, our boat". He looked at me and said "Gee Norrie I wonder what the bunch are doing at home tonight?" You see our hearts were still at home. He wasn't interested in the Teutonic then. After another moment of silence he blurted out "Let's take the next train home". We can sell our tickets to someone". I knew he meant every word. I said "Do you really mean it?" "Sure" he said, "we're young yet". (He was 17 and I would be 19 in August).

My heart was beating. Sure that we'd find someone to take our tickets and we could go home. *Home,* that seemed so far away even then. We looked up some older people that were at our house. They informed us that our luggage was already aboard and it was too late then. De said "Guess it's no use. Anyway Mother would be so mad as she wanted us to go to America".

About 10:30 I said goodnight to him, he was assigned to a room with some other young fellows and I with some girls from another country. We were called early next morning to get ready to be taken to the boat via a small steamer. I often wondered since what they at home would say if we had walked in on them that night. A few Irish musicians came on the packet or little boat with us, playing and singing old Irish tunes. I guess they did that with every trip to the large steamer.

When we got aboard De and I were separated. I had to go with the girls and he with the boys or men. We met after each meal and promenaded round and round the deck. De and I stood at the side watching the last glimpses of our dear land fade away in the distance. When I went below to my berth I felt like a lost sheep, everybody strangers around me. I finally got acquainted with two very nice girls from County Mayo, Mae McGann who was with her father and Maggie Finnigan.

The five of us, De and I and Mr. McGann and the girls seem to get along nicely. Mae's father took us all under his wing. When we were a few days out some one came up with an accordion which was just what De wanted. He played and we sang which brought the 2nd and 1st class passengers to their rail and they enjoyed it by shouting "More, More!" We danced a lot on the trip as long as the weather was fine.

It wasn't long before old man sea sickness hit us one after the other. First one and then another would heave to the side and part of our insides would go to the fishes. An Englishman by the name of Frank Keller took quite a shine to me and was very kind and full of sympathy for me. He had a small bottle of brandy which he passed around but couldn't get me to touch it as I said it burned my lips. Frank and De sang together too, so that's why he attached himself to our Crowd.

It was while we were all so sick that the big storm hit us. Everybody was ordered to their berths. I myself was passing through the worst of my spell of seasickness. The men's steward on board shouted an order "No one on deck". The ship was tossing bad and you slid across the floor only to be tossed back again. Most of the women and girls went to their berths but not me. I was deadly sick and knew I was going to die anyway. I wanted Dennie, but no men allowed. So I told myself if I'm to die I want the wind in my face. I knew I was white as a sheet. I tottered from my berth and made the companionway or stairs. I climbed it some way to the open deck and the wind felt good. Waves that were mountains high were smashing the deck. Everything was tied or bolted down. I wasn't supposed to be on deck, not a soul in sight. I saw a box and a big coil of rope go overboard. The ship heaved on her side and I grasped an iron bar which was fastened across a door. Just as I did a wave broke over again and the door behind me opened and a sailor came out. I was just sliding with the wave when he caught me and hung on to the iron bar himself. "My God", he shouted "what are you doing here?" (Remember I only weighed 98 lbs.) He was a middle aged man and when he managed to get me inside the stairway again I looked like a drowned rat. He had oilskins on and he called a steward to take care of me and said if he hadn't come through that door then I'd have been washed overboard. The news spread through the ship and there was a great to do. De heard of it and forced his way into our berth saying "that's my little sister and you can't keep me out". The stewardess put me to bed between wool blankets and took my clothes to be dried but I was all over my seasickness by morning. They said it was in the paper at home but my name wasn't mentioned.

The storm blew itself out. Finally the sun shone again and once more we were allowed on deck. One thing I noticed on the trip, was that there were a lot of foreign people sitting around in corners on deck with shawls over their heads. Women with babes in arms. A rumor went around that one of their babies had died and was buried at sea in the night. I don't know how true this was, but they seemed a strange lot of people sitting tailor fashion on the deck day after day never seeming to move around.

Of course we had more dancing and singing and Dennie was in great demand to play the accordion. We passed some very large icebergs on our way. They looked like white shiny castles sticking high up out of the water and once we saw a large whale or two spouting water like a fountain. Once in a while a gull or two would come flying over. I often wondered if they followed the steamers way across the ocean!

The days passed one by one and one evening the Steward told us "be up early" as we'd be sighting land. In the morning, sure enough, way off in the distance we saw a faint line in the ocean. Everybody was excited, of course. This was America and we had been nine days coming. We had made good time they said.

De and I watched that faint line get clearer and clearer till finally we were here. The old Statue of Liberty and Ellis Island where they landed at that time stood out clearly in sight. A few days before everybody had been vaccinated and we had very sore arms but had lots of fun with them, too, trying to keep one another from bumping them on our walks around the deck.

We had to stay on the boat one more night I guess for an inspection or something. We were landed at Ellis Island the next morning. De and I stuck together like glue wondering what would happen now. We were questioned by this one and that one till I nearly got mad at them. They almost took the eyes out of me poking and looking at them so often. I remember that I told one doctor "if you pull back my eyelid once more I'll hit you!" He only laughed at me and asked what kind of rouge I used which also made me mad as I didn't know what he was talking about.

They finally let us go but we had to stay there till our names were called. A Catholic priest finally gathered us under his wing. The boys were separated from us by then and I had to give Dennie half of the money I had. He took one suitcase and I the other. Finally the boys were turned loose to look out for themselves, but the priest took all the Catholic girls. Ferries were running constantly between Ellis Island and New York and someone told me that De had gone on alone which nearly got me crazy—as I knew he didn't know where to go although he had Jerry's address and also Uncle Johnny's.

A meal of some kind was finally served us. I thought if this is American food, I don't like it. Some kind of soup, and now I believe it must have been bean, and of course, I had never seen a bean in my life! I know it tasted horrible and I couldn't eat it but I was too excited to be hungry, anyway.

I had sat there for what seemed a very long time. Names were being constantly called and one by one a girl or lady left the table. Finally, "Nora O'Connor", that's me! I jumped up and grabbed my belongings and followed the officer. He put me in a kind of large cage. My God, I thought, what's going to happen to me now? I realized soon that the best looking man I ever saw was smiling at me through the bars "Jerry, Jerry", I cried. The man in uniform didn't take that for granted. He questioned me and said "Do you recognize this man?" I said "Why sure, that's my brother". He questioned Jerry a little and then let me out. Jerry put his arms around me and kissed me and said "Gee, little Sis, how you have grown! Quite a young lady, eh". He asked me where Dennis was. I said someone told me he had gone on. Jerry said you stay right here and don't move till I come back. He searched everywhere but no Dennis.

When we got aboard the ferry he searched every nook and corner, but Dennis was nowhere to be found and I could see that Jerry was worried. The ferry docked and the people streamed off and lo and behold, there stood poor De on the pier, watching and waiting for me, thinking I'd be first over on every ferry. Poor kid, he sure was in a state and was awfully glad to see us. He said some shabby man had approached him and asked him to go with him but he knew better. That's why he waited for me, thinking the man would kidnap me, I'm sure!

Jerry took us right to his home on 90th Street off Second Avenue. We rode on the elevated trains. I had carried my umbrella all the way from Ireland, only to leave it on the train. I never noticed in my excitement till I got on the street again that I had forgotten to pick it up with the rest of our luggage. Of course there was no way of locating it so I said "Oh, let's forget it". My sisters, Nellie and Mary were at Jerry's waiting to welcome us. Mary Ellen, Jer's wife had prepared a wonderful dinner. I remember it was just like home, ham and cabbage and it sure tasted good to De and I after the meals served us since we left home. There were the usual questions, as how the home folks were and Jerry sang for us his favorite song, "When you were sweet sixteen." For some reason De didn't seem to enjoy things in those days in New York. The man of the house went to the corner saloon and brought home his pail of beer, instead of standing at the bar like they do today. Jerry got an extra supply that evening to celebrate the coming of the "green horns", as they called us, and De didn't seem to like it. I saw his brown eyes flash at Jerry a few times and then he said like he was the oldest "Why do you have to drink that?" Jerry urged him with a lot of laughter, of course, to just taste it and did De get mad, which made me feel embarrassed. After all we weren't home now. I tried to get him to sing with me but nothing doing, so they made me sing alone. De and I had good voices then and enjoyed using them later when we got acquainted with all the cousins and friends, but we were tired anyway that evening and I know De wasn't happy for some reason.

I had never met Jerry's wife, Mary Ellen, although she too came from our part of Ireland and Jer had kept company with her at home. She was very nice, fair and good looking, but not well at the time as she was expecting her first child. She sure was nice to us—taking us into her house even though it was our brother's too.

The next evening after Jerry got home from work and supper was over, Jerry and Mary Ellen took us to see our Uncle John and family. They lived on East 88th Street, a few blocks from Jerry. My Uncle Johnny was a man whose features resembled our Mammie so much. When he took my hand to welcome me he said "Well, well here's the beauty of the family! Boy, but you're a motherly daughter", meaning that I looked like my mother when she was young. I always thought he was making fun of me as Nellie and Mary were sure very pretty girls. Mary fair, and Nell with chestnut hair and fair complexion and beautiful brown eyes. I with my coal black hair, white skin and awful red cheeks, which I hated, black ugly eyebrows and so *little*. I said "Uncle don't make fun of me, please". His wife, Auntie, as we called her, was a smart, trim woman. She had been a teacher in Ireland and was his second wife. His first had died leaving him with a family of very young children and Auntie had helped him raise them all, but she had none of her own. At that time he had lost them all but two girls, Margaret and Mamie who was in bad health at the time. She died later of T.B. but they were lovely girls then. Of course we were called green horns there too and Auntie had a parrot who could talk quite plain. It got to know our steps when we came to see them, which was quite often and would croak "Here's the green horns, Auntie"! It never called us anything else either while it lived. Auntie finally had to keep the thing covered when we were there as it always scolded us. Auntie said it was only jealous, but I hated it.

A few days after our arrival Jerry took De shopping and when I saw my little brother again I hardly knew him, all dressed up in his jaunty clothes, hat, suit and tie. I must tell of a funny incident which happened to him and the droll way he told it. Jerry was taking him somewhere and stopped at the corner of Second Avenue at a shoe shine stand. Jerry sat up in one chair and motioned De to sit in the other. In telling it to me De said "Gosh, I thought that it was another elevator or something, so I waited for the thing to move. When the colored man started to polish my shoes I said to myself, huh, Jer doesn't even clean his own shoes! What a country!" I laughed till I was sick at him, but he warned me to tell no one as they'd call him worse then a green horn then.

Chapter Six

Jerry got a job for De at the place where he worked. I think it was a wholesale furniture or rug and carpet house. That left me mostly lonely and I began to get home sick. I couldn't eat or sleep, thinking of home and wanting to be back there. Mrs. Leigh-White had given me excellent references but they didn't seem to matter much here and I couldn't get anything to do in my line of work. Mary, my sister, came and took me to the Employment Agency where she got her job. She introduced me to the lady that ran it, but of course, had to get back to her own job. I began to learn how to get back and forth as it was, I believe, on 34th or 35th Street. I learned to ride the street cars and elevated trains all by myself and I would sit at the agency with other girls waiting to be called to a job. Week after week went by and my heart was breaking to go home to the family. I knew I was homesick and it can make you sick. *Real sick*, I was that. Sometimes I'd walk all the way home to either Auntie's place or Jerry's with the news "No luck today". Yes, I'd walk all those blocks, all alone. Dennie of course was working every day and feeling good,

but I was sick, heartsick. I didn't like America. The heat was bad by this time
and those awful thunderstorms really put terror into my heart. I wasn't used
to them and I cringed at every streak of lightening. Mary Ellen did her best
to cheer me up. I had found where Maggie Finnegan lived with an old Aunt
and called on her. She was going to be married anyway to her Irish sweetheart
who had preceded her out here. I also found Mae McGann and visited her,
but nothing cheered me.

Finally in June, Mary came to Jerry's and said a friend of hers, a cook for
a family by the name of Runkle told her the family was going to the Adiron-
dack Mountains. They had a summer place there and wanted a kitchen girl to
help the cook. What a come down to what I had been trained for! I consented
to go since it was only for the summer months, anyway or maybe till October. I would be paid $16 a month, Imagine! Mary took me to see the lady one
evening and the day the family finally left for the mountains she took me to
Grand Central Station and I went by train with the rest of the help.

We arrived at the Saranac Inn in the morning, had breakfast there and
then a large launch took us up Saranac Lake to the Runkles camp. My heart
began to lighten a little, it reminded me of home. The blue lake water bor-
dered with beautiful fir and spruce trees. We were met at the dock by two
elderly men, guides they called them. They had been guides for the Runkles
family for years. They had been there for some time getting the place in order.
The camp consisted of several cabins with one large main house that had a
lounging room, a dining room and kitchen. The cook and I had a cabin to ourselves as did the laundress and waitress. It was beautiful there and I enjoyed
every moment of it. There was a boat for the use of the help and we sure used
it in the evenings when our work was done. Moonlight nights we'd go out on
the water and sing. The other girls had been with the family for some time
and so they knew the girls who worked for other families who had Camps
up the lake. It wasn't very far by water, but a mile and a half by land. I got to
know them all and we visited and played cards. There were men servants too
so it wasn't a hen party by any means! Mr. Runckle had a launch of his own
and a man to run it, besides his boats and canoes. The cook at Runckles was
Swedish, around 40 and very jolly. Her name was Lilly and I liked her very
much. We used to laugh a lot during our work and she'd always help me so
we'd finish our chores at the same time.

The two guides were very good to us taking us through the woods on
hikes when they had time off. One had the name of Jim (seems like all

through my life the name Jim followed me). Our Swedish cook called him Jimmy. To tell the truth I hated to leave Saranac Lake when October came and I vowed someday I'd go back again. I was hired only for the summer season so when I got back to New York City it would be the employment agency again, for me.

In September I had a letter from Jerry telling me they had a little daughter born on the 20th. He said that they had named her Eileen and what did I think of that for a good old Irish name!

I learned how to row a boat while there and often went out by myself on a still day. The boat was large though and hard to tip over. One night the whole bunch went out and Jim the guide took the cook with him, he had a light half-boat, half-canoe. We visited up the lake, it was a beautiful moonlit night. On the way home we could hear Lilly (the Cook) talking and laughing with Jim in her funny little broken English. Voices sound so clear on the water at night! When we caught up with them, Jim had drawn the boat up on the beach. Lilly was sitting on the land end. The boat was light and he had it almost on end with Lilly perched up high screaming "Jimmy, oh Jimmy". That's all she could say he had her so scared. He sat at his end way down in the water calmly watching her scream. "That will teach you", he said, "to tell me how to beach a boat". When he finally let the boat in the water again it took on water enough to give Lilly a partial bath. Jim was laughing by this time till the tears came to his eyes, and so were we.

I spent a wonderful summer and the days weren't really long enough. The woods were all in their glory. When we left in October, my job ended and then I had to look for another.

I went back to my brother Jerry's again to stay until I could find a job for the Winter season. The Society folks had already hired all their help as they had all come back to the city before we did. So I had to go and register at an employment bureau. Mary came to town and kind of introduced me to how to go about it. The office was way downtown in the 20's. I believe it was on 28th Street. I was quite used to riding the streetcars by this time, and also the elevated. Everyday I reported at the office and sat around with the rest of the applicants from 9 till 4. Applications came in for different types of help like cooks, housemaids, etc. One by one they would leave. Several weeks went by and no job for me. Many a day I walked home from there all the way to 90th Street, not because I didn't have the nickel for carfare but because I was lonely and discouraged and I wanted to be with people. (I am the same way now at

59!). I'd also stop and window shop. I'd stop in at Aunties on 88th Street and she always gave me encouragement.

Finally I got a job as a kitchen maid in a swank place on Fifth Avenue. The family's name was La Cheir, which was french I guess. I had to go interview with the lady of course to find out if I would suit her. I was shown in to her sitting room. She finally arrived clad in a beautiful negligee trimmed with fur and she had a poodle under her arm. She told me what she wanted me to do and the wages I would receive. I had all the passages leading to the kitchen, the laundry and the help's dining room to scrub every morning. Besides that, I was to help the cook and the assistant cook and do the help's dishes. It was some job. They entertained a lot and we were kept quite busy. I took the job and my wages were 20 dollars a month. I worked awful hard there and as the kitchen and laundry were one floor underground I soon began to lose my complexion. Jerry noticed it and stopped in one night on his way home from work to look the place over. Right away he said "you're quitting this job, it's no place for you". They, the help, all seemed to be afraid of the lady of the house. She had a habit of making a tour of the house to inspect it. No one ever knew when she'd make up her mind to come. Only her maid would let us know before hand if she had a chance. The poodle would always be under her arm. There were 7 of us to do for 2 people. The 2 sons were away at college, but the dinners they put on were large. They had a butler and a footman but it was the kitchen people that caught the worst, of course. I finally took Jerry's advice and left the place and came home, as we called Jerry's place.

In the spring I landed another summer job as a second laundress. That was around the time I met Bob Sullivan from my home town. He wouldn't even look at me at home as I was just a kid to him then. But over here he fell for me like a ton of bricks. I went with him steady, he asked me to marry him and go home to Ireland to live, anyway he planned it that way. I forgot to mention that Jim Hazel had come to America the winter before trying to find me but we never did see each other.

I spent the next summer in the beautiful Adirondacks again, this time as a laundress. While there I met a young fellow who got to like me also. He was the man who gave me an old gold signet ring for my birthday because I wanted to be innocent. I ran the mail launch, there too, just for fun. The mail boy used to take me with him on his trips across the lake for the mail. He'd start the launch and then I'd take charge and steer it. We had to go about three miles! I had lots of fun up there that summer.

I came back to New York in October to find out that Bob had been drinking a lot because I was gone. I told him then I'd never marry a man that drank. We kind of tagged along together all that Winter—danced a lot and went places together and he seemed better. In the spring I got a job at West Point with a Captain and Mrs. Marshall which suited me fine. They liked me very much and as it took me out of the city again, Bob started his drinking, so I gave up on him. I enjoyed myself at West Point very much—so many nice Cadets and soldier boys. It was wonderful there. Mrs. Marshall was very particular who I went with. We had the usual Hops (dances) on Saturday night and Effie, the other girl and I went to every one of them. Effie was much older than I, around 30 I believe and had a little girl around 8 or 9. Her husband was serving in the Philippine Islands. Her mother was caring for the little girl and lived in Highland Falls, a small town at the gates of the post.

I wasn't with Captain Marshall for very long when he got orders to go to Fort Ethan Allen, Vermont. We spent a winter up there which we didn't enjoy very much. There was an awful lot of snow that winter. Sunday afternoons I'd dress warm and plow through it all around the post. It was fun when you have a beau with you and I usually ran into some soldier I knew who liked to see me home. We had our Saturday night Hops there too and Effie and I went to dances in the towns surrounding the post. Some of the Barracks were closed there as the regiments were in the Philippine Islands. Even so, there were plenty of fellows to dance with.

When spring came Captain Marshall was again ordered to move—this time to Fort Sheridan. Mrs. Marshall gave us two weeks vacation so I visited the folks in New York City. Effie and I arrived together at Fort Sheridan one dark night. The lights at the depot were out and no one was meeting us (as we thought). Effie began to blow up like mad, cussed a little too, if I remember right. When out of the darkness, a voice said "never mind girls. I'm here to take you home". It was no one else but handsome Captain Marshall himself. Was Effie's face red! He took us to the house and the first thing I heard when I went to my room was the most beautiful Taps I had ever heard. I have never forgotten it all these years later.

That night Captain and Mrs. Marshall stayed at the Officer's quarters while waiting for their furniture. We had Army cots to sleep on at their new house, so we managed. We finally got settled as the furniture arrived the next day. The Army provided some furniture but not all, so we were busy for a few days. I had the fine glassware to take care of. Mrs. Marshall herself sometimes helped, too. She would never let me wash the dishes, only glasses. She wanted my hands pretty for waiting on the table. She was wonderful to us all the time I was with her. She was a little woman but quite pretty and the Captain was quite a tall, well built man. They were very much in love although she was 32 and he 38. There were no children but Mrs. Marshall's mother and father, Old General and Mrs. Page lived part of the time with them, along with their other daughter. Miss Marjorie was part invalid. I never did find out what her trouble was, but as far as I knew she never married although she had plenty of beaus. The Marshalls entertained constantly and I was kept quite busy. I had to order the pickles and sauces and kept them in my pantry, which was a room between the kitchen and dining room. Also, all drinks were mixed there. I often think of the drinks Captain Marshall and I mixed in that room. Sometimes we had 18 for dinner. It was at Ft. Sheridan that the ladies of the Post wanted to know from Mrs. Marshall what kind of rouge I used. She told them I didn't use it, but they didn't believe her. One afternoon she had them in for tea so they could see for themselves. One lady didn't believe and asked me if she could touch my face which made me mad, and my face flamed all the more. She believed it then and begged my pardon. I told Effie about it out in the kitchen and she said they were only jealous but I still was ashamed of my coloring.

We had a cute soldier mailman at the Post, his name was Jones. I had to take the mail from him, a nice boy, but slow. About that time we had a change of Commissary men. Each morning a man from the Post Exchange and one from the Commissary came for orders and delivered the goods in the afternoon. Anyway, this certain morning I pushed the swinging door into the kitchen to tell Effie something or other about breakfast and a soldier man was sitting at the table taking down orders. I said "No, nothing this morning" and skipped back to my post. I was fixing grapefruit for breakfast and was kind of late. I heard him say something as I disappeared. Later, Effie said, "Nora, do you know what he said"? I said "No". She answered like this. He said "that's the girl I'm going to marry some day". Effie told him he'd have to go some to get me. Why, I told her, "he's an old man. I'm not marrying my grandfather". But it seemed that he was one of the bunch of soldiers that had arrived from the Philippine Islands about a month before and the heat had really affected him. He had known Effie's brother who was also over there.

Each morning he came but I avoided him and always had my order slip on the kitchen table waiting for him. One afternoon he met me in the kitchen when he was delivering and stopped to chat. I really found he was quite nice and not that old. Finally he said, "Can I call on you ?" I said "oh, I guess so". So he made a date for the end of the week. Being busy I didn't think about it any more. The evening of the date came and I said to Effie, "guess I'll go to bed early tonight and read". Oh no you don't she said, you have a date tonight. And just as she said it there was a knock at the door. "There he is now" she said, "go to the door". I tried to get out of it as I had really forgotten. Anyway, in walked the neatest soldier I had ever seen so far, dressed in his blues. I had never seen him in his blues before. He usually wore khakis or fatigue uniforms while working. He did look neat now, his cap in his hand. He came right in. I told Effie I couldn't go out anywhere with him as I was on duty that evening, but she fixed that. She marched right in to Mrs. Marshall and said she'd answer bells so I could go out. It was alright with Mrs. Marshall too, so I had to give in. Effie handed me my coat and said "off you go". Oh we first just walked the post as he didn't have a pass to go out and he had to answer call to quarters at 10:45 p.m. He was like a big brother to me that night and always. Right now it's pretty hard to write about this as I'm alone again and still loving him so. He'll always kind of remain there in a very special place of his own in my heart. Anyway we spent a very nice evening together that spring night and I changed my mind about his age, he was only 26, really.

We had regular dates after that. Finally one morning I had a note from him from the hospital. He was taken there with a bad case of yellow jaundice. Effie and I had been calling on our soldier boy who helped at the house. While on drill practice, a horse had fallen on him and broke his leg so we had been constant visitors at the hospital. So now we had another patient to see. When we went, we generally took oranges and cigarettes and Stinie was really sick. Even his eyes were yellow. He was in the hospital two or three weeks. Finally he was released. The Post went on maneuvers about that time. Artillery, Cavalry and all were alerted to be on the move. They journeyed all the way to Toledo, Ohio and took my sweetheart along with them.

I had promised to marry him before he left. One evening in the kitchen he laid his whole life in front of me and asked me if I'd marry him when he was discharged in November. We were very much in love by that time and it would have been hard to say no, but I told him I was a Catholic. He answered by saying he would become one as he always went to the Catholic Church when he did go and even carried a prayer book around with him for years. I think I still have that little prayer book.

When he was ordered on the hike instead of going back to the Commissary it broke our hearts. But when you're in the Army you go where they tell you. So away my soldier boy went. We spent the evening before departure together, of course, and our promises were many. To write every day and so forth and that we did. I still treasure his letters and mine, as he saved his also.

The summer dragged along and my little mailman Jones started making eyes again seeing Stinie was gone. I told him while he was making time at the front door that the Stine man beat his time. Oh, I danced with him at the Hops but he never took me home but once. He was a swell dancer and I did like to waltz with him.

Effie kept telling me I was a fool not to go out with some one while Stine was away but I just couldn't see it that way. One evening she almost convinced me and made a blind date for me with a friend of her boyfriend. I really started out alright but when I got to the gates of the Post and saw the fellow I backed off like a stubborn mule. I said to Effie "I just can't do it". I told the fellow I was sorry and said goodnight. It was dark and we were standing by the Guard House. Then I turned and ran, and I could run in those days, believe me. I ran into a guard on duty and he grabbed me and nearly lost his rifle. "What's the matter?" he said, "why are you running?" and "why are you crying"? (I was sobbing my heart out). "Did somebody annoy you"? I said "no, I just wanted to get home fast". So he walked with me as far as his beat would allow him but he didn't ask any more questions. I never went on any more blind dates. I wrote my love letter every day and got one every day and that, in a way kept me kind of happy.

The mail, of course, followed the boys around. That's when the maneuvers were over in Toledo. After that, they were working their way back to Ft. Sheridan, town by town. Captain Marshall also was on the hike, being a Cavalry officer, so the entertaining at the house slacked up a bit. Finally in September the boys began to drift back. The Infantry were almost last as they really had to march. Captain Marshall came home and I began to look for the Artillery to move in as they had horses too. In those days nothing was mechanized.

I still danced with the boys that were left and enjoyed myself by visiting Childress, our stricken man, at the hospital. He still was there as his leg hadn't turned out so well and I guess he was due for discharge. The Artillery finally came home one Saturday and happiness, real happiness reigned in my heart.

My boyfriend, Jim, had given me a very nice engagement ring before he left. Two twin opals with chip diamonds. I was very proud of it but wasn't allowed to wear it when I served dinner at night, so I had the habit of leaving it on my dresser exposed to everyone who wanted to look at it.

The guard and the prisoners always put in screens and did such work as that around the Officer's Quarters. One day I went to my room after they had been there and my ring was gone. I reported it to Captain Marshall and right away he had the prisoners searched, but the ring couldn't be found. Our belief was that the guard himself took it and as he had gone off duty that noon with a 24 hour pass we never found the ring. But it broke my heart to lose it. Everything possible was done to find it, even to searching the shops in the towns surrounding the post, but to no avail. We never found it.

October passed and I gave Mrs. Marshall notice I was going to leave her, which made her feel bad. I hated to leave too as she was like a mother to me, really. The whole family took it hard but I was going to marry the man I loved and nobody could stop me. In November he was going to be discharged and go home to Howell, Michigan. I was to follow in a week or so.

One of the prisoners who was in for desertion had his wife on the Post somewhere. She was older than I was but the Marshalls hired her to take my place. She came to work a week or so before I left so I could kind of train her. Mrs. Marshall had trained me. The lady of the house was quite particular about things and liked even her breakfast served properly. I showed her a lot in those few days and she was quite grateful.

I was all packed by this time. I had gone to town and bought my wedding dress and hat, a soldier blue suit and blue velvet hat. My sweetheart had been discharged on the 9th day of November and had gone home and I was lost without him.

The family presented me with a set of silver for six which was to come to Howell after I got there. The day came when I had to leave. Mrs. Marshall grabbed me in the back hallway and kissed me with tears streaming down both our faces. She had come into the kitchen one evening before Stine had left and told him he better be good to me or else, and she really meant it.

I think I left Chicago in the morning and got into Howell around seven at night. As I went to step off the train at the depot a man in civilian clothes reached up to take me in his arms and I backed away from him. Finally he said "Why Hon, don't you know me"? and I really didn't as I had never seen him in civvies. In fact I hadn't seen very many young men in civilian clothes, always uniforms. I remember I said "Why didn't you wear your uniform and let me get used to it gradually?" His sister Cora was with him and I sure fell for her. She was a sweet person and is to this day.

They took me home to Cora's house and I met her husband Fred and their little boy, Don. In a few days I went to call on the parish priest to make arrangements for the marriage. Stine had called him already and Fr. Thornton told me he was a very nice fellow. And so we were to be married on Saturday evening, November 27 at 7:30. In those days a non catholic didn't have to take instructions before marrying a catholic. I made the usual preparations, Confession and Communion on that Saturday morning but I felt so alone. None of my own people to see me get married. Fr. Thornton had called some girl up and asked her and her boyfriend to stand up with us. Their names were Mary Dunne and Frank Meehan. He asked Mary if she would like to be bridesmaid for the cutest little Irish girl he ever saw. I wonder if he was making fun of me!

The 27th rolled around and everything was ready. All we had was ice cream and cake. We went across to the rectory and Frank and Mary were waiting for us. I didn't feel so nervous but I could feel my cheeks blaze. It didn't take as long as a Church wedding and after my new husband had slipped the ring on my finger, it was all over. Fr. Thornton had to ask him to kiss me which made us all laugh. He was very sweet and stood so straight, I was proud of him and always was, no matter what he did later. He never did kill that pride I had in him while watching him walk so straight down the street. And he kept that gait till the day he died. And I did love to watch him just walk down to the store, but he never knew it I guess. He did know about how proud I was of him. I loved him very much, all the 35 years we were married.

He got a job in Howell at a Poultry House and we went to live in a small cottage on what is now called Michigan Avenue. Oh, we were poor but very happy. It didn't matter what I didn't have as long as I heard that beloved step coming home to me. We were young and our whole life was ahead of us. (Right here I can't go on writing as the lump is rising in my throat).

We went without a lot of things in those days as work wasn't very steady but rent was due. I believe we paid $5.00 a month for our little house and food was cheap. But then again, wages were low, too, but we got along and by spring I discovered a lot of things I could do without.

We were planning by this time for the arrival of our baby due some time in August and I wasn't feeling so good. But summer came along and everything was different. I had gotten acquainted with more people. We had a grand time on the Lake and had lots of fish suppers during that summer.

I remember Decoration Day of that year. Jim was asked to take part in the parade. He put on his uniform which was blue with red trim and lighter blue pants. I stood on the side watching the parade pass and my soldier boy marching so proudly. Then a lady standing by me said "Gee whiz, I didn't know the Salvation Army marched in the Parade!" She said it loud enough for everyone to hear it. After that he never wore his uniform again. She must have been really stupid.

My husband's mother and stepdad lived in Howell also and that day we had a date for supper with them. We were to have strawberry shortcake for dessert and on our way there it started to snow. Believe it or not, imagine snow on the 30th of May and homegrown strawberries for supper!

As I said before, work was scarce for the laborer and sketchy, so Stinie was forced to take any kind of work. The owner of the Poultry House sent him to Perry, Michigan for a while. He was gone all week and came home weekends, which left me all alone although I had some very nice neighbors, all elderly women. But the nights were terribly lonely and I was scared stiff of storms. I lay awake all night waiting for one to come up. One neighbor who I really liked was an Irish lady I had met. She came from Cork, Ireland and she kind of adopted me as her own. If she heard a storm coming up in the night she'd come right up to the cottage I lived in to be with me. It was an awful hot summer, the summer of 1910.

The first Saturday Stinie came home for the weekend I heard him come. Somehow his footsteps hit the sidewalk just so. Anyway, I heard him coming and was so shy in meeting him. I ran for the privacy of the little house and he came to look for me there. I was thrilled to pieces to have him home again, even for a few days. He was soon sent back to Howell again and the Poultry business really got slack.

He got a job out in the country helping to build a brick school house next. I had a mandolin I used to kind of play on and sing along with a little in my single days. Having no more use for it, we traded it for a bicycle so Jim could get home once in a while, which he did 3 or 4 days a week.

I had written to my mother in Ireland in the spring and told her I wasn't feeling so good. Mother-like she guessed the cause, packed up and came over to America again. She had been over here before and got homesick, so we had sent her back home. My oldest sister Margaret had come with her the first time and she had remained in New York when Mother went back home.

Anyway, I had a letter from the folks in New York saying that Mother was on her way out to Michigan to be with me when my baby arrived. Stinie met her at the depot and recognized her at once. Family resemblance, I guess. I was awfully glad to see her and have her with me at this time.

The day arrived when I thought sure my hour had come. I wasn't scared and in those days you didn't have the hospitals like they have now. All babies were born at home. The doctor came and told me my baby would arrive the 25th of August. I said, "Oh no, that can't happen, we weren't married till the 27th of November!" Dr. Brown laughed at me and asked some questions and then explained some things to me that I had never heard before. It eased my mind somewhat.

The morning of the 25th arrived and in the early dawn I knew it was the right time. Mother went to the neighbor down the street and had them call the doctor. Stinie was still building the School house and didn't come home every night so Mother was with me. The doctor came and made an examination and told Mother it would be some time yet. He asked me if I wanted my husband with me. I was horrified. "No", I said, "please don't call him. I don't want him here at all". What a mistake I made that day. I weighed only 98 lbs. when I married so I was really having trouble now.

They finally sent for a neighbor across the street to give me the ether. My favorite neighbor was at my side, also. The baby had to be taken and the doctor told my mother it was either the mother or the child that could be saved, he couldn't promise that both would survive.

The ordeal ended about 7:30 in the morning with a half dead baby and an unconscious mother. At this moment another neighbor kept saying to herself "will I go or not?" She finally did come and came in the door as the doctor laid the baby aside. Both other neighbor women and mother were busy with the doctor and I had no one to take that baby and bring the spark of life to it. When God bless her, Liz Arnold walked in as if God had sent her, took that little bundle out in the kitchen and blew the breath of life into her and saved her. The poor little tyke had a crooked mouth and pointed head from the forceps. I never thought when I first saw her later that afternoon that she'd grow up into a beautiful baby girl and young woman.

Of course, the new Daddy was sent for and in the excitement, the party that called him told him in this manner "Better come home Jim, you have two now." He took it for granted we had twins. He got on the bicycle. A storm had been raging all morning with lightning, thunder and heavy rain. That didn't stop him. Finally a tire blew out. He still kept going. Another tire went out. That didn't stop him, either. He came home on the rims of the wheels, which of course, ruined the tires and also the wheels. I was dopey from the ether yet, and not quite awake. He washed, shaved, and tiptoed into the bedroom for clean clothes. He finally got up enough nerve to come to the bedside and speak to me. I had to giggle, as bad as I felt when he said "Gee, honey, where are they?" I said "They?" I turned back the blanket and said I have the homeliest baby ever and it wasn't a boy and then I let go and sobbed my heart out. Not because I had a girl instead of a boy but because I was so glad to see him, and knew everything would be alright. It was like that all through our life together. Whenever trouble or sickness came, when he came home and took over, I relaxed. I knew the children weren't going to die or whatever else was bothering us would clear away. Nothing or no one could harm us while he was around. (Oh, dear God, I must stop again. The heartache is coming back and I don't want tears here.)

Chapter Seven

At last I was up and around again but very shaky. My baby was beautiful. She had weighed over 7 lbs. at birth and gained weight daily. Her little face and head had become normal. She had the largest blue eyes and a lot of dark hair which turned blond as she grew. She looked like her Daddy, everyone said so. Three days after she was born, on a Sunday she was taken to the Church and christened. I gave her the name of Eileen and Fr. Thornton gave her Marie as he stood kind of pro tem as Godfather. Mother was the Godmother and was she proud when she came home from Church carrying my beautiful baby. She said she was good as gold. We had ice cream and cake then just like a birthday party, but they wouldn't give me any ice cream which made me mad. It wouldn't have hurt me but in those days they believed that anything other then chicken soup or broth, tea or toast could hurt a new mother. Today they give them everything!

The summer days drew to a close. Mother stayed with us. Jim got work in town and we were very happy. The baby grew fat and wonderful and so very much like her Daddy. She had the largest blue eyes and blond hair and was a great favorite with the growing girls in the neighborhood who often took her riding in her baby carriage, a wicker one with one of those sunshades instead of a hood. The winter of 1910 passed with a lot of snow which sometimes reached to almost under my arms. But then, I'm still only five foot two. No snowplows in those days. I remember Jim getting a case of sore throat which developed into quinsy, the bad kind. I finally had to walk through all that snow to town to get the doctor. When he saw me he gave me a good scolding and started out ahead of me to make a path. He was dressed for the snow with hip boots. He lanced Jim's throat with me acting as an assistant.

The spring of 1911 finally came, the awful heavy snow disappeared and pretty soon the warm weather came to cheer everybody. Our baby Eileen was a chubby armful by this time and a great favorite with her grandmother O'Connor who took wonderful care of her. By July I discovered that I was again to become a mother. The doctor said in December sometime, but by the 16th of October another sweet little girl arrived which surely surprised everybody. We named her Marguerite Elizabeth after my sister and Jim's mother. Two babies in less then 14 months! Mother stayed with me until the spring of 1912 when she went back to New York City. I was very lonely after Mother left. Due to the lack of work in Howell, Jim had gone to Lansing to work, he was lucky to get employment in a factory there. He boarded with his sister, Maude and came home weekends. Of course, after Mother left it was impossible for me to stay alone with two babies, the littlest one hadn't been well and in fact a little while before Mother left we nearly lost her. The doctor gave no hope for her recovery at the time, but somehow she did get well after a very bad spell. One afternoon she seemed to have breathed her last. A neighbor who was present said "Noreen she's gone". Her breathing had stopped and I thought I had lost my baby. But God gave her back to us, it seemed, and she seemed to gain new strength after her recovery. We decided to move to Lansing. We found a small apartment where the Lawrence Bakery is now and so we came to another milestone in our life. We had to send our household goods by freight, so we had to stay a few days with Jim's sister. Our goods came finally and we were very happy in again fixing our little home.

By the summer of 1912, the baby was well again, the oldest was a bundle of health anyway. So with Jim working steady our troubles seemed to cease. Although we didn't have the things young people have today, we were happy with what we did have. I remember that summer we sent away for a library table, dresser and rug, bought on time, of course. I was the proudest thing alive when they arrived. I made all our clothes and trimmed my own hats then and made the baby's too, without a sewing machine. We took trips to the park on Sundays on the street cars and spent nearly all day there. That, of course was our only entertainment. We were young, life was ahead of us, so what!

Around 1913 Jim got a job working for a contractor. He had learned the trade of a gas engine mechanic while at the factory and was sent out often on trouble trips. So he really worked for both places. When the factory sold an engine to run a cement mixer he had to go and instruct the men on how to run it. This contractor put in foundations for large buildings, and city sidewalks and such. Finally we found a real house to live in and Mother came back to visit us. Both babies were running around then and looked like twins by that time.

Life goes on, no matter what sorrow or joys you experience. We enjoyed all the birthdays, Christmases, holidays, anniversaries in our small way. Halloween with the kids bobbing for apples. We had nuts, candy and pumpkin lanterns (real ones), but we never allowed them to "beg" as they call it here. We always put on a party with Jim and Mother just like kids too. Of course, I engineered the plans (leave it to me). Birthdays, the fairy Godmother hid in the flowers and bushes and brought birthday gifts. On Christmas, Santa Claus came; every Christmas Eve without fail and I'll never forget the face on my first born when she saw him for the first time. The second hid as usual behind Mother's skirts, but Brave! Oh Boy! I, of course, had run to the neighbors while Santa made his appearance. When I came back I was met with "Oh Mama, Santa was here and look what he brought me." Such childish trust, and I enjoyed it too with them. I lived for them and wanted them happy above all! A happy childhood is something to remember, but something came into our lives later that kind of dimmed it that I will not speak of here as if I did I wouldn't be loyal to Jim. I do hope they don't remember. As years went by and they grew up, maybe they didn't understand. I hope so, if when they read this, they will guess what it was. I hope they too will forgive and overlook. We all have faults of some kind, we aren't all perfect. As they grew, I knew the love they had for Papa was O.K. regardless.

The first day of school came for Eileen. How I hated to give her up. I had taught the children their prayers and part of the small catechism. I took her to St. Mary's that morning. She, I guess, thought the end of the world had come for her. Poor kiddie, she actually turned pale when I left her. I watched from the corridor and I noticed no tears, but her big blue eyes were larger, and yet I was the one who had a lump in her throat.

School got to be quite a picnic for her later. The next year she took part in some patriotic programs and of course, I had to go see it. When she came out on the stage waving a small American flag and stood in line with the other children I said to my mother who sat alongside of me "My God, what is the matter with Eileen's face, her jaws are swollen"! I rushed to get her when the program was over only to find out she had a bad case of the mumps. The first childhood disease and I was frantic! She didn't seem to be sick and of course in due time, Babe (Marguerite Elizabeth) also had them. She hadn't even started school yet, she was to begin in the coming Fall!

In the meantime I realized another child was to come in June of the coming year. I was glad. Dad and I planned for that baby so much, but that's a long story. Babe started to school in September so I had the two of them to take in the morning. There was no kindergarten at St. Mary's, the kiddies went all day, so I took them in the mornings and walked down to meet them both there in the afternoon. Babe hadn't been attending school only a little while when she was taken sick with Scarlet Fever. So we were quarantined in the house with Dad shut out. It was very hard. She didn't seem too bad until the last when we nearly lost her, but due to the wonderful doctor we had, she pulled through. He had given her up, had done all he could do with the medicine. Finally her health returned and she went back to school, a frail little bit of humanity.

In June of 1916 a baby girl arrived on the evening of the 10th. A baby with dark hair, lots of it, and big blue eyes. We wanted a boy but were delighted with our new girl. They didn't tell me until the next day that she had been born with a ruptured spine, a hole had formed at the base of her little spine. Two doctors arrived to examine her. They didn't know much about such things then, so they planned to operate right away, blindly, uselessly, without knowing what they were doing. I insisted on Baptism first. She got the name of Nora Josephine to be called Nonnie, as I had been called in my childhood, if she lived. From the Church she was taken to the operating room at the Sparrow Hospital. My poor little babe. I nearly went insane waiting for them to come home. Every car that went by went over my heart. Finally they arrived. She had a cast on her little back, but she nursed. I had plenty of food in my own body for her.

The next three months I would like to forget, but memory brings back those awful days so vividly at times and I say "Why, oh why didn't they leave her alone"? She wouldn't have suffered so much, I know. I suffered every pang with her and died a thousand deaths. Many the cold dawn found me on my knees pleading with God to take her to Him. I sometimes look back on those hours while the rest of the family slept. I couldn't rest. There was to be no rest for me until she could rest in the arms of the Blessed Mother. I knew, too, that she stood by to take over at the last. She died on the 13th of September of that year and we laid her to rest at Mt. Hope in Lansing. Oh well, I have a little angel waiting for me when I go there. Every baby I saw after I lost her, I wanted to hold in my arms, they seemed so empty. I missed the feel of her little head against my shoulder. I suppose, if she had lived she would be an invalid in a wheelchair, but no matter what it would be, she was my baby and she had suffered so much.

Time heals all sorrows and as my Mother often said, little Nora Josephine wasn't to stay with us from the first, anyone could see that. But it's hard to part with loved ones even as time goes by and tears are dried in the eye. They are still shed in one's heart, that I know now so well! I had my two lovely healthy little girls. I thanked God for that and everybody admired them and how well behaved they were at all times.

On March 2nd, 1918, a big healthy boy arrived. Dad was overjoyed. A perfect baby with dark hair and eyes. We named him James Dennis. James for his Dad and Dennis for my brother who was fighting for his country in World War I. I little thought then that this baby boy would follow in his uncle's footsteps and go overseas to fight in World War II, but strange to say he did. Life is funny anyway you take it. Dad's boy, as he called him, was the apple of his eye. He dearly loved his children, nothing was too good for them. His boy was to be an Electrical Engineer. He'd come into the bedroom after waking up and hold him in his arms until Mother called him for supper.

Typed by Mary Lou Nelson 1995

Margaret McGuinness Elliott's memoir is entitled "My Life—An Adventure." She was born in Ballymote, Sligo, in 1887 and immigrated to New York City in 1904. Margaret wrote this text between 1972 and 1974 but died before completing it. A companion memoir was written by Margaret's niece, Alice McGuinness, between 1990 and 1991.

Chapter I

This is Christmas Eve, 1972, and I have just celebrated my 85th birthday on December 22nd, and being alone this evening my memory takes me back to a Christmas Eve in Ireland with my mother and sister. It must have been my last one there as it stands out so vividly in my mind. My mother made a fire of turf and coal, which burned brightly in our living room upstairs. We sat on the floor and enjoyed the warmth of the fire and then my mother made us a large pitcher of orangeade, which was so good I have never tasted anything like it since.

Then I thought of the last day I spent in Ireland before coming to America. It was an exciting day and yet I remember being rather lonely because it meant saying goodbye to my childhood friends; also old friends whom I had contact with through the years. Some of them had run the groceries, hardware and drygood[s][1] stores and were always so kind to me when I used to run errands for my mother and brothers. When I said goodbye to them, they had tears in their eyes and so did I as the thought came to me, as it must have to them, that we might never meet again.

Then there was the dance, which lasted until morning, which is the custom before one leaves for America. So many friends came and danced until it was time for me to leave for the train.

Then came the farewells to my mother, sister and brothers. My mother was so brave, even though she knew she was seeing me for the last time. She held back her tears and then turned to the friends around her and said: "I may never see her again but I always have this to remember—Margaret never said *no* to me," and I went on my way with those words ringing in my ears and in which in 67 years have never been forgotten.

Then I got on the train, which was going to take me to Queenstown, where I was to stay overnight and in the morning would have to take a ferry out to the ship which was to take me to America. That night for the first time I realized I was alone and away from home and there was no returning as I was on my way to the land of my dreams, America.

Chapter II

I don't remember how I got from the ferry to the ship but when I got there I was taken to my cabin with three other girls who were to share the cabin with me. The girls were all very nice, all about the same age. I had carried my little tin trunk with me, so must have found a place for it. I had a lower berth and I thought the bed looked quite comfortable. The girls and I sat around for a while and told our names. Then we talked about the night before in the lodging house and how we had to sleep on the floor and how tired we must have been to have fallen asleep so quickly, and it was morning before we knew it. We looked around our cabin and we all said we have a bed to sleep in tonight. We were all homesick and what a feeling that is. We felt we must eat and we looked around for a dining room. We found a great big room with long tables all set up for dinner. We four sat together and then others began to come in. A very nice elderly couple sat at the head of the table, and later on as the days passed I found them to be a great help to me as they had been in America before. In time we became good friends. They must have made quite an impression on me as I have never forgotten them. They were quite a help to me telling me about the American money; also about the different things to eat.

I don't remember what we did eat, if anything. But after leaving the dining room we looked around and eventually went up on deck. It being March it was quite cold and the waves were enormous, hitting up against the ship. It was a beautiful sight but I was beginning to feel a little sick which afterwards proved to be seasickness. I was very ill for five days. The girls told me afterwards that I was so sick they had to call the doctor whom they said poured brandy down my throat. I kept saying, "Please don't; I'll break my pledge." After the fifth day I was able to go to the dining room again and this time was able to enjoy the food. I went upon deck again several times, and I shall never forget those great big waves and at one time there was a hail storm which was the most beautiful thing I had ever seen. I shall never forget it.

We were to land in America on St. Patrick's Day but were several days overdue on account of the rough sea. It must have been about the 21st of March when we landed at Ellis Island safe and sound. I heard years later that my mother got a report through the papers that the *Cedric* had gone down and that she became ill from shock and never really recovered.

About the 20th of March we began to see land, which meant we were soon to land in America. Then it was farewells again to the people we became so attached to on board ship. The three girls who became my close friends asked for my address and of course I wanted theirs. In the course of exchanging addresses we found we were all going to different cities and although we were sure we would see each other again, we never did. So it was farewell forever again, and as I have said so many times "such is life".

Well, the ship landed at Ellis Island and I had to get a few things in my tin trunk and when that was done I asked where we were going to get out. A man in uniform asked if I were going to be met by someone. I said, yes, my brother was going to meet me. Then another man in uniform questioned me about money—asked me how much I had. All I had was in the palm of my hand and I showed it to him. He put his hand on my head and said "my, you're rich" and I really felt rich as I was going to land in America.

I was off the ship now and another man took me to what looked like a big cage and locked me in and said I must wait there until someone called for me. After a while they brought me a cup of coffee, which tasted good as I was very hungry.

And then the big moment—my brother came. I did not know him as he left Ireland when I was a little girl. But there was a family resemblance, so I knew he was my brother. He took me in his arms and from then on I knew I wouldn't feel alone anymore. My brother said, now you must meet my wife, so I met Alice, who from then on I was to know as my sister-in-law. I thought she looked lovely—she was dressed beautifully. Her hat, especially, must have been very becoming as that was the one thing I remembered so well. It had two different shades of ostrich plumes, which matched so well with the rest of her costume. We walked quite a distance until we got off the island. From there we took what must have been the subway. I was a little frightened going underground but was assured by my brother that it was quite safe. In about an hour we arrived at their home, which was an apartment in upper Manhattan [at] 43 East 131st Street. When I looked up and saw the big house, I thought they must be very rich but was told later that they only owned one apartment in the house. It was very difficult for me to get used to the way they lived—[with] the janitor and dumbwaiter, and having to walk up and [down] three flights of stairs. I was only there a few days when I met two girls who lived in other apartments in the house. They were about my own age and were just wonderful to me. They took me for walks on different streets and I learned about ice cream sodas and a lot of other things like how to tie my hair with a big bow and to carry a pocketbook. I began to feel like a real Yankee and that to me was a real accomplishment, and so I have never forgotten Josie Maul and Madeline Harrison.

Chapter III

My sister-in-law introduced me to another family, whom I became quite fond of—Mr. and Mrs. Duff. They had three children, May, Anne and Jim. They were younger than I but were so anxious to show me around. I guess it was because I was new in the neighborhood. There was a bakery near where they lived, which I remember so well because I learned about doughnuts and cream puffs, which I thought were wonderful. We paid a visit there at least once a day because the Duff girls liked them, too. I stayed with the Duff family once when my sister-in-law and brother went on vacation. I enjoyed being with them because having so many around reminded me of home. Jim Duff, the girls' brother, became quite interested in me, not because I was a girl but because I was an Irish immigrant. I wasn't too interested in him because I didn't like the way he combed his hair. It was quite long at the back and combed into what in those days they called a ducktail. The boys who combed their hair that way were called toughs. I imagine they were similar to our Hippies now. Those boys went around in groups of four or five and stood on street corners and if girls passed, they whistled. If May, Anne or I took a walk where we had to pass some of them, we were not whistled at because Jim was one of them. We were happy about that.

My brother and sister-in-law worried about my being so homesick and I know now that I must have [been] because even after 67 years I have that longing for my mother and the lovely walks we used to take in the fields which were close to our house and the hedges filled with primroses and buttercups and little hills covered with bluebells, which at a distance looked like a beautiful blue carpet. After a long walk we would sit on the grass, which felt so cool because there is so much moss in the grass in Ireland. It felt as if you were sitting on a soft rug. In the distance one could see the mountains covered with heather, and once in a while we would come across a little brook where we would pick watercress to take home for dinner. Oh, if I could only describe the beauty of the crabapple and sloe blossoms in the hedges. How beautiful it all was! No wonder the Irish immigrant wrote these words, of which I will now try to sing the chorus:

> Ireland, Ireland, though I am over the sea,
> Erin, my country, at night I am dreaming of thee.
> Dear little isle of the west, sweet spot of memories blest,
> Land of the bog and the shamrock, oh, how I long to be there.

My sister-in-law, being very anxious for me to get over being lonely, introduced me to many more nice friends. One family I remember quite well, the Barry family, who consisted of Mrs. Barry, a widow, whose husband was a very dear friend of my brother and who came from Ireland also. The family consisted of four children who were quite young when I met them. May was the oldest, then Kathleen, Francis and Madeline. I met them years later and they had grown into very charming ladies and gentleman. Many evenings my brother would take me to see Mrs. Barry and family, and I loved to go because she always served homemade chocolate layer cake and ice cream, which I liked very much.

My brother and sister-in-law one day asked me if I would like to go to work. I said I would like to very much, so we decided I should be a dressmaker. I answered an ad for an apprentice for a dressmaker on Fifth Avenue. I got the position. My hours were from 8:00 A.M to 6:00 P.M. and a half-hour for lunch. I got $2.00 a week. I walked to and from work but had to eat my lunch in the shop. I found out my boss was a Jewish woman who had a young sister who also worked there. They were born in Germany and spoke with an accent, but most of the time they spoke in German, which annoyed me, as I didn't know what they were talking about. I was there quite a while, but all I learned was sewing on hooks; then at six o'clock I would have to deliver a dress or something to someone miles away, which meant I would have to take a streetcar and not knowing the city, I nearly always got lost and then would arrive home for dinner very late, which provoked my brother and sister-in-law very much.

I finally rebelled and wouldn't go to work there any more. I told my brother I would rather be a maid. I was taken to an employment agency by a friend. A lot of Irish girls came there and you sat around waiting until you were called to fill some position. I sat there until every one else was called. Then a man came and told me I was too young for that kind of work and to try for something else.

I went home very disappointed and wondered what I should do next. My brother came to my rescue and got me into Siegel Cooper's Department store. A friend of his was a buyer there in the conservatory, which was on the sixth floor and where they sold all kinds of plants and bird and goldfish. It seemed like paradise to me as it was like being out in the country. The job I got was cashiering and as yet I wasn't well acquainted with the American money. However I met wonderful people in the department, one girl particularly whom God must have sent into my life. She was my guardian angel and indeed took me under her wing all the time I was in that department. Her name was Miss Wright and she remained Miss Wright until we parted which was months later. She left to get married. I missed her very much.

Shortly after that I was transferred to the main floor. I got on to the money quickly—that is why I was sent to a busier place, which pleased me very much as where they placed me was cashiering at the fountain. The fountain was a place that if you were shopping downtown and wanted to meet a friend, you would say "meet me at the fountain," where you could have a light luncheon or ice cream. It was a very busy place but I came in contact with very nice people.

Time went on and I became one of the cashiers who was placed in busy departments on the main floor. Then one day I was called to the office and they said I had a shortage of two dollars in my cash register. Oh, I felt so bad because I heard from some of the other girls who also were there because of a shortage that it would be taken out of my pay. I was getting four dollars a week and having two dollars taken out of that, I wouldn't have much left. And how could I go home and tell my brother. Well, I began to cry and felt as if the world had come to an end for me. But now I see that God had other things planned and that it was just the beginning of better things for me, because as I was sitting in the office, one of the young girls came over to me and said "don't cry—I also have a shortage, but perhaps we can find the mistake when we look over our tape." I'll never forget how kindly her voice sounded and immediately I knew that I had found a friend. Her name was Gertrude Cant. She was dressed in black and looked very pretty. Later I found out she was in mourning for her father who had just recently passed away. We didn't find our shortage but we did become close friends. We arranged to have lunch together every day and got to know each other quite well. Then we met another girl, Ann Muller, and the three of us became pals. New York was beginning to feel like home to me on account of meeting such nice girl friends.

Gertrude, Ann and I would meet on Sunday afternoons and take trolley rides to different parks. I remember Gertrude suggesting Pelham Bay Park, which in those days was in the country. I remember so well how wonderful it was to be out in the country. Gertrude told me that her father was a coachman for Knox the Hatter and the Knox family that lived in a beautiful home near the park. And that her family lived over the stable in a lovely apartment and she as a child played with the Knox children. Gertrude lived on 117th Street east and on some Sundays Ann and I would meet her there and since she lived near Central Park we very often took walks in the park and then to her house for tea.

One day when I got home from work, my brother told me I would have to go to my friends, the Duffs, for a few days as there was a baby coming to the house and when it arrived I could not come back. I was gone about two days when my brother came for me. On arriving home, I was taken to the bedroom and my sister-in-law showed me a lovely baby girl. I was so thrilled to know I had a niece and her name was going to be Alice.[2] The christening took place on Sunday and many friends came. It was a lovely party.

One day at work, Gertrude, Ann and I with several others, were called to the office and a very nice woman told us we were to have a week's vacation in Long Branch, New Jersey, a gift from the company. We were told to take our personal things in a suitcase and to be at the store on Saturday morning when we would be taken by trolley car to the ferry which would take us to Long Branch.

Chapter IV

Well, the great day arrived for us to meet and go to the boat which would be waiting for us at the Battery to take us to Long Branch. I met Gertrude and Anna at the store and with several other girls went on the subway to the Battery. We were told by someone there how to get on the boat and to find seats together, which we did. We were only on the boat a short time when we were on our way to a great adventure. I shall always remember how delightful that trip was. I cannot remember how long it took to get to Long Branch but I do know that I must have wished that it could go on forever and that there never would be anything more beautiful than what we were experiencing on that lovely summer day, going on a week's vacation in the country. We talked and laughed and sang some lovely old songs and then we got to our destination with a little regret that it was all too short but with great anticipation of the days to come.

When we got off the boat at Long Branch, a great big wagonette was waiting for us. We all got on and were driven to a lovely old home about a half-mile from the beach. We were greeted at the door by a lovely lady whom we found out later was to be our housemother. She, with two other women, showed us to our rooms. There were only two allowed in a room but Gertrude pleaded and she arranged to have a cot put in our room so that we could be together. The room was very homey and cool and big enough for two small beds and the cot, [which] Anna Muller without any persuasion said she would sleep on. We washed up and were quite ready to eat lunch when we got the call to go to the dining room. I cannot remember what we had to eat but I'm quite sure we were hungry enough to enjoy it. After lunch we went out on the lovely green lawns where we found all kinds of things, lounge chairs and swings and croquette sets. The one thing I remember so vividly was a wooden swing with room for four. We would sit in that for hours and sing all the popular songs of 1905. In the afternoon we could go to the beach, which was private. We were supplied with bathing suits, which were in the height of fashion for those days. They were cut with a round neckline and short puffed sleeves. The skirt was below the knee and with that you wore long black stockings, which had to be held up by an elastic garter, which was always too tight and very uncomfortable. On your head you wore a very fancy bathing cap. The beach was beautiful, so clean and cool, and for those who could swim it was ideal. Gertrude, Anna and I couldn't swim but one day we took a chance and went out a little farther than we were supposed and the lifesaver had to come out to get us.

The days flew by so quickly, each day bringing a new thrill. There were two lovely young ladies at the house, who in the evenings gave us book reviews and showed colored slides of the Rockies and Yellowstone Park. Refreshments would be served later. Then one day we were taken to Asbury Park, which was a lovely summer resort in those days. While on the boardwalk there we met some boys from Brooklyn, who were on vacation. At that time there was a cartoon in one of the papers. It was called "The Hall Room Boys." They were supposed to be boys who spent a lot of money on themselves and lived in hall rooms in boarding houses. I don't know why but we immediately figured that they were the Hall Room Boys—perhaps because they did not treat us to a soda—and so didn't become too interested in them. Some time later we met them in Brooklyn and they turned out to be very nice boys, not at all the Hall Room boys we thought they were. So we learned through that not to judge people until you know them better. The most memorable week of my days in America was drawing to a close. I had become so fond of my friends, Gertrude and Anna, that the thought of parting and never being so close to them again was frightening. How little I knew what God had planned for me: that Gertrude was to be my close friend for life and that now at 85, her children and grandchildren are calling me "Aunt Margie."

The last day of our vacation we were taken to Pleasure Bay, another lovely summer resort, with cool breezes from the ocean. We walked around and am sure made that last day a very happy one. The day had come for the farewells to the gracious people who entertained us and I'm sure the thought must have come to them that they were saying goodbye to some very nice girls whom they might never meet again. I said goodbye to Gertrude and Anna when we reached New York after another very enjoyable trip home.

I reached home and found my sister-in-law and brother waiting anxiously to hear all about my vacation. They seemed so pleased to have me back safely and I felt a sense of security, which no matter where we go, or what we do, we find only with our own. Little Alice also seemed to show that she was glad to have me back and I was so happy to see her that I took her for a ride in her baby carriage, which I did on many occasions while I lived with my brother.

I went to work Monday and as usual met Gertrude and Anna. We had lunch together and of course talked of nothing else but our vacation. We didn't mind getting back to work because we would plan so many nice things to do in the evenings, and no matter what we did, we always enjoyed it, if it were only having a soda.

Chapter V

The Christmas rush at the stores was drawing to a close and we were all very happy as the long hours (from 8:00 A.M. to 10:00 P.M.) were beginning to tire us out. When I got home one evening, my sister-in-law said she would meet me the next day at the fountain as she wanted to buy me a Christmas present. I met her the next day and she bought me the most beautiful red suit and a white velvet hat. I thought it was the lov[e]liest outfit I had ever seen. With the suit I wore a white blouse with a lace jabot, which I kept for years. I liked it so well I couldn't part with it. I was grateful to my brother and sister-in-law. I thought it was so kind of them to do that for me when I still had been unable to pay my board. I wore the suit to Mass on Christmas Day and afterwards my brother took me to call on some friends and they told me I looked like a real Yankee.

My sister-in-law had a very delicious dinner ready when we got home, my first Christmas dinner away from home. I was sorry to disappoint them but I really felt homesick and couldn't eat. However, as years went by I enjoyed many more delicious Christmas dinners at my brother's home with his family. I am sure those made up for the first Christmas dinner which I couldn't eat.

The winter went by quickly and I was seeing a lot of Josie Maul and Lillian Harrison. They were having nice parties at their homes and I was always invited. They invited boys from the neighborhood and we played games. Afterwards we were served ice cream and cake. I don't remember the names of the boys or the other girls at the parties but they must have made an impression as I have never forgotten them or the parties.

It was coming near Easter and we were beginning to be busy at the store. It was an exciting time. People were buying their Easter outfits and once again my sister-in-law met me at the store to buy me a suit. This time I chose a grey suit and a lovely red straw hat. I wore the outfit on Easter Sunday and after church I met Josie Maul and we walked over to Seventh Avenue where the uptown Easter parade took place. It was so colorful. The hats especially were so becoming and looked like flower gardens.

Coming home that day we walked on Fifth Avenue, which in those days had all brownstone homes. They were not the millionaires' homes of lower

Fifth Avenue but they had dignity, and as we walked along we saw in front of some of the houses a coachman sitting up in front of a lovely carriage waiting for some of the family who were going for a ride. Those were the lovely gay nineties.

I met Gertrude the next day at lunch. She was very sad. She said her older sister, Nellie, was taken to St. Luke's Hospital and she was very ill. Within a few weeks after she died of tuberculosis. She [Gertrude] stayed home with her mother for a few days, and I felt very lonely without her.

Then around that time we had a lot of excitement at our house. Little Alice became ill one night and was very sick. The doctor was called and he said she had pneumonia and was very ill. I remember he had to stay all night and worked in his shirtsleeves until early morning when he brought the good news that she was out of danger and would be quite well again.

I went to work the next day and met Gertrude for lunch as usual. As we talked, I knew there was something wrong. Then she told [me] that an aunt who lived in Brooklyn wanted her mother to move there and that she would find them an apartment near where she lived and that it was a very nice neighborhood. I said I was sure that would be a very good thing for them to do as their neighborhood was beginning to get run down (on the Lower East Side). More Jews and Italians were moving in, and the Irish were moving uptown, and I was sure her mother was unhappy about that. Then suddenly I happened to think—what will I do if I have to part with another close friend, because we had really become quite close. So that night I cried myself to sleep. But as had happened in my life before, I had an inspiration and when I met Gertrude at lunch the next day I said, if you move to Brooklyn, ask your mother if I can go with you.

Chapter VI

I was coming to the final decision about leaving my brother's home. I knew that Gertrude's mother's home was entirely different as Mrs. Cant had told me on Sunday when she had a talk with me about their being Protestant. For the first time I realized there was a difference in religion. However, I think I straightened that out by telling her a story my mother told me when I was a little girl. She said she had a friend living at her house who was Protestant. Her name was Miss Saunders and she was a piano teacher who had many Protestant friends coming to see her, including the Minister and his wife, whom she liked very much and they wanted to adopt me when I was a baby. I think Mrs. Cant liked me better after I told that story and she said, your mother must have been a very nice person, and at that moment I really think she reminded me a little of my mother and more than ever I wanted to live with her and take Nellie's place in her home. Many thoughts came to my mind that day as I walked home. Would I fit in with the other children— Harry, who was older than Gertrude and who worked for Knox the Hatter on Fifth Avenue, and Ted and Mabel who were still in school. But it seemed, regardless of results, I was determined to take this step.

Mrs. Cant had told me on Sunday to have a talk with my brother and sister-in-law and find out what they would think about my going to live with them. I seriously wanted to do that but was quite sure it would make trouble and I did not want that to happen. So the next day when Gertrude and I were having lunch we decided that it would be better not to tell my brother—and that I should pack my things and throw them out the window and she would be on the stoop and pick them up and I could walk out the door and not say anything.

Well, the memor[able] night came, and of course I was very nervous. But luckily my sister-in-law's sister was visiting that day. She was a very nice person who used to come to visit once a week. I liked her very much. She always gave me a dollar when she was going home and I usually walked to the trolley with her. But that night she served a purpose. After dinner, she and my sister-in-law sat in the kitchen talking, which gave me a chance to pack some of my things and throw them out the window to Gertrude. I saw them go flying as the paper I put them in fell apart. But I hoped we could get them together when I got downstairs. I went back to the kitchen and talked with Catherine for a few minutes. I told them I was going out for awhile and walked out the door. And that was how I left my brother's home for an entirely new life, which must have been in god's plan, as I never regretted what I had done.

I cannot remember that I ever found out how my brother must have felt when he discovered that I had gone to live with Mrs. Cant, but knowing him as I did, I am quite sure that he found out that I was in a good home and that I was happy. I seemed to fit in with Mrs. Cant and her family and I made myself quite at home, and then the preparations for moving to Brooklyn began. We were all very excited about that. It meant leaving Siegel Coopers and finding other jobs in Brooklyn and saying goodbye to all the nice people we had met while working there and wondering what the future would hold for us in our new jobs. Mrs. Cant completed the work of moving so well that it felt as if we just moved from one room to another, and yet what a responsibility it must have been for her.

We arrived in Brooklyn and loved it. The apartment was different from any in New York. It was over a drug store and in a very nice neighborhood on the corner of Monroe and Stuyvesant Avenue, which they now say is entirely black.

It didn't take us too long to get settled, and within a week, Gertrude and I got cashier jobs in a very nice department store on Fulton Street. The only thing we did not like about it was we had to work in the tube room, which was in the basement, and Mrs. Cant thought it might not be healthy and that we should try to find other jobs. Luckily Ted had found a job in Mills and Gibbs, a wholesale house on Broadway and Grand Street in New York. One evening while eating dinner, he said he was quite sure we would be able to get an office job there, so Gertrude immediately went to see the Office Manager and she got the job. I stayed on at Loes[e]r's [department store] for a short time, and then I think Gertrude was lonely taking that long trip to New York all by herself. So, she asked her boss if I could work there also, and in a few weeks I, too, was working at Mills and Gibbs. We liked the office work, which was taking care of the salesmen's books. The hours were shorter than in the stores, and we had Saturday afternoons off, which gave us a chance to get better acquainted in Brooklyn. We had an hour for lunch, and on nice days we could walk down Broadway to the Brooklyn Bridge where we found a Loft's candy store that made a wonderful ice cream soda for 5¢. We made that our lunch dessert and also enjoyed the walk. Mills & Gibbs was located in the wholesale district, which was on both sides of Broadway from Grand Street to Canal Street. We very quickly got acquainted with boys and girls who worked in the other wholesale houses along the street. It began to feel we were in a small town. We met the same people every morning and also at noon and in the evening. It made us feel so good to know that we were being noticed, perhaps it was because we were always together. Anyway, as time went [on] both older and young men stopped long enough to greet us with a nice "Good morning!" or just a smile. I am sure we made a good impression because, if by any chance one of us was alone, we would be asked, "Where's your friend?" Always it would have to be a good explanation.

Then the memorable day arrived when Ed Bradshaw was to come into my life. We were out for our walk at lunch time one day and we passed some boys who were standing outside of Calhoun & Robbins, and Gertrude asked me if I noticed a tall young man who was standing there. I said, No, but I would be sure to look tomorrow. But tomorrow came and I forgot to look again. However, on the third day I did look and found that a very handsome young man was smiling at me and, of course, I also smiled. And that was the beginning of a wonderful romance when I was 19 years, and later it grew into a great friendship for 52 years. I shall tell more about that friendship as I go on with my story. It will be very interesting.

Chapter VII

We were enjoying living in Brooklyn more as time went on. The young people in our neighborhood were very friendly. The houses on Monroe Street were mostly private homes, and the boys and girls who lived in them were especially well-behaved. We got to know them quite well and often took walks with both boys and girls. There was one boy in particular whom Gertrude liked very much, and I think he had a similar feeling for her also. His name was Bill Beckman,[3] and his mother owned the property where we lived. He and a boy named Charley Clark asked us for dates a few times. Once in particular, I remember it was on a Sunday. They wanted to take us to Coney Island, so Gertrude told them they would have to get permission from her mother. Will bravely went upstairs to ask Mrs. Cant if we could go. He talked to her for quite awhile but when he came down he said we were not allowed to go because it was Sunday. What a disappointment that was! But we were repaid, as later that evening when the boys came back from Coney Island, they called on us and presented us with two lovely bouquets, the first I had ever received from a boy friend.

When we got to work the next day, we told the other girls in our office, and I think they were a little bit jealous, but they, too, had many nice things to tell about their friends.

One evening when Gertrude and I were walking to the bridge to get our train to go home, two young men—one of them was the tall boy from Calhoun's who always smiled at me when I passed the store—asked if he and his friend could walk with us. I looked at Gertrude, and she at me, and in a very bored voice I said yes. And then he handed me a Jewish paper, which I accepted with thanks, and then they began to guess what our names were, but we got to the bridge and they still had not found an answer.

We saw them again the next evening and they still persisted trying to find out what our names were. So we promised we would tell them the next evening. That night we got Harry Cant to write both our names on a calling card, and when they met us the next evening I handed the tall fellow the card with Gertrude's name and he turned the card over and saw my name. He said, "I bet this is your name," and then he introduced himself as Ed Bradshaw and his friend as Joe Burke.

Then one evening, Ed handed me a letter addressed, "Miss Margie Mc-Guinness," and inside it said, "If I had your address, this would be delivered to your home and I would know where you lived and perhaps I could call on you." The next day at the office, Gertrude and I got together and wrote him a letter to Calhoun's and gave him our home address, which started a correspondence and his coming to see me twice a week. I had my first trip to Coney Island with him. He took me on all the different amusements. I remember one in particular was the Rocky Road to Dublin. I thought I was going to see a view of Ireland. Instead of that, we were seated in a rubber boat and sent on our way hitting against all kinds of great big what seemed to be rocks but we found out they also were some kind of rubber. The idea was that the boy would have to hold on to the girl in a protective way. When we got out of there, Ed asked if I would like something to eat. I really was hungry but when he suggested a club sandwich, I got angry because I thought that was some kind of a joke. But he explained what it was, and that was the first time I ever had a club sandwich.

Chapter VIII

Ed came quite often to see me. He had to come from 43rd Street in New York all the way to Brooklyn. He always came upstairs to visit the family, and one evening he asked Mrs. Cant if he could take me on a trip to Staten Island. He said we might be a little late but he would bring me home safely. She said, "I'll trust you, but don't be too late." That was another memorable trip. It was quite a distance from where I lived to the ferry. When we got on the boat, Ed looked around and found some seats where we could look out on the water. I remember it was a beautiful moonlight night in June and, as we got seated, Ed looked at me and said, "I'm sure you are going to enjoy this." The moon was shining on the water, and the waves all seemed to be silver-lined and beautiful colors which were hard to describe. And now, 57 years later, I am thinking of it as if it happened yesterday. There were other couples on the boat and they, too, must have been enjoying it as there was lots of laughter and singing. Ed told me about the house his family was building in Dumont, New Jersey. He said he would take me to see it when it was finished and to meet his mother whom he said was born in Ireland. And that I would be the first girl to see his new home in Dumont. Years later I did see his home in Dumont but under entirely different circumstances, which will come into the story later.

When we landed at Staten Island, it was a very beautiful trip. We could see the New York skyline and the Statue of Liberty at a distance, and the moonlight shining on the water made it look so colorful, and I think we must both have thought we might never see anything more beautiful again or be quite so happy. When we got off at Staten Island for a walk, and on leaving the bright lights it looked so dark, I hesitated for a moment, and Ed said, "I'm glad you did that, but don't be afraid—I have sisters of my own; I will never harm you," and he never did.

We got home quite late but everyone was up and Ed came upstairs to say goodnight to Mrs. Cant. She seemed quite pleased that he had done that and when he left she said, "He is a very nice boy—don't ever do anything to hurt him."

Well, life is not all sunshine and roses. Into our lives some rain must fall, and that year a little came into my life. I had a letter from home saying my mother was quite ill and there wasn't a thing I could do about [it] but hope and pray. That was one of the tragedies of the young Irish coming to America in those days—you never seemed to get enough money together to go back. I never did. Later when I could, there was no one left to welcome me home. Gone are the dear ones who loved me of old. There's no one to welcome me home.

Months were flying by and the lovely summer days were going fast. We were liking Brooklyn more all the time and we used to look forward to going to work in the mornings as the trip on the elevated train was always so exciting. We would meet the same people nearly every day and would usually have some of the boys get up and give us their seats, which meant conversation all the way to the Bridge. Once in a while, some of them would express a remark about our dresses, always a compliment. I remember I had a hat with a bird on it, and that brought the remark from one of the boys, "Oh, the saucy little bird on Nellie's hat." I didn't mind his saying it because I was flattered to know that someone even noticed it."

On Sunday, everyone went to church. The church nearest to me was on Madison Street, and I nearly always attended the eleven o'clock Mass because that was the time Mrs. Cant and the family went to their church. It was the custom in Brooklyn that the boys waited outside the church for their girl friends. I, of course, was one whose boyfriend was not there and had to walk home alone, until one day it was raining quite hard and I did not have an umbrella. But I heard a very nice voice ask if he could walk me home. I thanked him very kindly and he walked to the door with me. That started another nice friendship.

Chapter IX

The boy who walked me home from church introduced himself. His name was George Reuter. He said he wasn't a Catholic but that he went to that Church with his friend. I asked how they got out of church so quickly. He said it was because they always knelt on one knee in the vestibule and were the last ones in and the first out, and they were called the sharpshooters. I didn't hold that against him because I did see him a few times after that, and we were quite good friends. He was born in Brooklyn and seemed to know a lot about it, which was interesting, and perhaps if Ed hadn't come into my life, we might have seen more of each other.

Months were flying by and the lovely summer was drawing to a close, regretfully because it was an exciting summer for both Gertrude and me. Living in Brooklyn in itself was one of the nice things we both enjoyed. We found it so peaceful. The lovely trees and the small private homes with iron railings and little gates and lawns well taken [care] of all looked as if the people living in them were content and happy. We were very happy that summer and perhaps that is why we didn't want it to end. I wonder if we had a feeling that we might never be that happy again. I wonder.

Ed was coming twice a week to see me, and Gertrude was seeing Will Beckner[4] quite often, and now that the days were getting shorter and cooler we did more entertaining at home, and that meant including the whole family. Mrs. Cant nearly always found an excuse to spend the evening with her sister, who lived downstairs in the lower flat, but Harry, Teddy, and Mabel all wanted to help entertain, especially Mabel, who at six years old was taking dancing lessons. So, she always wanted to turn on the photograph, which must have been one of Edison's first. It had a large horn—I can see it now—dark blue with pink flowers painted on it; I think they must have been forget-me-nots. We bought disks, which cost about fifty cents. The singers then were mostly Irish tenors. I remember one of them was Chauncey [O]lcott; also Andrew Mack. They preceded John McCormack. They always sang lovely Irish songs. We also had some band music. When we put that music on, Mabel would show off her tap dancing, and we would do a little dancing with the boys, which always ended up with lots of laughter. And then off to our very homey kitchen with the coal stove nice and warm. We would all sit around a large square table and have tea and cookies, which Mrs. Cant would make for the occasion. Oh, those were lovely gay nineties. How wonderful they were!

Chapter X

I have heard people say they dislike the Fall because the fall of the leaves brings sadness. Well I have experienced some sorrow in the Fall and yet I cannot say that I blame it on the season any more than at any other time. I believe God has made a pattern for us to fill in with our free will, and the things we do are in God's plans and that they are all for the best, even though we cannot see it that way at the moment.

The Fall of 1907 was very colorful; the trees were turning into those beautiful shades of orange, yellow and red, and Gertrude and I took so many nice walks on a Sunday afternoon. One Sunday we passed a photograph[er]'s place and we went in and had our pictures taken together. I think they were six for fifty cents. I wanted one to give to Ed. That was the first picture I ever had of myself (I still have one here on the mantel in my dining room).

It was getting quite busy at the office. The salesmen were coming in after a very rewarding summer, which put them in good humor and made it very pleasant for us. One Monday morning we were greeted by two new salesmen. They were both quite good-looking and were introduced to us by our boss. I was assigned to John Wallace, who had been on the stage in a play called "The Red Mill." It was a musical and was very popular at that time. He told me it closed up for the summer and he was out of work until it opened up again. In the meantime he was learning to be a salesman and he often entertained us singing some of the songs from the play, which we enjoyed very much. He sometimes walked to the Bridge with us but otherwise he kept to himself and was very mysterious.

We also got a new office boy, whose name was Dick Burell, and who became quite friendly with Teddy Cant. We learned later that his mother was a nurse and that he was alone when she went to work[, a]nd especially on Sundays. [W]hen Mrs. Cant heard that, she usually invited him over for dinner. He was a very nice boy and he came into my life many years later and became a close friend, whom I will tell you about later.

One evening on arriving home from work, Mrs. Cant told us that her sister, Aunt Maggie, was taken to the hospital, which made us very sad. She said she had a very bad heart attack and wasn't expected to live. She died a few days later, and her husband took her body to New York and she was buried there. Joe moved out of the apartment shortly after, and within a month a new family came to live there. Mrs. Cant got acquainted with them as Mr. and Mrs. Platt and a daughter, Mae, who was ten years old. Mr. Platt was a Captain on a Merchant Marine ship and he was very seldom at home.

We became quite friendly with Mrs. Platt and Mae, and spent many interesting evenings with them. And I shall tell more about them as I go on with my story.

The lovely autumn was coming to an end and it was Halloween. We had a party at the house. It was Ed's birthday and he was invited. We played all kinds of tricks, and there was fun and laughter, and then came the end of a memorable evening. I went to the door with Ed and he made a date to take me to New York to a show on Election night. He said that he would come early so we would have lots of time to get to the show.

The days dragged on until finally the night arrived. I remember getting all dressed up. I had a pretty green dress, and Gertrude let me have a necklace of hers, which matched the dress. The family said I looked so nice. I was counting the minutes until he came because going to a show in New York would indeed be another great adventure for me and with Ed. I was sure it would be a very happy one, and Mrs. Cant and Gertrude were almost as excited as I was about it.

The minutes dragged by and an hour passed, which made it about 8:30, and I was beginning to think that even at this time it would be too late to go to a show. I was beginning to be a little disappointed and perhaps worried, fearing something might have happened, and then the bell rang. To this day I cannot remember how I felt when Teddy called from the door, "It's Bradge, Margie." I ran into the bedroom and sat there for a moment so as not to be in the living room when he came there. Mrs. Cant was there and asked him to sit down. And when I came to greet him, he said, "I'm sorry I'm late, but the trains were crowded." I don't remember what I said, but he looked at me and said, "[L]et's take a ride to New York." We got on the elevated, and he did most of the talking. When we got to the Bridge, he suggested that we go down and have a soda at Loft's. I said no, I wanted to go home. He really tried very hard to have me change my mind, but stubbornness conquered and he took me home. And that ended "what might have been," for better or worse.

However, fifty years later it did end up beautifully, and that will be another part of my story, which will be very interesting.

Chapter XI

Time marches on and the November days are coming to an end, and as I look back on those days, I think they must have been rather lone[l]y days for me as Ed wasn't coming to see me any more.

However, we must go on and face the future, hoping and praying that, in God's divine plan, the things that are best for us will be what the future will hold for us, and as I go on with my story, that is what happened to me.

It is coming near Christmas and everything has taken on a look of festivity. At work, the salesmen who are from out of town, are getting things in order so that they can go home for Christmas.

Gertrude and I are planning what we will do during the holidays. I know it will be a happy time as the boys and girls who come to the house are always so full of fun. However, I do feel a little sad when they brought Ed into the conversation and I began to think how nice it could have been.

Christmas came and the usual exchanging of gifts, and fancy handkerchiefs seemed to be the thing that year, and the most we could afford was a quarter. As I remember it, one could get a very pretty one for that price in those days.

It was the custom in Brooklyn that the girls on New Year's Day had to have a reception for their favorite boyfriends. A table was set up in the living room with fancy sandwiches and cookies (which you were supposed to make yourself) and a bottle of wine. We saved our pennies for a couple of weeks to get all the things together, and the table did look very nice. The reception was from 3:00 o'clock until 5:00. The boys we knew in the neighborhood brought some friends whom we had not met before. They were boys on vacation from college. They were very nice boys and for the moment very entertaining. One of them was from Yale and as he was a great big fellow, we surmised that he was a football player. So from then on, we were avid football fans, and the sports page of the morning paper was thoroughly scanned for reports of the football games of Yale, Princeton, Columbia and Harvard, which were the most popular colleges at that time.

Sunday afternoons during the winter months, we usually had callers or took walks on Bedford Avenue. Either way, it always ended up having tea and cake and music on the phonograph. How nice it was, and so wonderfully happy that we never had any idea of what the future would hold for us. And as I look back now, at 85, God's plans for me during the years were all for the best for me, even though at times I had my doubts.

Chapter 12[5]

A new year had begun—1908—and we were beginning to discard our winter clothing. The first and most important was our spats, which in those days were worn instead of rubbers or overshoes. And then came the thrill of getting new boots, which we usually got a size too small as small feet were very much admired then.

At the office the men were coming in from out of town and getting ready for the spring showing, which meant more work for us. We had to work overtime some evenings, but we didn't mind it at all as we were seeing all the new spring materials, which they were putting on display for the buyers who were coming in to buy for their stores. I remember one particular bolt of material, which caused a great deal of controversy because they thought it was too loud. Both Gertrude and I spoke up and said, "Oh, we would like it. It would make lovely dresses." So, one of the men said, "Well, girls, if it doesn't sell, we will give you enough to make two dresses." Time went on, and it didn't sell—and I think we were praying that it wouldn't. So, one day our boss told us we could have enough material to make two dresses. We got a pattern, and Mrs. Cant helped us to make them. They were beautiful when made up. They had gray and white large stripes, and we made them princess style. Mine had a wide red sash and red buttons. Gertrude's was black with black buttons. Every time we wore them we were complimented and told how lovely we looked in them. One day we wore them to the office, and there happened to be a buyer on the floor. Our boss asked one of us to go out and show him how the materials looked when made up. He bought a lot of it, and after that whenever a buyer was on the floor, if we happened to have the dresses on, we would have to go out and model to show off the material. In a short time it was bought up, and after that we got lots of beautiful material for dresses.

The days were getting longer and warmer, and in those days I longed for Ireland to be able to go out in the lovely green fields and see the colorful wild flowers. May was such a beautiful month. I remember telling Gertrude how I always put daisies and buttercups on the doorsteps of the people I liked on May Day in honor of Mary.

I remembered the tradition when I came to live in Buffalo, as I found a friend of whom I was very fond and, from walking home from Mass on May Day morning, if I happened to pass a lawn that had daisies on it, I would pick a few to put on her doorstep. Her name was Ethyl Hendryx and she was a very dear friend and one I miss very much. I shall tell you more about her later.

On arriving home from work one day, Mrs. Cant had a nice surprise for us. She had made arrangements for Gertrude and me to spend a week's vacation in a place called Pleasantville with a woman who belonged to her church [and] who had a small farm there. She had accommodations for six, and there were four other girls going who were about our age. We were delighted, so the next day we told our boss about it, and he said we could have a week off with [pay], which is what we needed to pay our board and give some to Mrs. Cant.

Oh, the excitement again of going to the country, and in 1908 Pleasant[ville] was in the country. We made some cotton dresses out of the material the salesmen gave us and were on our way one Monday morning on a New York Central train. I can't remember how long it took, but when we got off at Pleasantville we were met by a handsome young farmer whose name was Charles Ottinger. His father had a farm near where we were going to stay. He said he had met the other girls on Saturday, and that they were very nice girls.

It was a nice drive to the farmhouse and we were enjoying the buggy ride. We thought farm boys would be bashful, but he or the other boys whom we met later were not, as they were boys on vacation from college. It was lunchtime when we arrived at our destination, and it was fun meeting the other girls who were all from New York.

One of them was a comedian, and immediately we knew it was not going to be dull, which was proven definitely to us that night in bed. The six of us slept in one big room—I imagine it was a loft—with very comfortable beds. We just got settled down to sleep when someone screamed, "There is a mouse in the room." In a minute everyone was standing right up in bed and yelling,

"A mouse!" Each one thought it was in her bed. I'm quite sure nobody got any sleep that night.

However, when we got out in the lovely air the next day, we forgot all about the mice that might have been in the house.

As I remember Pleasantville, there was nothing spectacular about it. The one thing that has stood out in my memory was a lovely little bridge over a small brook, where we sat and enjoyed the lovely countryside.

Charley Ottinger called on several evenings. There were some other boys who came over just to set around and chat. But Charley nearly always asked me if I would go for a ride with him. I was never too interested in going alone so would always include Gertrude in the invitation. Together, we usually enjoyed the ride in the surrey with the fringe on top.

Gertrude was bitten by a caterpillar and it became infected. She was in great pain for two days and that, of course, spoiled the fun for the time being. However, the last two days were very enjoyable and we felt good as the country air gave us a lot of pep and we were always hungry and the food delicious.

Chapter 13

It was Saturday evening, the last evening we were going to be in Pleasantville, and as Charley said he would be over, Gertrude and the other girls said that I should go out alone with him for the last time.

Well, he did come, and sat around for a while, and then we went for the ride alone. It was delightful—we became better acquainted. He was telling about his plans for the future. One of them was that he hoped to take a trip to Australia when he got through school. He also wanted to know about Ireland, and it was then I really began to think I liked him.

When we got back to the house, the girls were sitting on the porch, so he sat for a while and then asked if he could ride home with me on Sunday. I, of course, said I would like that and for him to find out what time the train would be leaving. He said goodnight and left. Then the girls began to ask questions about the ride alone and if he proposed, and what my answer was. I said, "If you consider his asking me how I would like to go to Australia with him a proposal, than he did. But I said I would let him know on Sunday." We had lots of talk that night before going to bed—what a nice time we all had and how wonderful it was to have such a lovely week away from the heat of New York.

Then Sunday arrived, and it was more goodbyes to the four other girls, whom we knew we would never see again.

Charley came on Sunday with one of the other boys and they took care of our suitcases. It was another beautiful ride to the station in the charming little buggy, which to this day, 64 years later, I have never forgotten.

Charley got on the train with us and we said goodbye to the other boy who was going to take the horse and buggy back to the farm. We called to him and said we would be seeing him when we came back to Pleasantville, but we never saw him again. Charley sat beside me on the train, and I remember looking at him and thinking what a nice-looking boy he was. I know the feeling came to me that this would be the last time I would see him, because when we got home he stayed for the afternoon. We had lunch with the family and conversation, which led to religion once again, and then I knew it could never be anything but friendship. So when he was finally leaving, I went to the door with him and must have thought that I had reached the Pot of Gold at the end of the rainbow and didn't have to go to Australia to find it. And so it was goodbye and good luck to a very fine young man, whom I was sure would make good if he went to the end of the world. I never found out where he found his "pot of gold," but I am very sure he would be very happy wherever that would be.

Chapter 14

Gertrude and I talked of many things that night before going to bed. We nearly always had those heart to heart talks at that time. It must have been a time of consultation, which I know now we had many times during the years. It was a friendship, which meant implicit confidence in each other, and neither of us was ever disappointed.

Monday, and again back at the office. We knew it would be a day of adjustment trying to get our minds on office work once again. Our boss, John Dunn, was very lenient and he did try to make our first day from vacation with as little work as he possibly could, and we did appreciate that.

Days flew by and again the lovely summer was coming to an end and things were happening so quickly. Mrs. Cant told us one day that the rent was raised, and that she would have to find another place to live. After several weeks she did find an apartment quite a distance from where we lived on Monroe Street, which made us all feel sad. However, the day of moving arrived, and in a short time we were settled in our new home. It was on Gates Avenue, which was not as nice as Monroe Street, but Mrs. Cant said the rooms were larger and more airy, so that meant we would have to get used to the neighborhood. We, as young people, did make the best of it, but she didn't, because in a very short time she became ill. That made a great change in our lives. We took turns in caring for her, but it became impossible to go to work and to do the many things, which have to be done when illness comes into the home.

In those days nurses were few and far between, but we never gave up hope and said there must be some way out. As always, God does show a way, and through a contact with Aunt Maggie's husband, we found that somewhere in Canada a long-lost sister of Mrs. Cant was living. Through a boss of Harry Cant's at Knox, the Hatter's, who knew influential people, we were able to locate a Mrs. Gamble, whose husband was a prominent tailor in Toronto, and who turned out to be Aunt Annie.

She responded very quickly and in a short time she came to Brooklyn to take care of her sister. Of course, she had to live with the family and, since there wasn't an extra room, she had to share the room with Gertrude. I had to find a room somewhere else.

Once again, Aunt Maggie's husband came to our rescue and found me a small room in what seemed to be a very nice boarding house near Mrs. Cant's. Most important, it was within my means, which at that time was very little.

I adjusted to the change very quickly and tried to make the room more livable than it looked when I moved in. It was a room that had formerly been a storeroom, which only had a skylight for a window and had very little air. But for the winter, it was quite comfortable.

Once again I was on my own and hoped that the future would hold as many happy moments for me as I had experienced in the past. I called on Mrs. Cant and the family evenings after I got home from work and became better acquainted with Aunt Annie, who seemed to be a very fine person. She was taking over the responsibilities of the home and also nursing a lost sister. I remember two things outstanding about her. She was very refined and had a Canadian accent.

I missed Gertrude's company but I filled in the lonely hours by reading more and took many trips to the library. On one of those trips, I was fortunate to meet a very nice young girl about my own age. She, too, seemed to be rather lonely and was anxious to talk to me. We walked as far as her house one evening, and she invited me in to meet her family. I learned that he name was Rita Timmerman and she could play the piano beautifully. We became very good friends and, as she was Catholic, we quite often went to church together. She had a very nice home and a charming mother who, when she learned I lived in a small room, asked me to come often for dinner, which I was thankful for. I spent many very interesting evenings with Rita and her family.

Time passed quickly, and Mrs. Cant did not improve in health. She became very ill one evening and had to be taken to the hospital, and within a few days passed away.

Chapter 15

When I learned of Mrs. Cant's death, I knew I had lost a very special friend and one, I was sure, would never be replaced. Gertrude and the other children were brokenhearted as was Aunt Annie. But through it all, she had to make decisions, which were really quite difficult. First, it was what she could do to keep the family together, and, after a great deal of planning, she arrived at a decision. She got in touch with a relative in New York with whom she and her husband were quite friendly. She went to see them one Sunday and made plans for Gertrude, Ted and Mabel to live with them, and she would take Harry with her to Canada.

The time arrived again for goodbyes and hopes of better days to come. Gertrude found out later that the relative was a very sick woman with two children and a husband who worked nights. So, it meant she had to give up her office job and stay home to take care of a sick woman and two children, as well as Mabel and Teddy.

I went to see Gertrude one weekend, and she had just received a letter from Harry and also a letter from Aunt Annie to the effect that Harry was quite ill and a report from a doctor saying he had T.B. and should be placed in a sanitarium. We talked things over and came to the conclusion that she should consult her Minister. She did, and the people in the church made all the arrangements for him to get into a sanitarium in Brooklyn, and Aunt Annie took Ted and Mabel to Toronto with her. Gertrude had to remain with the sick relative until she was well enough to be out of bed and able to take care of the children.

It was at that time I received a letter from Ireland with the sad news of my mother's death, which, of course, brought all kinds of regrets—the regret of not having written to her more often and the feelings, which must have come to other young people who came to America in those days, that I was unable to keep the promises which I made to myself on leaving Ireland. I was going to come back as a Yankee and buy my mother silk dresses and a home where she and my sister could live, and that my brothers could get married to the girls I knew they loved, and deep down in my mother's heart, I knew that was what she hoped for. My brother, James, in his letter tried to describe in detail the very peaceful death of my mother and her last words, which left such an impression on me that, regardless of the many difficulties I encountered through the years, my mother's love, with God's help, gave me courage to go on. My brother said in his letter that my mother's last words were, "Maggie is back. She is standing at the end of the bed." I'm sure I was there in spirit because that is where I would like to have been.

I spent that weekend with my brother, Michael. We talked about Ireland, and I told him about all the nice things my mother, sister[6] and I did together. We both said how lonely my sister must be and we both wished that we could take a trip there, but at that time neither of us had that kind of money. So, I went back to Brooklyn to a lonely room and many memories.

Gertrude called me at the office the next day and said she had good news to tell me. So, I went to her friend's house that evening and we had dinner there. I met the husband of the woman who was ill and another young man from England, who seemed to be quite interested in Gertrude. He asked us to take a walk, and then he told me to persuade Gertrude to go back to her office job and for us to find a room together in Brooklyn. I was delighted at the idea, and within a short time we found a very nice room where we could get our own breakfast, and it will be so wonderful to be together once again. We paid a deposit on the room and then tried to figure out how we could move our things and how I could tell my landlady that I was going to move.

I didn't say anything for a few days, and as always through my mother's prayers I am guided to do the things which are right for me. This is what happened: for the first time since I had been in the house, I locked my door. I think that the reason was because at the dinner table that evening, there seemed to be more confusion than usual. I asked the maid what it was all about. She said they were having two men from the Belmont race track who were going to have dinner that evening and who were going to stay for a week.

I was introduced to one of them that evening, and he insisted upon my going out with him that night. I said, "No, I had a previous engagement." I did go to Rita Timmerman's house and stayed quite late. She walked home with me and said to lock my door, which I did. In the middle of the night, I was awakened by a slight twisting of the knob of my door. I got out of bed quickly and asked who was there. I got a whispered answer saying, "Open the door." I said, "No, I'm in bed and will not open the door." I prayed that whoever it was would go away. Then I remembered that, before I was awakened, I had a dream of a lovely lady in white over my bed, and to this day I am sure it was our Blessed Mother. I got dressed and sat in my room until daylight. Then I went downstairs and told the landlord what happened and that I could not stay in that room any longer.

I called Gertrude from the office the next day and made plans to move into our room immediately. She said she was quite sure her friend would see that she could move any time. However, I wasn't so lucky. That evening when I went to get my things, I found my room door locked, and I could not have them until I paid for a week's room and board. Luckily, I knew the policeman who was on the beat that evening, so I talked to him and he came to my rescue. I was so frightened, I'm sure I left some of my things there, but I was so glad to be out of there and in a very comfortable room with Gertrude again. What I left was never missed.

Chapter 16

Time was flying by and surely going more quickly since we were together again. Our evenings at home were quite interesting, as we were disclosing the events which occurred in our lives both at home and during business hours while we were separated. Gertrude had many more different things happen in her life than I had.

She told about how she met the young man from England, who I am sure made quite an impression as far as his intentions were concerned. His name was Thomas Napier Northcott, and his father was a bank clerk who expected his son to follow in his footsteps. Tom undoubtedly would have if he had not met and become friendly with a young wealthy American who was travelling in Europe and spending a lot of time in England. He was looking for a chauffeur who could fill in as a travelling companion. He felt that Tom had all the qualifications and asked him to come to America with him. [One day, Tom had] lunch at Shanley's restaurant, where Charley Abbot (... the husband of Gertrude's friend where she, Teddy and Mabel were staying) was a waiter. Shanley's in those days was very exclusive. [Charley] often waited on Lillian Russell, Anna Held, and many of the celebrities of the days of the Ziegfeld Follies. Charley and [Tom] became friends. [Tom] came to dinner one evening [at Charley's home] and met Gertrude and I did believe it was love at first sight.

I had very little to tell her except what was going on in the office, which at that time was uninteresting.

I must try to describe the room. It was what was called in those days a back parlor. The front parlor was designated as a reception room where we were allowed to entertain our friends. Our room had a large window where we had a view of the garden, which at the time we were there was very colorful. We both enjoyed that. We placed our dining table in front of the window and had our breakfast there every morning. I took the responsibility of grocery shopping, which meant going out every morning for hot rolls and milk and sometimes eggs. I don't think there was any such thing as an ice box in those days, so we just got enough food for each meal. We did not have to eat many dinners at home as we had found a very good restaurant quite near us, which served delicious meals and was very reasonable. We could purchase six tickets for a dollar and a half, and that usually lasted for a week as we were often treated to a dinner at that restaurant or perhaps at a more exclusive one. But no matter how delicious the meals were, we both always said their desserts could never compare with those lemon pies at Flarties. I have never forgotten how good they were. Many years later, Gertrude and I often told our friend[s] about them.

Tom was a frequent caller and often took both of us to dinner, which we appreciated, especially if it were the night before payday, as I was the only breadwinner at that time. However, very shortly Gertrude answered an ad in the evening paper and found a position with A. L. Reed's wholesale white goods house on White Street off Broadway and quite near Mills & Gibbs. She started to work immediately in the office at $8.00 a week and hours from 9:00 to 5:00. The work was very interesting, and the men with whom she worked were very kind, especially Mr. Reed.

One day, on arriving home, we got the sad news that Harry was very ill and that we should come immediately to the hospital. We went that evening and found a very sick boy. We remained at his bedside until the nurse came into the room and told us there was nothing more we could do and that they would notify us of any change. So we both kissed him goodbye. We received word later that night that he passed away a few hours after we left. Once again, Gertrude had to go through another sad period in her life. As I think of her now, these words come to me now from a poem we both knew years ago:

> And when memory seeks a pleasant trip
> And the choice of a pathway comes
> I'll choose the bridge of yesterday
> To the days when we were chums.

Notes

1. Corrections in brackets and all the notes below were made by Kerby Miller.

2. This was Alice L. McGuinness, who lived at Hampton Bays, New York, when she donated her aunt's memoir to Kerby Miller in 1990.

3. Later in the memoir, the author refers to this person as Bill (or Will) Beckner.

4. Or Beckman; see note 3 above.

5. Beginning here, the author switched to Arabic numerals in numbering her chapters.

6. Alice McGuinness wrote in the margin here: "The sister was blind."

BIBLIOGRAPHY

Abbas, Tahir, and Frank Reeves, eds. *Immigration and Race Relations: Sociological Theory and John Rex*. London: I. B. Tauris, 2007.

Addams, Jane. *Twenty Years at Hull-House*. 1910. Reprint. Champaign: University of Illinois Press, 1990.

Adorno, Theodor. *Minima Moralia: Reflections on a Damaged Life*. Translated by E. F. N. Jephcott. London: Verso, 2005.

Akenson, Donald. *The Irish Diaspora: A Primer*. Toronto: P. D. Meany, 1993.

———. *The Irish Education Experiment—The National System of Education in the Nineteenth Century*. London: Routledge & Kegan Paul, 1970.

———. "Remember Emmet." *Irish Studies Review* 12 (2004): 339–42.

Alba, Richard, and Victor Nee. *Remaking the American Mainstream: Assimilation and Contemporary Immigration*. Cambridge, MA: Harvard University Press, 2005.

Allen, Nicholas. "Autobiography and the Irish Literary Revival." In *A History of Irish Autobiography*, edited by Liam Harte, 149–63. Cambridge: Cambridge University Press, 2018.

Almeida, Linda Dowling. Review of *Irish-American Autobiography: The Divided Hearts of Athletes, Priests, Pilgrims, and More*, by James Silas Rogers. *American Catholic Studies* 128 (2017): 86–87.

Altınay, Ayşe Gül, María José Contreras, Marianne Hirsch, Jean Howard, Banu Karaca, and Alisa Solomon, eds. *Women Mobilizing Memory*. New York: Columbia University Press, 2019.

Anastasio, Thomas J. *Individual and Collective Memory Consolidation: Analogous Processes on Different Levels*. Cambridge, MA: MIT Press, 2012.

Anderson, Benedict. *Imagined Communities: Reflections on the Origin and Spread of Nationalism*. London: Verso, 1983.

Ansell-Pearson, Keith. "Bergson on Memory." In *Memory: Histories, Theories, Debates*, edited by Susannah Radstone and Bill Schwarz, 61–77. New York: Fordham University Press, 2010.

Antin, Mary. *From Plotzk to Bosto*. 2nd ed. Boston: W. B. Clarke, 1899.

———. *The Promised Land*. Leipzig: Bernhard Tauchnitz, 1913.

Ashton, Rosemary. *The Life of Samuel Taylor Coleridge: A Critical Biography*. London: John Wiley and Sons, 1996.

Assmann, Jan. "Communicative and Cultural Memory." In *Cultural Memory Studies: An International and Interdisciplinary Handbook*, edited by Astrid Erll and Ansgar Nünning, 109–18. Berlin: De Gruyter, 2008.

Avery, Cheryl J., and Mona Holmlund. *Better Off Forgetting?: Essays on Archives, Public Policy, and Collective Memory*. Toronto: University of Toronto Press, 2010.

Bachelard, Gaston. *The Poetics of Space*. Translated by Maria Jolas. Boston: Beacon, 1994.

Balée, Susan. "From the Outside In: A History of American Autobiography." *Hudson Review* 51, no. 1 (1998): 40–64.

Barbeau, J. W. "Romantic Religion, Life Writing, and Conversion Narratives." *Wordsworth Circle* 47 (2016): 32–39.

Barclay, Katie. "Place and Power in Irish Farms at the End of the Nineteenth Century." *Women's History Review* 21 (2012): 571–88.

Barclay, Katie, and Nina Javette Koefoed. "Family, Memory, and Identity: An Introduction." *Journal of Family History* 46 (2021): 3–12.

Beiner, Guy. *Forgetful Remembrance: Social Forgetting and Vernacular Historiography of a Rebellion in Ulster*. Oxford: Oxford University Press, 2018.

———. "Probing the Boundaries of Irish Memory: From Postmemory to Prememory and Back." *Irish Historical Studies* 39 (2014): 296–307.

———. *Remembering the Year of the French: Irish Folk History and Social Memory*. Madison: University of Wisconsin Press, 2007.

Bergland, Betty Ann. "Representing Ethnicity in Autobiography: Narratives of Opposition." *Yearbook of English Studies* 24 (1994): 67–93.

Bielenberg, Alan, ed. *The Irish Diaspora*. London: Pearson, 2000.

Bjorklund, Diane. *Interpreting the Self: Two Hundred Years of American Autobiography*. Chicago: University of Chicago Press, 1998.

Blaikie, Andrew. "Legacies of Perception: The Forgotten Places of Twentieth-Century Scotland." *Canadian Journal of Irish Studies* 39, no. 1 (2015): 64–91.

Blaiklock, E. M. *Out of the Earth: The Witness of Archaeology to the New Testament*. Milton Keynes, UK: Paternoster, 1957.

Blejmar, Jordana. "The Truth of Autofiction: Second-Generation Memory in Post-Dictatorship Argentine Culture." PhD thesis, University of Cambridge, 2012.

Bloom, Lynn Z. "Utopia and Anti-Utopia in Twentieth Century Women's Frontier Autobiographies." In *American Women's Autobiography: Fea(s)ts of Memory*, edited by Margo Culley. Madison: University of Wisconsin Press, 1992.

Blum, Matthias, Christopher L. Colvin, Laura McAtackney, and Eoin McLaughlin. "Women of an Uncertain Age: Quantifying Human Capital Accumulation in Rural Ireland in the Nineteenth Century." *Economic History Review* 70, no. 1 (2017): 187–223.

Boelhower, William. "The Brave New World of Immigrant Autobiography." *Multi-Ethnic Literature of the United States (MELUS)* 9, no. 2 (1982): 5–23.

———. Review of *American Autobiography*, by Rachel McLennan. *Biography* 36, no. 2 (2013): 397–401.

Boland, Eavan. *The Lost Land: Poems*. New York: W. W. Norton, 1998.

Bourke, Joanna. *Husbandry to Housewifery: Women, Economic Change, and Housework in Ireland, 1890–1914*. Oxford: Clarendon, 1993.

Bowen, Elizabeth. *Bowen's Court*. New York: Knopf, 1942.

Brah, Avtar. *Cartographies of Diaspora: Contesting Identities*. London: Routledge, 1996.

Bromell, Una. "The Creation of an Irish Culture in the United States: The Gaelic Movement, 1870–1915." *New Hibernia Review* 5, no. 3 (2001): 87–100.

Brown, Julia Prewitt. "The Feminist Depreciation of Austen: A Polemical Reading." *NOVEL: A Forum on Fiction* 23, no. 3 (1990): 303–13.

Brown, Thomas N. *Irish-American Nationalism, 1870–1890*. Philadelphia: J. B. Lippincott, 1966.

Brundage, David. *Irish Nationalists in America: The Politics of Exile, 1798–1998*. Oxford: Oxford University Press, 2016.

———. "Matilda Tone in America: Exile, Gender, and Memory in the Making of Irish Republican Nationalism." *New Hibernia Review / Iris Éireannach Nua* 14 (2010): 96–111.

Bruner, J. "The Autobiographical Process." In *The Culture of Autobiography: Constructions of Self-Representation*, edited by R. E. Folkenflik, 49–50. Stanford: Stanford University Press, 1993.

Bull, Philip. *Land, Politics and Nationalism: A Study of the Irish Land Question*. Dublin: Gill and Macmillan, 1996.

Burke, Peter. *Varieties of Cultural History*. Ithaca, NY: Cornell University Press, 1997.

Burton Kurtz, William. *Excommunicated from the Union: How the Civil War Created a Separate Catholic America*. New York: Fordham University Press, 2016.

Cahalan, James M. Review of Paul Hyland and Neil Sammells, eds., *Irish Writing: Exile and Subversion*; Otto Rauchbauer, ed., *Ancestral Voices: The Big House in Anglo-Irish Literature*; Jacqueline Gened, ed., *The Big*

House in Ireland: Reality and Representation; and John W. Purser, *The Literary Works of Jack B. Yeats, Modern Fiction Studies* 38, no. 4 (1992), 966–69.

Caldicott, C. E. J., and Anne Fuchs. *Cultural Memory: Essays on European Literature and History*. Bern: Peter Lang, 2003.

Campbell, Sean. "'Beyond Plastic Paddy': A Re-Examination of the Second Generation Irish in England." In *The Great Famine and Beyond: Irish Migrants in Britain in the Nineteenth and Twentieth Centuries*, edited by Donald MacRaild. Newbridge: Irish Academic Press, 2000.

Carney, Michael, and Gerard Hayes. *From the Great Blasket to America: The Last Memoir by an Islander*. Cork: Collins, 2013.

Carr, David. *Time, Narrative, and History*. Bloomington: Indiana University Press, 1986.

Carvalho, Solomon Nunes. *Incidents of Travel and Adventure in the Far West with Colonel Frémont's Last Expedition*. 1857. Edited by Ava F. Kahn. Lincoln: University of Nebraska Press, 2004.

Casey, Brian. *Class and Community in Provincial Ireland, 1851–1914*. London: Palgrave, 2018.

Casey, Edward S. *Getting Back into Place: Toward a Renewed Understanding of the Place-World*. 2nd ed. Bloomington: Indiana University Press, 2009.

———. *Remembering: A Phenomenological Study*. 2nd ed. Bloomington: Indiana University Press, 2000.

Casey, Janet Galligani. "Farm Women, Letters to the Editor, and the Limits of Autobiography Theory." *Journal of Modern Literature* 28, no. 1 (2004): 89–106.

Cashman, Ray. *Packy Jim: Folklore and Worldview on the Irish Border*. Madison: University of Wisconsin Press, 2016.

———. "Visions of Irish Nationalism." *Journal of Folklore Research* 45, no. 3 (2008): 361–81.

Chansky, Ricia Anne, ed. *Auto/Biography across the Americas: Transnational Themes in Life Writing*. London: Routledge, 2017.

Clarke, Clifford J. "The Bible Belt Thesis: An Empirical Test of the Hypothesis of Clergy Overrepresentation, 1890–1930." *Journal for the Scientific Study of Religion* 29 (1990): 210–25.

Clarke, Joseph. "Historians, Memory and Commemoration." Trinity Week Symposium 2016, Trinity College Dublin, April 12, 2016.

Clear, Caitriona. "Too Fond of Going: Female Emigration and Change for Women in Ireland, 1946–1961." In *Ireland in the 1950s: The Lost Decade*, edited by Dermot Keogh, Finbarr O'Shea, and Carmel Quinlan, 135–46. Cork: Mercier, 2004.

Cohen, Marilyn. *Linen, Family and Community in Tullylish, County Down, 1690–1914*. Dublin: Four Courts, 1997.

Corporaal, Marguérite. "From Golden Hills to Sycamore Trees: Pastoral Home-lands and Ethnic Identity in Irish Immigrant Fiction, 1860–75." *Irish Studies Review* 18, no. 3 (2010): 331–46.

———. *Global Legacies of the Great Irish Famine: Transnational and Interdisciplinary Perspectives.* Bern: Peter Lang, 2014.

———. "Moving towards Multidirectionality: Famine Memory, Migration and the Slavery Past in Fiction, 1860–1890." *Irish University Review* 47, no. 1 (2017): 48–61.

———. "Relocating Regionalism: The Fin-de-Siècle Irish Local Colour Tale in Transnational Contexts." *Irish Studies Review* 28, no. 2 (2020): 155–70. doi.org /10.1080/09670882.2020.1740429.

Corporaal, Marguérite, Christopher Cusack, and Lindsay Janssen. *Recollecting Hunger: An Anthology: Cultural Memories of the Great Famine in Irish and British Fiction, 1847–1920.* Newbridge: Irish Academic Press, 2012.

Corporaal, Marguérite, and Jason King. *Irish Global Migration and Memory: Transatlantic Perspectives of Ireland's Famine Exodus.* London: Routledge, 2016.

Corporaal, Marguérite, and Christina Morin. *Traveling Irishness in the Long Nineteenth Century.* London: Palgrave Macmillan, 2017.

Creedon, John. *That Place We Call Home.* Dublin: Gill, 2020.

Cronin, Maura. "Oral History, Oral Tradition and the Great Famine." In *Holodomor and Gorta Mór: Histories, Memories and Representation of Famine in Ukraine and Ireland*, edited by Lindsay Janssen, Christian Noack, and Vincent Comerford, 231–44. London: Anthem, 2014.

Cronin, Nessa, Séan Crosson, and John Eastlake, eds. *Anáil an Bhéil Bheo: Orality and Modern Irish Culture.* Newcastle, UK: Cambridge Scholars, 2009.

Crowe, Catriona. "The Commission and the Survivors." *Dublin Review* 83 (Summer 2021).

Crowe, Catriona, Margaret O'Callaghan, Caitriona Clear, Linda Connolly, and John Cunningham. "Recovering Imagined Futures." *Machnamh 100*, edited by Michael D. Higgins, May 2021.

Cullen, Fintan. "Representing the Irish Emigrant: Humour to Pathos?" *Visual Culture in Britain* 18, no. 2 (2017): 176–91.

Culley, Margo, ed. *American Women's Autobiography: Fea(s)ts of Memory.* Madison: University of Wisconsin Press, 1992.

Cusack, Tricia. "A 'Countryside Bright with Cosy Homesteads': Irish Nationalism and the Cottage Landscape." *National Identities* 3, no. 3 (2001): 221–38.

———. "'Enlightened Protestants': The Improved Shorescape, Order and Liminality at Early Seaside Resorts in Victorian Ireland." *Journal of Tourism History* 2, no. 3 (2010): 165–85.

Cusick, Christine. *Out of the Earth: Ecocritical Readings of Irish Texts.* Cork: Cork University Press, 2010.

Custer, Elizabeth Bacon. *Tenting on the Plains: General Custer in Kansas and Texas*. New York: Charles L. Webster, 1887.

Daly, Mary E. "Women in the Irish Workforce from Pre-Industrial to Modern Times." *Saothar* 7 (1981): 74–82.

Darnton, Robert. *The Great Cat Massacre and Other Episodes in French Cultural History*. London: Allen Lane, 1984.

Davis, Angela. *An Autobiography*. New York: Knopf, 1971.

Dekel, Sharon, and George A. Bonanno. "Changes in Trauma Memory and Patterns of Posttraumatic Stress." *Pyschological Trauma: Theory, Research, Practice and Policy* 5, no. 1 (2013): 26–34.

Delaney, Enda. *Irish Emigration since 1921*. Dublin: Economic and Social History Society of Ireland, 2002.

———. "Narratives of Exile and Displacement: Irish Catholic Emigrants and the National Past, 1850–1914." In *Ireland's Polemical Past: Views of Irish History in Honour of R. V. Comerford*, edited by T. A. Dooley, 102–22. Dublin: University College Dublin Press, 2010.

Delaney, Enda, and Donald MacRaild, eds. *Irish Migration, Networks and Ethnic Identities since 1750*. London: Routledge, 2007.

Delay, Cara. "'Deposited Everywhere': The Sexualized Female Body and Modern Irish Landscape." *Études-Irlandaises* 37 (2012): 71–86.

de Man, Paul. "Autobiography as De-facement." *Comparative Literature* 94, no. 5 (1979): 919–30.

Den Boer, Pim. "Loci Memoriae—Lieux de Mémoire." In *A Companion to Cultural Memory Studies*, edited by Astrid Erll and Ansgar Nünning, 19–27. Berlin: De Gruyter, 2008.

Derrida, Jacques. *Writing and Difference*. London: Routledge, 1981.

Dillane, Fionnuala, Naomi McAreavey, and Emilie Pine, eds. *The Body in Pain in Irish Literature and Culture*. London: Palgrave Macmillan, 2016.

Dillon, Brian. *In the Dark Room*. London: Fitzcarraldo, 2018.

Dillon, R. J. "Manufacturing the Past: Collective Memory and the Commodification of History as Popular Culture on British Television." PhD thesis, University of Lancaster, 2007.

Diner, Hasia R. *Erin's Daughters in America*. Baltimore, MD: Johns Hopkins University Press, 1983.

Doherty, Michael, and Hugh Garavan. "The Irish Mind Abroad: The Experiences and Attitudes of the Irish Diaspora." *Irish Journal of Psychology* 15, nos. 2 and 3 (1994): 15.

Dolan, Jay P. *The Irish Americans: A History*. London: Bloomsbury, 2008.

Donahoe, Patrick. *The Wearing of the Green Song Book*. Boston: Self-Published, 1869.

Donnan, Hastings. "Material Identities: Fixing Ethnicity in the Irish Borderlands." *Identities: Global Studies in Culture and Power* 12, no. 1 (2005): 69–105.

Donnelly, James. "Opposing the Modern World: The Cult of the Virgin Mary in Ireland, 1965–1985." *Eire-Ireland* 40, nos. 1 and 2 (2005): 183–245.

Dowling, Linda. "A Great Time to Be in America: The Irish in Post-Second World War New York City." In *Ireland in the 1950s: The Lost Decade*, edited by Dermot Keogh, Finbarr O'Shea, and Carmel Quinlan. Cork: Mercier, 2004.

Doyle, David Noel. "The Irish as Urban Pioneers in the United States, 1850–1870." *Journal of American Ethnic History* 10 (1990): 36–59.

Drannan, William F. *Capt. W. F. Drannan, Chief of Scouts, as Pilot to Emigrant and Government Trains, across the Plains of the Wild West of Fifty Years Ago*. Chicago: Rhodes and McClure, 1910.

———. *Thirty-One Years on the Plains and in the Mountains; or, I Last Voice from the Plains: An Authentic Record of a Life Time of Hunting, Trapping, Scouting and Indian Fighting in the Far West*. Chicago: Rhodes and McClure, 1900.

Drudy, P. J. *The Irish in America: Emigration, Assimilation, and Impact*. Cambridge: Cambridge University Press, 1985.

Duniway, Abigail Scott. *Path Breaking: An Autobiographical History of the Equal Suffrage Movement in Pacific Coast States*. Portland, OR: James, Kerns and Abbott, 1914.

Eakin, Paul John, ed. *American Autobiography: Retrospect and Prospect*. Madison: University of Wisconsin Press, 1991.

———. *How Our Lives Become Stories: Making Selves*. Ithaca, NY: Cornell University Press, 1999.

Earner-Byrne, Lindsey. "The Boat to England: An Analysis of the Official Reactions to the Emigration of Single Expectant Irish Women to Britain, 1922–1972." *Irish Economic and Social Review* 30 (2003): 52–70.

Eastlake, John. "Orality and Agency: Reading an Irish Autobiography from the Great Blasket Island." *Oral Tradition* 24, no. 1 (2009): 125–41. doi.org/10.1353/ort.0.0035.

Ebest, Ron. *Private Histories: The Writing of Irish Americans*. Notre Dame, IN: University of Notre Dame Press, 2005.

Ebest, Sally Barr. "Agency and Activism in Irish American Women's Memoirs." *Multi-Ethnic Literature of the United States (MELUS)* 44, no. 4 (2019): 177–96.

Ebner, Dean. *Autobiography in Seventeenth Century England*. Berlin: Mouton, 1971.

Edwards, R. Dudley. *The Great Famine: Studies in Irish History 1845–52*. With an introduction and bibliography by Cormac Ó Gráda. Dublin: Lilliput, 1994.

Enloe, Cynthia H. *Bananas, Beaches and Bases: Making Feminist Sense of International Politics*. 2nd ed. Berkeley: University of California Press, 2014.

Erll, Astrid. "Locating Family in Cultural Memory Studies." *Journal of Comparative Family Studies* 42 (2011): 303–18.

Erll, Astrid, and Ansgar Nünning, eds. *A Companion to Cultural Memory Studies*. Berlin: De Gruyter, 2010.

Fanning, Charles. "Dueling Cultures: Ireland and Irish America at the Chicago World's Fairs of 1933 and 1934." *New Hibernia Review* 15, no. 3 (2011): 94–110.

———. *The Exiles of Erin: Nineteenth-Century Irish-American Fiction.* 2nd ed. Chester Springs, PA: Dufour, 1997.

———. *New Perspectives on the Irish Diaspora.* Carbondale: Southern Illinois University Press, 2000.

Federici, Silvia. *Witches, Witch-Hunting and Women.* Oakland, CA: PM, 2018.

Feindt, Gregor, Félix Krawatzek, Daniela Mehler, Friedemann Pestel, and Rieke Trimçev. "Entangled Memory: Toward a Third Wave in Memory Studies." *History and Theory* 53, no. 1 (2014): 24–44.

Fentress, James, and Chris Wickham. *Social Memory.* Oxford: Blackwell, 1992.

Ferraro, Thomas. "Ethnicity and the Marketplace." In *The Columbia History of the American Novel*, edited by Emery Elliot, 380–406. New York: Columbia University Press, 1991.

Ferriter, Diarmaid. *The Transformation of Ireland, 1900–2000.* London: Profile, 2004.

Finerty, J. F. *War-Path and Bivouac: or, The Conquest of the Sioux: A Narrative of Stirring Personal Experiences and Adventures in the Big Horn and Yellowstone Expedition of 1876, and in the Campaign on the British Border, in 1879.* New York: Donohue Brothers, 1890.

Fitzpatrick, David. *Irish Emigration, 1801–1921.* Dublin: Economic and Social History Society of Ireland, 1984.

———. *Oceans of Consolation: Personal Accounts of Irish Migration to Australia.* Cork: Cork University Press, 1994.

———. "'A Share of the Honeycomb': Education, Emigration and Irishwomen." *Continuity and Change* 1, no. 2 (1986): 217–34.

Flannery, Eoin. *Versions of Ireland: Empire, Modernity and Resistance in Irish Culture.* Newcastle, UK: Cambridge Scholars, 2006.

Fleming, Rachel. "Resisting Cultural Standardization: Comhaltas Ceoltoirí Eireann and the Revitalization of Traditional Music in Ireland." *Journal of Folklore Research* 41, nos. 2 and 3 (2004): 30.

Foley, Timothy P. "Public Sphere and Domestic Circle: Gender and Political Economy in Nineteenth-Century Ireland." In *Gender Perspectives in Nineteenth-Century Ireland: Public and Private Spheres*, edited by Margaret Kelleher and James J. Murphy. Newbridge: Irish Academic Press, 1997.

Franklin, Benjamin. *Benjamin Franklin's Autobiography.* Edited by William B. Cairns. London: Longmans, Green, 1905.

Frawley, Oona. *Irish Pastoral: Nostalgia and Twentieth-Century Irish Literature.* Newbridge: Irish Academic Press, 2005.

———, ed. *Memory Ireland.* Vol. 1, *History and Modernity.* Syracuse, NY: Syracuse University Press, 2010.

———, ed. *Memory Ireland*. Vol. 2, *Diaspora and Memory Practice*. Syracuse, NY: Syracuse University Press, 2011.

———, ed. *Memory Ireland*. Vol. 3, *The Famine and the Troubles*. Syracuse, NY: Syracuse University Press, 2014.

Free, Marcus. "Keeping Them under Pressure: Masculinity, Narratives of National Regeneration and the Republic of Ireland Soccer Team." *Sport in History* 25, no. 2 (2005): 23.

Freeman, Mark. "Telling Stories: Memory and Narrative." In *Memory: Histories, Theories, Debates*, edited by Susannah Radstone and Bill Schwarz, 263–81. New York: Fordham University Press, 2010.

Frémont, John Benton. *Memoirs of My Life*. Belford: Clarke, 1887.

Galarza, Ernesto. *Barrio Boy: The Story of a Boy's Acculturation*. Notre Dame, IN: University of Notre Dame Press, 1971.

Gazzaniga, Michael. *The Mind's Past*. Berkeley: University of California Press, 1998.

Gerk, Sarah Rebecca. "Away O'er the Ocean Go Journeymen, Cowboys and Fiddlers: The Irish in Nineteenth-Century American Music." PhD thesis, University of Michigan, 2014.

Gillespie, Joanna Bowen. "'The Clear Leadings of Providence': Pious Memoirs and the Problems of Self-Realization for Women in the Early Nineteenth Century." *Journal of the Early Republic* 5 (1985): 197–221.

Gilmore, Leigh. *The Limits of Autobiography: Trauma and Testimony*. Ithaca, NY: Cornell University Press, 2001.

Gilpin, W. Clark. Review of *The Evangelical Conversion Narrative: Spiritual Autobiography in Early Modern England*, by D. Bruce Hindmarsh. *Spiritus: A Journal of Christian Spirituality* 6, no. 2 (2006): 257–60. doi.org/10.1353/scs.2006.0056.

Glassie, Henry. *Material Culture*. Bloomington: Indiana University Press, 1999.

———. *Passing the Time in Ballymenone: Culture and History of an Ulster Community*. Philadelphia: University of Pennsylvania Press, 1982.

———. *The Stars of Ballymenone*. Bloomington: Indiana University Press, 2006.

———. "Tradition." *Journal of American Folklore* 108, no. 430 (1995): 17.

Glassie, Henry, and Barbara Truessdell. "A Life in the Field: Henry Glassie and the Study of Material Culture." *Public Historian* 30, no. 4 (2008): 59–87.

Glazier, Michael, ed. *The Encyclopedia of the Irish in America*. Notre Dame, IN: Notre Dame University Press, 1999.

Goetsch, P. "The Country House in George Moore's *A Drama in Muslin*." In *Ancestral Voices: The Big House in Anglo-Irish Literature*, edited by Otto Rauchbauer, 79–92. Hildesheim, Germany: Georg Olms, 1992.

Gordon, Ann. "The Political Is the Personal: Two Autobiographies of Woman Suffragists." In *American Women's Autobiography: Fea(s)ts of Memory*, edited by Margo Culley, 111–28. Madison: University of Wisconsin Press, 1992.

Gray, Breda. *Women and the Irish Diaspora*. London: Routledge, 2004.

Gray, Jane. "The Circulation of Children in Rural Ireland during the First Half of the Twentieth Century." *Continuity and Change* 29 (2014): 399–421.

Gray, J. Glenn. "Heidegger on Remembering and Remembering Heidegger." *Man and World* 10 (1977): 62–78.

Greenwood, Annie Pike. *We Sagebrush Folks*. New York: Appleton, 1934.

Gribben, Arthur, ed. *The Great Famine and the Irish Diaspora in America*. Amherst: University of Massachusetts Press, 1999.

Grubgeld, Elizabeth. *Anglo-Irish Autobiography: Class, Gender and the Forms of Narrative*. Syracuse, NY: Syracuse University Press, 2004.

———. "Topography, Memory, and John Montague's *The Rough Field*." *Canadian Journal of Irish Studies* 14, no. 2 (1989): 25–36.

Guinnane, Timothy. *The Vanishing Irish: Households, Migration, and the Rural Economy in Ireland, 1850–1914*. Princeton, NJ: Princeton University Press, 1997.

Guinnane, Timothy W., and Ronald I. Miller. "The Limits to Land Reform: The Land Acts in Ireland, 1870–1909." *Economic Development and Cultural Change* 45 (1997): 591–612.

Hage, Ghassan. "Migration, Food, Memory and Home-Building." In *Memory: Histories, Theories, Debates*, edited by Susannah Radstone and Bill Schwarz, 416–28. New York: Fordham University Press, 2010.

Halbwachs, Maurice. *On Collective Memory*. Translated by Lewis A. Coser. Chicago: University of Chicago Press, 1992.

Halpern-Manners, Andrew. "The Effect of Family Member Migration on Education and Work among Nonmigrant Youth in Mexico." *Demography* 48, no. 1 (2011): 73–99.

Harris, Ruth Ann, and Sally K. Sommers Smith. "The Eagle and the Harp: The Enterprising Byrne Brothers of County Monaghan." *Irish Studies Review* 18 (2010): 173–83.

Harte, Liam, ed. *A History of Irish Autobiography*. Cambridge: Cambridge University Press, 2018.

———. "Migrancy, Performativity and Autobiographical Identity." *Irish Studies Review* 14, no. 2 (2006): 225–38.

———. "You Want to Be a British Paddy? The Anxiety of Identity in Post-War Irish Writing." In *Ireland in the 1950s: The Lost Decade*, edited by Dermot Keogh, Finbarr O'Shea, and Carmel Quinlan. Cork: Mercier, 2004.

Hatton, Timothy J., and Jeffrey Williamson. "After the Famine: Emigration from Ireland, 1850–1913." *Journal of Economic History* 53 (1993): 575–600.

Hazley, Barry. *Life History and the Irish Migrant Experience*. Manchester: Manchester University Press, 2020.

Hebel, Udo. "Sites of Memory in U.S.-American Histories and Cultures." In *A Companion to Cultural Memory Studies*, edited by Astrid Erll and Ansgar Nünning, 47–61. Berlin: De Gruyter, 2010.

Heidegger, Martin. *Being and Time*. Translated by John Macquarrie and Edward Robinson. Oxford: Blackwell, 1962.

Hemon, Alexander. *Nowhere Man*. London: Picador, 2004.

Higgins, Michael D., Ciarán Benson, Anne Dolan, Michael Laffan, and Joep Leerssen. "The Challenges of Public Commemoration." *Machnamh 100*. Dublin, December 2020. https://president.ie/en/diary/details/president-hosts -machnamh-100-event/.

Hirsch, Marianne. *The Generation of Post-Memory: Writing and Visual Culture after the Holocaust*. New York: Columbia University Press, 2012.

Hirsch, Marianne, and Valerie Smith. "Feminism and Cultural Memory: An Introduction." *Signs* 28, no. 1 (2002): 1–19.

Hobsbawm, E. J. *Nations and Nationalism since 1780: Programme, Myth, Reality*. Cambridge: Cambridge University Press, 1990.

Hobsbawm, E. J., and T. O. Ranger. *The Invention of Tradition*. Cambridge: Cambridge University Press, 1983.

Holt, Hamilton. *The Life Stories of Undistinguished Americans, as Told by Themselves*. New York: James Pott, 1906.

Hooper, Glenn, and Úna Ní Bhroiméil. *Land and Landscape in Nineteenth-Century Ireland*. Dublin: Four Courts, 2008.

Hoppen, K. Theodore. *Ireland since 1800: Conflict and Conformity*. 2nd ed. London: Longman, 1999.

Horne, John, Niamh Gallagher, Alvin Jackson, Eunan O'Halpin, Marie Coleman, and Michael D. Higgins. "Empire: Instincts, Interests, Power and Resistance." *Machnamh 100*, February 2021.

Horsman, Reginald. *Race and Manifest Destiny*. Cambridge, MA: Harvard University Press, 1986.

Hughes, Eamonn. "'The Fact of Me-Ness': Autobiographical Writing in the Revival Period." *Irish University Review* 33 (2003): 28–45.

Huyssen, Andreas. "Diaspora and Nation: Migration into Other Pasts." *New German Critique*, Winter 2003, 147–64.

Hyde, Douglas. *My American Journey*. Edited by Liam Mac Mathúna, Brian Ó Conchubhair, Niall Comer, Cuan Ó Seireadáin, and Máire Nic an Bhaird. Dublin: University College Dublin Press, 2019.

Hymes, Dell. *Foundations in Sociolinguistics: An Ethnographic Approach*. Philadelphia: University of Pennsylvania Press, 1989.

Ignatiev, Noel. *How the Irish Became White*. London: Routledge, 1995.

Inglis, Tom. "Local Belonging, Identities and Sense of Place in Contemporary Ireland." University College Dublin Institute for British-Irish Studies Discussion Paper, Politics and Identity Series, no. 4, 2009.

Izarra, Laura, and James Silas Rogers. "Life Writing and Diaspora I: Autobiographical Writings of the Irish in the USA and Latin America." In *History of*

Irish Autobiography, edited by Liam Harte, 315–31. Cambridge: Cambridge University Press, 2018.

Jacobson, Matthew Fyre. *Special Sorrows: The Diasporic Imagination of Irish, Polish and Jewish Immigrants in the United States.* Cambridge, MA: Harvard University Press, 1995.

Janssen, Lindsay. "Diasporic Identifications: Exile, Nostalgia and the Famine Past in Irish and Irish North-American Popular Fiction, 1871–1891." *Irish Studies Review* 26, no. 2 (2018): 199–216.

Jenkins, William. "In Search of the Lace Curtain: Residential Mobility, Class Transformation and Everyday Practice among Buffalo's Irish, 1880–1910." *Journal of Urban History* 35 (2009): 970–97.

Jensen, Richard. "'No Irish Need Apply': A Myth of Victimization." *Journal of Social History* 36, no. 2 (2002): 405–29.

Jones, Maldwyn A. "Scotch-Irish." In *Harvard Encyclopedia of American Ethnic Groups*, edited by Stephan Thernstrom. Cambridge, MA: Harvard University Press, 1980.

Kallan, Jeffrey. "Language, Space and Place." Trinity Week Annual Symposium, April 12, 2016.

Kaplan, Amy. "Manifest Domesticity." *American Literature* 70, no. 3 (1998): 581–606.

Keane, Molly. *Two Days in Aragon.* 1941. Reprint, London: Virago, 1993.

Kearney, Richard, ed. *Migrations: The Irish at Home and Abroad.* Dublin: Wolfhound, 1990.

———. "Narrative Hospitality: Three Pedagogical Experiments." In *Radical Hospitality*, edited by Richard Kearney and Melissa Fitzpatrick, 24–42. New York: Fordham University Press, 2021.

Keegan, Claire. *Walk the Blue Fields.* London: Faber, 2007.

Kelleher, Margaret. "'Ambassadors of Irish Taste': The Irish Lecture in America." Newberry Library Scholarly Series Irish Studies Seminar, Spring 2021.

———. "Famine and Commemoration, 1909–2017: Sites and Dynamics of Memory." *Canadian Journal of Irish Studies* 40 (2017): 21–37.

———. "Hunger and History: Monuments to the Great Irish Famine." *Textual Practice* 16 (2002): 249–76.

Kelleher, Margaret, and James H. Murphy, eds. *Gender Perspectives in Nineteenth-Century Ireland: Public and Private Spheres.* Newbridge: Irish Academic Press, 1997.

Kelly, Mary C. *Ireland's Great Famine in Irish American History: Enshrining a Fateful Memory.* Lanham, MD: Rowman and Littlefield, 2014.

Kelly, William, and John Young, eds. *Ulster and Scotland, 1600–2000: History, Language and Identity.* Dublin: Four Courts, 2004.

Kenneally, Michael. "The Autobiographical Imagination and Irish Literary Auto-biographies." In *Critical Approaches to Anglo Irish Literature*, edited by Michael Allen and Angela Wilcox, 111–31. Gerrards Cross, UK: Colin Smythe, 1989.

Kenny, Kevin. *The American Irish: A History*. London: Longman, 2000.

———. "Diaspora and Comparison: The Global Irish as a Case Study." *Journal of American History* 90, no. 1 (2003): 134–62.

———. "Twenty Years of Irish American Historiography." *Journal of American Ethnic History* 28, no. 4 (2009): 67–75.

Kerber, Linda K. "Separate Spheres, Female Worlds, Woman's Place: The Rhetoric of Women's History." *Journal of American History* 75, no. 1 (1988): 9–39.

Kerby, Anthony Paul. *Narrative and the Self*. Bloomington: Indiana University Press, 1991.

Kiberd, Declan. *Inventing Ireland: The Literature of a Modern Nation*. London: Jonathan Cape, 1995.

King, Jason. "Staging Famine Irish Memories of Migration and National Performance in Ireland and Quebec." *Comparative Literature and Culture* 18, no. 4 (2016).

Kingston, Maxine Hong. *The Woman Warrior: Memoirs of a Girlhood among Ghosts*. New York: Knopf, 1976.

Kleist, J. Olaf. *Political Memories and Migration: Belonging, Society, and Australia Day*. London: Palgrave Macmillan, 2017.

Klinkenborg, Verlyn. "The Definition of Home." *Smithsonian*, May 2012.

Koranyi, James, and Tricia Cusack. "The Making of Landscape in Modernity." *National Identities* 16, no. 3 (2014): 191–95.

Kurvet-Käosaar, Leena, Triuinu Ojamaa, and Aija Sakova. "Situating Narratives of Migration and Diaspora: An Introduction." *Trames* 23 (2019): 125–43.

Lauret, Maria. "When Is an Immigrant's Autobiography Not an Immigrant Autobiography? The Americanization of Edward Bok." *Multi-Ethnic Literature of the United States (MELUS)* 38, no. 3 (2013): 7–24.

Lee, J. J. *Ireland, 1912–1985: Politics and Society*. Cambridge: Cambridge University Press, 1989.

Lee, J. J., and Marion R. Casey. *Making the Irish American: History and Heritage of the Irish in the United States*. New York: New York University Press, 2006.

Lee, Robert, ed. *First Person Singular: Studies in American Autobiography*. New York: St. Martin's, 1988.

Lejeune, Philippe. *On Autobiography*. Translated by Katherine Leary. Minneapolis: University of Minnesota Press, 1989.

Llena, Carmen Zamorano. "Overcoming Double Exile: (Re)Construction of 'Inner- Scapes' in Contemporary Irish Women's Poetry." *Nordic Irish Studies* 3 (2004): 157–67.

Lochlainn, Sorcha Nic. "'Bear My Greetings across the Sea': Emigrant Experiences and the Gaelic Song Tradition." *Béaloideas* 82 (2014): 24–45.

Lovecraft, H. P. *A Means to Freedom: The Letters of H. P. Lovecraft & Robert E. Howard.* Vol. 2, 1933–36, edited by S. T. Joshi, David E. Schultz, and Robert E. Howard. New York: Hippocampus, 2009.

Lynch, Claire. *Irish Autobiography: Stories of Self in the Narrative of a Nation.* Bern: Peter Lang, 2009.

Lynch-Brennan, Margaret. *The Irish Bridget: Irish Immigrant Women in Domestic Service in America, 1840–1930.* Syracuse, NY: Syracuse University Press, 2009.

Mac Mathúna, Liam. "Letters in Irish from Utica: Pádraig Phiarais Cúndún Writes Home to Cork, 1834–1856." American Conference for Irish Studies Annual Conference. Chicago: April 2013.

———. *Pobal na Gaeilge.* Dublin: Coiscéim, 1987.

MacMullam, R. [Or a Looker On] "Sketches of the Highlands of Cavan, and of Shirley Castle, in Farney, Taken during the Irish Famine." Belfast: J. Reed, 1856.

MacRaild, Donald, ed. *The Great Famine and Beyond: Irish Migrants in Britain in the Nineteenth and Twentieth Centuries.* Newbridge: Irish Academic Press, 2000.

Madsen, Deborah. "The West and Manifest Destiny." In *A Concise Companion to American Studies,* edited by John C. Rowe. Malden, MA: Wiley-Blackwell, 2010.

Maher, Eamon, and Paul Butler. "John McGahern: His Time and His Places." *Canadian Journal of Irish Studies* 39, no. 2 (2016): 27–54.

Mahony, Patrick. *Recovering an Irish Voice from the American Frontier: The Prose Writing of Eoin Uu Cathail.* Denton: University of North Texas Press, 2021.

Maleney, Ian. *Minor Monuments.* Dublin: Tramp, 2019.

Mark-FitzGerald, Emily. *Commemorating the Irish Famine: Memory and the Monument.* Liverpool: Liverpool University Press, 2013.

Martin, Angela K. "The Practice of Identity and an Irish Sense of Place." *Gender, Place and Culture* 4, no. 1 (1997): 89–114. doi.org/10.1080/09663699725512.

Mason, Mary G. "Dorothy Day and Women's Spiritual Autobiography." In *American Women's Autobiography: Fea(s)ts of Memory,* edited by Margo Culley, 185–218. Madison: University of Wisconsin Press, 1992.

McBride, Ian. *History and Memory in Modern Ireland.* Cambridge: Cambridge University Press, 2001.

McCaffrey, Lawrence J. "The Catholic and Urban Profile of Irish America." *Irish Review* 14 (1986): 1–9.

———. *The Irish Diaspora in America.* Bloomington: Indiana University Press, 1976.

———. *Textures of Irish America.* Syracuse, NY: Syracuse University Press, 1992.

McCarthy, Mary. *Memories of a Catholic Girlhood*. 1947. Reprint, New York: Harcourt Brace Jovanovich, 1981.

McCarthy, Thomas. Introduction to *Bowen's Court*, by Elizabeth Bowen. Dublin: Collins, 1998.

McLennan, Rachel. *American Autobiography*. Edinburgh: Edinburgh University Press, 2013.

McMahon, Cian T. "Caricaturing Race and Nation in the Irish American Press, 1870–1880: A Transnational Perspective." *Journal of American Ethnic History* 33, no. 2 (2014): 33–56.

McWilliams, Ellen. "Looking for Irish America in the Memoirs of Mary McCarthy." *Women's Studies* 49 (2020): 391–404.

Meaghar, Timothy. *Inventing Irish America: Generation, Class, and Ethnic Identity in a New England City, 1880–1928*. Notre Dame, IN: University of Notre Dame Press, 2001.

Meaney, Geraldine, Mary O'Dowd, and Bernadette Whelan. *Reading the Irish Woman: Studies in Cultural Encounter and Exchange, 1714–1960*. Liverpool: Liverpool University Press, 2013.

Melgosa, B. D. "Memory and Trauma: Chicano Autobiographies and the Vietnam War." In *Landscapes of Writing in Chicano Literature*, edited by I. Martín-Junquera. London: Palgrave Macmillan, 2013.

Merwin, W. S. *The Shadow of Sirius*. Port Townsend, WA: Copper Canyon, 2009.

Miller, Kerby. *Emigrants and Exiles: Ireland and the Irish Exodus to North America*. New York: Oxford University Press, 1985.

———. *Ireland and Irish America: Culture, Class, and Transatlantic Migration*. Dublin: Field Day, 2008.

———. *The Shadow of Sirius*. Copper Canyon, 2009.

Miller, Kerby, Ellen Skerrett, and Bridget Kelly. "Walking Backward to Heaven?: Edmond Ronayne's Pilgrimage in Famine Ireland and Gilded Age America." In *Ireland's Great Famine and Popular Politics*, edited by Enda Delaney and Breandán Mac Suibhne. London: Routledge, 2015.

Miller, Perry. *Errand into the Wilderness*. Cambridge, MA: Harvard University Press, 1956.

Milner, Dan. "'Old Skibbereen': Fenian Anthem or Famine Lament?" *History Ireland* 24, no. 5 (2016).

Minczinger, Judit. "A Mass-Produced Muse: Gender and Late-Victorian Urban Developments in George Du Maurier's Trilby." *Gender Forum* 42 (2013): 15–34.

Mokyr, Joel, and Cormac Ó Gráda. "Poor and Getting Poorer?: Living Standards in Ireland before the Famine." *Economic History Review* 41, no. 2 (May 1988): 209–35.

Moore, George. *A Drama in Muslin*. London: Walter Scott, 1886.

Moran, Gerard. *Sending out Ireland's Poor: Assisted Emigration to North America in the Nineteenth-Century.* 2nd ed. Dublin: Four Courts, 2013.

Morash, Christopher. *Writing the Irish Famine.* Oxford: Clarendon, 1995.

Morash, Christopher, and Richard Hayes. *"Fearful Realities": New Perspectives on the Famine.* Newbridge: Irish Academic Press, 1996.

Moreno, Carolina P. Amador. "Remembering Language: Bilingualism, Hiberno-English and the Gaeltacht Peasant Memoir." *Irish University Review* 39, no. 1 (2009): 76–89.

Moynihan, Sinéad. *"Other People's Diasporas": Negotiating Race in Contemporary Irish and Irish American Culture.* Syracuse, NY: Syracuse University Press, 2013.

Napier, Taura. *Seeking a Country: Literary Autobiographies of Twentieth Century Irishwomen.* Lanham, MD: University Press of America, 2001.

Nash, Catherine. "Landscape, Body and Nation: Cultural Geographies of Irish Identities." PhD thesis, University of Nottingham, 1995.

———. "Remapping and Renaming: New Cartographies of Identity, Gender and Landscape in Ireland." *Feminist Review* 44, no. 1 (1993): 39–57. doi.org /10.1057/fr.1993.19.

Neiger, Mordechai, Oren Meyers, and Eyal Zandberg, eds. *On Media Memory: Collective Memory in a New Media Age.* London: Palgrave Macmillan, 2011.

Ní Bhroiméil, Úna. "Political Cartoons as Visual Opinion Discourse: The Rise and Fall of John Redmond in the Irish World." In *Ireland and the New Journalism,* edited by Karen Steele and Michael de Nie, 119–40. London: Palgrave, 2014.

Nic Dhiarmada, Briona. "Irish Language Autobiography." In *A History of Irish Autobiography,* edited by Liam Harte, 225–41. Cambridge: Cambridge University Press, 2018.

Nicholson, Asenath. *Lights and Shades of Ireland.* London: Charles Gilpin, 1850.

Nora, Pierre. *Realms of Memory: The Construction of the French Past.* Edited by Lawrence D. Kritzman. Translated by Arthur Goldhammer. 3 vols. New York: Columbia University Press, 1996–98.

Norris, Claire. "The Big House: Space, Place, and Identity in Irish Fiction." *New Hibernia Review / Iris Éireannach Nua* 8 (2004): 107–21.

O'Brien, George. "Memoirs of Irish Rural Life." In *A History of Irish Autobiography,* edited by Liam Harte, 193–209. Cambridge: Cambridge University Press, 2018.

O'Brien, Sarah. "Art, Oral History and Ireland's Mother and Baby Homes." *Oral History Review,* April 2, 2021.

———. "Irish Associational Culture and Identity in Post-War Birmingham." PhD dissertation, University of Limerick, 2009.

———. "Politics, Community and Nationhood in Irish-Argentine Oral Narrative." In *The Silent People? New Perspectives on the Irish Abroad,* edited by

Micháel O'hAodh and Mairtín O' Cathain. Lexington, KY: Rowman and Littlefield, 2013.

———. "The Stranger within My Gate: Irish Emigrant Narratives of Tradition, Modernity and Exile." In *Oral History: The Challenges of Dialogue*, edited by Marta Kurkowska-Budzan and Krzysztof Zamorski. Amsterdam: John Benjamins, 2009.

———. "Tom Brick of South Dakota, Irish Emigrant Life Writing, and the Dynamics of Storytelling." *New Hibernia Review* 22 (2018): 19–39.

O'Callaghan, Margaret. "Women's Political Autobiography in Independent Ireland." In *A History of Irish Autobiography*, edited by Liam Harte, 133–49. Cambridge: Cambridge University Press, 2018.

O'Carroll, Íde. *Models for Movers: Irish Women's Emigration to America*. Togher, Cork, Ireland: Attic, 2015.

O'Connor, Batt. *With Michael Collins in the Fight for Irish Independence*. London: Peter Davies, 1929.

O'Connor, Emmet. "The Autobiography of the Irish Working Class." In *A History of Irish Autobiography*, edited by Liam Harte, 209–25. Cambridge: Cambridge University Press, 2018.

Ó Crohan, Tomás. *The Islander*. Translated by Garry Bannister and David Sowby. Dublin: Gill and Macmillan, 2012.

Ó Foghludha, Risteárd, ed. *Pádraig Phiarais Cúndún*. Dublin: Oifig an tSoláthair, 1932.

Ó Gráda, Cormac. *Black '47 and Beyond: The Great Irish Famine in History, Economy, and Memory*. Princeton, NJ: Princeton University Press, 1999.

———. "Famine, Trauma and Memory." *Béaloideas* 69 (2001): 121–43. doi.org /10.2307/20520760.

———. *The Great Irish Famine*. Basingstoke, UK: Macmillan, 1989.

———. *Ireland Before and After the Famine: Explorations in Economic History, 1800–1925*. Manchester: Manchester University Press, 1988.

———. *Making Famine History*. Dublin: University College Dublin Press, 2006.

———. *The New York Irish in the 1850s: Locked in by Poverty?* Dublin: Centre for Economic Research, 2005.

———. "A Note on Nineteenth-Century Irish Emigration Statistics." *Population Studies* 29, no. 1 (1975): 143–9. doi.org/10.2307/2173431.

Olick, Jeffrey K. "Collective Memory: The Two Cultures." *Sociological Theory* 17, no. 3 (1999): 333–48.

———. *The Politics of Regret: On Collective Memory and Historical Responsibility*. London: Routledge, 2007.

Olick, Jeffrey K., and Joyce Robbins. "Social Memory Studies: From 'Collective Memory' to the Historical Sociology of Mnemonic Practices." *Annual Review of Sociology* 24 (1998): 105–40.

Olson, David. "Writing and the Mind." In *Sociocultural Studies of Mind*, edited by James V. Wertsch, Pablo del Río, and Amelia Alvarez, 95–123. Cambridge: Cambridge University Press, 1995.

Olson, David, and Nancy Torrance. "Conceptualizing Literacy as a Personal Skill and as a Social Practice." In *The Making of Literate Societies*, edited by David Olson and Nancy Torrance, 3–18. Malden, MA: Blackwell, 2001.

O'Neill, Kevin. "The Star Spangled Shamrock: Memory and Meaning in Irish America." In *History and Memory in Modern Ireland*, edited by Ian McBride. Cambridge: Cambridge University Press, 2001.

O'Neill, Peter. "Memory and John Mitchel's Appropriation of the Slave Narrative." *Atlantic Studies* 11 (2014): 321–43.

Ong, Walter. *Orality and Literacy: The Technologising of the Word*. London: Routledge, 1982.

O'Rourke, Maeve. "Ireland's Magdalene Laundries and the State's Duty to Protect." *Hibernian Law Journal* 10 (2011): 200–37.

Orwell, George. *Essays*. London: Penguin, 2000.

Ó Súileabháin, Muiris. *Fiche Blian Ag Fás*. Dublin: Clólucht an Talbóidigh, 1933.

O'Sullivan, Patrick. *Irish Women and Irish Migration*. Leicester, UK: Leicester University Press, 1995.

———, ed. *The Irish World Wide: History, Heritage, Identity*. Vol. 1, *Patterns of Migration*. Leicester, UK: Leicester University Press, 1992.

Palmer, Andrew William. "The Autobiographical Pact and the Selection of Self in Memoir." PhD thesis, University of Lincoln, 2016. http://eprints.lincoln.ac.uk/27879/.

Parfitt, Richard. "'Oh, What Matter, When for Erin Dear We Fall?': Music and Irish Nationalism, 1848–1913." *Irish Studies Review* 23 (2015): 480–94.

Parret, Herman. "The Communicative Value of Forgetting." *Empedocles: European Journal for the Philosophy of Communication* 2, no. 1 (2011): 95–107.

Pathe, Michael. *A Summer in Ireland*. Madison, WI: Cantwell, 1931.

Pavlenko, Aneka. "The Making of an American: Negotiation of Identities at the Turn of the Twentieth Century." In *Negotiation of Identities in Multilingual Contexts*, edited by Aneka Pavlenko and Adrian Blackledge, 34–67. Bristol, UK: Multilingual Matters, 2004.

Pine, Emelie. *The Politics of Irish Memory: Performing Remembrance in Contemporary Irish Culture*. London: Palgrave Macmillan, 2011.

Portelli, Alessandro. *The Order Has Been Carried Out: History, Memory, and the Meaning of a Nazi Massacre in Rome*. London: Palgrave Macmillan, 2003.

Power, John Logan. *Memoir of an Irish Pauper Who Became an American Humanitarian*. Edited by Joseph Kennedy. Callan, Ireland: Callan Heritage Society, 2020.

Pupin, Mihajlo Idvorsky. *From Immigrant to Inventor*. New York: Scribner, 1923.

Quiggin, E. C. "Prolegomena to the Study of the Later Irish Bards, 1200–1500." *Proceedings of the British Academy* 5 (1911).

Quinn, E. Moore. "Introduction: The Irish in the American Civil War." *Irish Studies Review* 18 (2010): 135–38.

———. "The Irish Rent . . . and Mended: Transitional Textual Communities in Nineteenth-Century America." *Irish Studies Review* 23 (2015): 209–24.

Radstone, Susannah, and Bill Schwarz, eds. *Memory: Histories, Theories, Debates.* New York: Fordham University Press, 2010.

Rauchbauer, Otto. "The Big House in Irish History: An Introductory Sketch." In *Ancestral Voices: The Big House in Anglo-Irish Literature,* edited by Otto Rauchbauer. Hildesheim, Germany: Georg Olms, 1992.

Ravage, Marcus Eli. *An American in the Making: The Life Story of an Immigrant.* 1917. Reprint, New Brunswick, NJ: Rutgers University Press, 2009.

Reader, Ian. *Pilgrimage: A Very Short Introduction.* Oxford: Oxford University Press, 2015.

Redmond, Jennifer. *Emigration to Britain from Independence to Republic.* Liverpool: Liverpool University Press, 2018.

Richards, Shaun. "'Saved in the Man and in the Nation': The Sacralization of the Soil in Twentieth-Century Irish Drama." *Worldviews* 5, no. 1 (2001): 80–95.

Ricoeur, Paul. *Memory, History, Forgetting.* Chicago: University of Chicago Press, 2004.

———. *Time and Narrative.* Chicago: University of Chicago Press, 1988.

Riis, Jacob A. *How the Other Half Lives: Studies among the Tenements of New York.* New York: Scribner, 1914.

———. *The Making of an American, with Numerous Illustrations.* New York: Macmillan, 1901.

Roberts, Elizabeth. *A Woman's Place: An Oral History of Working-Class Women, 1890–1940.* London: John Wiley and Sons, 1995.

Rogers, James Silas. "A Culture of Diffidence: Mid-Century Irish-American Priests' Autobiographies." *Studies: An Irish Quarterly Review* 96, no. 381 (2007): 69–79.

———. *Irish-American Autobiography: The Divided Hearts of Athletes, Priests, Pilgrims, and More.* Washington, DC: Catholic University of America Press, 2016.

Rose, Hilda. *The Stump Farm: A Chronicle of Pioneering.* Boston: Little, Brown, 1931.

Rossa, Jeremiah O'Donovan. *Rossa's Recollections, 1838–1898.* Shannon: Irish University Press, 1972.

Rothberg, Michael. *Multidirectional Memory: Remembering the Holocaust in the Age of Decolonization.* Stanford: Stanford University Press, 2009.

Rountree, Kathryn. "Tara, the M3, and the Celtic Tiger: Contesting Cultural Heritage, Identity, and a Sacred Landscape in Ireland." *Journal of*

Anthropological Research 68, no. 4 (2012): 519–44. doi.org/10.3998/jar.0521004 .0068.404.

Rudy, Kathryn. *Virtual Pilgrimages in the Convent: Imagining Jerusalem in the Late Middle Ages.* London: Brepols, 2011.

Ryan, Mary, Sean Browne, and Kevin Gilmour, eds. *No Shoes in Summer: Days to Remember.* Dublin: Merlin, 1995.

Rykwert, Joseph. *Remembering Places: A Memoir.* London: Routledge, 2017.

Rynne, Frank. "The Great Famine in Nationalist and Land League Propaganda, 1879–1882." *Mémoire(s), identité(s), marginalité(s) dans le monde occidental contemporain* 12 (2015). doi.org/10.4000/mimmoc.1864.

Sanders, Valerie. *The Private Lives of Victorian Women.* New York: St. Martin's, 1989.

Sayers, Peig. *Peig: The Autobiography of Peig Sayers of the Great Blasket Island.* Translated by Bryan MacMahon. Dublin: Talbot Press, 1973.

———. *An Old Woman's Reflections.* Translated by Seámus Ennis. Oxford: Oxford University Press, 1978.

———. *Scéalta ón mBlascaod.* Dublin: Cumann le Béaloideas Éireann, 1968.

Sayre, Robert. "Autobiography and the Making of America." *Iowa Review* 9, no. 2 (1978): 1–19.

Schama, Simon. *Landscape and Memory.* New York: HarperCollins, 1995.

Schiffrin, Deborah. "Linguistics and History: Oral History Discourse." In *Discourse and Beyond*, edited by Deborah Tannen and James Alatis. Washington, DC: Georgetown University Press, 2001.

Schofield, Ann. "The Returned Yank as a Site of Memory in Irish Popular Culture." *Journal of American Studies* 47, no. 4 (2013): 1175–95.

Schrier, Arnold. *Ireland and the American Emigration, 1850–1900.* Dublin: University College Dublin Press, 1997.

Scribner, S., and M. Cole. *The Psychology of Literacy.* Cambridge: Cambridge University Press, 1981.

Scully, Marc. "Plastic and Proud: Discourses of Authenticity among the Second Generation Irish in England." *Psychology and Society* 2, no. 2 (2009): 124–35.

Sheeran, Patrick. "Genius Fabulae: The Irish Sense of Place." *Irish University Review* 18, no. 2 (1988): 191–206. http://www.jstor.org/stable/25484245.

Shiels, Damian. "The Forgotten Irish Podcast." Soundcloud, 2021. https:// podcasts.apple.com/ie/podcast/the-forgotten-irish-podcast/id1397509508.

———. *The Irish in the American Civil War.* Dublin: History Press Ireland, 2014.

Smith, James M. "The Politics of Sexual Knowledge: The Origins of Ireland's Containment Culture and the Carrigan Report (1931)." *Journal of the History of Sexuality* 13, no. 2 (2004): 208–33.

Smith, Sally K. Sommers. "Landscape and Memory in Irish Traditional Music." *New Hibernia Review / Iris Éireannach Nua* 2, no. 1 (1998): 132–44. http://www .jstor.org/stable/20557478.

Smith, Sidonie. "Performativity, Autobiographical Practice, Resistance." *Auto/Biography Studies* 10 (1995): 17–33.

———. "Resisting the Gaze of Embodiment: Women's Autobiographies in the Nineteenth Century." In *American Women's Autobiography: Fea(s)ts of Memory*, edited by Margo Culley, 75–111. Madison: University of Wisconsin Press, 1992.

Smith, Sidonie, and Julia Watson. *Life Writing in the Long Run*. Ann Arbor: Michigan Publishing Services, 2016.

———. *Reading Autobiography: A Guide for Interpreting Life Narratives*. 2nd ed. Minneapolis: University of Minnesota Press, 2010.

Smith-Rosenberg, Carroll. "The Female World of Love and Ritual: Relations between Women in Nineteenth-Century America." *Signs* 1, no. 1 (1975): 1–29.

Solnit, Rebecca. *A Book of Migrations: Some Passages in Ireland*. London: Verso, 2011.

———. *Wanderlust: A History of Walking*. New York: Viking, 2000.

Soysal, Yasemin Nuho Flu. *Transnational Trajectories in East Asia: Nation, Citizenship, and Region*. London: Routledge, 2014.

Sproat, Richard. *Language, Technology, and Society*. Oxford: Oxford University Press, 2010.

Stanciu, Cristina. "Marcus E. Ravage's *An American in the Making*, Americanization, and New Immigrant Representation." *Multi-Ethnic Literature of the United States (MELUS)* 40, no. 2 (2015): 5–29.

Stanley, Liz. *The Autobiographical I: The Theory and Practice of Feminist Autobiography*. Manchester: Manchester University Press, 1995.

Stanton, Elizabeth Cady. *Eighty Years and More: Reminiscences, 1815–1897*. 1898. Reprint, New York: Schocken, 1971.

Stein, Gertrude. *The Autobiography of Alice B. Toklas*. New York: Harcourt Brace, 1933.

———. *Everybody's Autobiography*. 1937. Reprint, New York: Cooper Square, 1971.

Steiner, Edward Alfred. *From Alien to Citizen: The Story of My Life in America*. New York: Fleming H. Revell, 1914.

Stewart, Elinore Pruitt. *Letters of a Woman Homesteader*. Boston: Houghton Mifflin, 1914.

Swain, Kathleen. "'Come and Hear': Women's Puritan Evidences." In *American Women's Autobiography: Fea(s)ts of Memory*, edited by Margo Culley. Madison: University of Wisconsin Press, 1992.

Szpila, Kathleen. "Lest We Forget: Ellen Ryan Jolly and the Nuns of the Battlefield Monument." *American Catholic Studies* 123 (2012): 23–43.

Taves, Ann. "Self and God in the Early Memoirs of New England Women." In *American Women's Autobiography: Fea(s)ts of Memory*, edited by Margo Culley, 57–75. Madison: University of Wisconsin Press, 1992.

TeBrake, Janet. "Irish Peasant Women in Revolt: The Land League Years." *Irish Historical Studies* 28 (1992): 63–80.

Thuente, Mary Helen. "Development of the Exile Motif in Songs of Emigration and Nationalism." *Canadian Journal of Irish Studies* 26, no. 1 (2000): 8–23.

Tillson, Cristiana Holmes. *A Woman's Story of Pioneer Illinois*. Chicago: Donnelly, 1919.

Tobin, Robert. "'Tracing Again the Tiny Snail Track': Southern Protestant Memoir since 1950." *Yearbook of English Studies* 35 (2005): 171–85.

Tota, Anna, and Trevor Hagen, eds. *Routledge International Handbook of Memory Studies*. London: Routledge, 2016.

Trotter, Mary. "Re-Imagining the Emigrant/Exile in Contemporary Irish Drama." *Modern Drama* 46, no. 1 (2003): 35–54.

Tunc, Tanfer. "Manifest Destiny's Child: Mary Hazelton Blanchard Wade and the Literature of American Empire." *Children's Literature in Education* 48 (2017): 245–61.

Volpicelli, Robert. *Transatlantic Modernism and the US Lecture Tour*. Oxford: Oxford University Press, 2021.

Walsh, Tom. "The National System of Education, 1831–2000." In *Essays in the History of Irish Education*, edited by Brendan Walsh, 7–43. London: Palgrave 2016.

Walter, Bronwen. "Personal Lives: Narrative Accounts of Irish Women in the Diaspora." *Irish Studies Review* 13, no. 1 (2013): 37–54.

Warren, Craig A. "'Oh, God, What a Pity!': The Irish Brigade at Fredericksburg and the Creation of Myth." *Civil War History* 47 (2001): 193–221.

Watson, Julia. Review of Paul John Eakin, ed., *American Autobiography: Retrospect and Prospect*, and A. Robert Lee, ed., *First Person Singular: Studies in American Autobiography*. *Biography* 16, no. 2 (1993): 161–68.

Welzer, Harald. "Communicative Memory." In *Companion to Cultural Memory Studies*, edited by Astrid Erll and Ansgar Nünning, 285–301. Berlin: De Gruyter, 2010.

Whelan, Bernadette. "Women on the Move: A Review of the Historiography of Irish Emigration to the USA." *Women's History Review* 24 (2015): 900–16.

White, Eva Roa. "Emigration as Emancipation: Portrayals of the Immigrant Irish Girl in Nineteenth-Century Fiction." *New Hibernia Review* 9, no. 1 (2005): 95–108.

Wills, Clair. *The Best Are Leaving: Emigration and Post-War Irish Culture*. Cambridge: Cambridge University Press, 2015.

Wilson, Christine. "Illegible Ethnicity and the Invention of Scots-Irish Narratives on the Stages of Belfast and Appalachia." *Irish Studies Review* 23 (2015): 194–208.

Wilson, H. W. "Language and Identity in Twentieth Century Irish Culture." *Eire Ireland* 38, no. 1/2 (2003): 4–197.

Winkler, Justin, and Peter Burke. "Cultural Displacements and Intellectual Moorings—a Conversation with Peter Burke." *Mobile Cultural Studies* 2 (2016): 153–64.

Wong, Sau-Ling Cynthia. "Immigrant Autobiography: Some Questions of Definition and Approach." In *American Autobiography: Retrospect and Prospect*, edited by Paul John Eakin, 142–70. Madison: University of Wisconsin Press, 1991.

Wood, Curtis, and Tyler Blethen. *Ulster and North America: Transatlantic Perspectives on the Scotch-Irish*. Tuscaloosa: University of Alabama Press, 1997.

Sarah O'Brien is Lecturer at Mary Immaculate College, Limerick, Ireland, and codirector of the college's Oral History Centre. She is author of *Linguistic Diasporas, Narrative and Performance: The Irish in Argentina.*

For Indiana University Press

Tony Brewer, *Artist and Book Designer*
Allison Chaplin, *Acquisitions Editor*
Sophia Hebert, *Assistant Acquisitions Editor*
Samantha Heffner, *Marketing and Publicity Manager*
Brenna Hosman, *Production Coordinator*
Katie Huggins, *Production Manager*
Darja Malcolm-Clarke, *Project Manager/Editor*
Dan Pyle, *Online Publishing Manager*
Pamela Rude, *Senior Artist and Book Designer*

www.ingramcontent.com/pod-product-compliance
Lightning Source LLC
Chambersburg PA
CBHW030353120726
47901CB00007B/2004